MICROBEHAVIORAL ECONOMETRIC METHODS

MICROBEHAVIORAL ECONOMETRIC METHODS

Theories, Models, and Applications for the Study of Environmental and Natural Resources

S. NIGGOL SEO
Muaebak Institute of Global Warming Studies
Seoul, Korea

ELSEVIER

Amsterdam • Boston • Heidelberg • London
New York • Oxford • Paris • San Diego
San Francisco • Singapore • Sydney • Tokyo
Academic Press is an imprint of Elsevier

Academic Press is an imprint of Elsevier
125 London Wall, London EC2Y 5AS, United Kingdom
525 B Street, Suite 1800, San Diego, CA 92101-4495, United States
50 Hampshire Street, 5th Floor, Cambridge, MA 02139, United States
The Boulevard, Langford Lane, Kidlington, Oxford OX5 1GB, UK

Notices
Knowledge and best practice in this field are constantly changing. As new research and experience
broaden our understanding, changes in research methods, professional practices, or medical treatment
may become necessary.

Practitioners and researchers must always rely on their own experience and knowledge in evaluating
and using any information, methods, compounds, or experiments described herein. In using such
information or methods they should be mindful of their own safety and the safety of others, including
parties for whom they have a professional responsibility.

To the fullest extent of the law, neither the Publisher nor the authors, contributors, or editors, assume
any liability for any injury and/or damage to persons or property as a matter of products liability,
negligence or otherwise, or from any use or operation of any methods, products, instructions, or ideas
contained in the material herein.

British Library Cataloguing-in-Publication Data
A catalogue record for this book is available from the British Library

Library of Congress Cataloging-in-Publication Data
A catalog record for this book is available from the Library of Congress

ISBN: 978-0-12-804136-9

For information on all Academic Press publications
visit our website at https://www.elsevier.com/

  Working together
to grow libraries in
developing countries

www.elsevier.com • www.bookaid.org

Publisher: Nikki Levy
Acquisition Editor: J. Scott Bentley
Editorial Project Manager: Susan Ikeda
Production Project Manager: Julie-Ann Stansfield
Designer: Matthew Limbert

Typeset by Thomson Digital

CONTENTS

ABOUT THE AUTHOR

S. NIGGOL SEO

Professor S. Niggol Seo is a natural resource economist who specializes in the study of global warming. Born in a rural village in South Korea in 1972, he studied at a doctoral degree program at the University of California at Berkeley and received a PhD degree in Environmental and Natural Resource Economics from Yale University in May 2006 with a dissertation on microbehavioral models of global warming. Since 2003, he has worked with the World Bank on various climate change projects in Africa, Latin America, and Asia. He held professorial positions in the UK, Spain, and Australia from 2006–15. Professor Seo has published three books and over 45 international journal articles on global warming. He frequently serves as a journal referee for more than 30 international journals and has been on the editorial boards of the two journals: Food Policy, Applied Economic Perspectives and Policy. He received an Outstanding Applied Economic Perspectives and Policy Article Award from the Agricultural and Applied Economics Association in Pitsburgh in June 2011.

PREFACE

Environmental and natural resources provide humanity with shelters and basic materials to live on. Human beings have survived and flourished on this Earth by appropriating and enjoying environmental surroundings and natural resources. During the past two centuries, it is noted that humanity's influences on nature and the environment have vastly increased. Notwithstanding the remarkable growth in economic well-being realized over this time period, there are many signs that citizens of Earth are concerned about how humans utilize and care for natural and environmental endowments on the planet. In order to answer many pressing concerns and scholarly inquiries, a large array of research fields on environmental and natural resources has emerged.

This book presents a full spectrum of microbehavioral econometric methods that can be applied to a large variety of studies of environmental and natural resources. The microbehavioral econometric methods are concerned with how an individual makes decisions, taking into account given circumstances, to make the best use of concerned resources. This book places the ensemble of microbehavioral econometric and statistical methodologies in the context of how an individual, a community, or a society makes decisions on essential natural resources and environmental assets.

The present author puts together a large number of theories, models, and empirical studies that fall into the literature of microbehavioral methods and studies. The approach of the book is therefore encompassing, covering economics, statistics, psychology, public policy, finance, environmental science, ecology, climate science, and global affairs. The descriptions of the statistical methods are taken purposefully to cover the entire range of methodological advances that are pertinent to modeling individual decisions and outcomes.

This book provides applications of the microbehavioral methodologies to natural resource managers' decision problems faced with global warming and climatic changes. The nature of the problem of global warming is reviewed succinctly. The present author provides detailed explanations of how the microbehavioral methodologies developed in the first three chapters of the book can be applied to examine behaviors of individuals, communities, and societies in response to changing external climate conditions. The book utilizes the rural farm household survey data collected at the continental level in Latin America, Africa, and India. These low-latitude regions are on their own of great interest to environmental and natural resource researchers for their unique economies, societies, ecologies, and climates.

The present author hopes that the book will provide a valuable resource to the students and professionals of environmental and natural resource studies. The book is ideal for a textbook of a range of microbehavioral statistics courses in the school of environment, school of agricultural and natural resources, and school of public policy. The book also unfolds many important academic frontiers in the studies of microbehavioral statistics which are hoped to serve as an attraction for the scholars and professionals of microbehavioral statistics and economics.

Finally, the present author wishes to thank all those involved directly or indirectly in the publication of this book. Many professors at Yale University and the University of California Berkeley have given invaluable comments, albeit informally, on various aspects of the book. Their contributions are acknowledged in the first chapter and throughout the book. The present author also expresses gratitude to many who sponsored the Muaebak Institute of Global Warming Studies in Seoul where this book has been written.

Wish you a great journey!

S. Niggol Seo
Muaebak Institute of Global Warming Studies
Seoul, Korea
http://www.muaebakinstitute.org

CHAPTER 1

Introduction to the Microbehavioral Econometric Methods for the Study of Environmental and Natural Resources

This book is written as a textbook of the microbehavioral econometric methods applicable to the studies of environmental and natural resources. This book covers the microeconometrics literature in a comprehensive manner, both from the perspective of an individual agent's economic decisions and from the perspective of statistical modeling. The full range of statistical methods to be presented in the book are elucidated through empirical applications to the research questions on global climate changes, agricultural and natural resource enterprises, changes in ecosystems, and economic development in low-latitude developing countries.

This book can be used as a textbook for graduate-level courses in the environmental studies such as environmental and ecological statistics, environmental research methods, valuation methods, environmental and natural resource economics, agricultural economics. The book can also be adopted as a full or supplementary textbook in any graduate-level econometrics courses, especially in the courses related to microeconometrics and discrete choice modeling.

The book is written for the scholars, practitioners, and policy-makers of global and local environmental, developmental, and natural resource issues, with empirical applications drawn from the researches on global warming and an individual's adaptation decisions to global warming. The book pays special attention to natural resources and ecosystems in low-latitude developing countries in Sub-Saharan Africa, Latin America, and Asia and explains how changes in these systems and natural resources are an integral part of the microbehavioral econometric models applied to the studies of environmental and natural resources.

Although microeconometric methods have been widely applied to the applied economics research questions since seminal publications by McFadden, Hackman, and their colleagues (McFadden, 1974; Heckman, 1979; Dubin and McFadden, 1984), there are still few, if not none, microeconometrics textbooks available that have a clear objective of addressing local and global environmental and natural resource issues.

Notwithstanding, recent efforts across the environmental and resource research communities have increasingly unraveled that behavioral decisions and responses of individuals lie at the heart of today's major environmental problems as well as solutions for such problems (Mendelsohn, 2000, 2012; Seo, 2006, 2015a). This field of research is still emerging and the present author believes that it has high potential to offer a major theoretical and practical breakthrough in the studies of environmental and natural resource problems, which have long shackled intellectual endeavors and policy dialogues, with global warming research and negotiations being only one example.

From another angle, the unique opportunities that local and global environmental studies present in advancing the current state and quality of the microeconometrics literature have been by and large overlooked or unnoticed. Among the econometricians and applied statisticians, there is little awareness of environmental and natural resource studies that apply a variety of microeconometric tools to address numerous problems that are of major policy issues of today. One of the objectives of the book is, therefore, to highlight a new frontier in the microeconometrics literature that has been advanced in the environmental and resource research communities.

This is not to say that the book will be a dictionary of microeconometrics. The present author does not intend to cover all the minute details of the microeconometrics literature, which may be accessed through other sources such as McFadden (1984, 1999a,b); Train (2003); and Cameron and Trivedi (2005). Rather, the book has a focus on what decisions are made by an individual agent in the face of environmental changes and constraints and how these decisions and economic outcomes can be modeled empirically by employing a battery of statistical methods to yield economically meaningful policy conclusions. The book will highlight a number of advances achieved through the studies of individual's decisions on managing environmental and natural resources.

This does not mean that the book will only deal with the microeconometric concepts and methods in a perfunctory manner. The entire array of methodological options available in the microeconometrics and statistics literature will be elaborated throughout the book in the contexts of individuals' decision-makings and economic consequences of such decisions with regards to the environmental choices and tradeoffs. In an endeavor to write a crisp, accessible, and interesting book on microbehavioral econometric methods, however, the present author will put an emphasis on some methodological options and treat other methodological options rather lightly.

What are micro decisions taken by the individuals in responding to environmental and natural changes and/or constraints? To natural resource scientists and economists are known numerous decisions that are conditioned by environmental constraints such as global climatic changes and pollution of the environment (Tietenberg and Lewis, 2014; Seo, 2015a). Some of these decisions and the consequences of such decisions have been contentiously debated in the research communities as well as in the international policy roundtables on environmental and natural resource problems.

Let's consider several examples. A farmer makes a large number of decisions in consideration of the climate and weather conditions of the region where her/his farm is located, which have consequences on the revenues and costs that she/he can generate (Mendelsohn et al., 1994). Farmers in Sub-Saharan Africa are observed to switch an agricultural system from a crops-only to a mixed crops-livestock system or a livestock-only system when the climate becomes hotter and more arid (Seo, 2010a,b). If climate becomes more variable and risky through an increase in the coefficient of variation in precipitation (CVP) over a 30 year period, they are observed to switch to a mixed system (Seo, 2012c).

These changes in individuals' behaviors or strategies would occur because of changes in net incomes that can be earned by the individual farms due to an alteration in the climate condition. That is, farmers at present manage their farms in order to maximize the profit from farming and natural resource activities given climate, soil, and other external conditions. When the climate condition is altered due to global warming in the next decades and centuries, farmers and natural resource managers are expected to adjust their practices and enterprises to cope with, that is, adapt to such changes in the environmental conditions (Mendelsohn, 2000; Seo, 2006, 2013, 2014a).

Another example is choices of animals by rural households. In hotter climate zones, African farmers are observed to switch from cattle, both beef cattle and dairy cattle, to goats and sheep (Seo and Mendelsohn, 2008a). Farmers in Africa are also found to switch from cattle and sheep to goats and chickens in humid climate conditions, the phenomenon which is also observed in Australian agriculture (Seo and Mendelsohn, 2008a; Seo, 2015d).

This means that farmers prefer to raise sheep in a hot and arid climate zone (Seo and Mendelsohn, 2008a; Seo et al., 2010). In the high variability and risk zones resulting from the monsoon climate in India, Indian rural households are found to increase the number of goats owned (Seo, 2016).

Rural areas of the world rely heavily on forests and forest products for income, forest services, and various trades (Peters et al., 1989; Vedeld et al., 2007). The amount of forest resources varies across the continents: in South America, a forest-cover as defined by >50% forest cover over the land area is as large as 44% of the total land area of the continent (WRI, 2005). In the tropical countries of Africa and Latin America, rural residents adopt a variety of forest-related enterprises, either specialized or diversified, in order to utilize the large amount of available forest resources (Seo, 2010c, 2012a). In a hotter and wetter climate zone, rural residents are found to rely more often on forest resources and adopt forest-related enterprises (Seo, 2012b). That is, rural households are observed to switch away from the other enterprises such as crops-based or animals-based to forest-related enterprises such as a forest-only enterprise, a forests-crops enterprise, or a crops-livestock-forests enterprise (Seo, 2012a).

An ocean-based example of microbehavioral decisions is decisions by the residents in the coastal zones. If the sea levels in many important coastal zones were to rise due to an increase in sea surface temperature and global warming as projected by climate scientists, coastal residents may either build a coastal wall or decide to leave the coastal city or town if expected damage is too high or the cost of protection is too high (Yohe and Schlesinger, 1998; Ng and Mendelsohn, 2006; IPCC, 2014).

Coastal towns and residents that are frequently in the path of deadly hurricanes should make not a few decisions in order to reduce the vulnerability and damages from hurricane strikes, especially if the severity and frequency of hurricanes were to increase due to global warming (Emanuel, 2013). For example, concerned municipalities may issue an early warning, evacuate the residents, build bunkers and shelters, educate the residents on specific protective measures, or prevent the residents from walking outside during the hurricane landfalls. A more sophisticated hurricane trajectory prediction, a more wind-resistant building, and a sound levee system will help vulnerable individuals make right decisions (Seo, 2015e; Bakkensen and Mendelsohn, 2015).

A response to a change in external factors sometimes calls for a community level cooperative action. For example, a sea wall to protect from a sea level rise is unlikely to be built by a single coastal resident. A construction of a sea wall to protect a coastal zone has a characteristic of a community good. The sea wall should cover the entire coastal line; a single crack or an empty space in the stretch of the sea wall will render the rest of the sea wall ineffective in stopping an inundation.

Another example of a community response in managing agricultural and natural resources is the construction of a public irrigation system. A majority of irrigation schemes are privately built and managed. If, however, an irrigation system can service an entire community while a private irrigation is too costly, it would be more efficient to construct the irrigation system jointly by community members rather than individually (Coman, 1911; Seo, 2011a). For the same reason, it may be more efficient for a local government to provide a public irrigation system. A public irrigation scheme, however, can also result in inefficiencies.

In managing environmental and natural resources, a community-level decision with an informal agreement and coordination can play a pivotal role in providing a local public good and efficiently allocating a common pool resource, especially in a tightly-knit community (Ostrom, 2009). For example, a commons in a village can be managed through an informal agreement among the village members in order to prevent excess utilization. This book will place community-level decisions in the context of microbehavioral decisions by a community which are apposite for applications of the microbehavioral econometric methods.

Numerous decisions made by individuals or rural managers in response to climatic changes or environmental constraints have been studied empirically in the past two decades through applications of microeconometric methods (Seo, 2006). Over time, policy implications of empirical studies of individual decisions have rapidly become clearer owing to fast-paced changes in a global negotiation landscape on global warming.

It dawned on the researchers and policy-makers that we cannot know quantitatively how much damage global warming will incur without a full consideration of these micro decisions (Adams et al., 1990; Rosenzweig and Parry, 1994; Mendelsohn et al., 1994). The magnitude of expected damage from global warming will by and large determine the level of carbon tax and the level of reduction in the emissions of greenhouse gases called for, the two critical policy variables (Nordhaus, 1994, 2013). What it implies is that quantitative results from the microbehavioral models presented in this book often turn out to be a key input variable for policy dialogues on various issues.

On a more practical side, the micro decisions some of which were briefed above are increasingly recognized in the policy communities as a center-piece of policy responses to global environmental challenges (Seo, 2015a,c). Reflecting the gradual awakening, the focal point of global negotiations has gradually shifted from a mitigation focus in the early years to an adaptation focus in the recent years (UNFCCC, 1992, 1998, 2011b, 2013). Many countries which have rejected the Kyoto Protocol's mitigation commitments, including the United States, China, and South Korea, have voluntarily pledged billions of dollars to the United Nations' adaptation finance known as the Green Climate Fund.

The gravity of the research on microbehavioral decisions in the face of global environmental challenges has been elucidated by the ever increasing influences the microbehavioral studies have had on numerous policy discussions of global warming as demonstrated in part by the above-referenced international policy documents (UNFCCC, 2015). This again demonstrates the prominence of the microbehavioral econometric methods in the policy-relevant areas of research such as global environmental problems and natural resource uses.

There are a number of specialized microeconometrics textbooks that are widely adopted in relevant courses including Train (2003); Cameron and Trivedi (2005); and Agresti (2013). There are more than a few major econometrics textbooks that have had success in the past decade and are widely adopted as a textbook for econometrics courses, which contain microeconometric methods as one chapter of the book such as Johnston and Dinardo (1997); Wooldridge (2010); and Greene (2011). Relying on the extensive literature on econometrics, microeconometrics, behavioral economics, and environmental and natural resource studies, this book offers a number of new advances that separate this book from the earlier mentioned textbooks.

First, this book deals with the full extent of microdecisions. That is to say, the microbehavioral methods introduced in this book explicitly account for all the phases of decision-making: reasons, options, alternative classifications of options, consequences, and welfare changes (Seo, 2010b, 2015b). At this point of the book, readers may not have a clear understanding of what these phases are and imply, but will certainly become acquainted gradually with each of these phases as they go further through the book. This approach of the book, curiously, differs from those approaches adopted in the other textbooks in which the emphasis is laid heavily on modeling choice decisions (Train, 2003; Cameron and Trivedi, 2005).

Second, this book provides an illuminating description and analysis of the relationship between the whole system and the subsystems of economic activities. An individual economic agent's choice of an occupation from the full variety of available options inevitably leads to the formations of subsectors of the economy within the whole economic system. Available microeconometric textbooks pay little attention to this important subject. This is despite the fact that the seminal study by Heckman was pointing a finger to this development (Heckman, 1979, 2000). This book will unravel numerous whole system-subsystem relationships that arise through microdecisions, the ways that the microbehavioral econometric methods can capture them, and constraints and implications for microbehavioral models (Seo, 2015b).

Third, this book provides a fresh perspective on human decisions and natural systems through microbehavioral econometric models. The warming of the Earth is viewed as a change in the natural systems. Individuals' decisions will reflect changes in the natural ecosystems as these changes are embedded in the varied profitabilities of natural resource intensive enterprises such as crop agriculture, animal husbandry, and forestry. The present author will highlight the exquisite interconnections that exist between ecological systems and human behaviors and anthropogenic systems (Seo, 2011b, 2012b, 2014a). What this modeling perspective will lead to is that natural systems are not independent of anthropogenic natural resource systems and simultaneously the manmade systems are rooted on the natural ecological systems.

Fourth, this book offers an elegant microbehavioral econometric framework for modeling risk and uncertainties that arise from the environmental changes and the microbehavioral decisions undertaken to deal with and adapt to such changes in risk and uncertainties (Seo, 2012c, 2014b). Making decisions under risk and uncertainties has long been a prominent economics subject in the context of financial and investment decisions (Markowitz, 1952; Tobin, 1958; Sharpe, 1964; Black and Scholes, 1973). Recent experiences of the financial crises in the first decade of the 21st century, that is, the dotcom bubble burst in 2000 and the global financial crisis that began in 2008, have given much weight to the behavioral and psychological factors that influence market indices such as critical value, framing, irrational exuberance, bubble, and speculation (Kahneman and Tversky, 1979; Shiller, 1981, 2000, 2005; Case and Shiller, 2003).

In the natural resources intensive sectors, the literature has focused on irreversibility of capital investments and threshold events beyond which prethreshold states are not recoverable (Arrow, 1971; Arrow and Fisher, 1974; Weitzman, 2009; IPCC, 2012). In the extreme case, the risk involved is undefined

(Mandelbrot, 1963; Mandelbrot and Hudson, 2004, Weitzman, 2009). That is, the threshold event occurs when no one expects it. However, in most cases of reality, individuals and communities can deal with the risk and uncertainties in a rational manner by employing an array of coping strategies (von Neumann and Morgenstern, 1947; Fama, 1970; Udry, 1995; Nordhaus, 2011; Mendelsohn, 2012).

The microeconometrics literature has, by and large, not explored the aspects of risk and uncertainties in an individual's decisions (Train, 2003; Cameron and Trivedi, 2005). A unique feature of this book is that the present author provides a category of risk and uncertainties in the context of environmental and natural changes faced by microagents who make decisions. For example, rainfall swings from severe drought years to heavy rainfall years and vice versa are examined as one of the risk factors faced by Sub-Saharan farmers faced with climatic changes (Janowiak, 1988; Hulme et al., 2001; Shanahan et al., 2009; Seo, 2012c). Another example of risk factors is a monsoon climate system, which dominates the regional climate system in India and South Asia. A monsoon brings exceedingly high rainfall in the monsoon season which is often more than 100 times the nonmonsoon season rainfall, which leads to unique behavioral decisions by Indian farmers (Meehl and Hu, 2006; IPCC, 2014, Seo, 2016).

This book comprises eight chapters. In Chapters 2 and 3, the present author provides a full description of microbehavioral methods for modeling microdecisions in the context of environmental and natural changes. Chapter 2 describes the microeconometric methods from the perspectives of economics, that is, economic options, choices, outcomes, and welfare changes that are involved in and arise from decision-making. Comparisons and contrasts with alternative methodological approaches are made in this chapter whenever needed in order to highlight the micro and behavioral aspects of the book.

Chapter 3 has the same objective as Chapter 2 of describing the microbehavioral econometric methods, but the emphasis is laid on the statistical assumptions and considerations which call for numerous adjustments in empirical models. The chapter will also provide mathematical proofs and simulations as necessary of the key equations and formulations that are applied throughout this book.

Topics discussed in Chapter 3 include binary choice models, polychotomous choice models (McFadden, 1974), choices of discrete choice methods (Wooldridge, 2010; Greene, 2011), simulation-based methods for discrete choice models (McFadden and Train, 2000; Train, 2003), selection bias correction methods when binary or multiple choices are involved (Heckman, 1979; Lee, 1983; Dubin and McFadden, 1984; Schmertmann, 1994; Dahl, 2002), Monte Carlo simulations for selection bias correction models (Schmertmann, 1994; Bourguignon et al., 2004), spatial spillover and neighborhood effects (Moran, 1950a,b; Anselin, 1988; Case, 1992; Beron and Vijverberg, 2004), identification strategies (Fisher, 1966; Johnston and Dinardo, 1997; Manski 1995), applications to panel data (Train, 2003; Cameron and Trivedi, 2005), modeling successive choices (McFadden, 1978; Chib and Greenberg, 1998), and bootstrap methods for estimating uncertainties (Efron, 1981; Andrews and Buchinsky, 2000).

From Chapter 4–7, applications of the microbehavioral econometric methods developed in the previous chapters are presented. Using the empirical data collected in South American households, these chapters show quantitative estimates of various measures and concepts of the microbehavioral methods. The present author highlights the critical and unique insights that result from modeling microdecisions using microeconometric methods by comparing with the results from alternative methodologies.

Chapter 4 provides an application of the microbehavioral methods to South American agriculture data which contain the observed farmer decisions collected from seven countries across the continent (Seo and Mendelsohn, 2008b). This chapter will showcase all the phases of the microbehavioral decisions, natural constraints faced by individuals, and results from such decisions. Being the first chapter with the empirical data, the chapter will for the first time delineate the environmental problems to be dealt with in the book and the natural and anthropogenic aspects that are connected with the problems (IPCC, 2014).

The application in Chapter 5 further develops the concepts and methodologies presented in Chapter 4. It deals with the relationship between the subsystems and the whole system. The whole system is defined to be the family of agricultural and natural resource enterprises. A subsystem is one of these enterprises that an individual chooses. For example, a subsystem may be a livestock-only enterprise. This chapter examines how and why a microbehavioral modeling of subsystems is similar to a direct modeling of the whole system in some aspects and different from it in other aspects (Seo, 2015b).

In Chapter 6, the present author provides another application of the microbehavioral methods by constructing a more complex structure of the microbehavioral model (Seo, 2012b, 2014b). A more complex structure is constructed in tandem with the natural systems, ecosystems, or ecological systems that are predicted to undergo changes under external forces. An external force in the chapter is anthropogenic footprints on the natural systems through accumulation of Carbon Dioxide emissions that result from industrial activities and land use changes. This chapter couples changes in the natural systems with changes in microbehavioral decisions, which is a novel concept for both microeconometricians and biogeophysical scientists.

In Chapter 7, the present author provides another application of the microbehavioral methods with a focus on the risk and uncertainties that arise due to environmental changes (Seo, 2012c, 2015f). The present author examines a variety of ways for modeling environmental risk and uncertainties that have been well known to the environmental and natural resource researchers. One of the risk factors, mentioned already earlier, is the fluctuation of yearly rainfall from severe drought years to extremely heavy rainfall years and vice versa, which is common in the Sahelian region. Another example is a monsoon climate in South Asia in which the amount of rainfall swings drastically back and forth from an extremely high monsoon rainfall to an extremely low nonmonsoon rainfall. Using the empirical data from the relevant regions, the present author explains how an individual manager makes a set of decisions to cope with such environmental risk and uncertainties.

In describing the concepts and modeling experiences on risk and uncertainties, the present author draws insights from the financial and investment economics literature. Major concepts that are reviewed are a portfolio theory (Markowitz, 1952; Tobin, 1958), attitudes towards risk (Arrow, 1971), capital asset pricing models (Sharpe, 1964), insurance (Sumner and Zulauf, 2012), futures (Fabozzi et al., 2009), options (Black and Scholes, 1973), prospect theory (von Neumann and Morgenstern, 1947; Kahneman and Tversky, 1979), and a speculation and bubble theory (Fama, 1970; Shiller, 1981, 2014).

In the final chapter, Chapter 8, the present author delves on and endeavors to advance policy aspects of the microbehavioral models (Seo, 2014c, 2015c; UNFCCC 2011a, 2011b). Being the primary empirical question of this book, global warming is at the center of the discussions of policy implications, relevance, and impacts of the microbehavioral applications. The importance of adaptation literature in the contexts of global warming policy decisions is elaborated in detail (Seo, 2015f). However, the present author extends the descriptions to other environmental and natural resource issues of our time including energy uses, air pollution, transportation systems and automobile pollution, water management, and agricultural and resource subsidies.

The empirical data used in the book for applications of the microbehavioral methods are drawn from the studies of global warming and adaptation strategies (Seo, 2015b). Many readers of this book, for example, graduate students in the economics or statistics department may have only intermittent observations on the science and economic problems of global warming. And some of them may not even have had any prior experience on any other environmental issues. For these readers who pick up this book for study, it will be worthwhile for the present author to give a brief introduction to the central environmental issue that is addressed throughout this book.

The phenomenon of global warming is sometimes referred to as the defining issue of our times. Although, there are also many people who would argue against such an emphatic claim, there are many reasons why the dialogues on global warming have become a deeply troubling issue in the world. First and foremost, it is because the science of global warming challenges the ways and foundations that the modern societies have been built: industrialization, division of labor, specialization, mass productions, extensive appropriations of natural resources, urbanization, transportation, communication, and globalization (Smith, 1776; Nordhaus and Tobin, 1972; Nordhaus, 1977).

The theory of greenhouse effects states that the increases in greenhouse gases in the atmosphere in the process of industrializations and natural resource appropriations form a greenhouse-like blanket in the atmosphere, which blocks and reflects back the infrared solar radiation from the Earth surfaces (Le Treut et al., 2007; IPCC, 2014). The greenhouse level serving as a thermostat, the greenhouse effect leads to an increase in the global average temperature of the atmosphere. The most powerful greenhouse gas in altering the Earth's temperature is carbon dioxide (CO_2). Other potent greenhouse gases are Methane (CH_4), Nitrous Oxides (N_2O), water vapor (H_2O), and fluorinated gases such as HFCs (hydroflurocarbons), PFCs, and SF6.

An increase in the level of Carbon Dioxide in the atmosphere was first systematically recorded by Charles D. Keeling from the Scripps Institute of Oceanography. His record began in the late 1950s and has continued until today in the observatory set up in the top of the Mauna Loa Mountain in

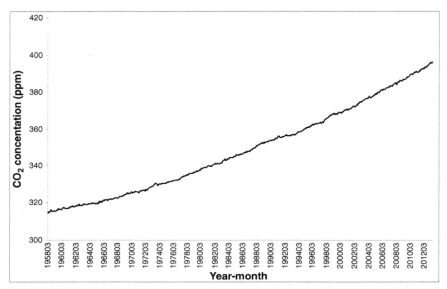

Figure 1.1 *Atmospheric carbon dioxide concentration since 1950s in the Mauna Loa Observatory. (The figure is drawn by the author from the data recorded at the Mauna Loa Observatory as compiled in the Carbon Dioxide Information and Analysis Center of the Oak Ridge National Laboratory at http://cdiac.ornl.gov).*

Hawaii (Keeling et al., 2005). His record shown in Fig. 1.1 above is called the "Keeling Curve" and is one of the most fundamental findings of global warming science. The figure shows that the atmospheric concentration of Carbon Dioxide was below 320 ppm (parts per million) in the 1950s and has increased since then to around 400 ppm in 2014, overriding seasonal fluctuations.

Carbon Dioxide is the primary greenhouse gas accounting for more than 80% of the greenhouse effects (Global Carbon Project, 2014). CO_2 is the most troublesome greenhouse gas because it is the byproduct of burning of fossil fuels such as coal, oil, and natural gas (US EPA, 2011). The burning of these fossil fuels produces more than 90% of the energy used in the United States and elsewhere (US EIA AEO, 2014). The energy produced from low-carbon or zero-carbon energy sources such as solar energy, wind energy, geothermal energy accounts for less than 2% of the total energy produced in the United States. This low-carbon energy production percentage is not significantly higher in any other countries of the world.

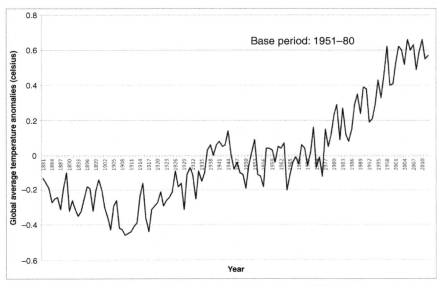

Figure 1.2 *Global average temperature anomalies since 1880. (The figure is drawn from the data provided by the Goddard Institute of Space Studies (GISS) as compiled in the Carbon Dioxide Information and Analysis Center of the Oak Ridge National Laboratory at http://cdiac.ornl.gov).*

What this means is that the world has no alternative but to rely on burning of fossil fuels to power economic growth and sustain livelihoods of people. Technological options such as fusion energy have turned out to be extremely expensive to develop and the pace of development has been slow (ITER, 2015, LLNL, 2015). A carbon capture and storage technology has been employed locally, but is not an economical option for any country (IEA, 2013).

How much temperature rise can the increase in Carbon Dioxide concentration in the atmosphere cause? The records of global average temperature are available since 1880s when instrumental records began. The Fig. 1.2 above shows the temperature record kept by the Goddard Institute of Space Studies (GISS) of the National Aeronautic and Space Administration (NASA) of the United States (Hansen et al., 2006). The figure shows that the global average temperature has increased by 0.6°C from the 20th century average temperature. The figure plots the anomalies, that is, yearly deviations from the 20th century annual average temperature which is about 14°C (Le Treut et al., 2007). Celcius is an international unit for temperature. A conversion formula from Fahrenheit (°F) is C = 5/9 × (F − 32).

A contentiously debated key question on the science of global warming is whether the observed temperature trend shown in Fig. 1.2 is just a reflection of natural fluctuations of temperature caused by changes in the nature. Natural causes for global temperature fluctuations are numerous: inter alia, changes in the Earth's orbit around the Sun, changes in Sunspots, multidecadal fluctuations in ocean currents, and changes in dust in outer space.

To separate the changes in global temperature caused by natural variations from the changes in global temperature caused by an anthropogenic increase in Carbon Dioxide, climate scientists put together all the causes of temperature changes and attribute them to either natural causes or anthropogenic causes.

The IPCC attribution exercise is shown in Fig. 1.3. In the two figures, the record of global temperature presented in Fig. 1.2 is reproduced. The top figure simulates the changes in global average temperature using both natural causes and anthropogenic causes and overlay them to the observed trend in temperature. In the bottom figure, scientists simulate the changes in global average temperature using only natural causes, leaving out changes in anthropogenic greenhouse gases, and overlay them to the observed trend in global temperature. As readers can verify, the bottom figure with only natural causes taken into account cannot explain the changes in the observed global temperature. This means that anthropogenic causes of global warming must be added to explain the observed increase in global average temperature in the 20th century.

There is no doubt that the greenhouse effects will lead not only to changes in global average temperature but also to other weather and climatic variables, the most prominent of which is precipitation changes (Hansen et al., 2012). A global precipitation is harder to measure than a global temperature since it varies greatly even across a small geographical area, for example, a small city. This means that a global estimate of rainfall is more difficult to quantify. Empirical data on regional historical rainfall amounts do not suggest historical variations in changes in precipitation patterns: there is no single trend in global precipitation similar to the global temperature trend shown in Fig. 1.2.

Along with changes in temperature, alteration in precipitation amounts and patterns have grave consequences on microbehavioral decisions of those

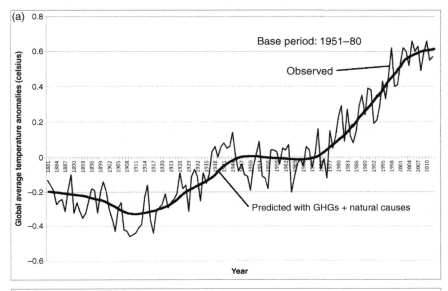

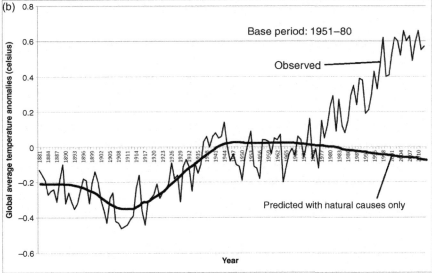

Figure 1.3 *Attribution of global warming to natural and anthropogenic causes.* (a) Predicted with both anthropogenic and natural causes; (b) Predicted with natural causes only. *(These figures are drawn by the present author by approximating the means in the figure in the IPCC 2014 report).*

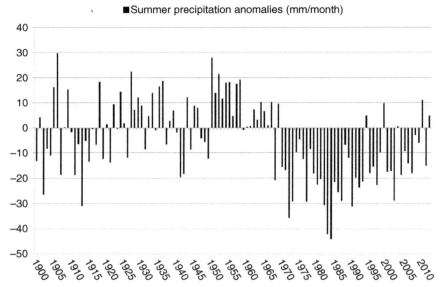

Figure 1.4 *Precipitation changes in the Sahelian region. (The figure was drawn from the data provided by the Joint Institute for the Study of Ocean and the Atmosphere (JISOA), University of Washington, JISOA, 2015).*

who manage natural and environmental resources. In Fig. 1.4, the present author draws the changes in summer season precipitation in the Sahelian region (Janowiak, 1988; Hulme et al., 2001). The Sahel is the ecoclimatic and biogeographic zone of transition in Africa between the Sahara Desert to the north and the Sudanian Savanna to the south. For the period from 1900 to 2013, the figure shows summer precipitation anomalies from the summer season mean precipitation constructed from the 30 year period rainfall data from 1950–79. In the figure, the summer is defined to range from Jun. to Oct.

As shown in the figure, average summer precipitation has fluctuated greatly in the Sahelian region since the beginning of the 20th century. In the early decades of the past century, precipitation often had swung wildly from year to year. A severe drought year is often followed by a heavy rainfall year. The most notable is the prolonged drought period in the 1970s and the 1980s. In the 2000s, precipitation has been relatively higher than the previous three decades. The severe drought decades in the late 20th century is preceded by the high rainfall decades from the 1920s–50s.

This swing from the heavy rainfall decades to the severe drought decades in the Sahel is well known among the climate scientists. This particular

pattern in precipitation is attributed to changes in the ocean circulation known as the Atlantic Multidecadal Oscillation (Hulme et al., 2001;
Shanahan et al., 2009). This particular pattern does not appear in other
continents or regions which exhibit their own unique characteristics in
precipitation patterns.

A key scientific question on global warming is how large and how fast
temperature change will be by the end of 21st century. According to the
recent IPCC report, the prediction is riddled with uncertainties: it ranges
from 1–4.6°C (IPCC, 2001, 2014). The best guess estimate of climate sensitivity is 3°C in response to a Carbon Dioxide doubling.

The IPCC prediction has a wide range because of different assumptions
on the future economy and energy use patterns on which fixed probabilities
cannot be assigned (Nakicenovic et al., 2000; Gordon et al., 2000; Schmidt
et al., 2005). In addition, there are more than a dozen global climate models
called the Atmospheric Oceanic General Circulation Model (AOGCM)
used for the IPCC prediction. These AOGCM models differ from one to
another in the model's structure and a large number of sensitivity parameters (IPCC, 2007; Le Treut et al., 2007).

This book has come to fruition through about one and a half decades'
research by the present author on the economics of global warming. Directly and indirectly, many people have contributed to the development
of the theories and empirical models presented in this book. The present
author had the honor to learn personally from Professors Robert Mendelsohn and William Nordhaus. The economic theories on global warming
presented in this book were by and large laid out by the two distinguished
economists, for which the author would like to express heart-felt gratitude
to them (Nordhaus, 1994; Mendelsohn et al., 1994). The microbehavioral
econometric framework presented in this book was conceived initially by
the present author with the advice from Professor Robert Mendelsohn
(Seo, 2006; Seo and Mendelsohn, 2008a,b).

The presentations of the microeconometrics literature throughout the
book draw heavily from the lifetime works by the two distinguished econometricians: Daniel McFadden at the University of California Berkeley and
James Heckman at the University of Chicago. The present author would
like to acknowledge the enduring contribution of their works to environmental and natural resource fields.

Finally, I owe thanks to the editorial team at Elsevier and Academic Press
for superbly managing the publication of this book. J. Scott Bentley coordinated the review process of the book proposal and Susan Ikeda and Julie-Ann

Stansfield coordinated the editorial and production works for the publication of the book. The present author would like to thank also more than five anonymous reviewers who provided valuable comments on the proposal.

In closing this chapter, the present author wishes to underscore that the entire book is written with the ongoing international policy negotiations on climate change in mind. The success of an international policy intervention will certainly hinge on how well a policy or a set of policies is designed to capture and alter microdecisions of individuals. A family of microbehavioral econometric methods presented throughout this book will provide an essential tool for the policy-makers of global warming and for the researchers who care to look into the behaviors of individuals.

Exercises
1. From the historical record of global temperature anomalies shown in Fig. 1.2 measured and calculated by the Goddard Institute of Space Studies, fit a linear trend line or a nonlinear trend line after employing several different definitions of climate normals. Is it possible to confirm statistically that there has been a significant climate change over this time period?
2. Continuing with the question 1, is it possible to reject statistically that there has been a significant climate change over a subset of the time period?

REFERENCES

Adams, R., Rosenzweig, C., Peart, R.M., Ritchie, J.T., McCarl, B.A., Glyer, J.D., Curry, R.B., Jones, J.W., Boote, K.J., Allen, L.H., 1990. Global climate change and US agriculture. Nature 345, 219–224.

Agresti, A., 2013. Categorical Data Analysis, third ed. John Wiley & Sons, New Jersey.

Andrews, D.K., Buchinsky, M., 2000. A three-step method for choosing the number of bootstrap repetitions. Econometrica 68, 23–51.

Anselin, L., 1988. Spatial econometrics: Methods and models. Kluwer Academic Publishers, Dordrecht.

Arrow, K.J., 1971. Essays in the theory of risk bearing. Markham Publishing Co, Chicago.

Arrow, K.J., Fisher, A.C., 1974. Environmental preservation, uncertainty, and irreversibility. Q. J. Econ. 88, 312–319.

Bakkensen, L.A., Mendelsohn, R., 2015. Risk and adaptation: evidence from global hurricane damages and fatalities. J. Assoc. Environ. Res. Econ. Available from: http://www.laurabakkensen.com/wp-content/uploads/2016/01/Risk-and-Adaptation.pdf

Beron, K.J., Vijverberg, W.P.M., 2004. Probit in a spatial context: a Monte Carlo approach. In: Anselin, L., Florax, R.J.G.M., Rey, S.J. (Eds.), Advances in Spatial Econometrics: Methodology, Tools and Applications. Springer-Verlag, Heidelberg, Germany, pp. 169–192.

Black, F., Scholes, M., 1973. The pricing of options and corporate liabilities. J. Polit. Econ. 81 (3), 637–654.

Bourguignon, F., Fournier, M., Gurgand, M., 2004. Selection bias corrections based on the multinomial Logit model: Monte-Carloc. DELTA Working Paper No. 20, Département et Laboratoire d'Economie Théorique et Appliquée. (DELTA).

Cameron, A.C., Trivedi, P.K., 2005. Microeconometrics: Methods and Applications. Cambridge University Press, Cambridge.

Case, A., 1992. Neighborhood influence and technological change. Reg. Sci. Urban Econ. 22, 491–508.

Case, K.E., Shiller, R.J., 2003. Is there a bubble in the housing market? Brookings Pap. Econ. Act. 2003, 299–342.

Chib, S., Greenberg, E., 1998. Analysis of multivariate Probit models. Biometrika 85, 347–361.

Coman, K., 1911. Some unsettled problems of irrigation. Am. Econ. Rev. 1 (1), 1–19.

Dahl, G.B., 2002. Mobility and the returns to education: testing a Roy model with multiple markets. Econometrica 70, 2367–2420.

Dubin, J.A., McFadden, D.L., 1984. An econometric analysis of residential electric appliance holdings and consumption. Econometrica 52 (2), 345–362.

Efron, B., 1981. Nonparametric estimates of standard error: the jackknife, the bootstrap and other methods. Biometrika 68, 589–599.

Emanuel, K., 2013. Downscaling CMIP5 climate models shows increased tropical cyclone activity over the 21st century. Proc. Nat. Acad. Sci. 110 (30), 12219–12224.

Fabozzi, F.J., Modigliani, F.G., Jones, F.J., 2009. Foundations of Financial Markets and Institutions, fourth ed. New York, Prentice Hall.

Fama, E.F., 1970. Efficient capital markets: a review of empirical work. J. Finance 25 (2), 383–417.

Fisher, F.M., 1966. The Identification Problem in Econometrics. McGraw-Hill, New York.

Global Carbon Project, 2014. Global Carbon Budget 2014. Available from: http://cdiac. ornl.gov/GCP/.

Gordon, C., Cooper, C., Senior, C.A., Banks, H.T., Gregory, J.M., Johns, T.C., Mitchell, J.F.B., Wood, R.A., 2000. The simulation of SST, sea ice extents and ocean heat transports in a version of the Hadley Centre coupled model without flux adjustments. Clim. Dynam. 16, 147–168.

Greene, W.H., 2011. Econometric Analysis. Prentice Hall, New York.

Hansen, J., Sato, M., Reudy, R., Lo, K., Lea, D.W., Medina-Elizade, M., 2006. Global temperature change. Proc. Nat. Acad. Sci. 103, 14288–14293.

Hansen, J., Sato, M., Reudy, R., 2012. Perception of climate change. Proc. Nat. Acad. Sci. 109 (37), E2415–E2423.

Heckman, J., 1979. Sample selection bias as a specification error. Econometrica 47, 153–162.

Heckman, J., 2000. Microdata, heterogeneity and the evaluation of public policy. Nobel Prize Lecture for Economic Sciences. Stockholm University, Sweden.

Hulme, M., Doherty, R.M., Ngara, T., New, M.G., Lister, D., 2001. African climate change: 1900-2100. Clim. Res. 17, 145–168.

International Energy Agency (IEA), 2013. Technology Roadmap: Carbon Capture and Storage. IEA, France.

Intergovernmental Panel on Climate Change (IPCC), 2001. Climate Change 2001 the Physical Science Basis, the Third Assessment Report. Cambridge University Press, Cambridge.

IPCC, 2007. Climate Change 2007 the Physical Science Basis, the Fourth Assessment Report. Cambridge University Press, Cambridge.

IPCC, 2012. Managing the risks of extreme events and disasters to advance climate change adaptation. A Special Report of Working Groups I and II of the Intergovernmental Panel on Climate Change. Cambridge University Press, Cambridge.

IPCC, 2014. Climate Change 2014 the Physical Science Basis, The Fifth Assessment Report of the IPCC. Cambridge University Press, Cambridge.

ITER, 2015. ITER: The World's Largest Tokamak. Available from: https://www.iter.org/mach.

Janowiak, J.E., 1988. An investigation of interannual rainfall variability in Africa. J. Clim. 1, 240–255.

Johnston, J., Dinardo, J., 1997. Econometric Methods, Fourth ed. McGraw-Hill, New York.

Joint Institute for the Study of Ocean and the Atmosphere (JISOA), 2015. Sahel Precipitation Index. JISOA, University of Washington, Seattle, WA.

Kahneman, D., Tversky, A., 1979. Prospect theory: an analysis of decision under risk. Econometrica 47, 263–291.

Keeling, C.D., Piper, S.C., Bacastow, R.B., Wahlen, M., Whorf, T.P., Heimann, M., Meijer, H.A., 2005. Atmospheric CO_2 and $^{13}CO_2$ exchange with the terrestrial biosphere and oceans from 1978 to 2000: observations and carbon cycle implications. In: Ehleringer, J.R., Cerling, T.E., Dearing, M.D. (Eds.), A History of Atmospheric CO_2 and its Effects on Plants, Animals, and Ecosystems. SpringerVerlag, New York.

Lawrence Livermore National Laboratory (LLNL), 2015. How NIF Works. Available from: https://lasers.llnl.gov/about/how-nif-works.

Le Treut, H., Somerville, R., Cubasch, U., Ding, Y., Mauritzen, C., Mokssit, A., Peterson, T., Prather, M., 2007. Historical overview of climate change. In: Solomon S., Qin D., Manning M., Chen Z., Marquis M., Averyt K.B., Tignor M., Miller H.L. (Eds.), Climate Change, 2007, The physical science basis. Contribution of working group I to the fourth assessment report of the intergovernmental panel on climate change. Cambridge University Press, Cambridge.

Lee, L.F., 1983. Generalized econometric models with selectivity. Econometrica 51, 507–512.

Mandelbrot, B., 1963. The variation of certain speculative prices. J. Bus. 36 (4), 394–419.

Mandelbrot, B., Hudson, R.L., 2004. The (Mis)Behaviour of Markets: A Fractal View of Risk, Ruin, and Reward. Profile Books, London.

Manski, C.F., 1995. Identification Problems in the Social Sciences. Harvard University Press, Cambridge, MA.

Markowitz, H., 1952. Portfolio selection. J. Finance 7, 77–91.

McFadden, D.L., 1974. Conditional logit analysis of qualitative choice behavior. In: Zarembka, P. (Ed.), Frontiers in Econometrics. Academic Press, New York, pp. 105–142.

McFadden, D.L., 1978. Modeling the choice of residential location. In: Karlqvist, A., Lundqvist, L., Snickars, F., Weibull, J., (Eds.), Spatial interaction theory and residential location. North Holland, Amsterdam, pp. 349–353.

McFadden, D.L., 1984. Econometric analysis of qualitative response models. Grilliches, Z., Intrilligator, M.D. (Eds.), Handbook of Econometrics, Vol. II, Elsevier Science Publishers BV, Amsterdam.

McFadden, D., 1999a. Discrete Response Models. Lecture Note. University of California, Berkeley, Chapter 1.

McFadden D, 1999b. Sampling and Selection. Lecture Note. University of California, Berkeley, Chapter 2.

McFadden, D., Train, K., 2000. Mixed MNL models for discrete response. J. Appl. Econ. 15, 447–470.

Meehl, G.A., Hu, A., 2006. Megadroughts in the Indian monsoon region and southwest North America and a mechanism for associated multidecadal Pacific sea surface temperature anomalies. J. Clim. 19, 1605–1623.

Mendelsohn, R., 2000. Efficient adaptation to climate change. Clim. Change 45, 583–600.

Mendelsohn, R., 2012. The economics of adaptation to climate change in developing countries. Clim. Change Econ. 3, 1–21.

Mendelsohn, R., Nordhaus, W., Shaw, D., 1994. The impact of global warming on agriculture: a Ricardian analysis. Am. Econ. Rev. 84, 753–771.

Moran, P.A.P., 1950a. Notes on continuous stochastic phenomena. Biometrika 37, 17–23.

Moran, P.A.P., 1950b. A test for the serial dependence of residuals. Biometrika 37, 178–181.

Nakicenovic, N., Davidson, O., Davis, G., Grübler, A., Kram, T., La Rovere, E.L., Metz, B., Morita, T., Pepper, W., Pitcher, H., Sankovski, A., Shukla, P., Swart, R., Watson, R., Dadi, Z., 2000. Emissions Scenarios, A Special Report of Working Group III of the Intergovernmental Panel on Climate Change. IPCC, Geneva.

Ng, W.S., Mendelsohn, R., 2006. The economic impact of sea-level rise on nonmarket lands in Singapore. Ambio 35, 289–296.

Nordhaus, W.D., Tobin, J., 1972. Is Growth Obsolete? In Economic Growth. National Bureau of Economic Research, Boston.

Nordhaus, W., 1977. Economic growth and climate: the carbon dioxide problem. Am. Econ. Rev. 67, 341–346.

Nordhaus, W., 1994. Managing the Global Commons. The MIT Press, Cambridge, MA.

Nordhaus, W., 2011. The economics of tail events with an application to climate change. Rev. Environ. Econ. Policy 5, 240–257.

Nordhaus, W., 2013. The Climate Casino: Risk, Uncertainty, and Economics for a Warming World. Yale University Press, New Haven, CT.

Ostrom, E., 2009. Beyond Markets and States: Polycentric Governance of Complex Economic Systems. Nobel Lecture. The Royal Swedish Academy of the Sciences, Sweden.

Peters, C.M., Gentry, A.W., Mendelsohn, R.O., 1989. Valuation of an Amazonian rainforest. Nature 339 (6227), 655–656.

Rosenzweig, C., Parry, M., 1994. Potential impact of climate change on world food supply. Nature 367, 133–138.

Schmertmann, C.P., 1994. Selectivity bias correction methods in polychotomous sample selection models. J. Econom. 60, 101–132.

Schmidt, G.A., Ruedy, R., Hansen, J.E., Aleinov, I., Bell, N., Bauer, M., Bauer, S., Cairns, B., Canuto, V., Cheng, Y., DelGenio, A., Faluvegi, G., Friend, A.D., Hall, T.M., Hu, Y., Kelley, M., Kiang, N.Y., Koch, D., Lacis, A.A., Lerner, J., Lo, K.K., Miller, R.L., Nazarenko, L., Oinas, V., Perlwitz, J., Rind, D., Romanou, A., Russell, G.L., Sato, M., Shindell, D.T., Stone, P.H., Sun, S., Tausnev, N., Thresher, D., Yao, M.S., 2005. Present day atmospheric simulations using GISS ModelE: comparison to in-situ, satellite and reanalysis data. J. Clim. 19, 153–192.

Seo, S.N., 2006. Modeling Farmer Responses to Climate Change: Climate Change Impacts and Adaptations in Livestock Management in Africa. PhD Dissertation, Yale University, New Haven.

Seo, S.N., 2010a. Is an integrated farm more resilient against climate change?: a microeconometric analysis of portfolio diversification in African agriculture? Food Policy 35, 32–40.

Seo, S.N., 2010b. A microeconometric analysis of adapting portfolios to climate change: adoption of agricultural systems in Latin America. App. Econ. Perspect. Policy 32, 489–514.

Seo, S.N., 2010c. Managing forests, livestock, and crops under global warming: a microeconometric analysis of land use changes in Africa. Austr. J. Agric. Resour. Econ. 54 (2), 239–258.

Seo, S.N., 2011a. An analysis of public adaptation to climate change using agricultural water schemes in South America. Ecol. Econ. 70, 825–834.

Seo, S.N., 2011b. A geographically scaled analysis of adaptation to climate change with spatial models using agricultural systems in Africa. J. Agr. Sci. 149, 437–449.

Seo, S.N., 2012a. Adapting natural resource enterprises under global warming in South America: a mixed logit analysis. Econ. J. Lat. Am. Caribb. Econ. Assoc. 12, 111–135.

Seo, S.N., 2012b. Adaptation behaviors across ecosystems under global warming: a spatial microeconometric model of the rural economy in South America. Papers Reg. Sci. 91, 849–871.

Seo, S.N., 2012c. Decision making under climate risks: an analysis of sub-Saharan farmers' adaptation behaviors. Weather Clim. Soc. 4, 285–299.

Seo, S.N., 2013. An essay on the impact of climate change on US agriculture: weather fluctuations, climatic shifts, and adaptation strategies. Clim. Change 121, 115–124.

Seo, S.N., 2014a. Evaluation of Agro-Ecological Zone methods for the study of climate change with micro farming decisions in sub-Saharan Africa. Eur. J. Agron. 52, 157–165.

Seo, S.N., 2014b. Coupling climate risks, eco-systems, anthropogenic decisions using South American and Sub-Saharan farming activities. Meteorol. Appl. 21, 848–858.

Seo, S.N., 2014c. Adapting sensibly when global warming turns the field brown or blue: a comment on the 2014 IPCC Report. Econ. Aff. 34, 399–401.

Seo, S.N., 2015a. Micro-Behavioral Economics of Global Warming: Modeling Adaptation Atrategies in Agricultural and Natural Resource Enterprises. Springer, Cham, Switzerland.

Seo, S.N., 2015b. Modeling farmer adaptations to climate change in South America: a microbehavioral economic perspective. Environ. Ecol. Stat. 23 (1), 1–21.

Seo, S.N., 2015c. Adaptation to global warming as an optimal transition process to a greenhouse world. Econ. Aff. 35, 272–284.

Seo, S.N., 2015d. Adapting to extreme climate changes: raising animals in hot and arid ecosystems in Australia. Int. J. Biometeorol. 59, 541–550.

Seo, S.N., 2015e. Fatalities of neglect: adapt to more intense hurricanes? Int. J. Climatol. 35, 3505–3514.

Seo, S.N., 2015f. Helping low-latitude poor countries with climate change. Regulation. Winter 2015-2016 Issue: 6–8.

Seo, S.N., 2016. Untold tales of goats in deadly Indian monsoons: adapt or rain-retreat under global warming? J. Extreme Events 3. doi: 10.1142/S2345737616500019.

Seo, S.N., Mendelsohn, R., 2008a. Measuring impacts and adaptations to climate change: a structural Ricardian model of African livestock management. Agric. Econ. 38, 151–165.

Seo, S.N., Mendelsohn, R., 2008b. A Ricardian analysis of the impact of climate change impacts on South American farms. Chil. J. Agric. Res. 68, 69–79.

Seo, S.N., McCarl, B., Mendelsohn, R., 2010. From beef cattle to sheep under global warming? An analysis of adaptation by livestock species choice in South America. Ecol. Econ. 69, 2486–2494.

Shanahan, T.M., Overpeck, J.T., Anchukaitis, K.J., Beck, J.W., Cole, J.E., Dettman, D.L., Peck, J.A., Scholz, C.A., King, J.W., 2009. Atlantic forcing of persistent drought in West Africa. Science 324, 377–380.

Sharpe, W.F., 1964. Capital asset prices: a theory of market equilibrium under conditions of risk. J. Finance 19, 425–442.

Shiller, R.J., 1981. Do stock prices move too much to be justified by subsequent changes in dividends? Am. Econ. Rev. 71 (3), 421–436.

Shiller, R.J., 2000. Irrational Exuberance. Princeton University Press, Princeton, NJ.

Shiller, R.J., 2003. From efficient markets theory to behavioral finance. J. Econ. Persp. 17, 83–104.

Shiller, R.J., 2004. The New Financial Order: Risk in the 21st Century. Princeton University Press, Princeton, NJ.

Shiller, R.J., 2005. Irrational Exuberance, second Ed. Princeton University Press, Princeton, NJ.

Shiller, R.J., 2014. Speculative asset prices. Am. Econ. Rev. 104 (6), 1486–1517.

Smith, A., 1776. An Inquiry into the Nature and Causes of the Wealth of Nations. W. Strahan and T. Cadell, London.

Sumner, D.A., Zulauf, C., 2012. Economic & Environmental Effects of Agricultural Insurance Programs. The Council on Food, Agricultural & Resource Economics (C-FARE), Washington DC.

Tietenberg, T., Lewis, L., 2014. Environmental & Natural Resource Economics. Prentice Hall, New York.

Tobin, J., 1958. Liquidity preference as behavior toward risk. Rev. Econ. Stud. 25 (2), 65–86.

Train, K., 2003. Discrete Choice Methods with Simulation. Cambridge University Press, Cambridge.

Udry, C., 1995. Risk and saving in Northern Nigeria. Am. Econ. Rev. 85, 1287–1300.

United Nations Framework Convention on Climate Change (UNFCCC), 1992. The United Nations Framework Convention on Climate Change. New York.

United Nations Framework Convention on Climate Change (UNFCCC), 1998. Kyoto Protocol to the United Nations Framework Convention on Climate Change. UNFCCC, Geneva.

United Nations Framework Convention on Climate Change (UNFCCC), 2011a. The Durban Platform for Enhanced Action. UNFCCC, Geneva.

United Nations Framework Convention on Climate Change (UNFCCC). 2011b. Report of the transitional committee for the design of Green Climate Fund. UNFCCC, Geneva.

United Nations Framework Convention on Climate Change (UNFCCC), 2013. Report of the Green Climate Fund to the Conference of the Parties and guidance to the Green Climate Fund. UNFCCC, Warsaw.

United Nations Framework Convention on Climate Change (UNFCCC), 2015. The Paris Agreement. Conference Of the Parties (COP) 21, UNFCCC, Geneva.

United States Energy Information Administration (US EIA), 2014. Annual Energy Outlook 2014. Washington, DC: USEIA.

United States Environmental Protection Agency (US EPA), 2011. Inventory of US greenhouse gas emissions and sinks: 1990-2009. US EPA, Washington DC.

Vedeld, P., Angelsen, A., Bojø, J., Sjaastad, E., Kobugabe, G.K., 2007. Forest environmental incomes and the rural poor. Forest Policy Econ. 9, 869–879.

von Neumann, J., Morgenstern, O., 1947. Theory of Games and Economic Behavior, second ed. Princeton University Press, Princeton, NJ.

Weitzman, M.L., 2009. On modeling and interpreting the economics of catastrophic climate change. Rev. Econ. Stat. 91, 1–19.

Wooldridge, J.M., 2010. Econometric Analysis of Cross Section and Panel Data. MIT Press, MA.

World Resources Institute (WRI), 2005. World Resources 2005: The Wealth of the Poor: Managing Ecosystems to Fight Poverty. WRI, Washington, DC.

Yohe, G.W., Schlesinger, M.E., 1998. Sea level change: the expected economic cost of protection or abandonment in the United States. Clim. Change 38, 337–342.

CHAPTER 2

Modeling Microbehavioral Decisions: Economic Perspectives

An individual makes many decisions during his/her lifetime in the form of a choice from multiple discrete alternatives (McFadden, 1984, 1999a). In many of these decisions, a chosen alternative determines the path and economic outcome of the individual's life over a long time horizon. For example, an individual makes a choice decision on which university she/he will attend to earn a degree. A woman makes a decision on whether she/he will enter into a labor market or work at home. One makes a choice of which city she/he will live for her/his life. One decides whether she/he will take a bus or a train to the workplace for daily commutes. Microeconometrics is a field of statistics which quantitatively explains individuals' choices using a probabilistic theory (Train, 2003; Cameron and Trivedi, 2005).

In choosing one of the many alternatives, an individual relies on an indicator which informs her of the final outcome of the choice. This may be the total discounted net return expected from the selected alternative in the long term. She will choose the alternative which earns her the highest net return among all the alternatives available. An indicator should be defined in the broadest sense to include all the possible outcomes of the decision that are valued by an individual.

Of the many choice decisions that an individual makes, some decisions are a participation decision, that is, a decision on whether one will participate in a certain market (or group) or not. An individual will decide to enter the market if the total net return from the market participation is expected to exceed a reference value which is unique to the decision maker. In a situation where there are multiple alternatives from which an individual can choose, she/he will choose one option only if the total discounted net return from the alternative of choice would exceed those expected from the other available alternatives.

In environmental and natural resource studies, discrete choice decisions of individuals have been treated as a key factor in explaining market and environmental outcomes (Freeman, 2003; Mendelsohn and Olmstead, 2009). For example, a hedonic property method explains the variation in property values by, inter alia, individuals' varied preferences and choices of a certain

Microbehavioral Econometric Methods

environmental quality such as cleaner air free of smog. Similarly, a hedonic wage method explains the variation in observed wages by, *inter alia*, individuals' varied preferences and choices of job-related risks and compensations. Nevertheless, modeling probabilistic choices of individuals have been set aside as secondary in the past environmental and natural resource studies. Instead, the focus of the literature laid on the variation of prices or wages.

In the environmental and natural resource literature, microdecisions of individuals have become a major field of scientific inquiry through the heated debates on whether and how societies can adapt to global warming challenges (Seo, 2013b, 2014a, c). Early studies argued that the magnitude of damage from global warming will depend on whether, how, and how easily farmers will adapt to global climate changes (Rosenberg, 1992; Mendelsohn, 2000; Hanemann, 2000). The seminal paper by Mendelsohn et al. (1994) showed empirically that the impact of climate warming by about 2–3°C may not harm the American agriculture if farmers adapt by substituting inputs and switching customary practices.

However, adaptation strategies were never studied or quantified for a decade since the seminal paper until, Seo and Mendelsohn (Seo, 2006; Seo and Mendelsohn, 2008a) presented an empirical adaptation model using African farmers' choices of household animals in response to climatic conditions in the continent. The authors reported that African farmers will switch from cattle and chickens to more heat tolerant livestock species of goats and sheep when climate becomes hotter. The authors also found that African farmers switch from cattle and sheep to goats and chickens when precipitation increases due to global warming.

The initial model of microadaptations to global warming has been further developed since then to explain a variety of agricultural systems: a crops-only, a mixed crops-livestock, a livestock-only, irrigated agriculture, rainfed agriculture (Seo, 2010a, b, 2011a). The adaptation model has been further advanced to include all natural resource intensive enterprises. That is, forest-based activities, which constitute a major fraction of the South American rural economy such as a crops-forests, a crops-livestock-forests, and a forests-only enterprise are explicitly integrated into the model structure (Seo, 2012a, b).

This book describes the literature of microbehavioral econometric methods that is pertinent and therefore can be applied to the research endeavors on a large array of environmental and natural resource problems that face today's societies. The book elaborates economic and behavioral theories, developments of microbehavioral models, and applications to empirical environmental and natural resource data. The present author integrates multiple disciplines of research such as climate science, environmental and ecological science, economics and finance, econometrics, and statistics to put forth the literature of microbehavioral econometric methods for environmental and natural resource studies.

Empirical applications of the microbehavioral models are presented in Chapters 4–7 with the rural households' environmental and natural resource decisions collected in a large number of low-latitude developing countries in three continents. The surveys of household decisions were taken from Africa, Latin America, and South Asia (Seo and Mendelsohn, 2008b; Seo et al., 2009; Seo, 2016). In Africa, eleven countries were included: Burkina Faso, Senegal, Niger, Ghana from West Africa; Cameroon from Central Africa; Egypt from North Africa; Ethiopia, Kenya from East Africa; Zimbabwe, Zambia, South Africa from Southern Africa. Household surveys from Latin America were collected from seven Latin American countries: Argentina, Brazil, Chile, Uruguay from the Southern Cone region; Ecuador, Colombia, Venezuela from the Andean region. For South Asian studies, agricultural data from Sri Lanka and India are used.

An agricultural and natural resource manager chooses a portfolio of farm products she/he manages given climatic and geographic conditions. A large number of crops are planted around the world (Reilly et al., 1996; Mata et al., 2001). In addition, there are many different types of crops. Some of the major grain crops are maize, wheat, rice, barley, millet, and sorghum. Some of the major bean crops are soybeans, legumes, pulses, and lentil. Some of the major root crops are potatoes, sweet potatoes, cassava, carrots, and radish. Some of the major oil seeds are sunflower, canola, mustard seeds, and sesame seeds. Some of the major vegetables are lettuce, spinach, tomatoes, egg plants, Chinese cabbage, onions, green onions, garlic, pepper, cucumber, zucchini, and broccoli. Other specialty crops include sugarcane, sugar beet, tobacco, ginseng, etc.

Besides the large portfolio of crops which has received dominant attention from agricultural as well as development researchers at the expense of other salient rural activities, an agricultural and natural resource manager most often owns domesticated animals, that is, livestock (Nin et al., 2007; World Bank, 2008). Major animals raised by farmers are beef cattle, dairy cattle, goats, sheep, chickens, pigs, horses, ducks, and turkeys. Other animals include donkeys, dogs, camels, Asian water buffalo, beehives etc. Some of these animals are a ruminant. Some farmers sell livestock products such as eggs, wool, meat, milk, cheese, butter, skins, and others.

In the United States, 53% of farms own at least some livestock while live-stock management accounts for 49% of agricultural income (USDA, 2007). In Africa and South America, more than two thirds of the farms own at least some livestock (Seo and Mendelsohn, 2008a; Seo et al., 2010). In South America, almost 15% of the total farms are a specialized livestock farm while only 3–4% farms in Sub Saharan Africa are a livestock-only farm (Seo, 2010a, b). Of the total agricultural lands, pastures used for livestock are four to eight times larger than the croplands in South American countries (Baethgen, 1997; WRI, 2005).

Besides a large number of crops and animals, the pool of portfolios held by natural resource managers includes forest-based portfolios. The income earned from forests and forest products accounts for 22% of rural income in South and Central America (Peters et al., 1989; Vedeld et al., 2007). The forest income is earned from sales of wild foods such as mushroom, tree fruits, fuel wood, fodder, timber, grass/thatch, wild medicine, and others. Nontimber forest products are many and diverse including fruits, nuts, plants, resins, barks, and fibers.

In South America, the forest-covered ecosystem, defined as >50% forest cover, is a dominant ecosystem accounting for 44% of the total land area (WRI, 2005). In South America, 19% of the total farms have forest-based activities: 10% of the farms are a crops-livestock-forests enterprise, 8% a crops-forests enterprise, and 1% is a forests-only farm (Seo, 2012b). Common trees in South America are palm, cacao, cashew, mango, pineapple, citrus, banana, shea nut, apple, Kola, peach, almond, prune, apricot, avocado, cherry, hickory, eucalyptus, lemon, and Brazil nuts (Seo, 2012a). Other common farm trees include coffee, gum acacia in the Sahel; date, persimmons, papaya, guava, guanabana, tea, coconut, chestnut, oak, nut pines, and rubber in South and East Asia (Seo et al., 2005; Seo, 2010c). Besides being sources of income and livelihoods of rural managers, forests provide a sink for Carbon dioxide in the atmosphere as well as settlements for birds and animals (Houghton, 2008; Convention on Biological Diversity, 2010).

Table 2.1 summarizes key features of agricultural and natural resource enterprises that are held in low-latitude developing countries across the world. Arable and permanent crop lands account for 7–8% of the total land area in Sub Saharan Africa and South America. The 35% of the total land area in Sub Sahara is permanent pasture while the 29% of the total land area in South America is permanent pasture. The farms that own some livestock account for 49% in the United States, but about 70% farms own livestock in South America and Sub Sahara. Almost 20% of the farms in South America own livestock only. In South America, about 13% of the rural farms own forests and forest products.

Table 2.1 Key statistics on natural resource enterprises in low-latitude countries

	Crops	Animals	Forests
Major products	Grains (maize, wheat, rice, barley, millet, sorghum); Bean crops (soybeans, legumes, pulses, lentil); Root crops (potatoes, sweet potatoes, cassava, carrots, radish); Oil seeds (sunflower, canola, mustard seeds, sesame seeds); Vegetables (lettuce, spinach, tomatoes, egg plants, Chinese cabbage, onions, green onions, garlic, pepper, cucumber, zucchini, Kale, broccoli); Other specialty crops (sugarcane, sugar beet, tobacco, ginseng, gourds).	Livestock: Beef cattle, dairy cattle, goats, sheep, chickens, pigs, turkey, donkey, ducks, horses, dogs, beehives, llama, etc. Livestock products: Wool, eggs, milk, butter, cheese, hides.	Palm, cacao, cashew, mango, pineapple, citrus, banana, sheanut, apple, Kola, peach, almond, prune, apricot, avocado, cherry, hickory, eucalyptus, lemon, Brazil nuts, coffee, gum acacia date, persimmons, papaya, guava, guanabana, tea, coconut, chestnut, oak, rubber, nut pines, pear, Korean dogwood, plum, blue berry.
Land use percentages	Arable and permanent cropland accounts for 8% of total land area in Sub Sahara and 7% in South America.	Permanent pasture accounts for 35% of total land area in Sub Sahara and 29% of total land area in South America.	Forested area (defined as >50% forest cover) accounts for 44% of the total land area in South America and 18% of the total land area in Sub Sahara.
Ownership percentages	95% in Sub Saharan African rural farms. 80% in South American rural farms.	49% of the US farms. About 70% of Sub Saharan farms. About 70% of South American farms.	13% of rural farms in South America.
Income percentages			22% of rural household income South and Central America.

Note: Data sources are WRI (2005), USDA (2007), Seo (2015a).

From a large number of products and portfolios, a rural manager chooses a portfolio which is composed of any of the products explained earlier (Seo, 2015a). A portfolio of choice can be either a specialized portfolio or a diversified (mixed) portfolio. For example, a farmer may choose a portfolio composed of some crops and some animals. Or, she/he may choose a portfolio composed of some crops, some animals, and some trees. Alternatively, one may choose to specialize in one of these categories of assets, that is, a crops-only, a livestock-only, a forests-only enterprise.

In this particular classification system, the following family of portfolios constitutes the choice set of the rural managers:

Portfolio 1: A crops-only enterprise;

Portfolio 2: A livestock-only enterprise;

Portfolio 3: A forests-only enterprise;

Portfolio 4: A crops-forests enterprise;

Portfolio 5: A crops-livestock enterprise;

Portfolio 6: A livestock-forests enterprise;

Portfolio 7: A crops-livestock-forests enterprise.

The first three portfolios are a specialized portfolio and the latter four portfolios are a diversified portfolio across the three types of assets. It is important to note that diversification is an economic decision which is driven by a motive to deal with risk in returns (Markowitz, 1952; Tobin, 1958). That is, one will choose a diversified portfolio if and only if it gives a higher return than the other specialized portfolios, conditional on the same risk. Equivalently, a farmer will choose a diversified portfolio if and only if it has a lower risk than the other portfolios, conditional on the same return.

Further, diversification is a different behavior from selection or choice. That is, diversification is another dimension of microbehavioral decisions made by individuals. Whereas selection is a behavior to choose one asset, diversification is a behavior to choose a pool of assets. Therefore, a decision maker must consider, among other things, correlations among the assets in the pool in the ways they react to a shock, complementarity of inputs across the assets, and dietary demands for foods.

In agricultural and natural resource industries, a diversification decision can arise for many reasons. For example, a farmer may decide to diversify across crops and animals, so that she/he can graze farm animals when croplands are left fallow in an effort to improve the quality of soils of the croplands during the fallow period. A farmer may diversify across crops and animals since the total profit earned from the diversified portfolio is higher than either of those earned from specialized portfolios in either crops or livestock.

Besides diversification across multiple asset types, that is, crops, livestock, or forests, diversification can take place within each of the seven enterprises. In a crops-only portfolio, for example, a farmer may use inter-cropping or crop rotations, both of which are widely practiced by the farmers across the world. It is commonly believed that diversification through these practices increases the total production and return from the given land (Zilberman, 1998).

A natural resource manager chooses only one of the seven enterprises, as will be formally explained later, in order to earn the highest return, given external conditions, considering the characteristics of risks. Conditional on the choice of one of these enterprises, she/he will make further decisions on the levels of numerous inputs, outputs, farm practices to maximize the profit in the long-term (Seo, 2006, 2015a, b).

If the external condition, for example, a climate system, were to be altered, yields and profitabilities of the seven natural resource enterprises would be changed. These changes would occur through physical changes in Carbon Dioxide concentration in the atmosphere, average temperature, average rainfall, temperature variability, rainfall variability, and shifting seasons (Schlesinger, 1997; Tubiello and Ewert 2002; Ainsworth and Long, 2005; Denman et al., 2007; Hahn et al., 2009). Indirectly, an alteration in the climate system leads to changes in disease occurrences and prevalence which affect animal and plant productivities (Ford and Katondo, 1977; Fox et al., 2012) or influence changes in insects, pests, and weeds (Porter et al., 1991; Ziska 2003).

The changes in yields and returns of the enterprises would be varied across the enterprises. Therefore, a natural resource manager should be allowed in the microbehavioral models to make switch decisions simultaneously on enterprises, production inputs such as labor and capital, production practices, and outputs. To put it differently, the microbehavioral econometric framework which will be presented shortly must capture a full array of adaptations across the enterprises as well as within each enterprise.

Let the observed profit (π) from enterprise 1 by an individual manager n be written as a function of exogenous factors as follows (McFadden, 1999a; Train, 2003):

$$\pi_{n1} = X_n \xi_1 + \varphi_{n1}. \tag{2.1}$$

In the reduced form equation above, X is a vector of explanatory variables that determine the profit from enterprise 1. The second term on the right-hand side is an error term which is assumed to be a white noise. This reduced form equation exists in certain conditions, for example, if there is no selectivity in enterprise 1.

However, since the profit data are only available when enterprise 1 is chosen, the latent (true) profit may differ from the observed profit. Let the latent profit ($\breve{\pi}$) from enterprise j by an individual manager be written as a function of exogenous factors as follows:

$$\breve{\pi}_{nj} = Z_n \zeta_j + \eta_{nj}, \ j = 1, ..., J. \tag{2.2}$$

In the earlier equation, Z is a vector of explanatory variables that determine the profits of not only enterprise 1, but also all the other enterprises. The second term on the right-hand side is an error term which is again assumed to be a white noise. Note that $\breve{\pi}$ is latent, therefore, not observable by a researcher or a resource manager. Therefore, we cannot estimate Eq. (2.2) directly.

Researchers are often concerned with estimating Eq. (2.1) by employing a proper statistical procedure (Greene, 2011). The difficulty arises because, since the profit data of enterprise 1 are available only if that enterprise is chosen, the observed profit data and the latent profit data must be correlated. The estimation of Eq. (2.1) therefore must correct for the correlation that arises from a selection process from multiple alternatives. Otherwise, estimated parameters of Eq. (2.1) will be biased and inconsistent (Heckman, 1979).

In an optimization problem over a long time horizon such as a natural resource manager's optimization decisions under global warming, the profit measure in the left-hand side of Eq. (2.1) is a profit measure over a long time horizon. Such a measure has been a signature feature of the climate change economics literature. Land rent is an annual profit of a farm and land value is defined as the discounted present value of the infinite stream of land rents in the future with flexible discount rates (Ricardo, 1817; Fisher, 1906, 1930; Mendelsohn et al., 1994; Seo, 2015b).

For the purpose of estimating Eq. (2.1) consistently, let's assume the classical error term for Eq. (2.1) for the moment, given X, Z. That is, it has a zero mean and homoscedastic as follows (Bourguignon et al., 2004):

$$\begin{aligned} E(\varphi_{n1} \mid X_n, Z_n) &= 0, \\ Var(\varphi_{n1} \mid X_n, Z_n) &= \sigma^2. \end{aligned} \tag{2.3}$$

The profit data for enterprise 1 are observed only if this enterprise is chosen by an individual manager from the pool of available enterprises. Enterprise 1 will be chosen only if the latent profit from this enterprise exceeds those from all the other enterprises (For simplicity, from now on we will drop the subscript indicating an individual manager as long as there is no ambiguity in reading the equations). That is,

$$\breve{\pi}_1 - \breve{\pi}_k > 0, \forall k \neq 1. \tag{2.4}$$

The probability of enterprise 1 to be chosen by an individual manager is then expressed as follows:

$$
\begin{aligned}
P_1 &= P[\breve{\pi}_1 > \breve{\pi}_k, \forall k \neq 1] \\
&= P[Z\zeta_1 + \eta_1 > Z\zeta_k + \eta_k, \forall k \neq 1] \\
&= P[\eta_k < Z\zeta_1 - Z\zeta_k + \eta_1, \forall k \neq 1].
\end{aligned}
\tag{2.5}
$$

This probability can be solved into a succinct form if we assume a certain distribution for the error term. Let $(\eta_{nj})'s$ be identically and independently Gumbel distributed after spatial resampling (Anselin, 1988; Case, 1992; Seo, 2011b). This is so called Independence from Irrelevant Alternatives (IIA) hypothesis to which we will come back again later in this chapter. A rationale and procedure for spatial resampling will be given in the next chapter.

Then, the probability of enterprise 1 to be chosen by an individual manager is written in a succinct form as a Logit (McFadden, 1974):

$$P_1 = \frac{\exp(Z\zeta_1)}{\displaystyle\sum_{j=1}^{J} \exp(Z\zeta_j)}. \tag{2.6}$$

That the Logit formula in Eq. (2.6) is handily derived from the Gumbel distribution is intuitively clear, given that the third line in Eq. (2.5) is simply the cumulative distribution of the Gumbel distribution. The Gumbel distribution is defined by the following cumulative distribution function (G) and the density function (g):

$$
\begin{aligned}
G(\eta) &= \exp(-e^{-\eta}), \\
g(\eta) &= \exp(-\eta - e^{-\eta}).
\end{aligned}
\tag{2.7}
$$

The sample log-likelihood function is defined as follows:

$$LL = \sum_{n=1}^{N}\sum_{i-1}^{J} d_{ni} \cdot \ln P_{ni} \tag{2.8}$$

where P_{ni} is defined by Eq. (2.6) and d_{ni} is an indicator function whose value equals 1 if the farm household chose alternative i or zero otherwise.

The parameters $(\zeta_j, j = 1,...,J)$ are estimated using a Maximum Likelihood method by maximizing the log-likelihood function in Eq. (2.8). A nonlinear iterative optimization technique such as a Newton–Raphson method is used to find the estimated parameters which maximize the log-likelihood function (Johnston and DiNardo, 1997). The Newton–Raphson method, as in many other optimization techniques, calculates the Score matrix and the Hessian matrix from the log-likelihood function and uses them to find the shortest distance to climb to a certain target level of the log-likelihood function.

The vector Z is a set of explanatory variables in the determination of the profits earned from managing natural resources. In the studies of global warming and climatic changes, primary variables in this vector are climate variables. The climate of a given farming region is identified by climate normals such as a temperature normal or a precipitation normal. For example, a precipitation normal is a 30 year average precipitation of a given region (IPCC, 2014). Note that a climate normal is different from a yearly weather variable.

The distinction between climate and weather is a key concept for understanding individuals' behaviors in response to climatic changes. The distinction is clear in the comparison between annual rainfall and a 30 year average rainfall. An amount of precipitation fluctuates interannually (Rosenzweig et al., 2001). A heavy rainfall year is often followed by a low rainfall year which is again often followed by a high rainfall year. A natural resource manager makes numerous decisions to cope with the amount of rainfall in a specific year. At the same time, a natural resource manager makes many decisions to deal with the long-term average rainfall, that is, rainfall normals.

The decisions to cope with climate normals are by and large different from the decisions to cope with the weather in a specific year. The responses to the weather in a specific year are likely to be dependent upon the decisions taken to cope with a long-term weather pattern, that is, climate normals. Researchers should be careful in defining climate variables which must not be confused for annual weather (Seo, 2013b).

Another aspect of climate and weather is seasons. In capturing behavioral decisions of individuals in response to climate conditions, definition of seasons matters. Many economic activities are seasonally arranged: crops are planted in spring, grown in summer, harvested in autumn, and stored in winter. The climate change impact and adaptation literature has relied on multiple definitions of seasons. A traditional four-season approach is widely used: spring, summer, autumn, and winter (Mendelsohn et al., 1994). In the tropical countries, two seasons were used: summer and winter (Seo and

Mendelsohn, 2008a, b). In the monsoon climate regime, two seasons were used: monsoon period and nonmonsoon period (Seo, 2016).

In the Southern Hemisphere, a summer season corresponds approximately to a winter season in the Northern Hemisphere which falls upon Dec., Jan., and Feb. (Kurukulasuriya et al., 2006; Seo and Mendelsohn, 2008a). As an example, summer precipitation in the Southern Hemisphere can be defined as follows. With PR_t^s being average precipitation for season s and year t:

$$PR_{sum} = \frac{\sum_{t=1}^{30}(PR_t^{Dec} + PR_t^{Jan} + PR_t^{Feb})}{30 \star 3}. \tag{2.9}$$

Instead of using seasons as described earlier, agronomic or statistical crop studies often rely on the concept of growing degree days (Schenkler et al., 2006; Schlenker and Roberts, 2009; Deschenes and Greenstone, 2007). The concept of growing degree days builds upon several key assumptions: (1) there is a base temperature below which the organism does not grow; (2) the growth rate increases with temperature above the base temperature; (3) growth and development of crops are closely related to daily temperature mean accumulations above the base temperature.

Formally, the growing degree days (GDD) is defined as follows:

$$GDD = \frac{TE_{max} + TE_{min}}{2} - TE_{base} \tag{2.10}$$

where TE_{max} is maximum daily temperature and is set equal to 86°F when temperatures exceed 86°F, TE_{min} is the minimum daily temperature and is set equal to 50°F when temperatures fall below 50°F, and TE_{base} is the base temperature for the organism (US EPA 2014).

The GDD concept is useful for understanding crop growth. One of the original uses of the GDD concept was characterization of corn development. Corn (maize) has a base temperature of 50°F and each corn hybrid has a certain GDD requirement to reach maturity. Those varieties grown in the central Corn Belt in the United States require anywhere from 2,100–3,200 GDD depending on the hybrid. The GDD requirement varies across the varieties and the crops. In addition, the GDD requirement event of the same crop variety varies across the crop growing regions. Hence, the GDD concept is less meaningful in microbehavioral studies, which are concerned on the whole range of portfolios farmers hold, not a single grain crop.

Besides climate variables, the vector Z includes other determinants of farm profit and choices such as soils, topography, hydrology, household characteristics, market access, and country-specific variables (Seo and Mendelsohn, 2008b, Seo 2012c). A dominant soil type in any given region of the world is available from the FAO (Driessen et al., 2001; FAO, 2003). Elevation data are available from the Global Multi-resolution Terrain Elevation Data 2010 (GMTED2010) dataset developed by the United States Geological Survey (USGS) and the National Geospatial-Intelligence Agency (NGA) (Danielson and Gesch, 2011). The elevation data are constructed from a large number of source data sets which are often available at 1 arc-second resolution. Hydrology data capture the amounts of seasonal waterflows and the amounts of seasonal runoffs in a given region, which are available from, for example, the University of Colorado hydrology model (Strzepek and McCluskey, 2006). Accessibility to the markets is measured by a travel time or a travel distance to a major city or a major port for purchases of inputs or sales of products, which are available from the World Bank spatial dataset constructed from the World Bank Project on Africa Infrastructure and Country Diagnostic (AICD) (World Bank, 2009a). Detailed explanations of these nonclimate explanatory variables will be given in the application chapters of the book, that is, Chapters 4–7.

A natural resource manager, having chosen an enterprise, say enterprise 1, chooses the bundle of inputs and outputs at the same time to maximize the profit earned from the chosen enterprise over a long time horizon. A researcher who attempts to estimate the profit function of enterprise 1 using the observed profit data of the enterprise and the other observed data of the explanatory variables may estimate the following equation:

$$\pi_{n1} = X_n \tilde{\xi}_1 + v_{n1}. \tag{2.11}$$

This is the same equation as in Eq. (2.1) except the error term which can be defined by a concerned researcher more generally than the error term in Eq. (2.1). That is, the researcher may assume v_{n1} to have the following general variance-covariance matrix structure with heteroscedastic or autocorrelated error terms:

$$COV[v] = COV[v_1, v_2, \ldots, v_J] = \Sigma = \begin{bmatrix} \sigma_{11} & \sigma_{12} & \cdots & & \sigma_{1J} \\ \sigma_{21} & \sigma_{22} & \cdots & & \\ \cdots & \cdots & \cdots & & \\ & & & \cdots & \\ \sigma_{J1} & & & & \sigma_{JJ} \end{bmatrix} \tag{2.12}$$

However, any specification from the whole variety of specifications that is contained in Eqs. (2.11) and (2.12) will end up with a bias due to the selection process involved in estimating Eq. (2.11). That is to say, regardless of how general the specification of the covariance matrix is, a researcher cannot avoid the fundamental problem that the error term in Eq. (2.11) must be correlated with the error term in the selection equation, that is, Eq. (2.2). When selectivity is present, a direct estimation of the outcome equation results in biased parameter estimates (Heckman, 1979, 2000).

To see concretely what the problem is, let's assume that the error term in Eq. (2.11) and the error term in Eq. (2.2) have the following correlation structure:

$$Corr[\eta, v_1] = \begin{bmatrix} Corr(\eta_1, v_1) \\ Corr(\eta_2, v_1) \\ . \\ Corr(\eta_j, v_1) \\ . \\ Corr(\eta_J, v_1) \end{bmatrix} = \begin{bmatrix} \omega_1 \\ \omega_2 \\ . \\ \omega_j \\ . \\ \omega_J \end{bmatrix}, \text{with } \omega_j \neq 0, \forall j. \tag{2.13}$$

Then, the error term in Eq. (2.11) can be rewritten instead by $\eta'_j s$:

$$v_1 = \omega_1 \cdot \eta_1 + \omega_2 \cdot \eta_2 + \cdots + \omega_j \cdot \eta_j + \cdots + \omega_J \cdot \eta_J. \tag{2.14}$$

Therefore, the estimated equation in Eq. (2.11) is not unbiased, therefore not consistent under the general structure of η distribution. That is to say,

$$E[v_1] \neq 0. \tag{2.15}$$

The same conclusion can be drawn to the estimation of the profit function of the other enterprises. When selection is an economic decision, the outcome function of the selected alternative cannot be estimated in an unbiased way. Note that the value of the expectation in the above equation can be either positive or negative since the correlation coefficient ω_j can be either negative or positive. This means the outcome equation can be biased either downward or upward.

Is there a way to estimate without bias the outcome equation of the selected alternative? This is the question that James Heckman asked and provided an answer, for which the Nobel Prize in Economic Science was awarded in the year 2000, along with Daniel McFadden (Heckman, 2000). In the Heckman's seminal paper, the choice decision was dichotomous.

Heckman provided a selection bias correction method for the estimation of the women's wage function in which there are two groups of women: those work at home and those who are paid wages for the jobs they are employed.

In the Heckman problem where the choice is yes/no, the correlation matrix in Eq. (2.13) has only one element which can be identified. Then, a selection bias can be expressed in a simple manner by capturing the single correlation term. Since the Heckman method is also important in a multinomial choice setting to be described later in this chapter, the present author will write down the Heckman problem and method in the following, which can be based on a slighted revised version of Eq. (2.1) and Eq. (2.2):

$$\pi_{n1} = X_n \xi_1 + v_{n1}. \tag{2.1$\star$}$$

$$\tilde{\pi}_{nj} = Z_n \zeta_j + \eta_{nj}, \; j = 0 \quad \text{or} \quad 1. \tag{2.2$\star$}$$

Equations marked with ($\star$) denotes the revised version of Eq. (2.1) and (2.2).

The selection bias correction term for the Heckman binomial problem is derived from the following manipulations:

$$\begin{aligned} E[v_1 \mid \tilde{\pi}_1 > 0] &= E[v_1 \mid Z\zeta_1 + \eta_1 > 0] \\ &= E[v_1 \mid \eta_1 > -Z\zeta_1]. \end{aligned} \tag{2.16}$$

If v_1 and η_1 are uncorrelated, the selection bias term in the above equation is equal to zero. However, since the two error terms are correlated, Eq. (2.17) can be written as follows using the inverse-mills ratio (λ_1) (Greene, 2011):

$$E[v_1 \mid \tilde{\pi}_1 > 0] = \omega_1 \cdot \sigma_{v_1} \cdot \lambda_1(\alpha_{\eta_1}) \tag{2.17}$$

$$\text{where} \quad \lambda_1(\alpha_{\eta_1}) = \frac{\phi(Z\zeta_1 / \sigma_{\eta_1})}{\Phi(Z\zeta_1 / \sigma_{\eta_1})}. \tag{2.18}$$

A consistent estimation of Eq. (2.1)$\star$ in the Heckman problem takes the following form with the white-noise error term (τ_{n1}):

$$\pi_{n1} = X_n \xi_1 + E[v_{n1} \mid \tilde{\pi}_{n1} > 0] + \tau_{n1} \tag{2.19}$$

$$= X_n \xi_1 + \omega_1 \cdot \sigma_{v_1} \cdot \frac{\phi(Z\zeta_1 / \sigma_{\eta_1})}{\Phi(Z\zeta_1 / \sigma_{\eta_1})} + \tau_{n1}. \tag{2.20}$$

In a multinomial choice setting, there are $J-1$ correlation terms. Therefore, the correction of selection bias becomes more complicated as all these terms should be part of the selection bias correction.

In a polychotomous (multinomial) choice setting, the Dubin–McFadden method is known to provide a selection bias correction that outperforms other methods such as the Lee's or the semi-parametric Dahl's method (Dubin and McFadden, 1984; Schmertmann, 1994; Bourguignon et al., 2004). The Dubin–McFadden method outperforms the other methods because it allows for a more flexible correlation structure than the other methods (Lee, 1983; Dahl, 2002). For instance, the Lee's method assumes the same correlation coefficient among all the alternatives in the choice set.

The Lee's method is a generalization of the Heckman method to a multinomial choice situation and assumes the following highly restrictive correlation structure:

$$Corr[\eta_j, v_1] = \omega, \quad \forall j. \tag{2.21}$$

This restrictive correlation structure means that the selection bias term can be expressed as a single parameter, as in the Heckman method for a binomial choice situation (Lee, 1983; Bourguignon et al., 2004).

$$E[v_1 \mid \varepsilon_1 = \underset{j \neq 1}{Max}(\tilde{\pi}_j - \tilde{\pi}_1) < 0, \Gamma] = \omega \cdot \sigma_{v_1} \cdot \frac{\phi(J_{\varepsilon_1}(0 \mid \Gamma))}{F_{\varepsilon_1}(0 \mid \Gamma)}. \tag{2.22}$$

Note the similarity between Eq. (2.22) and Eq. (2.17). In the Eq. (2.22), F is a cumulative distribution of ε_1, Γ is the vector of explanatory variables, and J is a transformation of F. In the next chapter, we will revisit this equation and the Lee's method. For now, it is sufficient to note that the Lee's method is a generalization of the Heckman method to the multinomial choice situations and is a restrictive model because it assumes implicitly that all correlations among the alternatives in the choice set are identical.

Dubin and McFadden (1984) suggested an alternative method which does not impose such a restrictive assumption on the correlation structure. Instead, they assumed the following linearity condition with all the unique correlation parameters included in the equation:

$$E(v_1 \mid \eta_1, \ldots, \eta_J) = \sigma_{v_1} \sum_{j=1}^{J} \omega_j (\eta_j - E(\eta_j)),$$

$$\text{with} \quad \sum_{j=1}^{J} \omega_j = 0, \tag{2.23}$$

$$\text{where} \quad \omega_j = corr(v_1, \eta_j).$$

Eq. (2.23) can be simplified and rewritten as follows:

$$E(v_1 \mid \eta_1, \ldots, \eta_J) = \sigma_{v_1} \sum_{j=2}^{J} \omega_j \cdot (\eta_j - \eta_1). \tag{2.24}$$

If the choice model is the multinomial Logit model as in Eq. (2.6), the expectation of the term in the parenthesis on the right-hand side of the Eq. (2.24) can be derived as follows:

$$E(\eta_j - \eta_1 \mid \breve{\pi}_1 > \max_{j \neq 1} \breve{\pi}_j, \Gamma) = \frac{P_j \cdot \ln P_j}{1 - P_j} + \ln P_j, \quad \forall j \neq 1. \tag{2.25}$$

Then, the conditional long-term profit for enterprise 1 can be estimated consistently after correcting for selection biases (the second term on the right hand side below) with the white-noise error term (δ_1) as follows:

$$\pi_1 = X\xi_1 + \sigma_{v_1} \sum_{j \neq 1}^{J} \omega_j \cdot \left[\frac{P_j \cdot \ln P_j}{1 - P_j} + \ln P_1 \right] + \delta_1. \tag{2.26}$$

Note that there are $J - 1$ selection bias correction terms in the outcome equation in Eq. (2.26) of enterprise 1. Similarly, there will be $J - 1$ selection bias correction terms in the outcome equation of any of the other enterprises. This is in contrast to the generalized Heckman method, that is, the Lee's method, which has only one selection bias correction term for any of the outcome equations.

The sign of each of the selection bias correction terms will reveal the sign of the correlation coefficient between the corresponding two alternatives. This is because σ is always positive while ω_j can be positive or negative. A positive estimate of the selection bias correction term $(\sigma \omega_j)$ will mean that the correlation between η_j and v_1 is positive. A negative estimate of the bias correction term will mean that the correlation between the two error terms is negative.

The estimated bias correction terms tell important economic stories. A negative estimate for the selection bias correction term in Eq. (2.26) for alternative j means that an error term, which increases the choice of alternative j, will decrease the long-term profit of alternative 1. On the other hand, a positive estimate for the selection bias correction term for alternative j means that an error term which increases the choice of alternative j will increase the long-term profit of alternative 1.

To be more concrete, let's say that alternative 1 is a specialized enterprise in crops, alternative 2 is a mixed enterprise of crops and animals, and alternative 3 is a specialized enterprise in animals. Let's assume that we estimated Eq. (2.26) for enterprise 1. Then, there are two selection bias correction terms in the estimated function: one for the mixed enterprise and the other for the specialized enterprise in animals. A negative selection bias correction term that belongs to enterprise 2, if assumed so, would mean that an error term that increases the adoption of the mixed enterprise would decrease the profit of the crops-only enterprise. Similarly, a positive selection bias correction term that belongs to enterprise 3, if assumed so, would mean that an error term that increases the adoption of the specialized enterprise in animals increases the profit of the specialized enterprise in crops.

This again means that, if these parameter estimates are assumed, a farm that is more likely to choose a mixed crops-livestock enterprise has a lower crops-only enterprise profit. Similarly, a farm that is more likely to choose a specialized livestock enterprise has a higher crops-only enterprise profit. This is of course if these farmers were to be managed for the crops-only enterprise instead.

The outcome (profit) equations for the other enterprises are estimated in the same manner. In total, there will be J conditional outcome (profit) equations to be estimated. It is extremely important not to miss the feature that a microbehavioral econometric methodology enables researchers to model component systems of the whole system. Let's say the whole system here is the natural resource system. The whole system comprises numerous natural resource enterprises that are mutually exclusively and exhaustively defined. The seven portfolios introduced in the beginning of this chapter is one such categorization of the natural resource system.

In the microbehavioral econometric methodology described up to now, two sets of equations are estimated simultaneously: the set of choice equations and the set of outcome equations. When there are J alternatives in the choice set to choose from, J outcome equations should be estimated. Note from Eqs. 1 and 2 that the vector of explanatory variables (Z) in the choice equations is different from the vector of explanatory variables (X) in the outcome equation.

In estimating the system of equations, the set of choice equations should be identified from the set of outcome equations (Koopmans, 1949; Fisher, 1966; Manski, 1995). In a nonparametric identification strategy which is most often used by researchers, the vector of explanatory variables in the choice equations should include the subset of explanatory variables that are significant variables for choices among the alternatives but do not affect the outcome (profit) equations. The identification variables should enter only the choice equations and be dropped from the outcome equations.

The identification problem arises when you observe a person and her mirror image at the same time (Manski, 1995). The two objects move at the same time. Does a person cause the mirror image to move? Does the mirror image cause the person to react? You cannot identify one from the other.

In the research contexts, the identification problem occurs when a researcher attempts to estimate J behavioral functions when there are in fact more than J behavioral relations that bring about the J behavioral functions (Johnston and DiNardo, 1997). The J behavioral functions must be identified by employing an identification strategy.

To understand this, let's examine the estimation problem of market demand. A researcher observes only one market data of the numbers of a product sold and prices sold of the product. In Fig. 2.1, an example scatter plot of market data of observed prices and quantities sold of the item is drawn.

A researcher observes the changes in the price over time and the changes in the quantity sold over time. This plot puts together price data and

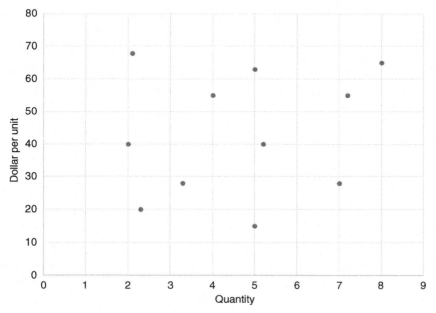

Figure 2.1 *Observed market data on prices and quantities sold of a product.*

quantity data in one space. From the plot, a researcher can identify neither the demand function nor the supply function of the product, although each point in the plot has been determined in the market by the demand and the supply at that point of time. The researcher does not see either a downward sloping demand curve or an upward sloping supply curve in Fig. 2.1.

In order to identify either equation, the researcher needs to know more about changes in the markets, for example, changes in income, changes in other prices, and changes in demographics. For example, one way to identify the demand equation from the above plot is to analyze changes in the equilibrium points during the time period when the demand curve has remained stable. By tracing the changes in the equilibrium supply points along the stable demand curve, one will be able to establish the demand equation. When the demand curve is shifted to another line due to, for example, changes in income level, she/he can estimate another demand curve for the time period when the demand curve remains stable.

Alternatively, the demand equation (or the supply equation) can be identified in the system of equations by adding an explanatory variable that is unique to the demand equation (or the supply equation). For example, an income variable can enter the demand equation and a price of an important input for the product can enter the supply equation. This process prevents the demand equation from being determined by the supply equation, and vice versa.

Let Q_D be the demand amount, Q_S be the supply amount, and x and y are two explanatory variables that determine both dependent (outcome) variables. Let's suppose that a researcher estimates the following structural equation with the classical error terms, ε_D and ε_S:

$$
\begin{aligned}
Q_D &= \alpha_D + \beta_1 x + \beta_2 y + \varepsilon_D, \\
Q_S &= \alpha_S + \varphi_1 x + \varphi_2 y + \varepsilon_S.
\end{aligned}
\tag{2.27}
$$

Since the researcher observes only the quantities sold at certain prices, there is only one quantity at one transaction point, that is, $Q = Q_D = Q_S$. Given the data points in Fig. 2.1, neither of the two equations in Eq. (2.27) can be estimated. A change in one explanatory variable in the supply function also causes a change in the demand function. That is to say, the demand equation is unidentified, so is the supply equation.

An identification of the demand equation can be achieved nonparametrically (Johnston and DiNardo, 1997). Let z be an independent variable which influences the demand function, but not the supply function. Then the following system of equations can be estimated:

$$Q_D = \alpha_D + \beta_1 x + \beta_2 y + \beta_3 z + \varepsilon_D,$$
$$Q_S = \alpha_S + \varphi_1 x + \varphi_2 y + \varepsilon_S.$$
$$(2.28)$$

The system of equations in Eq. (2.28) is said to be exactly identified, which occurs when $J-1$ identification variables are entered in the system of J equations. In simple terms, when there are two equations to be estimated, one unique variable identifies one equation and therefore the other equation too. The system of equations can be over-identified or under-identified when the number of identification variables (NI) satisfies the following equations:

$$\text{Over-identified if } NI > J - 1;$$
$$\text{Under-identified if } NI < J - 1.$$
$$(2.29)$$

Getting back to the microbehavioral model in Eq. (2.2) and Eq. (2.26), there are J alternatives to choose from in the choice model as well as J outcome equations. Choices of enterprises influence profits earned from enterprises while profits of enterprises influence choices. To exactly identify the choice equations from the outcome equations or vice versa, there should be $J-1$ identification variables.

The $J-1$ identification variables will be chosen so that they affect the choice of an individual agent from the pool of options, but do not affect the long-term profits of the options that are chosen. To give an example, the present author will build a microeconometric model outlined so far for the study of agricultural systems, which is presented in Chapter 4 of this book. In the first stage of the model, an individual agents' choice of one of the three agricultural systems is modeled: a crops-only, a livestock-only, a mixed. In the second stage, land value of one of the systems is estimated after correcting for selection biases. The choice equations were identified using two identification variables. One was the topographic variable indicating whether the terrain was flat or not. Another was the distance to the nearest coast (Seo, 2010b, 2015b).

The chosen identification variables were effective in explaining the choice of agricultural systems in the past studies. That is, a farmer is more likely to choose a livestock-only system in a flat terrain than the other systems. Also, a farmer is more likely to choose a crops-only system if the farm is located near the coast due to export considerations, for example, refrigeration costs of livestock products (Seo, 2010b, 2011b). The identification variables turned out insignificant in explaining the land values of these systems of agriculture with other explanatory variables controlled.

From the choice probabilities estimated in Eq. (2.6) and the conditional long-term profit equations estimated in Eq. (2.26), a researcher can estimate the expected profit from natural resource enterprises at the microlevel. This is done by multiplying the probability of each enterprise to be adopted to the conditional profit of that enterprise, repeating the procedure for all the enterprises in the model, and summing these products across all the natural resource enterprises in the model. Formally, let C be the vector of climate variables and Π be expected long-term profit. Then, the expected long-term profit for farm n is written as follows:

$$\Pi_n(C) = \sum_{j=1}^{J} P_{nj}(C) \cdot \pi_{nj}(C). \tag{2.30}$$

Note that the Π is not observed by a researcher, nor by a manager. It is the welfare measure pertinent to each microagent. It is the expected profit given the full array of enterprises available as an option to each agent. It is the weighted sum of all enterprise unbiased profits using the estimated probabilities of adopting enterprises.

The change in this welfare measure, $\Delta\Pi$, resulting from a change in the climate vector from C_0 to C_1 can be measured as the difference in the expected profit before and after the change:

$$\Delta\Pi_n = \Pi_n(C_1) - \Pi_n(C_0). \tag{2.31}$$

The change in the welfare measure in Eq. (2.31) captures both the changes in adoption probabilities of natural resource enterprises and the changes in the conditional profit equations of all the enterprises (Seo, 2013b, 2014c). That is, the microbehavioral models can capture both changes in systems or enterprises as well as changes in economic activities within each of the systems. This can be clarified by rewriting Eq. (2.31) using individual components:

$$\Delta\Pi_n = \sum_{j=1}^{J} P_{nj}(C_1) \cdot \pi_{nj}(C_1) - \sum_{j=1}^{J} P_{nj}(C_0) \cdot \pi_{nj}(C_0). \tag{2.32}$$

Note that all the components in the above welfare equation, if climate is shifted, contribute to the change in the total welfare. In the flow diagram in Eq. 2.33, a change in climate leads to simultaneous changes in the choice probabilities, changes in the conditional profits, and the cross-products of the two terms (denoted as ⋆ below). All these changes lead to the change in the welfare of the microagent:

$$
\Delta C \longrightarrow
\begin{bmatrix}
 & \Delta P_{n1} & \Delta P_{n2} & \cdots & \Delta P_{nJ} \\
\Delta \pi_{n1} & \star & \star & & \star \\
\Delta \pi_{n2} & \star & \star & & \star \\
\cdots & & & & \\
\Delta \pi_{nJ} & \star & \star & & \star
\end{bmatrix}
\longrightarrow \Delta \Pi_n.
\tag{2.33}
$$

A microbehavioral model can be contrasted with a so-called "black box" model in which these changes are all implicitly included. Let ϑ_n be land value observed at the microagent level, that is, farm n. The value of this captures the highest income that can be earned over time at the farm given climate and soil conditions. A researcher can estimate the land value function using climate (C_n) and other exogenous factors (M_n) as explanatory variables as follows:

$$
\frac{\vartheta_n}{w_n} = g\left(\frac{C_n}{w_n}, \frac{M_n}{w_n}\right) + o_n.
\tag{2.34}
$$

All the variables are weighted by w_n. This equation is known as the Ricardian model (Mendelsohn et al., 1994; Deschenes and Greenstone, 2007). A full explanation and analysis of the Ricardian model will be given in Chapter 5, which is one of the primary subjects of this book. The Ricardian model itself or the conceptual basis of the model has been applied widely across the world from the United States to India, Canada, Sri Lanka, Africa, Brazil, South America, China, and Mexico (Mendelsohn et al., 1994; Kumar and Parikh, 2001; Reinsborough, 2003; Seo et al., 2005; Schenkler et al., 2005; Kelly et al., 2005; Kurukulasuriya et al., 2006; Seo and Mendelsohn, 2008b; Sanghi and Mendelsohn, 2008; Wang et al., 2009; Mendelsohn et al., 2010). The Ricardian model is also applied to the panel data of US agriculture with time-varying random effects (Massetti and Mendelsohn, 2011).

The strength of the Ricardian model arises from its conceptual foundation which allows for all adaptive changes to be captured in the model.

The model was developed more than two decades ago in response to agronomic crop models which did not allow for a large number of adaptive measures that farmers routinely take to cope with natural changes (Adams et al., 1990; Rosenzweig and Parry, 1994; Parry et al., 2004; Butt et al., 2005). However, the Ricardian model does not reveal any of the adaptation changes embedded in the model. They are implicit in the model (Seo and Mendelsohn, 2008a).

The microbehavioral model introduced in this book makes adaptation strategies taken by the natural resource managers which are implicitly included in the Ricardian model explicit. To be more concrete, an operation of Eq. (2.6) reveals changes in individuals' adoptions of enterprises as a climate condition is altered. This is achieved while not compromising the capability of the model to encompass a full array of adaptation behaviors in the model. That is, an operation of Eq. (2.26) will capture the full range of adaptation strategies in the corresponding natural resource enterprise.

Given this background on the Ricardian model, Eqs. (2.6, 2.26, and 2.31) can be understood to be tools that unlock the Ricardian black box which contains the full range of adaptation activities. In the above-presented microbehavioral model framework, some adaptation strategies are explicitly modeled while other adaptation strategies are implicitly included. The changes in choices of natural resource enterprises are modeled as an explicit adaptation strategy in the model described in this chapter.

What are the implicit adaptation strategies in the microbehavioral model of this chapter? All other adaptation strategies besides the choices of enterprises are implicit. For example, individuals' choices of crops or crop varieties are included implicitly (Seo and Mendelsohn, 2008c). A farmer can switch animals, for example, from cattle to goats and sheep in a hotter temperature regime or from cattle and sheep to goats and chickens in a wetter climate regime (Seo and Mendelsohn, 2008a). A farmer can adopt an irrigation system as an existing climate regime becomes drier or hotter or more variable (Seo, 2011a). A farmer more likely chooses a mixed portfolio of crops and livestock in order to cope with a hotter or drier climate (Seo, 2010a, 2010b). Similarly, a farmer may change many of cropping and animal husbandry practices including crop rotations, fertilization, chemical uses, farming machines, intercropping, sprinkling, shades, barns, and feedlots in order to cope with numerous climate-related risks (Hahn, 1981; Ruttan, 2002; Mader and Davis, 2004; FAO 2009). A farmer can also adopt a new variety of crops or livestock species which are more heat tolerant or drought resistant (Evenson and Gollin, 2003; Zhang et al., 2013).

That these adaptation strategies are implicitly included in the microbehavioral model presented in this chapter does not mean that one cannot model these adaptation strategies explicitly. As the above referred articles indicate, these strategies can be modeled as an explicit adaptation strategy by developing an apposite model structure. The upshot is that microbehavioral econometric methods are excellent tools that enable environmental and natural resource researchers to examine and quantify the behaviors of individuals observed in the markets and the rural operations. Using these tools, a researcher can model the full range of adaptation strategies explicitly and show quantitatively the impact of each of these adaptation strategies on the microagent's ability to deal with external changes in the environment and nature.

The Eq. (2.32) can capture the impact of a climatic change on an individual with full adaptation strategies employed by the microagent accounted for. A critique, however, can be leveled that a rural manager may not be able to switch from one enterprise to another in response to a climate change from C_0 to C_1 for various reasons (Hanemann, 2000). For example, a farmer may be a subsistence farmer who does not have means and finance to adjust from one enterprise to another enterprise which calls for a substantial investment of capital. In the market economy, she/he may be able to loan money to make adaptive changes and pay back at later years. Let's say that such a financial system is not available, nor is any similar kind of banking systems (World Bank, 2008, 2009b). Then, she/he may end up with the current system unchanged even if the climate is altered.

The microbehavioral econometric models in this chapter have the flexibility to capture such constraints that are faced by decision makers (Seo, 2010b). Let's call this situation a constrained optimization case. In this constrained optimization case, the impact of a climatic change can be calculated by, for example, fixing choice probabilities:

$$\Delta \tilde{\Pi}_n = \sum_{j=1}^{J} P_{nj}(C_0) \cdot \pi_{nj}(C_1) - \sum_{j=1}^{J} P_{nj}(C_0) \cdot \pi_{nj}(C_0). \qquad (2.35)$$

In the above equation, a decision-maker sticks to the adoption probabilities of the enterprises that are currently existent even if the climate is altered from C_0 to C_1 That is, she/he does not make any switch to another enterprise although the climate has changed. In the constrained optimization case, the impact of a climatic change would turn out to be severer than that in the full optimization case captured in Eq. (2.32). Formally,

$$| \Delta\tilde{\Pi}_n | \geq | \Delta\Pi_n | . \tag{2.36}$$

Behavioral and psychological factors that constrain an optimization decision of an individual decision-maker has been an important research field in both economics and psychology since the seminal work by Kahneman and Tversky (1979, 1984) for which the Nobel Prize was awarded in 2002. The seminal papers were directed to the psychological barriers that force an individual to make a seemingly irrational decision. They argued that individuals have a different attitude toward winning and losing in a gamble situation. An individual has a distinct value function and there is a shifting critical value at which attitudes of a decision-maker diverge.

The degree of dominance of psychological factors varies across the range of choices to be made and the situations in which the choices are put into. The psychological factors may not matter much to individuals' decisions with regard to global warming. The rationale for this is that an individual's decision is not motivated by a single year outcome in the global warming case. One must consider long-term changes in the climate and the effects of such changes on her/him in the long-term. That is, one should consider not just a single outcome, but more than a decade long outcomes. A rational decision is more likely to be expected in decisions with regards to global warming and climate change.

On the other hand, behavioral and psychological factors have been reported to have a powerful sway in market indices of stocks, commodities, and real estates, causing the great depression in the 1930s as well as the great recession in the 2000s (Galbraith, 1954; Shiller, 2003, 2005, 2014). Behavioral and psychological elements set forth irrational exuberance among market participants, which lead to a bubble for a sustained period of time after which it bursts eventually, leaving painful experiences to a large fraction of individuals in the society of losses, bankruptcies, foreclosures, and debts. A market bubble arises from the interactions among market participants through which a success story spreads rapidly with envy and exaggeration.

In the economics of global warming, irrationality and/or a bubble can play an important role occasionally. For example, a farmer's high profit from a certain crop, say, garlic, in a certain year may influence the whole village to decide to plant garlic the next year, causing a price drop in a local market due to excess supply. However, it is not easy to imagine that such behavioral factors strongly sway agricultural market prices of an entire country, given information and extension services available. A fuller description of the theory and applications of the behavioral economics and finance which is beyond the scope of this chapter will be taken up in Chapter 7.

The uncertainty on the estimated welfare change in Eq. (2.32) can be quantified by the size of standard error and the confidence interval constructed using the standard error. Since it is difficult to estimate parametrically the standard error of the estimate in Eq. (2.32) due to numerous terms of probabilities and profits involved in the equation, one should prefer to proceed nonparametrically. That is, one can bootstrap the result by calculating the bootstrap standard error (Efron, 1979, 1981).

The bootstrap method interprets the sample data that is available to a researcher as one representation of the population or the universe. A researcher resamples the original sample to obtain a bootstrap sample and she/he repeats the resampling for a sufficiently large number of times (B) (Andrews and Buchinsky, 2000). The resampling is done randomly or based on alternative assumptions of the distribution of the sample data (McFadden, 1999b). The number of observations in each bootstrap sample can be the same as N, the number of data points in the original sample, or a different number. From each of the B samples, one can obtain the estimate of the impact in Eq. (2.32):

$$\left\{ \Delta\Pi^{B_1}, \Delta\Pi^{B_2}, ..., \Delta\Pi^{B_B} \right\}. \tag{2.37}$$

From the impact estimates in Eq. (2.37) obtained from the B bootstrap samples, the researcher can calculate the mean (μ) and the standard deviation (σ) of the estimates. Then, the 95% confidence interval of the impact estimate can be provided as follows, with $P(|x| \geq Z_{0.025}) = 0.05$:

$$\left(\mu^B_{\Delta\Pi} - z_{0.025} \star \sigma^B_{\Delta\Pi}, \mu^B_{\Delta\Pi} + z_{0.025} \star \sigma^B_{\Delta\Pi} \right). \tag{2.38}$$

The same bootstrap procedure can be used to calculate the 95% confidence intervals of the probability estimates in Eq. (2.6) and the conditional profit estimates in Eq. (2.26). Formally, the confidence intervals for P_1 and π_1 can be constructed as follows:

$$\left(\mu^B_{P_1} - z_{0.025} \star \sigma^B_{P_1}, \mu^B_{P_1} + z_{0.025} \star \sigma^B_{P_1} \right) \tag{2.39}$$

$$\left(\mu^B_{\pi_1} - z_{0.025} \star \sigma^B_{\pi_1}, \mu^B_{\pi_1} + z_{0.025} \star \sigma^B_{\pi_1} \right). \tag{2.40}$$

The Eqs. (2.31) and (2.32) make it possible for a researcher to measure the impact of climate change—or other environmental changes—on the welfare of an individual enterprise. A remaining question that needs to be addressed is how to capture a climate system and identify the changes in a climate system (Le Treut et al., 2007). Earlier in this chapter, the present author explained the differences between climate and weather. The author also explained the ways to capture a climate system using climate normals. A climate normal is defined as the 30 year average of temperature or precipitation.

One may argue that this question falls on the realm of science, not economic models (IPCC, 2014; Gordon et al., 2000; Schmidt et al., 2005). The question is one of the key economic questions with regard to global warming and climate changes. Economists have labored painstakingly to identify the most pertinent climate characteristics that determine behavioral decisions of individuals (Mendelsohn et al., 1994; Schenkler et al., 2006; Deschenes and Greenstone, 2012; Welch et al., 2010; Lobell et al., 2011; Seo, 2012c, 2016).

A climate system can be defined in more than one ways. For example, we may define the climate system by characteristics of risk and variability in yearly weather variables. Indeed, climate scientists have increasingly focused on climate risks and extremes, shifting away from the efforts to quantify changes in the average climate, that is, climate normals. Climate scientists have warned the world of the possibilities of increased risks associated with global warming, for example, more frequent extreme weather events, more destructive hurricanes, and disruptions in rainfall patterns in major farming areas, and abrupt climatic shifts (Easterling et al., 2000; IPCC 2001, 2012; Emanuel, 2005; Tebaldi et al., 2007; UNFCCC 2009; Rahmstorf and Coumou, 2011; Hansen et al., 2012; NRC 2013; Titley et al. 2016). Economists are debating about the existence of a climate threshold beyond which a climatic shift turn quickly into a global catastrophe (Weitzman, 2009; Nordhaus, 2011). Changes in climate risk and variability will lead to major changes in yields of plants and crops (Aggarwal and Mall, 2002; Porter and Semenev, 2005). Some argue that agriculture will be severely harmed if climate thresholds for major staple crops were to be crossed (Schlenker and Roberts, 2009).

The microbehavioral econometric methods introduced in this book provide an outstanding scientific framework to model and explain changes in individuals' behaviors in response to changes in risk factors caused by a climatic shift (Seo, 2012c). In making everyday decisions, an individual takes risk, whether small or large, as a fact of life. Always people are forced to make decisions under uncertainty and in consideration of risks involved.

Naturally, economists have long delved into decision-making under risks when financial returns are concerned (Fisher, 1930; Markowitz, 1952; Tobin, 1958; Fama, 1970; Arrow, 1971; Arrow and Fisher, 1974; Kahneman and Tversky, 1979; Shiller, 2003, 2014). Agricultural economists have studied farm management decisions under various farm risks including weather risks (Udry, 1995; Zilberman, 1998; Kazianga and Udry, 2006; Wright, 2011; Sumner and Zulauf, 2012).

Climate risk is a new type of risk that confronts environmental and natural resource managers now and in the future. A rigorous study of climate risk and strategies to cope with it has begun only recently (Reilly et al., 1996; Easterling et al., 2007; Seo, 2012c, 2014b, 2015c, 2016; Bakkensen and Mendelsohn, 2015; Kala, 2015). Nevertheless, characteristics and alterations of climate risks have received substantial attention from researchers in some communities of the globe. The multidecadal swings in precipitation in the Sahelian region over the past millennium are one of the best known examples of climate risk, which is attributed to changes in the ocean known as the Atlantic Multidecadal Oscillation (Janowiak, 1988; Hulme et al., 2001; Shanahan et al., 2009). Another example is the El Nino Southern Oscillation (ENSO) that alternates multidecadally over the Pacific Rim countries, affecting rainfall patterns, droughts, and wild fires (Ropelewski and Halpert, 1987; Curtis et al., 2001).

Many studies of agricultural development in Africa have focused on understanding the weather risks to farmers in Africa (Udry, 1995; Kazianga and Udry, 2006). It should be emphasized once again that climate risk is not the same phenomenon as weather risk. A rural village, which is visited from time to time by a weather shock such as a severe drought or an intense rainfall can still be said to be a low climate risk zone if the number of weather shocks over many decades turn out to be smaller in the village than in the other villages. A high climate risk village is one in which weather shocks occur more frequently and more surprisingly from a sustained period of time, for example, 30 years.

From this point on, the present author explains three indicators of climate risk that affect agricultural and natural resource enterprises: coefficient of variation in precipitation, diurnal temperature range, and monsoon variability index. The risk in the climate regime that an individual farmer faces takes the form of either temperature risk or precipitation risk or both.

A long-term risk in a rainfall regime can be captured by the degree of dispersion in precipitation amounts over a long time period. The Coefficient of Variation in Precipitation (CVP) is a measure of precipitation dispersion over a defined period of time that is independent of the absolute amount of measurement. A seasonal CVP is defined as an average of corresponding monthly CVPs, with PR_{kj} being monthly precipitation in month j and year k and $\bar{R}_j$ being a 30 year average rainfall for month j:

$$CVP_j = \breve{\sigma}_j / \bar{R}_j$$

$$\text{where} \quad \breve{\sigma}_j = \sqrt{\sum_{k=1}^{K} (PR_{kj} - \bar{R}_j)^2 \Big/ (K-1)}. \tag{2.41}$$

The seasonal CVPs are measured from the many decades' data on monthly precipitation normals. A global database of the seasonal CVPs is, for example, constructed from many decades' weather observations, that is, for the 40 year period from 1961 to 2000, at more than 26,000 ground weather stations scattered all parts of the world (New et al., 2002).

The CVP measure is found to be effective in capturing a climate system in the regions where multidecadal and cyclical fluctuations in precipitation exist due to either changes in ocean circulations or other reasons. The seasonal CVPs in Sub Saharan Africa are found to correlate well with the cyclical multidecadal fluctuations in the Sahelian region which are dominated by the Atlantic Multi-decadal Oscillation (Seo, 2012c). The precipitation fluctuations in South American countries caused by the ENSO cycles are explained well by the seasonal CVPs in the continent (Seo, 2014b).

Table 2.2 summarizes the distribution of annual CVP across the Agro-Ecological Zones (AEZ) of Sub Saharan Africa. There are 16 AEZs in the continent according to the AEZ classification system proposed by the Food and Agriculture Organization (FAO) based on the concept of the Length of Growing Periods for crops which is again defined by soil and climate conditions of a spatial location (Dudal, 1980; FAO, 2005; Seo et al., 2009; Seo, 2014a).

The table reveals that the lowland dry savannah zones and the lowland semiarid zones exhibit the highest CVPs, 198% and 226% respectively. The two zones are located in the Sahelian region which lies just below the Sahara Desert. In the desert zones, the CVP is 144%. On the other hand, humid zones have the lowest CVPs. Highland humid forest zones and mid-elevation humid forest zones exhibit 69% of the CVP (Seo, 2012c).

As reported in the earlier referenced articles, the variation in the CVP across the continent leads to drastically different farming decisions made

Table 2.2 CVPs across the AEZs in Sub Saharan Africa

AEZs	Number of sampled households	Coefficient of variation in precipitation (%)	
		Mean	Std
Desert	193	144.8	51.7
High elevation dry savanna	75	97.5	14.9
High elevation humid forest	224	69.1	14.1
High elevation moist savannah	135	90.1	15.1
High elevation semi-arid	20	99.8	0.001
High elevation subhumid	153	77.9	16.7
Lowland dry savannah	1395	198.4	34.5
Lowland humid forest	1061	71.3	12.5
Lowland moist savannah	826	148.1	34.0
Lowland semiarid	1272	226.2	21.7
Lowland subhumid	299	84.2	13.9
Mid-elevation dry savannah	195	145.8	41.8
Mid-elevation humid forest	291	68.5	13.3
Mid-elevation moist savannah	1086	185.5	41.3
Mid-elevation semiarid	27	156.5	33.1
Mid-elevation subhumid	381	89.9	29.7

by rural natural resource managers. In the high CVP zones of Sub Saharan Africa, farmers more often diversify their portfolios into a varied array of crops and animals than the farmers in the low CVP zones do. The high CVP zones therefore show a higher rate of adoption of the mixed system of agriculture.

Another major climate risk variable is a Diurnal Temperature Range (DTR). Scientists are concerned that global warming will unfold with more frequent extreme temperature occurrences. Extreme temperature events are, inter alia, an extremely hot day, an extremely cold day, and a more volatile temperature (IPCC, 2001, Tebaldi et al., 2007). The increases in the intensities and frequencies of these extreme temperature events lead to an increase in the long-term range between daily maximum temperature and daily minimum temperature, that is, the DTR. The changes in the DTR would affect natural resource managers through the changes in growing periods for crops and changes in the frequency and severity of a heat wave event or a cold spell event (Easterling et al., 2000; FAO, 2005; Schlenker and Roberts, 2009; US EPA 2014).

The daily temperature range is measured by the DTR. The DTR data are provided as a monthly average DTR (New et al., 2002). The average monthly DTR in a spatial location for the 40 year period, a DTR normal, can be constructed by averaging the 40 year monthly DTR data. Let TE_{max} be a daily maximum temperature, TE_{min} a daily minimum temperature, j an index for day, m for month, and k for year. Then, the DTR normal for month m is defined as follows:

$$
\text{DTR}_m = \frac{\sum_{k=1}^{K} \sum_{j=1}^{J} (TE_{k,m,j,\max} - TE_{k,m,j,\min})}{J \star K} \tag{2.42}
$$

where J = number of days per month, K = 40 years.

The DTR normal captures temperature volatility over a sustained period of time. Table 2.3 summarizes the seasonal DTR normals across the major land covers in South America. The classification of major land covers is based on satellite imageries and an extensive collection of ground-level studies of land uses, which is available at the Goddard Institute for

Table 2.3 Seasonal DTR normals in South America

Major land covers	Summer DTR (°C)	Winter DTR (°C)
Cold-deciduous forest, with evergreens	13.12	8.6
Tall/medium/short grassland, < 10% woody cover	7.16	11.48
Tall/medium/short grassland, shrub cover	12.05	9.92
Tall/medium/short grassland, 10–40 % woody cover	10.19	14.62
Meadow, short grassland, no woody cover	10.86	11.09
Subtropical evergreen rainforest	12.05	11.74
Tall grassland, no woody cover	13.63	11.19
Temperate/subpolar evergreen rainforest	12.81	7.99
Tropical evergreen rainforest	9.67	11.05
Tropical/subtropical broad forest	9.85	11.38
Tropical/subtropical drought-deciduous forest	9.41	11.93
Xeromorphic forest/woodland	12.04	9.92
Xeromorphic shrubland/dwarf shrubland	13.9	12.01
Water	8.12	7.58

Space Studies (GISS) at the National Aeronautic and Space Administration (NASA) or other similar space programs (Matthews, 1983).

The DTR is high in the xeromorphic forests, tall grasslands with no woody cover, and cold-deciduous forests. In these land covers, summer DTR exceeds 13°C. The DTR is lowest in the water body such as coastal zones, rivers, and lakes. Winter DTR is highest in the grasslands with 10–40% woody cover and lowest in the temperate evergreen forests (Seo, 2014b).

In Sub Saharan lowlands, temperature volatility expressed as the DTR is highest in the lowland arid zones and the lowland semiarid zones which fall most notably upon the Sahelian region. The volatility of temperature is lower in the humid zones of Sub Sahara and in the lowland humid zones (Seo, 2012c).

A third climate risk indicator is identified from a unique regional climate system known as a monsoon. The monsoon is a regional climate phenomenon which is salient in South Asia including Sri Lanka, India, and Thailand (IPCC, 2014). It is characterized by an exceptionally heavy rainfall during a monsoon season and a scarcity of rainfall during a nonmonsoon season (Meehl and Hu, 2006; Goswami et al., 2006; IITM, 2012). Evidently, a monsoon-driven precipitation pattern dominates agricultural activities in these South Asian countries. That is, almost every crop varieties must be harvested before or early in the monsoon season. Otherwise, all left on the fields will be swept away. Growing crops is virtually impossible in a severe monsoon season.

In Table 2.4, the average monsoon season rainfall and the average non-monsoon season rainfall in each state of India for the 40 year period from 1971 to 2010 are summarized. The 40 year rainfall record indicates that the monsoon season, that is, the heaviest rainfall months of the year, ranges from Jun. to Sep. while the nonmonsoon season falls on Dec., Jan., and Feb. In the Gujarat state, the monsoon season rainfall reaches 2126 mm/month, but the nonmonsoon season rainfall drops precipitously to 22 mm/month. In the state of Karnataka, the monsoon season rainfall is as high as 3356 mm/ month but the nonmonsoon season rainfall is as low as 44 mm/month. In Goa, the monsoon rainfall is 5661 mm/month while the nonmonsoon rainfall is 17 mm/month. On the other hand, in the State of Tamil Nadu, the monsoon rainfall is 790 mm/month relative to 430 mm/month for the nonmonsoon season, a much milder transition from one season to another (Seo, 2016).

To identify the risk characteristics of the monsoon climate system, a Monsoon Variability Index (MVI) is created as follows. In the first step,

Table 2.4 Indian monsoon and nonmonsoon season rainfall by State

State and union territories	Average monsoon precipitation (mm/month)	Average nonmonsoon precipitation (mm/month)
Andhra Pradesh	1393	113
Assam	3610	204
Bihar	2550	116
Chhattisgarh	2699	99
Goa	5661	17
Gujarat	2126	22
Haryana	1192	143
Jharkhand	2732	151
Karnataka	3356	44
Kerala	4616	195
Madhya Pradesh	4706	234
Maharashtra	1810	67
Manipur	3097	177
Meghalaya	3610	204
Mizoram	3097	177
Nagaland	3097	177
Odisha	2855	114
Punjab	1340	222
Rajasthan	1078	44
Tamil Nadu	782	435
Tripura	3097	177
Uttar Pradesh	2042	129
West Bengal	3008	161
Dadra and Nagar	2126	22
Daman and Diu	2126	22

based on the 40 year period (from 1971 to 2010) monthly weather data compiled by a weather agency, the ratio of a monsoon season rainfall (PR_t^M) over a nonmonsoon season rainfall (PR_t^{NM}) for each year (t) is calculated:

$$\Phi_t = \frac{PR_t^M}{PR_t^{NM}}. \tag{2.43}$$

In the second step, the coefficient of variation in this ratio for the 40 year period which is defined to be the MVI is calculated:

$$\sum = \sigma^M(\Phi_t)/\overline{\Phi}. \tag{2.44}$$

The MVI (Σ) is a measure of variability in the ratio Φ_t independent of the long-term average where σ^M is the standard deviation in the 40 year rainfall data of the ratio in Eq. (2.43). The MV Index is not a risk measure for a single year. It is a measure of variability (risk) for a 40 year time period, a climate risk normal.

The MVI is a key indicator which encapsulates a monsoon climate risk and has the power to explain South Asian farmers' decisions in response to the monsoon climate system. This point can be elucidated by Fig. 2.2, which plots the numbers of goats per farm across Indian States against the MVI values defined in Eq. (2.44). Overlaid to the two-dimensional plot is the log-linear relationship between the two measures. The estimated relationship shows that South Asian farmers increase the number of goats owned as the MVI increases. This behavioral response is of course an endeavor by the farmers to deal with an increase in climate risk.

The three indicators—CVP, DTR, and MVI—introduced in this chapter capture a riskiness in the climate system as well as uncertainty in the system. As the value of one of these indicators increases, a climate-related uncertainty becomes amplified. Changes in choices and resultant long-term profits from the decisions made in the face of the changes in these risk indicators would capture adaptation strategies adopted by the individual farmers in order to reduce the harmful effects and take advantage of beneficial effects.

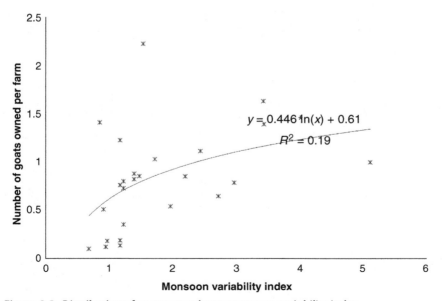

Figure 2.2 *Distribution of goats owned over monsoon variability index.*

In applying the microbehavioral econometric methods to the environmental and natural resource problems, identification of an indicator(s) of the external factor of concern is a crucial statistical procedure. The identification problem has long been regarded as one of the pillar areas of biological, environmental, and ecological statistics. Notwithstanding, this literature has in general made microbehavioral implications from proposed and conventional indicators a secondary consideration (Gregoire and Valentine, 2004). The three indicators of climate risk are, by contrast, developed in order to reveal microbehavioral decisions and consequences that are induced by external changes.

There is a greater understanding among concerned researchers that the microbehavioral econometric methods elaborated thus far depend critically on the reliability and accuracy of available climate and climate risk data. However, it has turned out to be a no minor scientific task (Le Treut et al., 2007). Climate scientists have measured climate variables through observed data from either ground weather stations dispersed around the world or Earth-orbiting satellites (Basist et al., 1998; New et al., 2002). A high resolution data on climate, soils, and geography can play a prominent role in capturing numerous microbehaviors taken by individuals (Adams et al., 2003; Mendelsohn et al., 2007; Fisher et al., 2012; Seo, 2013a).

This completes the presentation of the microbehavioral econometric methods from the perspectives of economic motives and behavioral decisions. In the next chapter, we will continue our journey with an alternative presentation of the microbehavioral econometric methods from the perspectives of the mathematical and statistical considerations and sophistications that go into the microbehavioral models applied to a large variety of unique problems.

Exercises

1. Referring to the microbehavioral econometric model framework presented in this chapter, explain that nonmarket benefits and costs of economic decisions can be accommodated handily in this framework. Explain what nonmarket benefits and costs are pertinent to agricultural and natural resource managers.

2. Referring to the Heckman selection bias correction term for a binomial choice situation, prove that the parameter estimates of the model are attenuated by correcting the selection bias. In other words, show that, using a simple model of selectivity, the OLS estimates overestimate the treatment effect. Explain the implications of this attenuation in terms of the magnitude of the impact of a change in climate on the outcome (profit) variable.

REFERENCES

Adams, R., Rosenzweig, C., Peart, R.M., Ritchie, J.T., McCarl, B.A., Glyer, J.D., Curry, R.B., Jones, J.W., Boote, K.J., Allen, L.H., 1990. Global climate change and US agriculture. Nature 345, 219–224.

Adams, R.M., McCarl, B.A., Means, L.O., 2003. Effects of spatial scale of climate scenarios on economic assessments: an example from the US agriculture. Clim. Change 60, 131–148.

Aggarwal, P.K., Mall, P.K., 2002. Climate change and rice yields in diverse agro-environments of India. II. Effect of uncertainties in scenarios and crop models on impact assessment. Clim. Change 52, 331–343.

Ainsworth, E.A., Long, S.P., 2005. What have we learned from 15 years of free-air CO_2 enrichment (FACE)? A meta-analytic review of the responses of photosynthesis, canopy properties and plant production to rising CO_2. New Phytol. 165, 351–371.

Andrews, D.K., Buchinsky, M., 2000. A three-step method for choosing the number of bootstrap repetitions. Econometrica 68, 23–51.

Anselin, L., 1988. Spatial Econometrics: Methods and Models. Kluwer Academic Publishers, Dordrecht.

Arrow, K.J., 1971. Essays in the Theory of Risk Bearing. Markham Publishing Co, Chicago.

Arrow, K.J., Fisher, A.C., 1974. Environmental preservation, uncertainty, and irreversibility. Q. J. Econ. 88, 312–319.

Baethgen, W.E., 1997. Vulnerability of agricultural sector of Latin America to climate change. Clim. Res. 9, 1–7.

Bakkensen, L.A., Mendelsohn, R., 2015. Risk and Adaptation: Evidence From Global Hurricane Damages and Fatalities. Yale University, New Haven, CT.

Basist, A., Peterson, N., Peterson, T., Williams, C., 1998. Using the special sensor microwave imager to monitor land surface temperature, wetness, and snow cover. J. Appl. Meteorol. 37, 888–911.

Bourguignon, F., Fournier, M., Gurgand, M., 2004. Selection bias corrections based on the Multinomial Logit Model: Monte-Carlo comparisons. DELTA Working Paper No. 20, Département et Laboratoire d'Economie Théorique et Appliquée.(DELTA).

Butt, T.A., McCarl, B.A., Angerer, J., Dyke, P.T., Stuth, J.W., 2005. The economic and food security implications of climate change in Mali. Clim. Change 68, 355–378.

Cameron, A.C., Trivedi, P.K., 2005. Microeconometrics: Methods and Applications. Cambridge University Press, Cambridge.

Campbell, B.D., Smith, D.M.S., Ash, A.J., Fuhrer, J., Gifford, R.M., Hiernaux, P., Howden, S.M., Jones, M.B., Ludwig, J.A., Manderscheid, R., Morgan, J.A., Newton, P.C.D., Nösberger, J., Owensby, C.E., Soussana, J.F., Tuba, Z., Zhong, C.Z., 2000. A synthesis of recent global change research on pasture and rangeland production: reduced uncertainties and their management implications. Agri. Ecosyst. Environ. 82, 39–55.

Case, A., 1992. Neighborhood influence and technological change. Reg. Sci. Urban Econ. 22, 491–508.

Convention on Biological Diversity, 2010. Global Biodiversity Outlook 3. Secretariat of the Convention on Biological Diversity, Montréal.

Curtis, S., Adler, R.F., Huffman, G.J., Nelkin, E., Bolvin, D., 2001. Evolution of tropical and extratropical precipitation anomalies during the 1997 to 1999 ENSO cycle. Int. J. Climatol. 21, 961–971.

Dahl, G.B., 2002. Mobility and the returns to education: testing a Roy model with multiple markets. Econometrica 70, 2367–2420.

Danielson, J.J., Gesch, D.B., 2011. Global multi-resolution terrain elevation data 2010 (GMTED2010). US Geological Survey Open-File Report 2011-1073, 26 p.

Denman, K.L., Brasseur, G., Chidthaisong, A., Ciais, P., Cox, P.M., Dickinson, R.E., Hauglustaine, D., Heinze, C., Holland, E., Jacob, D., Lohmann, U., Ramachandran, S., da Silva Dias, P.L., Wofsy, S.C., Zhang, X., 2007. Couplings between changes in the climate system and biogeochemistry. In: Solomon, S., Qin, D., Manning, M., Chen, Z.,

Marquis, M., Averyt, K.B., Tignor, M., Miller, H.L. (Eds.), Climate Change 2007, the Physical Science Basis. Contribution of Working Group I to the Fourth Assessment Report of the Intergovernmental Panel on Climate Change. Cambridge University Press, Cambridge.

Deschenes, O., Greenstone, M., 2007. The economic impacts of climate change: evidence from agricultural output and random fluctuations in weather. Am. Econ. Rev. 97, 354–385.

Deschenes, O., Greenstone, M., 2012. The economic impacts of climate change: evidence from agricultural output and random fluctuations in weather: reply. Am. Econ. Rev. 102, 3761–3773.

Driessen, P., Deckers, J., Nachtergaele, F., 2001. Lecture Notes on the Major Soils of the World. Food and Agriculture Organization, Rome.

Dubin, J.A., McFadden, D.L., 1984. An econometric analysis of residential electric appliance holdings and consumption. Econometrica 52 (2), 345–362.

Dudal, R., 1980. Soil-related constraints to agricultural development in the tropics. International Rice Research Institute, Los Banos, Philippines.

Easterling, D.R., Evans, J.L., Groisman, P.Y., Karl, T.R., Kunkel, K.E., Ambenje, P., 2000. Observed variability and trends in extreme climate events: a brief review. Bull. Am. Meteorol. Soc. 81, 417–425.

Easterling, W.E., Aggarwal, P.K., Batima, P., Brander, K.M., Erda, L., Howden, S.M., Kirilenko, A., Morton, J., Soussana, J.-F., Schmidhuber, J., Tubiello, F.N., 2007. In: Parry, M.L., Canziani, O.F., Palutikof, J.P., van der Linden, P.J., Hanson, C.E. (Eds.), Food, Fibre and Forest Products. Climate Change 2007: Impacts, Adaptation and Vulnerability. Contribution of Working Group II to the Fourth Assessment Report of the Intergovernmental Panel on Climate Change. Cambridge University Press, Cambridge.

Efron, B., 1979. Bootstrap methods: another look at the jackknife. Ann. Stat. 7, 1–26.

Efron B, 1981. Nonparametric estimates of standard error: the jackknife, the bootstrap and other methods. Biometrika 68, 589–599.

Emanuel, K., 2005. Increasing destructiveness of tropical cyclones over the past 30 years. Nature 436, 686–688.

Evenson, R., Gollin, D., 2003. Assessing the impact of the Green Revolution 1960-2000. Science 300, 758–762.

Fama, E.F., 1970. Efficient capital markets: a review of empirical work. J. Finance 25 (2), 383–417.

Fisher, F.M., 1966. The Identification Problem in Econometrics. McGraw-Hill, New York.

Fisher, I., 1906. The Nature of Capital and Income. Macmillan, New York.

Fisher, I., 1930. The Theory of Interest. Macmillan, New York.

Fisher, A.C., Hanemann, W.M., Roberts, M.J., Schlenker, W., 2012. The economic impacts of climate change: evidence from agricultural output and random fluctuations in weather: comment. Am. Econ. Rev. 102, 3749–3760.

Ford, J., Katondo, K.M., 1977. Maps of tsetse fly (Glossina) distribution in Africa, 1973, according to subgeneric groups on a scale of 1 5000000. Bull. Anim. Health Prod. Afr. 15, 187–193.

Fox, N.J., Marion, G., Davidson, R.S., White, P.C.L., Hutchings, M.R., 2012. Livestock Helminths in a changing climate: approaches and restrictions to meaningful predictions. Animals 2, 93–107.

FreemanIII, A.M., 2003. The Measurements of Environmental and Resource Values: Theory and Practice, second ed. RFF Press, Washington DC.

Food and Agriculture Organization (FAO), 2003. The digital soil map of the world (DSMW) CD-ROM, Rome.

Food and Agriculture Organization (FAO), 2005. Global agro-ecological assessment for agriculture in the twenty-first century (CD-ROM). FAO Land and Water Digital Media Series. FAO, Rome.

FAO, 2009. The state of food and agriculture 2009: livestock in the balance. FAO, Rome.

Galbraith, J.K., 1954. The Great Crash 1929. Houghton Mifflin, Boston.

Gordon, C., Cooper, C., Senior, C.A., Banks, H.T., Gregory, J.M., Johns, T.C., Mitchell, J.F.B., Wood, R.A., 2000. The simulation of SST, sea ice extents and ocean heat transports in a version of the Hadley Centre coupled model without flux adjustments. Clim. Dyn. 16, 147–168.

Goswami, B.N., Venugopal, V., Sengupta, D., Madhusoodanan, M.S., Xavier, P.K., 2006. Increasing trend of extreme rain events over India in a warming environment. Science 314, 1442–1445.

Greene, W.H., 2011. Econometric Analysis. Prentice Hall, New York.

Gregoire, T.G., Valentine, H.T., 2004. Sampling Strategies for Natural Resources and the Environment. Chapman and Hall/CRC Press, Florida.

Hahn, G.L., 1981. Housing and management to reduce climate impacts on livestock. J. Anim. Sci. 52, 175–186.

Hahn, G.L., Gaughan, J.B., Mader, T.L., Eigenberg, R.A., 2009. Chapter 5 Thermal indices and their applications for livestock environments. In: DeShazer, J.A., (Eds.), Livestock Energetics and Thermal Environmental Management, St. Joseph, Mich.: ASABE. Copyright 2009 American Society of Agricultural and Biological Engineers. ASABE # 801M0309. ISBN 1-892769-74-3, pp. 113–130.

Hanemann, W.M., 2000. Adaptation and its management. Clim. Change 45, 511–581.

Hansen, J., Sato, M., Reudy, R., 2012. Perception of climate change. In: Proceedings of the National Academy of Sciences of the United States of America 109, pp. E2415–2423.

Heckman, J., 1979. Sample selection bias as a specification error. Econometrica 47, 153–162.

Heckman, J., 2000. Microdata, heterogeneity and the evaluation of public policy. Nobel Prize Lecture for Economic Sciences. Stockholm University, Stockholm, Sweden.

Houghton, R.A., 2008. Carbon flux to the atmosphere from land-use changes. In: Trends: A Compendium of Data on Global Change. Carbon Dioxide Information Analysis Center, Oak Ridge National Laboratory, US Department of Energy, Oak Ridge, TN, USA, pp. 1850–2005.

Hulme, M., Doherty, R.M., Ngara, T., New, M.G., Lister, D., 2001. African climate change: 1900-2100. Clim. Res. 17, 145–168.

Indian Institute of Tropical Meteorology (IITM), 2012. Homogeneous Indian Monthly Rainfall Data Sets & Indian Regional Monthly Surface Air Temperature Data Set. IITM. Pune, India.

Intergovernmental Panel on Climate Change (IPCC), 2001. Climate change 2001 the physical science basis, the third assessment report. Cambridge University Press, Cambridge.

IPCC, 2012. Managing the risks of extreme events and disasters to advance climate change adaptation. A special report of working groups I and II of the Intergovernmental Panel on Climate Change. Cambridge University Press, Cambridge

IPCC, 2014. Climate change 2014 the physical science basis, the fourth assessment report, Cambridge University Press, Cambridge.

Janowiak, J.E., 1988. An investigation of interannual rainfall variability in Africa. J. Clim. 1, 240–255.

Johnston, J., DiNardo, J., 1997. Econometric Methods, 4th Ed. McGraw-Hill, New York.

Kahneman, D., Tversky, A., 1979. Prospect theory: an analysis of decision under risk. Econometrica 47, 263–291.

Kahneman, D., Tversky, A., 1984. Choices, values and frames. Am. Psychol. 39 (4), 341–350.

Kala, N., 2015. Ambiguity aversion and learning in a changing world: The potential effects of climate change from Indian agriculture. Ph.D. dissertation, Yale University, New Heaven, CT.

Kazianga, H., Udry, C., 2006. Consumption smoothing? Livestock, insurance, and drought in rural Burkina Faso. J. Dev. Econ. 79, 413–446.

Kelly, D.L., Kolstad, C.D., Mitchell, G.T., 2005. Adjustment costs from environmental change. J. Environ. Econ. Manag. 50, 468–495.

Koopmans, T., 1949. Identification problems in economic model construction. Econometrica 17, 125–144.

Kumar, K.S.K., Parikh, J., 2001. Indian agriculture and climate sensitivity. Global Environ. Change 11, 147–154.

Kurukulasuriya, P., Mendelsohn, R., Hassan, R., Seo, S.N., Dinar, A., et al., 2006. Will African agriculture survive climate change? World Bank Econ. Rev. 20, 367–388.

Le Treut, H., Somerville, R., Cubasch, U., Ding, Y., Mauritzen, C., Mokssit, A., Peterson, T., Prather, M., 2007. Historical overview of climate change. In: Solomon, S., Qin, D., Manning, M., Chen, Z., Marquis, M., Averyt, K.B., Tignor, M., Miller, H.L., (Eds.), Climate Change 2007 The Physical Science Basis. Contribution of Working Group I to the Fourth Assessment Report of the Intergovernmental Panel on Climate Change. Cambridge University Press, Cambridge.

Lee, L.F., 1983. Generalized econometric models with selectivity. Econometrica 51, 507–512.

Lobell, D., Schlenker, W., Costa-Roberts, J., 2011. Climate trends and global crop production since 1980. Science 333, 616–620.

Mader, T.L., Davis, M.S., 2004. Effect of management strategies on reducing heat stress of feedlot cattle: feed and water intake. J. Anim. Sci. 82, 3077–3087.

Manski, C.F., 1995. Identification Problems in the Social Sciences. Harvard University Press, Cambridge.

Markowitz, H., 1952. Portfolio selection. J. Finance 7, 77–91.

Massetti, E., Mendelsohn, R., 2011. Estimating Ricardian models with panel data. Clim. Change Econ. 2, 301–319.

Mata, L.J., Campos, M., et al., 2001. Latin America. In: Climate Change 2001 Impacts, Adaptation, and Vulnerability—Contribution of Working Group II to the Third Assessment Report of the Intergovernmental Panel on Climate Change, Cambridge University Press, Cambridge.

Matthews, E., 1983. Global vegetation and land use: new high-resolution data bases for climate studies. J. Clim. App. Meteorol. 22: 474–487. Available from: http://data.giss.nasa.gov/landuse/vegeem.html.

McFadden, D.L., 1974. Conditional logit analysis of qualitative choice behavior. In: Zarembka, P. (Ed.), Frontiers in Econometrics. Academic, New York, pp. 105–142.

McFadden, D.L., 1984. Econometric analysis of qualitative response models. In: Grilliches, Z., Intrilligator, M.D., (Eds.) Handbook of Econometrics, vol. II, Elsevier Science Publishers BV.

McFadden, D., 1999a. Chapter 1. Discrete Response Models. Lecture Note. University of California at Berkeley, CA.

McFadden, D., 1999b. Chapter 2. Sampling and selection. Lecture Note. University of California at Berkeley, CA.

Meehl, G.A., Hu, A., 2006. Megadroughts in the Indian monsoon region and southwest North America and a mechanism for associated multidecadal Pacific sea surface temperature anomalies. J. Clim. 19, 1605–1623.

Mendelsohn, R., 2000. Efficient adaptation to climate change. Clim. Change 45, 583–600.

Mendelsohn, R., Nordhaus, W., Shaw, D., 1994. The impact of global warming on agriculture: a Ricardian analysis. Am. Econ. Rev. 84, 753–771.

Mendelsohn, R., Kurukulasuriya, P., Basist, A., Kogan, F., Williams, C., 2007. Measuring climate change impacts with satellite versus weather station data. Clim. Change 81, 71–83.

Mendelsohn, R., Olmstead, S., 2009. The Economic Valuation of Environmental Amenities and Disamenities: Methods and Applications. Ann. Rev. Resour. 34, 325–347.

Mendelsohn, R., Arellano-Gonzalez, J., Christensen, P., 2010. A Ricardian analysis of Mexican farms. Environ. Dev. Econ. 15, 153–171.

National Research Council (NRC), 2013. Abrupt impacts of climate change: anticipating surprises. The National Academies Press, Washington DC.

Nin, A., Ehui, S., Benin, S., 2007. Livestock productivity in developing countries: an assessment. Evenson, R., Pingali, P. (Eds.), Handbook of Agricultural Economics, Vol. 3, Oxford, North Holland.

New, M., Lister, D., Hulme, M., Makin, I., 2002. A high-resolution data set of surface climate over global land areas. Clim. Res. 21, 1–25.

Nordhaus, W., 2011. The economics of tail events with an application to climate change. Rev. Environ. Econ. Policy 5, 240–257.

Parry, M.L., Rosenzweig, C.P., Iglesias, A., Livermore, M., Fischer, G., 2004. Effects of climate change on global food production under SRES emissions and socioeconomic scenarios. Global Environ. Change 14, 53–67.

Peters, C.M., Gentry, A.W., Mendelsohn, R.O., 1989. Valuation of an Amazonian rainforest. Nature 339 (6227), 655–656.

Porter, J.H., Parry, M.L., Carter, T.R., 1991. The potential effects of climatic change on agricultural insect pests. Agri. Forest Meteorol. 57, 221–240.

Porter, J.R., Semenev, M., 2005. Crop responses to climatic variation. Phil. Trans. R. Soc. B 360, 2021–2035.

Rahmstorf, S., Coumou, D., 2011. Increase of extreme events in a warming world. In: Proceedings of the National Academy of Sciences of the United States of America 108:17905–17909.

Reilly, J., Baethgen, W., Chege, F., Van de Geijn, S., Enda, L., Iglesias, A., Kenny, G., Patterson, D., Rogasik, J., Rotter, R., Rosenzweig, C., Sombroek, W., Westbrook, J., 1996. Agriculture in a changing climate: impacts and adaptations. In: Watson, R., Zinyowera, M., Moss, R., Dokken, D. (Eds.), Climate Change 1995: Impacts, Adaptations, and Mitigation of Climate Change. Intergovernmental Panel on Climate Change (IPCC). Cambridge University Press, Cambridge.

Ricardo, D., 1817. On the principles of political economy and taxation. John Murray, London, England.

Rosenberg, N.J., 1992. Adaptation of agriculture to climate change. Clim. Change 21, 385–405.

Reinsborough, M.J., 2003. A Ricardian model of climate change in Canada. Can. J. Econ. 36, 21–40.

Ropelewski, C.F., Halpert, M.S., 1987. Global and regional precipitation patterns associated with the El Nino/Southern Oscillation. Mon. Weather Rev. 115, 1606–1626.

Rosenzweig, C., Parry, M., 1994. Potential impact of climate change on world food supply. Nature 367, 133–138.

Rosenzweig, C., Iglesias, A., Yang, X.B., Epstein, P.R., Chivian, E., 2001. Climate change and extreme weather events: implications for food production, plant diseases, and pests. Global Change Hum. Health 2 (2), 90–104.

Ruttan, V.W., 2002. Productivity growth in world agriculture: sources and constraints. J. Econ. Perspect. 16, 161–184.

Sanghi, A., Mendelsohn, R., 2008. The impacts of global warming on farmers in Brazil and India. Global Environ. Change 18, 655–665.

Schenkler, W., Hanemann, M., Fisher, A., 2005. Will US agriculture really benefit from global warming? Accounting for irrigation in the hedonic approach. Am. Econ. Rev. 95, 395–406.

Schenkler, W., Hanemann, M., Fisher, A., 2006. The impact of global warming on U.S. agriculture: an econometric analysis of optimal growing conditions. Rev. Econ. Stat. 88 (1), 113–125.

Schlenker, W., Roberts, M., 2009. Nonlinear temperature effects indicate severe damages to crop yields under climate change. In: Proc. Nat. Acad. Sci. USA, 106(37), 15594–15598.

Schlesinger, W.H., 1997. Biogeochemistry: An Analysis of Global Change, second ed. Academic Press, San Diego.

Schmertmann, C.P., 1994. Selectivity bias correction methods in polychotomous sample selection models. J. Econ. 60, 101–132.

Schmidt, G.A., Ruedy, R., Hansen, J.E., Aleinov, I., Bell, N., Bauer, M., Bauer, S., Cairns, B., Canuto, V., Cheng, Y., DelGenio, A., Faluvegi, G., Friend, A.D., Hall, T.M., Hu, Y., Kelley, M., Kiang, N.Y., Koch, D., Lacis, A.A., Lerner, J., Lo, K.K., Miller, R.L., Nazarenko, L., Oinas, V., Perlwitz, J., Rind, D., Romanou, A., Russell, G.L., Sato, M., Shindell, D.T., Stone, P.H., Sun, S., Tausnev, N., Thresher, D., Yao, M.S., 2005. Present day atmospheric simulations using GISS ModelE: comparison to in-situ, satellite and reanalysis data. J. Clim. 19, 153–192.

Seo, S.N., 2006. Modeling Farmer Responses to Climate Change: Climate Change Impacts and Adaptations in Livestock Management in Africa. PhD Dissertation, Yale University, New Haven.

Seo, S.N., 2010a. Is an integrated farm more resilient against climate change?: a microeconometric analysis of portfolio diversification in African agriculture? Food Policy 35, 32–40.

Seo, S.N., 2010b. A microeconometric analysis of adapting portfolios to climate change: adoption of agricultural systems in Latin America. App. Econ. Perspect. Policy 32, 489–514.

Seo, S.N., 2010c. Managing forests, livestock, and crops under global warming: a microeconometric analysis of land use changes in Africa. Aust. J. Agri. Resour. Econ. 54 (2), 239–258.

Seo, S.N., 2011a. An analysis of public adaptation to climate change using agricultural water schemes in South America. Ecol. Econ. 70, 825–834.

Seo, S.N., 2011b. A geographically scaled analysis of adaptation to climate change with spatial models using agricultural systems in Africa. J. Agri. Sci. 149, 437–449.

Seo, S.N., 2012a. Adapting natural resource enterprises under global warming in South America: a mixed logit analysis. Economia J. 12, 111–135.

Seo, S.N., 2012b. Adaptation behaviors across ecosystems under global warming: a spatial microeconometric model of the rural economy in South America. Pap. Reg. Sci. 91, 849–871.

Seo, S.N., 2012c. Decision making under climate risks: an analysis of sub-Saharan farmers' adaptation behaviors. Weather Clim. Soc. 4, 285–299.

Seo, S.N., 2013a. Refining spatial resolution and spillovers of a microeconometric model of adapting portfolios to climate change. Mitig. Adapt. Strategies Glob. Chang. 18, 1019–1034.

Seo, S.N., 2013b. An essay on the impact of climate change on US agriculture: weather fluctuations, climatic shifts, and adaptation strategies. Clim. Change 121, 115–124.

Seo, S.N., 2014a. Evaluation of Agro-Ecological Zone methods for the study of climate change with micro farming decisions in sub-Saharan Africa. Eur. J. Agron. 52, 157–165.

Seo, S.N., 2014b. Coupling climate risks, eco-systems, anthropogenic decisions using South American and Sub-Saharan farming activities. Meteorol. Appl. 21, 848–858.

Seo, S.N., 2014c. Adapting sensibly when global warming turns the field brown or blue: a comment on the 2014 IPCC Report. Econ. Affairs 34, 399–401.

Seo, S.N., 2015a. Micro-Behavioral Economics of Global Warming: Modeling Adaptation Strategies in Agricultural and Natural Resource Enterprises. Springer: Cham, Switzerland.

Seo, S.N., 2015b. Modeling farmer adaptations to climate change in South America: a microbehavioral economic perspective. Environ. Ecol. Stat. 23 (1), 1–21.

Seo, S.N., 2015c. Fatalities of neglect: adapt to more intense hurricanes? Int. J. Climatol. 35, 3505–3514.

Seo, S.N., 2016. Untold tales of goats in deadly Indian monsoons: adapt or rain-retreat under global warming? J. Extreme Events 3. doi: 10.1142/S2345737616500019.

Seo, S.N., Mendelsohn, R., Munasinghe, M., 2005. Climate change and agriculture in Sri Lanka: a Ricardian valuation. Environ. Dev. Econ. 10, 581–596.

Seo, S.N., Mendelsohn, R., 2008a. Measuring impacts and adaptations to climate change: a structural Ricardian model of African livestock management. Agri. Econ. 38, 151–165.

Seo, S.N., Mendelsohn, R., 2008b. A Ricardian analysis of the impact of climate change impacts on South American farms. Chil. J. Agri. Res. 68, 69–79.

Seo, S.N., Mendelsohn, R., 2008c. An analysis of crop choice: adapting to climate change in South American farms. Ecol. Econ. 67, 109–116.

Seo, S.N., Mendelsohn, R., Dinar, A., Hassan, R., Kurukulasuriya, P., 2009. A Ricardian analysis of the distribution of climate change impacts on agriculture across Agro-Ecological Zones in Africa. Environ. Resour. Econ. 43, 313–332.

Seo, S.N., McCarl, B., Mendelsohn, R., 2010. From beef cattle to sheep under global warming? An analysis of adaptation by livestock species choice in South America. Ecol. Econ. 69, 2486–2494.

Shanahan, T.M., Overpeck, J.T., Anchukaitis, K.J., Beck, J.W., Cole, J.E., Dettman, D.L., Peck, J.A., Scholz, C.A., King, J.W., 2009. Atlantic forcing of persistent drought in West Africa. Science 324, 377–380.

Shiller, R.J., 2003. From efficient markets theory to behavioral finance. J. Econ. Perspect. 17, 83–104.

Shiller, R.J., 2005. Irrational Exuberance, 2nd Ed. Princeton University Press, Princeton, NJ.

Shiller, R.J., 2014. Speculative asset prices. Am. Econ. Rev. 104 (6), 1486–1517.

Strzepek, K., McCluskey, A., 2006. District level hydroclimatic time series and scenario analyses to assess the impacts of climate change on regional water resources and agriculture in Africa. CEEPA Discussion Paper No. 13. Centre for Environmental Economics and Policy in Africa, University of Pretoria, Pretoria.

Sumner, D.A., Zulauf, C., 2012. Economic & environmental effects of agricultural insurance programs. The Council on Food, Agricultural & Resource Economics (C-FARE), Washington DC.

Tebaldi, C., Hayhoe, K., Arblaster, J.M., Meehl, G.E., 2007. Going to the extremes: an intercomparison of model-simulated historical and future changes in extreme events. Clim. Change 79, 185–211.

Titley, D.W., Hegerl, G., Jacobs, K.L., Mote, P.W., Paciorek, C.J., Shepherd, J.M., Shepherd, T.G., Sobel, A.H., Walsh, J., Zwiers, F.W., Thomas, K., Everett, L., Purcell, Gaskins, R., Markovich, E., 2016. Attribution of Extreme Weather Events in the Context of Climate Change. National Academies of Sciences, Engineering, and Medicine. National Academies Press, Washington, DC.

Tobin, J., 1958. Liquidity preference as behavior toward risk. Rev. Econ. Stud. 25 (2), 65–86.

Train, K., 2003. Discrete Choice Methods with Simulation. Cambridge University Press, Cambridge.

Tubiello, F.N., Ewert, F., 2002. Simulating the effects of elevated CO_2 on crops: approaches and applications for climate change. Eur. J. Agron. 18, 57–74.

Udry, C., 1995. Risk and saving in Northern Nigeria. Am. Econ. Rev. 85, 1287–1300.

United States Department of Agriculture (USDA), 2007. Census of agriculture 2007. Available from: http://www.agcensus.usda.gov/Publications/2007/index.php.

United Nations Framework Convention on Climate Change (UNFCCC), 2009. Copenhagen Accord. UNFCCC, New York.

United States Environmental Protection Agency (US EPA), 2014. Heating and cooling degree days. US EPA, Washington DC.

Vedeld, P., Angelsen, A., Bojø, J., Sjaastad, E., Kobugabe, G.K., 2007. Forest environmental incomes and the rural poor. Forest Policy and Econ. 9, 869–879.

Wang, J., Mendelsohn, R., Dinar, A., Huang, J., Rozelle, S., Zhang, L., 2009. The impacts of climate change on China's agriculture. Agri. Econ. 40, 323–337.

Weitzman, M.L., 2009. On modeling and interpreting the economics of catastrophic climate change. Rev. Econ. Stat. 91, 1–19.

Welch, J.R., Vincent, J.R., Auffhammer, M., Moya, P.F., Dobermann, A., Dawe, D., 2010. Rice yields in tropical/subtropical Asia exhibit large but opposing sensitivities to minimum and maximum temperatures. In: Proc. Natl. Acad. Sci. USA 107, 14562–14567.

World Bank, 2008. World development report 2008: agriculture for development. World Bank Washington DC.

World Bank, 2009a. Africa Infrastructure and Country Diagnostics (AICD). World Bank, Washington DC. Available from: http://www.infrastructureafrica.org/aicd/.

World Bank, 2009b. Awakening Africa's sleeping giant: prospects for commercial agriculture in the Guinea Savannah Zone and Beyond. World Bank and FAO Washington DC.

World Resources Institute (WRI), 2005. World Resources 2005: The wealth of the poor—managing ecosystems to fight poverty. WRI, Washington DC.

Wright, B., 2011. The economics of grain price volatility. App. Econ. Perspect. Policy 33, 32–58.

Zhang, W., Hagerman, A.D., McCarl, B.A., 2013. How climate factors influence the spatial distribution of Texas cattle breeds. Clim. Change 118, 183–195.

Zilberman, D., 1998. Agricultural and environmental policies: economics of production, technology, risk, agriculture, and the environment. The State University of New York - Oswego, NY.

Ziska, L.H., 2003. Evaluation of yield loss in field-grown sorghum from a C3 and C4 weed as a function of increasing atmospheric Carbon Dioxide. Weed Sci. 51, 914–918.

CHAPTER 3

Modeling Microbehavioral Decisions: Statistical Considerations

The previous chapter explained the microbehavioral econometric methods from the standpoint of economics of decision-making by a microagent: availabilities of natural resources, economic options, choices, systems, values, risk, diversification, uncertainties, psychology, climate change, energy uses, and others. The objective of this chapter is to elaborate statistical and mathematical considerations in modeling microbehavioral decisions of individuals. The previous chapter already dealt with many of the statistical issues in microbehavioral models, but this chapter will expand those discussions and have a focus on the statistical variations of microbehavioral models while keeping economic dimensions of decision-making to a minimum.

This chapter draws from various textbooks and articles on discrete choice and selection models, including McFadden (1984, 1999a, b); Bourguignon et al. (2004); Train (2003); and Anselin (1998).

3.1 BINOMIAL CHOICE MODELS

Let's start with an individual who is faced with a binary choice. A binary—dichotomous—choice is an important economic decision in many real life situations. One has to choose whether to attend a college or not. One has to decide whether to marry or not. One has to decide whether to live in the rural area or in the city. A firm must decide whether it will enter into a business or not. A firm must decide whether it will go public or remain private. A firm must decide whether it should shut down its operations or not.

An individual will choose one alternative over the other considering all the factors that matter to him/her, including the variables that are related with her economic, social, and psychological states; the variables that are related with the choice set of alternatives; the variables that are related with the policies and society; the variables that are related with natural conditions such as climate and geography.

Let an individual's profit (π_i^*) from making a binary choice, for example, choice of living in a rural area against living in an urban area, be written as follows:

$$\pi_i^* = x_i\beta - \varepsilon_i. \tag{3.1}$$

Both x_i and β are a vector of variables and of parameters. The above equation assumes that the profit can be written as a linear function of the parameters, plus the error term. The profit should be seen to include both monetary rewards and nonmonetary rewards from the decision that are accrued in the long-term.

Suppose that the disturbance term ε_i is known to the individual who makes the choice decision but unknown to a statistician/modeler. But, the disturbance term can be assumed by the modeler up to the Cumulative Distribution Function (CDF) of the error term.

An individual agent will choose the option if the profit from choosing that option is greater than zero. The probability that this occurs, given x, is

$$\begin{aligned} P(\pi_i^* > 0) &= P(\varepsilon_i < x_i\beta) \\ &= F(x_i\beta). \end{aligned} \tag{3.2}$$

Note that π_i^* is a latent variable, that is, it is not directly observed by a researcher. Define $\pi_i = 1$ if the option is chosen, $\pi_i = -1$ otherwise. Then, π_i is an observed indicator for the event that $\pi_i^* > 0$. The probability rule is summarized as follows:

$$P(\pi_i \mid x_i\beta) = \begin{cases} F(x_i\beta) & \text{if } \pi_i = 1, \\ 1 - F(x_i\beta) & \text{if } \pi_i = -1. \end{cases} \tag{3.3}$$

Let's assume that ε is symmetrically distributed about zero. This is not an essential component of the choice model, but only for the purpose of simplifying the notation. With this assumption, the probability rule in Eq. 3.3 can be rewritten in an even simpler form (McFadden, 1999a):

$$P(\pi_i \mid x_i\beta) = F(\pi_i x_i\beta). \tag{3.4}$$

A researcher is interested in estimating β, for which an obvious approach is a Maximum Likelihood (ML) method (Casella and Berger, 2001; Andrews, 2001; Hogg et al., 2012). The log likelihood of an observation is expressed as

$$l(\beta \mid \pi_i, x_i) = \log P(\pi_i \mid x_i\beta) = \log F(\pi_i x_i\beta). \tag{3.5}$$

If the researcher has a random sample with I observations ($i = 1, 2,\ldots,I$), then the sample log likelihood is expressed as

$$LL(\beta) = \sum_{i=1}^{I} \log F(\pi_i x_i \beta). \tag{3.6}$$

The ML estimation will search for β that maximizes the sample log likelihood in the above equation. A nonlinear optimization technique such as the Newton-Raphson method which is embedded in any statistical programming package used nowadays is used to find β (Maddala, 2001; Train, 2003).

Conceptually, the maximization of Eq. 3.6 calls for the calculations of the first-order derivative and the second-order derivative of Eq. 3.6 with respect to the parameter vector β. The score, the first-order derivative, and the Hessian, the second-order derivative, of the log likelihood are obtained by successively differentiating Eq. 3.6 with regard to β (Johnston and DiNardo, 1997; McFadden, 1999a):

$$\nabla_\beta LL(\beta) = \sum_{i=1}^{I} \pi_i x_i' F'(\pi_i x_i \beta)/F(\pi_i x_i \beta), \tag{3.7}$$

$$\nabla_{\beta\beta} LL(\beta) = \sum_{i=1}^{I} x_i' x_i \{F''(\pi_i x_i \beta)/F(\pi_i x_i \beta) - [F'(\pi_i x_i \beta)/F(\pi_i x_i \beta)]^2\}. \tag{3.8}$$

An application of a Maximum Likelihood Estimation (MLE) procedure will find local maxima, using the score in Eq. 3.7 and the Hessian in Eq 3.8, at the points where $\nabla_\beta LL(\beta) = 0$ and $\nabla_{\beta\beta} LL(\beta) \leq 0$. A global maximum will be searched and found from the local maxima which are in most cases more than one.

A Newton-Raphson method, on the other hand, is one of the numerical algorithms available for a nonlinear optimization. The algorithm will begin from a starting point from which the shortest distance is sought to reach a predetermined increase in the value of the objective function, that is, the sample log-likelihood function in Eq. 3.6 (Maddala, 2001; Train, 2003).

The score and the Hessian can be rewritten in a different but more conventional way. That is, let $d_i = (\pi_i + 1)/2$ (McFadden, 1999a). The dummy variable d_i becomes an indicator for the choice of the alternative. That is, $d_i = 1$ if an individual chooses the alternative and $d_i = 0$ otherwise. Then, the log-likelihood function in Eq. 3.5 above becomes

$$l(\pi_i \mid x_i, \beta) = d_i \cdot \log F(x_i \beta) + (1 - d_i) \cdot \log F(-x_i \beta). \tag{3.9}$$

Differentiating the log-likelihood function again with respect to β, and noting that $F'(x_i\beta) = F'(-x_i\beta)$, we get

$$\nabla_\beta l = x_i F'(x_i\beta)\{d_i/F(x_i\beta) - (1-d_i)/F(-x_i\beta)\} \tag{3.10}$$
$$= w(x_i\beta) \cdot x_i \cdot [d_i - F(x_i\beta)]$$

where $w(x_i\beta) = F'(x_i\beta)/F(x_i\beta)F(-x_i\beta)$.

The sample score matrix is then

$$\nabla_\beta LL = \sum_{i=1}^{I} w(x_i\beta) \cdot x_i' \cdot [d_i - F(x_i\beta)]. \tag{3.11}$$

The first-order condition for the MLE is that the sample score be equal to zero can be interpreted as a weighted orthogonality condition between a residual $[d_i - F(x_i\beta)]$ and the vector of explanatory variables x_i. This interpretation is equivalent to those in the extreme estimators of a regression model such as the Least Squares method, the Maximum Likelihood method, or the Generalized Method of Moments (Johnston and DiNardo, 1997; Greene, 2011).

This weighted orthogonality condition means that the weighted Nonlinear Least Squares (NLLS) regression run on Eq. 3.12 below with each observation i is weighted by $w(x_i\beta)^{1/2}$ and with η_i being the classical error term is equivalent to the ML estimation of this choice model (McFadden, 1999a):

$$d_i = F(x_i\beta) + \eta_i. \tag{3.12}$$

The Hessian matrix can also be rewritten using d_i as follows:

$$\nabla_{\beta\beta} ll = -x_i'x_i \cdot s(x_i\beta), \quad \text{where}$$
$$s(x_i\beta) = \frac{F'(x_i\beta)^2}{F(x_i\beta)F(-x_i\beta)} \tag{3.13}$$
$$- [d_i - F(x_i\beta)]\left\{\frac{F''(x_i\beta)}{F(x_i\beta)F(-x_i\beta)} - \frac{F'(x_i\beta)^2(1-2F(x_i\beta))}{F(x_i\beta)^2 F(-x_i\beta)^2}\right\}.$$

Note that $E[s(x_i\beta)] = \dfrac{F'(x_i\beta)^2}{F(x_i\beta)F(-x_i\beta)}$ is always positive at the true value of β, say, $\beta*$, since the CDF is always positive. Note also that $[d_i - F(x_i\beta)]$

approaches zero in a sufficiently large sample, as in Eq. 3.12. Then, the sample sum of the Hessians of the observations (in the first line of Eq. 3.13) in sufficiently large samples will eventually become almost certainly negative definite in the neighborhood of $\beta*$, the condition which must be satisfied for a maximum value point (McFadden, 1999a).

In estimating the parameters of the choice model, a researcher must know the distribution function, $F(\varepsilon)$. That is, there remains the CDF, $F(\varepsilon)$, in the sample score in Eq. 3.10, which means that the cumulative distribution function enters the sample log-likelihood function which must be maximized in an intrinsic way. Therefore, unlike linear regression models, she/he cannot estimate the vector of parameters, β, relying only on the assumptions about the first two moments of the distribution (Johnston and DiNardo, 1997; Greene, 2011).

In principle, the researcher can deduce a form of the CDF, $F(\varepsilon)$, from a particular application, which would in many cases be conditioned on the observed explanatory variables (Albert and Chip 1993; Allenby and Lenk 1994). In most applied economic studies, however, one (or several) of the following standard distributions is assumed by the researchers, which are not conditioned on the explanatory variables x (Agresti, 2013; Train, 2003). Based on the assumption on the CDF, a choice model is called a Probit, a Logit, a Linear, or a Log-linear model:

$$\text{Probit: } F(\varepsilon) \text{ is the standard normal CDF,} \tag{3.14a}$$

$$\text{Logit: } F(\varepsilon) = 1/(1 + e^{-\varepsilon}), \quad \text{the standard logistic CDF,} \tag{3.14b}$$

$$\text{Linear: } F(\varepsilon) = \varepsilon, \text{ for } 0 \leq \varepsilon \leq 1, \quad \text{the standard uniform distribution,} \tag{3.14c}$$

$$\text{Log-linear: } F(\varepsilon) = e^{\varepsilon}, \text{ for } \varepsilon \leq 0, \quad \text{a standard exponential CDF.} \tag{3.14d}$$

The CDFs of these standard distributions are drawn in Fig. 3.1. The CDF of the Probit model, that is, the standard normal CDF, is symmetric around zero. So is the CDF of the Logit model, that is, the standard logistic CDF. As can be seen in the figure, the CDF of the Logit model has fatter tails than the CDF of the Probit model. In other words, the density function of the standard normal distribution has thinner tails than the density of the standard logistic probability density function. Other than this, the two distributions are nearly identical. This is one of the reasons that the Logit model is widely adopted in applied economic studies.

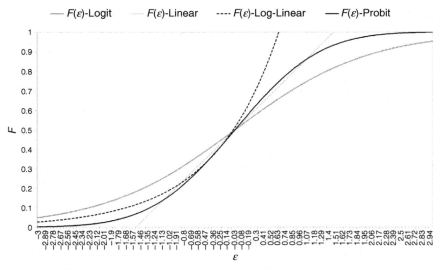

Figure 3.1 *CDFs of standard distributions in binomial choice models.*

A tail behavior of a distribution function varies substantially from one distribution to another (Schuster, 1984). A fat-tailed distribution is interpreted to capture a larger uncertainty in the occurrence in an event and is introduced to economics for the first time by Benoit Mandelbrot for the analysis of speculative price changes in crops (Mandelbrot, 1963). Recent debates on catastrophic possibility of global warming are centered around the tail behavior of the distribution of expected global warming (Weitzman, 2009; Nordhaus, 2011). The present author will further discuss this issue shortly.

Under the assumptions about the CDF, the probability of choice in Eq. 3.3 can be written succinctly using the CDFs earlier:

$$\text{Logit model: } P(\pi_i = 1 \mid x_i\beta) = F(x_i\beta) = \frac{1}{1 + e^{-x_i\beta}} \tag{3.15}$$

$$\text{Probit model: } P(\pi_i = 1 \mid x_i\beta) = F(x_i\beta)$$
$$= \int_{-\infty}^{x_i\beta} f(\varepsilon_i)\, d\varepsilon_i = \int_{-\infty}^{x_i\beta} \frac{1}{2\pi} e^{-\varepsilon_i^2/2}\, d\varepsilon_i. \tag{3.16}$$

As can be observed from Eqs. 3.15 and 3.16, one of the advantages of the Logit model is the handiness in calculating the probability since it does not call for any integration. There is no easy way, on the other hand, to calculate the probability in the Probit model since the integration must be done using a numerical method.

A general form of the CDF of the logistic distribution is expressed as follows (Hastings and Peacock, 1975; Casella and Berger, 2001):

$$F(\varepsilon_i) = \frac{1}{\left(1 + e^{-\frac{\varepsilon_i - \mu}{s}}\right)}. \tag{3.17}$$

The cumulative distribution function of the logistic distribution is a logistic function, for which reason the distribution is called a logistic distribution. The term "Logit" model comes from the logistic distribution. In the above equation, μ is the mean and s is a scale parameter proportional to the standard deviation, as shown shortly.

The probability density function (PDF) of a logistic distribution has the same shape as that of the normal distribution with the same mean and standard deviation. The only difference between the two distributions is that the logistic distribution has fatter tails than the standard normal distribution (Hastings and Peacock, 1975).

The first two moments of the general form of the logistic distribution in Eq. 3.17 are as follows:

$$E(\varepsilon_i) = \mu,$$
$$Var(\varepsilon_i) = \frac{s^2 \pi^2}{3}. \tag{3.18}$$

From the general form of the logistic distribution function, it is not difficult to see that the logistic CDF used in Eq. 3.14b is a special case of the general form of the logistic CDF in which $\mu = 0$ and $s = 1$.

Also from the general form of the logistic CDF, a researcher can calibrate a fatter-tailed, also sometimes called heavier-tailed, logistic distribution in comparison with a thinner-tailed logistic distribution (Schuster, 1984; Nordhaus, 2011). In Fig. 3.2, the two logistic distribution functions are drawn: one with fatter tails and the other with thinner tails. From the general logistic distribution function, the CDF with the fatter tails is drawn with $\mu = 0$ and $s = 1$. The CDF with thinner tails is drawn with $\mu = 0$ and $s = 1/2$. The larger the scale parameter, the fatter the tails of the logistic distribution become.

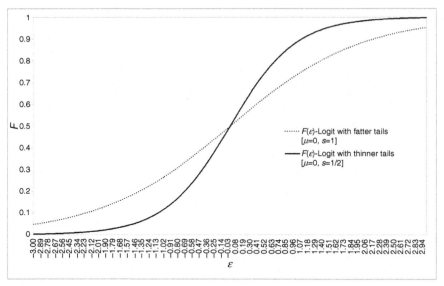

Figure 3.2 *Fatter and thinner tails of the CDF of the logit model.*

Let $\hat{\beta}$ be Maximum Likelihood estimators of β. The probability of choosing the alternative in the Logit model is then calculated as

$$P(\pi_i = 1 \mid x_i \beta) = \frac{1}{1 + e^{-x_i \hat{\beta}}}$$

$$= \frac{e^{x_i \hat{\beta}}}{1 + e^{x_i \hat{\beta}}}. \tag{3.19}$$

Suppose that the researcher suspects three explanatory variables in the choice model, that is, $x_i = (x_{1i}, x_{2i}, x_{3i})$. Then, the expanded form of $x_i \hat{\beta}$ is written as follows:

$$x_i \hat{\beta} = \hat{\beta}_0 + \hat{\beta}_1 x_{1i} + \hat{\beta}_2 x_{2i} + \hat{\beta}_3 x_{3i}. \tag{3.20}$$

How can the researcher test whether each of the parameter estimates is significant, say, $\beta_3 = 0$? This null hypothesis can be tested by estimating the model twice, first without the null hypothesis imposed and second with the null hypothesis imposed. There are three statistical tests commonly used: the Wald test statistic, the Likelihood Ratio (LR) test statistic, and the Lagrange Multiplier (LM) test statistic (McFadden, 1999a; Casella and Berger, 2001; Hogg et al., 2012).

The Wald test statistic is the quadratic form:

$$Wald = (\hat{\beta}_3 - \beta_3)'Var(\hat{\beta}_3)^{-1}(\hat{\beta}_3 - \beta_3). \qquad (3.21a)$$

This is just the square of the t-statistic for the one-dimensional hypothesis. The Wald test statistic is asymptotically Chi-square distributed with one degree of freedom when the null hypothesis is true (Casella and Berger, 2001).

An alternative to the Wald test statistic that is computationally easier to estimate is the Likelihood Ratio (LR) statistic:

$$LR = 2 * [LL(\hat{\beta}_3) - LL(\beta_3)]. \qquad (3.21b)$$

In the above, $LL(\hat{\beta}_3)$ is the sample log-likelihood without the null hypothesis imposed and $LL(\beta_3)$ is the sample log-likelihood with the null hypothesis imposed. This statistic is asymptotically equivalent to the Wald statistic.

The third test statistic is the Lagrange Multiplier (LM) test statistic. This is obtained by estimating the model under the null hypothesis, evaluating the score of the unrestricted model at the restricted estimates, and then testing whether this score is zero (Casella and Berger, 2001). With the estimate of the error term for the unrestricted model $\hat{\varepsilon}$ and that for the restricted model $\tilde{\varepsilon}$:

$$LM = \frac{n(\tilde{\varepsilon}'\tilde{\varepsilon} - \hat{\varepsilon}'\hat{\varepsilon})}{\tilde{\varepsilon}'\tilde{\varepsilon}}. \qquad (3.21c)$$

A broader statistical question is whether the model in Eq. 3.1 is correctly specified. A number of statistical tests that are available for general specification tests are applicable: the White test, the Wu–Hausman test, the Engle's exogeneity test, and the Granger causality test (White, 1980; Granger, 1969; Engle, 1984; Wooldridge, 2010). For example, the Wu–Hausman procedure provides a test for the following null hypothesis (Wu, 1973; Hausman, 1978):

$$H_0 : plim\left(\frac{1}{n}x'\varepsilon\right) = 0. \qquad (3.22)$$

3.2 SELECTION BIAS PROBLEM

The previous section described the model of a binomial choice: how an individual's choice of one of two alternatives is made and can be modeled. Most often, however, a researcher is interested in estimating the outcome function by which the choice is ultimately guided. The problem of estimating the outcome function when selection is an important economic decision in the first place was first explained by Heckman using the classic example of the wage function of working women (Heckman, 1979, 2000). Heckman noted that the female wages are observed only for employed women, but the factors that determine the wages of employed women also influence the decision of a woman to enter the workforce. To give an example, an unobserved (by a researcher) factor that increases Ms Brown's potential wage and decreases Ms Jones's potential wage at the same time is more likely to increase the relative probability that Ms. Brown joins the workforce against Ms Jones's. Then, a regression of women's wages over family and individual characteristics using data for working females will result in the potential wage function of working females which is biased and will typically overestimate the potential wage of nonworkers (McFadden, 1999b).

To understand the selection problem more formally, we will continue with the example of the female wage function. The description in this section is drawn from Daniel McFadden's description on selection bias problem in choice models (McFadden, 1999b). Let y_i be the observed variable for whether a woman is in the labor market or works at home and π_i be the observed variable of the wage of an individual worker. The latent variables can be modeled as functions of exogenous variables and the disturbance terms (Greene, 2011):

$$
\begin{aligned}
y_i^* &= x_i \beta + \varepsilon_i \\
\pi_i^* &= z_i \gamma + \sigma \eta_i
\end{aligned}
\tag{3.23}
$$

where x, z are vectors of exogenous variables; β, γ are parameter vectors; and σ is a positive parameter. The vectors x, z are not necessarily identical. The dependent variable $y*$ is latent desired hours of work and $\pi*$ is the latent potential wage in logarithm. The error terms ε, η are assumed to have a standard bivariate normal distribution:

$$
\begin{aligned}
\varepsilon_i &\sim N(0,1) \\
\eta_i &\sim N(0,1) \\
Corr(\varepsilon_i, \eta_i) &= \rho.
\end{aligned}
\tag{3.24}
$$

In this setting, the observation rule is such that a woman has a job and her wage is observed if desired hour of work is greater than zero (McFadden, 1999b):

$$y_i = 1 \quad \text{and } \pi_i = \pi_i^* \text{ if } y_i^* > 0;$$
$$y_i = 0 \quad \text{and } \pi_i \text{ is not observed if } y_i^* \leq 0. \tag{3.25}$$

Let the probability of working be provided by a Probit model that was described in the previous section or a Mixed Logit model which will be explained in a later section in this chapter:

$$P(y_i = 1 \mid x_i) = \Phi(x_i\beta). \tag{3.26}$$

In the bivariate model, the conditional density of one normal variable given another normal variable is univariate normal (Hogg et al., 2012):

$$\varepsilon_i \mid \eta_i \sim N(\rho\eta_i, 1 - \rho^2)$$
$$f_1(\varepsilon_i \mid \eta_i) = \frac{1}{1 - \rho^2} \varphi\left(\frac{\varepsilon_i - \rho\eta_i}{\sqrt{1 - \rho^2}}\right). \tag{3.27}$$

And, the same holds for the other direction:

$$\eta_i \mid \varepsilon_i \sim N(\rho\varepsilon_i, 1 - \rho^2)$$
$$f_2(\eta_i \mid \varepsilon_i) = \frac{1}{1 - \rho^2} \varphi\left(\frac{\eta_i - \rho\varepsilon_i}{\sqrt{1 - \rho^2}}\right). \tag{3.28}$$

Given the conditional density functions in Eqs 3.27 and 3.28, the joint density between the two error terms can be written as the product of the marginal density of η_i times the conditional density of ε_i given η_i. Alternatively, it can be written as the product of the marginal density of ε_i times the conditional density of η_i given ε_i (Hogg et al., 2012):

$$g(\varepsilon_i, \eta_i) = \begin{pmatrix} \varphi(\eta_i) \cdot \dfrac{1}{1 - \rho^2} \cdot \varphi\left(\dfrac{\varepsilon_i - \rho\eta_i}{\sqrt{1 - \rho^2}}\right) \\[2em] \varphi(\varepsilon_i) \cdot \dfrac{1}{1 - \rho^2} \cdot \varphi\left(\dfrac{\eta_i - \rho\varepsilon_i}{\sqrt{1 - \rho^2}}\right). \end{pmatrix} \tag{3.29}$$

The joint density of (y_i^*, π_i^*) can then be written (McFadden, 1999b):

$$h(y_i^*, \pi_i^*)$$

$$= \frac{1}{\sigma} \varphi\left(\frac{\pi_i^* - z_i\gamma}{\sigma}\right) \cdot \frac{1}{\sqrt{1-\rho^2}} \cdot \varphi\left(\frac{y_i^* - x_i\beta - \rho(\pi_i^* - z_i\gamma)/\sigma}{\sqrt{1-\rho^2}}\right) \qquad (3.30)$$

$$= \varphi(y_i^* - x_i\beta) \cdot \frac{1}{\sigma\sqrt{1-\rho^2}} \cdot \varphi\left(\frac{\pi_i^* - z_i\gamma - \rho\sigma(y_i^* - x_i\beta)}{\sigma\sqrt{1-\rho^2}}\right).$$

The parameters of these models, both the job participation model and the wage model, can be estimated, as explained in the previous section, by the Maximum Likelihood method. The sample log-likelihood function can be constructed based on the log likelihood function of an observation, $l(\beta, \gamma, \sigma, \rho)$. The log-likelihood for the worker and the nonworker are written as follows (McFadden, 1999b):

$$e^{l(\beta,\gamma,\sigma,\rho)}$$

$$= \begin{cases} \Phi(-x_i\beta) & \text{if } y_i = 0, \\[3mm] \dfrac{1}{\sigma}\varphi\left(\dfrac{w_i - z_i\alpha}{\sigma}\right) \cdot \Phi\left(\dfrac{x_i\beta + \rho\left(\dfrac{w_i - z_i\alpha}{\sigma}\right)}{\sqrt{1-\rho^2}}\right) & \text{if } y_i = 1. \end{cases} \qquad (3.31)$$

An alternative to the Maximum Likelihood estimation is a Generalized Method of Moments (GMM) procedure. The GMM method is computationally lighter as it relies only on the first two moments of π_i, therefore, is the method of choice for most applied microeconometric works. The GMM estimators can be obtained in an illuminating manner making use of the following two basic statistical properties (McFadden, 1999b; Hogg et al., 2012). First, the conditional expectation of η_i given $y_i = 1$ equals the conditional expectation of η_i given ε_i, integrated over the density of ε_i given $y_i = 1$. The second property is that if ε_i follows a normal distribution, then

$$\frac{d\varphi(\varepsilon_i)}{d\varepsilon_i} = -\varepsilon_i\varphi(\varepsilon_i). \qquad (3.32)$$

Relying on these two properties, the expected value of the wage of the employed woman can be calculated as follows:

$$
\begin{aligned}
E[\pi_i \mid z_i, y_i = 1] &= z_i\gamma + \sigma \cdot E[\eta_i \mid y_i = 1] \\
&= z_i\gamma + \sigma \int_{-x_i\beta}^{+\infty} E[\eta_i \mid \varepsilon_i]\varphi(\varepsilon_i)d\varepsilon_i / \Phi(x_i\beta) \\
&= z_i\gamma + \sigma \int_{-x_i\beta}^{+\infty} \varepsilon_i\varphi(\varepsilon_i)d\varepsilon_i / \Phi(x_i\beta) \\
&= z_i\gamma + \sigma\rho\varphi(x_i\beta)/\Phi(x_i\beta) \\
&= z_i\gamma + \lambda M(x_i\beta)
\end{aligned}
\tag{3.33}
$$

where $\lambda = \sigma\rho$ and $M(c) = \varphi(c)/\Phi(c)$.

The M is called the inverse Mills ratio. Again, relying on the basic statistical properties, the following result is obtained:

$$
\begin{aligned}
E[\eta_i^2 \mid \varepsilon_i] &= Var[\eta_i \mid \varepsilon_i] + \left\{ E[\eta_i \mid \varepsilon_i] \right\}^2 \\
&= 1 - \rho^2 + \rho^2\varepsilon_i^2.
\end{aligned}
\tag{3.34}
$$

And, apply the integration by parts formula:

$$
\begin{aligned}
\int_{-c}^{+\infty} \varepsilon^2\varphi(\varepsilon)d\varepsilon &= -\int_{-c}^{+\infty} \varepsilon\varphi'(\varepsilon)\,d\varepsilon = -c\varphi(c) + \int_{-c}^{+\infty} \varphi(\varepsilon)\,d\varepsilon \\
&= -c\varphi(c) + \Phi(c).
\end{aligned}
\tag{3.35}
$$

One obtains that

$$
\begin{aligned}
E[(\pi_i - z_i\gamma)^2 \mid z_i, y_i = 1] \\
&= \sigma^2 E[\eta_i^2 \mid y_i = 1] \\
&= \sigma^2 \int_{-x_i\beta}^{+\infty} E[\eta_i^2 \mid \varepsilon_i]\varphi(\varepsilon_i)d\varepsilon_i / \Phi(x_i\beta) \\
&= \sigma^2 \int_{-x_i\beta}^{+\infty} \{1 - \rho^2 + \rho^2\varepsilon_i^2\}\varphi(\varepsilon_i)d\varepsilon_i / \Phi(x_i\beta) \\
&= \sigma^2 \{1 - \rho^2 + \rho^2 - \rho^2 x_i\beta\varphi(x_i\beta)/\Phi(x_i\beta)\} \\
&= \sigma^2 \{1 - \rho^2 x_i\beta\varphi(x_i\beta)/\Phi(x_i\beta)\} \\
&= \sigma^2 \{1 - \rho^2 x_i\beta \cdot M(x_i\beta)\}.
\end{aligned}
\tag{3.36}
$$

Then,

$$
\begin{aligned}
E\{[(\pi_i - z_i\gamma) - E(\pi_i - z_i\gamma \mid z_i, y_i = 1)]^2 \mid z_i, y_i = 1\} \\
= E\{(\pi_i - z_i\gamma)^2 \mid z_i, y_i = 1\} - \{E[(\pi_i - z_i\gamma) \mid z_i, y_i = 1]\}^2 \\
= \sigma^2\{1 - \rho^2 x_i\beta\varphi(x_i\beta)/\Phi(x_i\beta) - \rho^2\varphi(x_i\beta)^2/\Phi(x_i\beta)^2\} \\
= \sigma^2\{1 - \rho^2 M(x_i\beta)[x_i\beta + M(x_i\beta)]\}.
\end{aligned}
\tag{3.37}
$$

A GMM estimator for this problem can be obtained by applying the NLLS method, for the observations with $y_i = 1$, to the equation:

$$
\pi_i = z_i\gamma + \sigma\rho M(x_i\beta) + \xi_i
\tag{3.38}
$$

where ξ_i is a disturbance term. The disturbance term satisfies $E[\xi_i \mid y_i = 1] = 0$. The regression is consistent, but nonetheless ignores the problem of heteroscedasticity of ξ_i. The procedure to correct the problem of heteroscedasticity of the disturbance term will be explained shortly.

The regression in Eq. 3.38 estimates only the product $\lambda = \sigma\rho$. Since σ is a positive parameter, the estimate of λ has the same sign with the correlation parameter ρ. If the estimates of both σ and ρ are of interests to a researcher, she/he can obtain consistent estimates of σ and ρ with an additional procedure to estimate the variance of ξ_i which should then be used to remove heteroscedasticity of the error term. From Eq. 3.37, the variance of ξ_i is

$$
Var[\xi_i \mid x_i, z_i, y_i = 1] = \sigma^2\left\{1 - \rho^2 M(x_i\beta)[x_i\beta + M(x_i\beta)]\right\}.
\tag{3.39}
$$

In the above equation, σ^2 is separated. Using the Eq. 3.39, one can obtain an estimate of σ^2 by regressing the square of the estimated residual, ξ_i, on one and the variable $M(x_i\hat{\beta})[x_i\hat{\beta} + M(x_i\hat{\beta})]$ where $\hat{\beta}$ is the estimated parameter vector from the choice probability model in Eq. 3.26. That is, one estimates the following equation with the OLS or MLE:

$$
\hat{\xi}_i^2 = a + b \cdot M(x_i\hat{\beta})[x_i\hat{\beta} + M(x_i\hat{\beta})] + \zeta_i,
\tag{3.40}
$$

from which the researcher can obtain the consistent estimated coefficients of a,b of σ^2 and $\sigma^2\rho^2$, respectively.

The GMM estimator in Eq. 3.38 is asymptotically inefficient, although consistent, because it fails to correct for heteroscedasticity as can be seen in Eq. 3.39 (Greene, 2011; Wooldridge, 2010). This can be corrected for by a GLS (Generalized Least Squares)-type transformation. From the first step of the NLLS regression and the second step for the estimate of σ explained earlier, the following weight is calculated:

$$\tau_i^2 = 1 - \hat{\rho}^2 M(x_i\hat{\beta})[x_i\hat{\beta} + M(x_i\hat{\beta})]. \tag{3.41}$$

Applying this weight to the NLLS regression, a researcher can run a weighted regression as follows:

$$\frac{\pi_i}{\tau_i} = \frac{z_i}{\tau_i}\gamma + \sigma\rho\frac{M(x_i\hat{\beta})}{\tau_i} + \frac{\xi_i}{\tau_i}. \tag{3.42}$$

Owing to the contribution by James Heckman, a selection bias correction model can be estimated in the following two steps with only a standard statistical software when the choice in the first stage is binomial (Heckman, 1979):

In the first stage, estimate the binomial Probit model by a Maximum Likelihood method:

$$P(\gamma_i \mid x_i, \beta) = \Phi(\gamma_i x_i \beta). \tag{3.43}$$

In the second stage, estimate the linear regression model:

$$\pi_i = z_i\gamma + \lambda M(x_i\hat{\beta}) + \xi_i \tag{3.44}$$

where $\lambda = \sigma\rho$ and the inverse Mills ratio is evaluated with the parameters obtained from the first stage (Eq. 3.43).

A researcher can further obtain the estimates of σ and ρ, based upon which she/he can run a weighted NLLS regression, after obtaining the weights, to increase the efficiency of the regression model, as explained earlier in Eqs. 3.40, 3.41, and 3.42.

3.3 MULTINOMIAL LOGIT MODELS

In most situations of managing natural resources, an individual has more than one alternative to choose from. The examples introduced in Chapter 2 are multinomial choices, that is, to choose one enterprise from available natural resource enterprises (Seo, 2010, 2012a, b). It is conceptually straightforward to move from modeling a binomial response to a multinomial response. The descriptions in the above sections on dichotomous choice and selection bias will turn out to be useful in modeling a choice in a multiple alternative situation.

Suppose that there are J alternatives in the choice set, $C = \{1,\ldots,J\}$. An individual agent, n, wants to choose an alternative that gives the highest return, namely, profit:

$$\underset{j}{\text{ArgMax}} \quad \{\pi^*_{n1}, \pi^*_{n2}, \ldots, \pi^*_{nJ}\}. \tag{3.45}$$

To explain what can be included in this multinomial choice set, let's suppose C comprises natural resource enterprises introduced in the previous chapter. If the choice set C includes the "no choice" alternative, the model can describe the choice of not choosing any of the enterprises. That is, the model can explain opting out of natural resource enterprises. If $i \in C$ identifies a mixed portfolio composed of two specialized enterprises, then it can explain the holding of a mixed enterprise. For example, a mixed portfolio of a crops-only and a livestock-only can be modeled.

The choice set should be exhaustive. In other words, it should include all the options in the choice situation. Further, alternatives should be defined in a mutually exclusive fashion. That is, choice of an alternative by an individual excludes any possibility of choosing the other alternatives in the choice set.

Suppose the latent profit of alternative j can be expressed as the sum of the observable component and the unobservable component by a researcher. The unobservable component may be known to an individual who makes a choice decision, but unknown to the researcher. Further, let's assume that the observable component can be written linearly in the parameters (McFadden, 1974; Chow, 1983). Then, the model is written as follows:

$$\pi^*_{nj} = Z_n \beta_j + \varepsilon_{nj}. \tag{3.46}$$

The vector of explanatory variables, Z, includes the characteristics of alternative j, the characteristics of the microagent who makes a decision, and the characteristics of the geographic features in the place where the individual is located. The vector includes the factors that vary across the alternatives as well as that vary across the individual agents.

In a choice model of transportation modes, for example, travel time is an explanatory variable that varies across the modes of transportation such as car, bus, boat, and subway. The age of an individual decision-maker is a variable that varies across the individual agents (Train, 2003). In a choice model of natural resource enterprises, climate and soils are explanatory variables that vary across the individuals located in different geographic zones. Prices of natural resource products are variables that vary across the alternatives (Seo and Mendelsohn, 2008; Seo, 2015a).

The choice rule for an individual is to choose alternative 1 if it earns the highest profit among the alternatives. Then, the probability of the choice is expressed as:

$$
\begin{aligned}
P_{n1} &= \mathrm{Prob}[\pi_{n1}^* > \pi_{nk}^*, \forall k \neq 1] \\
&= \mathrm{Prob}[Z_n\beta_1 + \varepsilon_{n1} > Z_n\beta_k + \varepsilon_{nk}, \forall k \neq 1] \\
&= \mathrm{Prob}[\varepsilon_{nk} - \varepsilon_{n1} < Z_n\beta_1 - Z_n\beta_k, \forall k \neq 1].
\end{aligned}
\tag{3.47}
$$

This probability is a cumulative distribution function of the residual. Using the density function, $f(\varepsilon_n)$, and the indicator function, $I(\cdot)$, this probability can be rewritten as

$$
P_{n1} = \int_{\varepsilon} I(\varepsilon_{nk} - \varepsilon_{n1} < Z_n\beta_1 - Z_n\beta_k, \forall k \neq 1) f(\varepsilon_n) d\varepsilon_n.
\tag{3.48}
$$

This is a multidimensional integral over the density, $f(\varepsilon_n)$, where $\varepsilon_n = (\varepsilon_{n1}, \varepsilon_{n2}, \ldots, \varepsilon_{nJ})$. Different discrete choice models result from different assumptions on this density function. Most widely used models are a Probit model and a Logit model. The former is derived when the density function follows a multivariate normal distribution while the latter is derived when the density function follows an independently and identically distributed (iid) extreme value distribution. In the mixed Logit model, the disturbance term consists of a part that follows any distribution specified by a researcher and a part that follows an iid extreme value distribution.

The closed-form expression of the probability in Eq. 3.48 exists only for the Logit model in which the disturbance term is assumed to follow an iid extreme value distribution. In the Probit and the mixed Logit models, the probability does not have a closed-form and is evaluated numerically through simulation. The present author will explain the Logit model now and come back to the Probit and the mixed Logit models later in this chapter.

The probability in Eq. 3.48 is a J dimensional integral over the density of J error terms in $\varepsilon_n = (\varepsilon_{n1}, \ldots, \varepsilon_{nJ})$. The Logit model is derived by assuming ε_{nj} is independently and iid extreme value. This distribution is also called a Gumbel distribution or a type I extreme value distribution. The density function and the cumulative distribution of a Gumbel distribution is as follows (Casella and Berger, 2001; Hogg et al., 2012):

$$F(\varepsilon_{nj}) = \exp(-e^{-\varepsilon_{nj}}), \tag{3.49}$$

$$f(\varepsilon_{nj}) = e^{-\varepsilon_{nj}} \exp(-e^{-\varepsilon_{nj}}). \tag{3.50}$$

The variance of a Gumbel distribution is $\pi^2/6$ where π is an irrational number, that is, not a notation for profit. The mean of this distribution is not zero, but the mean does not matter since only the differences in profits matter in making a choice of one over the others. That is, absolute magnitudes of profits from alternatives would not matter in selecting one alternative over the others, but relative profits among the alternatives would matter. The difference between the two random terms that have the same mean is zero. In other words, the difference between the two residual terms that follow an iid Gumbel distribution has a distribution with mean zero.

The difference between the two extreme value variables is distributed logistic. That is, if ε_{nj} and ε_{ni} are iid extreme value distributed, then $\varepsilon_{nji}^* = \varepsilon_{nj} - \varepsilon_{ni}$ follows the logistic distribution which has the following cumulative distribution function:

$$F(\varepsilon_{nji}^*) = \frac{e^{\varepsilon_{nji}^*}}{1 + e^{\varepsilon_{nji}^*}}. \tag{3.51}$$

Continuing from Eq. 3.47, the probability can be written as the CDF of the Gumbel distribution, ε_{nk}, evaluated at $\varepsilon_{n1} + Z_n\beta_1 - Z_n\beta_1$ for all $k \neq 1$:

$$P_{n1} = \text{Prob}[\varepsilon_{nk} < \varepsilon_{n1} + Z_n\beta_1 - Z_n\beta_k, \forall k \neq 1]. \tag{3.52}$$

If ε_{n1} is considered given, since $\varepsilon_{nk}'s$ are independent, this cumulative distribution over all $k \neq 1$ is the product of independent distributions:

$$P_{n1} \mid \varepsilon_{n1} = \prod_{k \neq 1} \exp(-e^{-(\varepsilon_{n1} + Z_n\beta_1 - Z_n\beta_k)}). \tag{3.53}$$

The probability is then the integral over this conditional probability over all values of ε_{n1} weighted by the density of ε_{n1}:

$$P_{n1} = \int \left(\prod_{k \neq 1} \exp(-e^{-(\varepsilon_{n1} + Z_n\beta_1 - Z_n\beta_k)}) \right) \cdot e^{-\varepsilon_{n1}} \exp(-e^{-\varepsilon_{n1}}) d\varepsilon_{n1}. \tag{3.54}$$

The following manipulations of Eq. 3.54 lead to a succinct Logit formula (Train, 2003):

$$P_{n1} = \int_{s=-\infty}^{+\infty} \prod_k \exp(-e^{-(s+Z_n\beta_1-Z_n\beta_k)})e^{-s}\, ds$$

$$= \int_{s=-\infty}^{+\infty} \exp\left(-\sum_k e^{-(s+Z_n\beta_1-Z_n\beta_k)}\right)e^{-s}\, ds \qquad (3.55)$$

$$= \int_{s=-\infty}^{+\infty} \exp\left(-e^{-s}\sum_k e^{-(Z_n\beta_1-Z_n\beta_k)}\right)e^{-s}\, ds.$$

Define $t = e^{-s}$. The first derivatives of both sides lead to $dt = -e^{-s}ds$. As s approaches infinity, t approaches zero; as s approaches negative infinity, t approaches infinity. Using this relation,

$$P_{n1} = \int_{t=\infty}^{0} \exp\left(-t\sum_k e^{-(Z_n\beta_1-Z_n\beta_k)}\right)(-dt)$$

$$= \int_{t=0}^{\infty} \exp\left(-t\sum_k e^{-(Z_n\beta_1-Z_n\beta_k)}\right)dt$$

$$= \frac{\exp\left(-t\sum_k e^{-(Z_n\beta_1-Z_n\beta_k)}\right)\Big|^{\infty}_0}{-\sum_k e^{(-Z_n\beta_1-Z_n\beta_k)}} \qquad (3.56)$$

$$= \frac{1}{\sum_k e^{-(Z_n\beta_1-Z_n\beta_k)}}.$$

The final manipulation of the last line of Eq. 3.56 leads to the Logit probability formula from a multinomial choice setting (McFadden, 1974).

$$P_{n1} = \frac{e^{Z_n\beta_1}}{\sum_{k=1}^{K} e^{Z_n\beta_k}}. \qquad (3.57)$$

The odds of the probability P_1 is the ratio between probability of choice and probability of no choice, that is, $P_1/(1-P_1)$. The log-odds is the logarithm of the odds (Hilbe, 2009, Agresti, 2013):

$$\text{Log}-\text{odds} = \log\left(\frac{P_1}{1-P_1}\right). \qquad (3.58)$$

The Logit of a probability is the log-odds (Hilbe, 2009; Agresti, 2013):

$$\text{Logit}(P_j) = \log\left(\frac{P_j}{1-P_j}\right) = -\log\left(\frac{1}{P_j}-1\right)$$

$$= -\log\left(e^{-Z_n\beta_j + \sum_{k\neq j} Z_n\beta_k}\right) \qquad (3.59)$$

$$= Z_n\beta_j - \sum_{k\neq j} Z_n\beta_k.$$

The logarithm of the odds ratio is the difference between the logits of two of two probabilities:

$$\log(\text{odds ratio}) = \log\left(\frac{P_1/{1-P_1}}{P_2/{1-P_2}}\right) \qquad (3.60)$$

$$= \text{Logit}(P_1) - \text{Logit}(P_2).$$

As explained in the review of history of the Logit models (Cramer, 2003), the Logit model was first developed in the process of biological modeling by Joseph Berkson in 1944 who coined the term (Berkson, 1944, 1951). He used the term "Logit" by analogy from the Probit model which had been developed earlier by Chester Bliss in 1934 (Bliss, 1934a, b). Daniel McFadden developed the Multinomial Logit model as elaborated in this section to explain behavioral processes using mathematical statistics, for which he was awarded the Nobel Prize in Economics in 2000 (McFadden, 1974).

The multinomial choice model described in this section is formulated as a choice by an individual of one alternative from the set of alternatives at once and for all. There are choice situations, however, that a different modeling perspective is needed. One such situation exists when an individual makes a binary choice multiple times successively (Chib and Greenberg, 1998). A situation can be imagined in which a consumer makes purchase decisions on multiple items separately. She/he would make a binary choice on the first item in the first decision, then make another binary choice on the second item in the second decision, and then make another binary choice on the third item in the third decision, and so on. This modeling approach is called a multivariate Probit model.

Another such situation is when an individual makes a binary (or polychotomous) choice in the first stage and makes another binary (or polychotomous) choice in the second stage conditional on the choice in the first stage. A situation can be imagined in which an individual chooses a housing location to live. She/he would make a choice on which city (or State) she/he would live considering available information on characteristics of the cities in the choice set. Conditional on the choice in the first stage, she/he would make another choice on which type of dwelling units she/he would live: an apartment unit, an apartment unit with a good view, a detached house, a detached house with a swimming pool, a detached house with a large yard, and so on. This model is called a nested Logit model (McFadden, 1978; Train, 2003).

3.4 MULTINOMIAL SELECTION BIAS CORRECTION MODELS

Often, researchers are interested in estimating the outcome function. For example, a researcher may be interested in the profit function of one of the natural resource enterprises introduced in the previous chapter such as a crops-only enterprise because, for example, many scientists are worried about negative effects of changes in climate on major staple crops. In the same way that there is selection problem in the binomial choice situation, selection bias will arise from simple estimation of an outcome function based on observed profits.

Continuing with the specification in Eq. 3.46, let's consider the following model in which the researcher is attempting to estimate the profit function of alternative 1:

$$\begin{aligned}
\pi_1 &= X\gamma_1 + \eta_1, \\
\pi_j^* &= Z\beta_j + \varepsilon_j, \quad j = 1, 2, \dots, J.
\end{aligned} \tag{3.61}$$

The researcher may attempt to estimate the first equation of Eq. 3.61 using observed profit data and explanatory variables. He may specify the disturbance term parametrically with

$$\begin{aligned}
E[\eta_1 \mid X, Z] &= 0, \\
Var[\eta_1 \mid X, Z] &= \sigma^2.
\end{aligned} \tag{3.62}$$

where the vector Z represents the maximum set of explanatory variables from all the alternatives, $j = 1, 2, \ldots, J$, and the vector X contains all the determinants of alternative 1.

The problem of estimating the first equation of Eq. 3.61 arises because the error term in the first equation, η_j, is not independent of all the error terms in the second equation, $(\varepsilon_j)'s$. This would introduce some correlation between the explanatory variables and the error term in the first equation of Eq. 3.61 (Lee 1983, Dubin and McFadden 1984, Dahl 2002). Because of this, least squares estimates of γ_1 would not be consistent.

To explain the bias due to selection, let's start with the definitions of Γ and ς_1 as follows:

$$\Gamma = \{Z\beta_1, Z\beta_2, \ldots, Z\beta_J\}, \tag{3.63}$$

$$\varsigma_1 = \max_{j \neq 1}\{\pi_j^* - \pi_1^*\}. \tag{3.64}$$

The selection bias can be based on the conditional mean of η_1:

$$E(\eta_1 \mid \varsigma_1 < 0, \Gamma) = \int\int_{-\infty}^{0} \frac{\eta_1 \cdot f(\eta_1, \varsigma_1 \mid \Gamma)}{P(\varsigma_1 < 0 \mid \Gamma)} d\varsigma_1 d\eta_1 = \lambda(\Gamma). \tag{3.65}$$

Let P_k be the probability that alternative k is selected:

$$P_k = \frac{e^{Z\beta_k}}{\displaystyle\sum_{j=1}^{J} e^{Z\beta_j}}. \tag{3.66}$$

Then, the relation between J components of Γ and J corresponding probabilities is invertible. Therefore, there exists a unique function μ such that:

$$E(\eta_1 \mid \varsigma_1 < 0, \Gamma) = \lambda(\Gamma) = \mu(P_1, P_2, \ldots, P_J). \tag{3.67}$$

The consistent estimate of the outcome equation can be estimated from either of the following equations:

$$\begin{aligned}
\pi_1 &= X\gamma_1 + \mu(P_1, P_2, \ldots, P_J) + \psi_1 \\
\text{or} \quad \pi_1 &= X\gamma_1 + \lambda(\Gamma) + \psi_1
\end{aligned} \tag{3.68}$$

where ψ_1 is a residual which is mean-independent of the regressors.

Lee proposed a generalization of the two-step selection bias correction method proposed by Hackman that allows for any parameterized error distribution (Lee, 1983). Let $F_{\varsigma_1}(\cdot \mid \Gamma)$ be the cumulative distribution function of ς_1 and define $J_{\varsigma_1}(\cdot \mid \Gamma)$ by the following transformation:

$$J_{\varsigma_1}(\cdot \mid \Gamma) = \Phi^{-1}(F_{\varsigma_s}(\cdot \mid \Gamma)) \tag{3.69}$$

where Φ is a standard normal cumulative distribution. $J_{\varsigma_1}(\cdot \mid \Gamma)$ has a standard normal cumulative distribution.

Lee assumes that η_1 and $J_{\varsigma_1}(\cdot \mid \Gamma)$ is linearly related with correlation parameter ρ_1. That is, the two assumptions are:

1) Correlation assumption:

$$Corr(\eta_1, J_{\varsigma_1}(\varsigma_1 \mid \Gamma)) \text{ does not depend on } \Gamma. \tag{3.70}$$

2) Linearity assumption:

$$E(\eta_1 \mid \varsigma_1, \Gamma) = -\sigma \rho_1 J_{\varsigma_1}(\varsigma_1 \mid \Gamma). \tag{3.71}$$

Then, the expected value of the disturbance term conditional on the choice of alternative 1 is given by:

$$E(\eta_1 \mid \varsigma_1 < 0, \Gamma) = -\sigma \rho_1 \frac{\phi(J_{\varsigma_1}(0 \mid \Gamma))}{F_{\varsigma_1}(0 \mid \Gamma)} \tag{3.72}$$

where ϕ is the density function of the standard normal distribution.

A consistent estimator for γ_1 is obtained by running least squares regression on the following equation:

$$\pi_1 = X\gamma_1 - \sigma \rho_1 \frac{\phi(J_{\varsigma_1}(0 \mid \Gamma))}{F_{\varsigma_1}(0 \mid \Gamma)} + \psi_1. \tag{3.73}$$

The two-step estimation of the above equation is implemented by (1) obtaining $(\beta_j)'s$ from running a multinomial choice model and forming $\dfrac{\phi(J_{\varsigma_1}(0 \mid \hat{\Gamma}))}{F_{\varsigma_1}(0 \mid \hat{\Gamma})}$ and (2) including this into the regression in Eq. 3.73 which is estimated by a least squares method.

The problem in the Lee's model is that the joint distribution between η_1 and ς_1 originates in the possible correlation between η_1 and all $(\varepsilon_j)'s$, and thus generally depends on Γ. Eq. 3.70, however, requires that the correlation between η_1 and $J_{\zeta_1}(\varsigma_1 \mid \Gamma)$ is independent of Γ. This is in general not the case even with the transformation of the variable (Bourguignon et al., 2004).

This has strong practical implications (Schmertmann, 1994). This implies that the correlation between η_1 and $\varepsilon_j - \varepsilon_1$ be the same sign for all j. That is to say, the unobservable determinants in the choice of alternative 1 against any other alternative should be correlated in the same direction with the unobservable determinants of the outcome, π_1.

This assumption further implies that the correlations are identical if the residual terms $\varepsilon_j - \varepsilon_1$ are assumed to be identically distributed (Schmertmann, 1994). The residual terms are assumed to be identically distributed in the Multinomial Logit model. For most empirical studies, this is a strong assumption.

Dubin and McFadden proposed a different approach based on the following linearity assumption, expressed in terms of the original $(\varepsilon_j)'s$, which overcomes the strong correlation assumption in the Lee model:

$$E(\eta_1 \mid \varepsilon_1, \varepsilon_2, ..., \varepsilon_J) = \sigma \sum_{j=1,2,...,J} r_j (\varepsilon_j - E(\varepsilon_j)),$$

with $\quad \sum_{j=1}^{J} r_j = 0$

and $\quad r_j = Corr(\eta_1, \varepsilon_j).$

(3.74)

The linearity assumption implies

$$E(\eta_1 \mid \varepsilon_1, \varepsilon_2, ..., \varepsilon_J) = \sigma \sum_{j=2,...,J} r_j (\varepsilon_j - \varepsilon_1). \tag{3.75}$$

With the multinomial Logit model,

$$E(\varepsilon_j - \varepsilon_1 \mid \pi_1^* > \max_{s \neq 1}(\pi_s^*), \Gamma) = \frac{P_j \ln P_j}{1 - P_j} + \ln P_1, \forall j > 1. \tag{3.76}$$

Eq. 3.76 is obtained by the following manipulations from Eq. 3.77 to Eq. 3.83:

$$E(\varepsilon_j - \varepsilon_1 \mid \pi_1^* > \max_{s \neq 1}(\pi_s^*), \Gamma)$$

$$= E(\varepsilon_j \mid \pi_1^* > \max_{s \neq 1}(\pi_s^*), \Gamma) - E(\varepsilon_1 \mid \pi_1^* > \max_{s \neq 1}(\pi_s^*), \Gamma)$$

$$= \int_{\varepsilon_j} \varepsilon_j f(\varepsilon_j \mid \pi_1^* > \max_{s \neq 1}(\pi_s^*), \Gamma) d\varepsilon_j - \int_{\varepsilon_1} \varepsilon_1 f(\varepsilon_1 \mid \pi_1^* > \max_{s \neq 1}(\pi_s^*), \Gamma) d\varepsilon_1$$

$$= \int_{\varepsilon_j} \varepsilon_j \left\{ \frac{1}{1-P_j} \left[g(\varepsilon_j) - g(\varepsilon_j) \cdot \exp(e^{-\varepsilon_j}) \cdot \exp\left(-\frac{e^{-\varepsilon_j}}{P_j} \right) \right] \right\} d\varepsilon_j$$

$$- \int_{\varepsilon_1} \varepsilon_1 \cdot \frac{e^{-\varepsilon_1}}{P_1} \cdot \exp\left(-\frac{e^{-\varepsilon_1}}{P_1} \right) d\varepsilon_1$$

$$= \int_{\varepsilon_j} \left\{ \frac{\varepsilon_j g(\varepsilon_j)}{1-P_j} - \frac{\varepsilon_j}{1-P_j} e^{-\varepsilon_j} \exp\left(-\frac{e^{-\varepsilon_j}}{P_j} \right) \right\} d\varepsilon_j \qquad (3.77)$$

$$- \int_{\varepsilon_1} \frac{\varepsilon_1}{P1} \cdot e^{-\varepsilon_1} \cdot \exp\left(-\frac{e^{-\varepsilon_1}}{P_1} \right) d\varepsilon_1.$$

Let $\varepsilon_j g(\varepsilon_j) = k$. Then the last line of Eq. 3.77 equals the following:

$$= \int_{\varepsilon_j} \left\{ \frac{k}{1-P_j} - \frac{\varepsilon_j P_j}{1-P_j} g(\varepsilon_j + \ln P_j) \right\} d\varepsilon_j - \int_{\varepsilon_1} \varepsilon_1 g(\varepsilon_1 + \ln P_1) d\varepsilon_1. \qquad (3.78)$$

Let $\vartheta_j = \varepsilon_j + \ln P_j$. Then the last line of Eq. 3.78 equals the following:

$$= \int_{\vartheta_j} \left\{ \frac{k}{1-P_j} - \frac{(\vartheta_j - \ln P_j) \cdot P_j \cdot g(\vartheta_j)}{1-P_j} \right\} d\vartheta_j - \int_{\vartheta_1} (\vartheta_1 - \ln P_1) \cdot g(\vartheta_1) d\vartheta_1$$

$$= \int_{\vartheta_j} \left\{ \frac{k(1-P_j)}{1-P_j} - \frac{kP_j - P_j \cdot \ln P_j \cdot g(\vartheta_j)}{1-P_j} \right\} d\vartheta_j - \int_{\vartheta_1} \left\{ k + \ln P_1 \cdot g(\vartheta_1) \right\} d\vartheta_1 \qquad (3.79)$$

$$= \int_{\vartheta_j} \frac{P_j \cdot \ln P_j}{1-P_j} g(\vartheta_j) d\vartheta_j + \int_{\vartheta_1} \ln P_1 \cdot g(\vartheta_1) d\vartheta_1$$

$$= \frac{P_j \cdot \ln P_j}{1-P_j} + \ln P_1.$$

From Eqs. 3.77, 3.78, and 3.79, we get Eq. 3.76. However, the fourth line of Eq. 3.77 still needs an explanation. In other words, we need to explain how the conditional density of ε_1 as well as that of ε_j is obtained given the choice of alternative 1. That is,

$$f(\varepsilon_1 \mid \pi_1^* > \max_{s \neq 1}(\pi_s^*), \Gamma)$$

$$= f(\varepsilon_1 \mid \varepsilon_1 > \max_{s \neq 1}(Z\beta_s + \varepsilon_s) - Z\beta_1)$$

$$= \frac{g(\varepsilon_1)}{P(\pi_1^* > \max_{s \neq 1}(\pi_s^*))} \int \cdots \int I[\varepsilon_1 > (Z\beta_2 + \varepsilon_2) - Z\beta_1] \cdot g(\varepsilon_2) \cdots$$

$$...I[\varepsilon_1 > (Z\beta_j + \varepsilon_j) - Z\beta_1] \cdot g(\varepsilon_j) d\varepsilon_2 d\varepsilon_3 ... d\varepsilon_J$$

$$= \frac{g(\varepsilon_1)}{P(\pi_1^* > \max_{s \neq 1}(\pi_s^*))} \prod_{s>1} G(\varepsilon_1 + Z\beta_1 - Z\beta_s). \tag{3.80}$$

In the above equation, G is the cumulative of the Gumbel distribution and g is the density function of the Gumbel distribution. Note that

$$\prod_{s>1} G(\varepsilon_1 + Z\beta_1 - Z\beta_s) = \exp\left(-e^{-\varepsilon_1} \frac{\sum_{s>1} e^{Z\beta_s}}{e^{Z\beta_1}} \right). \tag{3.81}$$

After some transformations, it follows that:

$$f(\varepsilon_1 \mid \pi_1^* > \max_{s \neq 1}(\pi_s^*), \Gamma)$$

$$= \frac{e^{-\varepsilon_1}}{P_1} \cdot \exp\left(-\frac{e^{-\varepsilon_1}}{P_1} \right) \tag{3.82}$$

$$= g(\varepsilon_1 + \ln P_1).$$

The conditional density of ε_j can be obtained in the same manner:

$$f(\varepsilon_j \mid \pi_1^* > \max_{s \neq 1}(\pi_s^*), \Gamma)$$

$$= \frac{1}{1-P_j}\left[g(\varepsilon_j) - g(\varepsilon_j) \cdot \exp(e^{-\varepsilon_j}) \cdot \exp\left(-\frac{e^{-\varepsilon_j}}{P_j} \right) \right]$$

$$= \frac{1}{1-P_j}\left[g(\varepsilon_j) - \varepsilon^{-\varepsilon_j} \cdot \exp\left(-\frac{e^{-\varepsilon_j}}{P_j} \right) \right] \tag{3.83}$$

$$= \frac{1}{1-P_j}\left[g(\varepsilon_j) - P_j g(\varepsilon_j + \ln P_j) \right].$$

Eqs. 3.77–3.83 provides the necessary proofs for Eq. 3.76. These proofs provide that the model can be estimated consistently with selection bias correction as follows:

$$\pi_1 = X\gamma_1 + \sigma \sum_{j=2,...,J} r_j \left(\frac{P_j \ln P_j}{1-P_j} + \ln P_1 \right) + \psi_1. \tag{3.84}$$

In contrast to the Lee's model, the Dubin–McFadden method does not impose an assumption on the correlations between η_1 and the error terms in the selection equation, $(\varepsilon_j)'s$. They are only assumed to sum up to zero. Each of correlation parameters is estimated through Eq. 3.84 (Seo and Mendelsohn, 2008; Seo, 2010, 2015a, b).

Eq. 3.84 is estimated through a two-step procedure. A researcher estimates the choice probabilities of all the alternatives in the first step. The estimated probabilities are used to form the following bias terms for each of the observations:

$$\Omega_j = \frac{\hat{P}_j \ln \hat{P}_j}{1 - \hat{P}_j} + \ln \hat{P}_1, \forall j > 1. \qquad (3.85)$$

In the second step, this quantity is entered as one of the regressors along with the explanatory variables X to obtain the least squares estimates. The only technical difficulty in deriving the Dubin–McFadden model is to show how Eq. 3.76 is obtained.

The choice equations should be identified from the outcome equations (Fisher, 1966; Manski, 1995; Cropper and Oates, 1992; Johnston and DiNardo, 1997; Freeman et al., 2014). Either parametrically or nonparametrically, identification can be done (Cropper and Oates, 1992). In a nonparametric approach, a researcher uses the same set of explanatory variables in both the choice equations and the outcome equations with $J - 1$ variables dropped from the outcome equations as identification variables, which was explained at length in the previous chapter (Seo and Mendelsohn, 2008; Seo, 2010, 2015b).

3.5 MIXED LOGIT AND SIMULATION-BASED METHODS

The Multinomial Logit model is probably most widely used to model a polychotomous choice situation because of its compact expression for probabilities, as shown in Eq. 3.57, and computational ease (Seo and Mendelsohn, 2008; Agresti, 2013). Other multinomial choice models, for example, the Multinomial Probit model, require a multidimensional integration of a density function relying on the use of various simulation methods, hence these models are computationally intensive (Train, 2003). Despite this advantage, the Multinomial Logit model has several well-known limitations in capturing choice behaviors.

The most cited of these limitations is that the Multinomial Logit model imposes a certain substitution pattern among the alternatives, which is known as the Independence from Irrelevant Alternatives (IIA) hypothesis (Luce, 1959; McFadden, 1999a). That is, when the attributes of one alternative are improved, the probability of this alternative being chosen increases. Some of the people who chose one of the other alternatives under the original attributes would now choose this alternative instead. Since probabilities should sum up to one across the alternatives, an increase in the choice of one alternative necessarily means a decrease in the choice probabilities of the other alternatives. In this process, the Multinomial Logit model imposes a certain type of substitution pattern across the alternatives, that is, the ways how the probabilities of the other alternatives should be rearranged.

To see the IIA hypothesis more concretely, let's consider again the Multinomial Logit model which is based solely on the explanatory variables that vary across the alternatives (Train, 2003). Then, the ratio of Logit probabilities of two alternatives is

$$\frac{P_{ni}}{P_{nk}} = \frac{e^{Z_i\beta} \Big/ \sum_{i=1}^{J} e^{Z_i\beta}}{e^{Z_k\beta} \Big/ \sum_{k=1}^{J} e^{Z_k\beta}} = \frac{e^{Z_i\beta}}{e^{Z_k\beta}} = e^{Z_i\beta - Z_k\beta}. \tag{3.86}$$

Note in the above equation that the ratio of choice probabilities of two alternatives does not depend on any alternatives other than i and k. That is, the other alternatives are irrelevant to how the ratio between the probability to choose i and the probability to choose k is determined in any state of attributes of alternatives.

This behavioral hypothesis is unrealistic in many choice situations of real life (Chipman, 1960; Debreu, 1960). Let's consider the well-known red bus and blue bus example. In the present state, let's assume that an individual can go to work either by a red bus or by a car. Further, assume that the probability to choose a car and the probability to choose a red bus are the same. That is, the probability to choose a car equals 1/2 and the probability to choose a red bus equals 1/2. The ratio of the two probabilities is 1.

Now, the blue bus is introduced and is considered by the individual to be exactly same as the red bus. That is, the probability to choose a red bus and the probability to choose a blue bus must be the same. In the IIA hypothesis, the only possible outcome in which the ratio between the probability to choose a car and the probability to choose a red bus remains 1 while the ratio between the probability to choose a blue bus and the probability to choose a red bus is 1 is when the probability to choose a car equals 1/3, the probability to choose a blue bus equals 1/3, and the probability to choose a red bus equals 1/3.

In real life, however, we would expect that the introduction of a blue bus reduces mostly the choice of a red bus, but not much of the choice of a car. That is, a more realistic outcome may be when the probability of a car equals $1/2$, the probability of a blue car equals $1/4$, and the probability of a red car equals $1/4$.

The simulation-based probability models such as the Probit, the mixed Logit, or the mixed Probit overcome this problem, that is, the IIA hypothesis (Train, 2003). In the Probit model, the integration in Eq. 3.48 becomes a multidimensional integration of the density function since the error term $\varepsilon'_n = (\varepsilon_{n1},...,\varepsilon_{nJ})$ is assumed to be distributed normal with a mean vector of zero and a covariance matrix Ω. The density of ε_n is written as follows:

$$\phi(\varepsilon_n) = \frac{1}{(2\pi)^{J/2}|\Omega|^{1/2}} e^{-\frac{1}{2}\varepsilon'_n\Omega^{-1}\varepsilon_n}. \tag{3.87}$$

The integration in Eq. 3.48 under the Probit model can be completed using simulation methods such as the Accept-Reject simulator, the smoothed Accept-Reject simulator, or the GHK (Geweke, Hajivassiliou, and Keane) simulator (Geweke, 1989, 1991; Hajivassiliou and McFadden, 1998; Keane, 1990, 1994). Kenneth Train provides an excellent review of these various simulation methods, so the readers are encouraged to refer to his book for these various simulation methods (Train, 2003). The basic idea of simulation methods is simple: draw from a relevant density function and calculate probabilities. The present author will cover some of these simulation methods in the discussion of the mixed Logit models, which is ensued presently.

A Mixed Logit model is a highly flexible choice model that can approximate any random utility model, the proof of which was given by McFadden and Train and can be reproduced with some degree of mathematical manipulations (McFadden and Train, 2000). Similarly with the Probit model, the mixed Logit model has been known for many years but has become fully applicable only since the advent of simulation (Train, 2003). Early applications of the mixed Logit were Boyd and Mellman (1980) and Cardell and Dunbar (1980) applied to automobile demand models. Train et al. (1987) and Ben-Akiva et al. (1993) developed the mixed Logit models at the individual decision maker level.

The mixed Logit model combines the Logit model with simulation techniques (Seo, 2010, 2011a). The mixed Logit probability is a weighted average of the Logit formula evaluated at different values of β, with weights given by the density function $f(\beta)$. In the statistics literature, the weighted average of several functions is called a mixed function and the density function that provides the weights is called a mixing distribution. The Mixed Logit is a mixture of the Logit function evaluated at different $\beta's$ with $f(\beta)$ as the mixing distribution, which is why this method is called a Mixed Logit.

In the mixed Logit model, choice probabilities can be expressed as integrals of standard Logit probabilities over a density of parameters:

$$P_{ni} = \int L_{ni}(\beta) f(\beta) d\beta. \tag{3.88}$$

With L_{ni} being a Logit probability, the mixed Logit model can be written as follows:

$$P_{ni} = \int \left(\frac{e^{Z_n \beta_i}}{\sum_{j=1}^{J} e^{Z_n \beta_j}} \right) f(\beta) d\beta. \tag{3.89}$$

In the above equation, $f(\beta)$ is a density function and $L_{ni}(\beta)$ is a Logit probability evaluated at the parameters $\beta. f(\beta)$ is called a mixing distribution. In the mixed Logit model, this mixing distribution can take any form. That is, it can be assumed to be a normal distribution which is most common. But, any other distributions such as lognormal, triangular, uniform, and gamma distribution can be used as a mixing distribution (Train, 2003). The choice of a mixing distribution is made by a researcher considering the nature of choice behaviors in the given problem. Again, Kenneth Train provides an excellent account of how to choose from various mixing distributions.

The mixing distribution, $f(\beta)$, can be discrete. Suppose that β take on a finite number of values labeled $b_1, b_2, \ldots, b_M$ and the probability to take on each of these values is $s_m = P(b_m)$. This is a special case of the mixed Logit model and known as the latent class model which has long been popular in psychology and marketing research (Kamakura and Russell, 1989; Chintagunta et al., 1991). In the latent class model, the choice probability is expressed as

$$P_{ni} = \sum_{m=1}^{M} s_m \left(\frac{e^{Z_n b_{im}}}{\sum_{j=1}^{J} e^{Z_n b_{jm}}} \right). \tag{3.90}$$

The latent class model is meaningful if a researcher has a strong evidence to believe that there are M segments in the concerned population and each of these segments make distinct choice decisions. For example, the population may be grouped by religious affiliation, race, gender, or social caste. The share of the population in each segment m is s_m. The group-wise parameters b_m is estimated in the respective segment, m, of the population.

A standard Multinomial Logit model is a special case of the Mixed Logit model where the mixing distribution is degenerate at fixed parameters b. That is,

$$f(\beta) = \begin{pmatrix} 1 & \text{if } \beta = b \\ 0 & \text{if } \beta \neq b \end{pmatrix}. \tag{3.91}$$

Given this degenerate mixing distribution, the Mixed Logit model in Eq. 3.89 collapses to the multinomial Logit model in Eq. 3.57.

In most cases of the Mixed Logit modeling, the mixing distribution is specified to be continuous, neither discrete nor degenerate. Let's suppose that β is distributed Normal with mean b and covariance W. The Mixed Logit probability is expressed as follows:

$$P_{ni} = \int \frac{e^{Z_n \beta_i}}{\displaystyle\sum_{k=1}^{J} e^{Z_n \beta_k}} \phi(\beta \mid b, W) d\beta, \tag{3.92}$$

where $\phi(\beta \mid b, W)$ is the normal density with mean vector b and covariance vector W. A researcher estimates the probability in Eq. 3.89 and b and W through simulation by drawing from the normal distribution.

The Mixed Logit model is well suited for a variety of simulation methods for estimating probabilities. Let's start with the model in Eq. 3.61 again and assume that the coefficients β are distributed with the density $f(\beta \mid \theta)$ which is conditioned by θ, the parameters of the distribution such as the mean and covariance of β. A researcher specifies the form of the density function and estimates the parameters θ.

The Mixed Logit probabilities are estimated through simulation by drawing from a density function for any given value of θ. The simulation proceeds as follows:

Step 1: Given a value of θ, draw a value of β from the assumed distribution $f(\beta \mid \theta)$. Label it β^r with the superscript r referring to the number of draws. For the first draw, $r = 1$.

Step 2: Calculate the Logit formula $L_{ni}(\beta^r)$ shown in Eq. 3.57 with the drawn value β^r.

Step 3: Repeat the steps 1 and 2 for a large number of times (R) and average the Logit probabilities. This average is the simulated probability:

$$\tilde{P}_{ni} = \frac{1}{R} \sum_{r=1}^{R} L_{ni}(\beta^r). \qquad (3.93)$$

The variance of the simulated probability decreases as the number of simulation increases. $\tilde{P}_{ni}$ is strictly positive and is smooth (twice differentiable) in the parameters θ and variables Z. Also, $\tilde{P}_{ni}$ sums to one across the alternatives (Train, 2003).

A Simulated Log-Likelihood (SLL) function is constructed by inserting the simulated probabilities into the log-likelihood function:

$$SLL = \sum_{n=1}^{N} \sum_{j=1}^{J} d_{nj} \ln \tilde{P}_{nj}, \qquad (3.94)$$

where $d_{ni} = 1$ if individual n chooses alternative i and zero otherwise.

The Maximum Simulated Log-Likelihood Estimator (MSLE) is the value of θ that maximizes SLL. While the Multinomial Logit model calculates the value of β, the Mixed Logit model yields the distribution of β conditioned by $\theta = (b, W)$.

3.6 SPATIAL ECONOMETRIC MODELS

In the discrete choice models introduced up to now, spatial effects are by land large left unexplained. Spatial effects refer to spatial dependence in empirical data including spatial autocorrelation and spatial heterogeneity (Anselin, 1988, 1998; Case 1992; Beron and Vijberberg, 2004). Spatial dependence can arise because of an omitted variable that is correlated with spatial locations of sample data, for example, uncaptured county characteristics (Deschenes and Greenstone, 2007, 2012). Spatial dependence can take the form of spatial heterogeneity of observations as some farms are located in primarily rural areas while other farms are located in suburban areas (Mendelsohn et al., 1994).

Following Anselin (1998), let S be a set composed of N geographical units (eg, districts, counties, census tracts). The set S can be partitioned into R nonoverlapping spatially-defined subsets S_r (with $r = 1, 2, \dots, R$) such that for any $r, q(r \neq q)$, $S_r \cap S_q = 0$ and $\underset{r=1,\dots,R}{\cup} S_r = S$. In other words, the subsets are mutually exclusive and exhaustive. Spatial heteroscedasticity across the spatially-defined subsets is defined as follows:

$$Var(\varepsilon_i) = \sigma_r^2, \forall\ i \in S_r. \tag{3.95}$$

Spatial autocorrelation refers to the coincidence of value similarity with location similarity. It takes the form of nonzero covariance between the observations from two distinct spatially-defined groups r, q:

$$Cov(\pi_i, \pi_j) = \sigma_{ij} > 0, \ \forall i, j\ s.t.\ i \in S_r, j \in S_q. \tag{3.96}$$

Furthermore, let s denote a specific spatial location and h a directional distance from a specific location. Then, we can define the following variance $V_s(h)$ using profit (π) differences in two locations:

$$V_s(h) = \frac{1}{2}Var[\pi(s+h) - \pi(s)]. \tag{3.97}$$

If there is spatial continuity in the observed profits, the profits observed in two closer locations should exhibit smaller differences than the profits observed in two farther apart locations. The larger the h, the larger the $V_s(h)$. That is, the farther apart are two locations, the larger the variance in the profit differences.

A spatial weights matrix is used to code spatial dependence, both spatial heterogeneity and spatial autocorrelation (Anselin, 1998; Schlenker et al., 2006; Schlenker and Roberts 2009). Spatial dependence can take a variety of forms, so does a spatial weights matrix. To give an example, a spatial weights matrix can be defined based on the defined neighborhoods. Let W be an $N * N$ matrix with c_{ij} as its component. For each location i (as the row) which belongs to the predefined neighborhood S_i, the columns in the neighborhood of S_i are assigned nonzero values and the columns not in the neighborhood are assigned zero values. That is, for each row i, the matrix elements c_{ij} are given the following values, with S_i defined to be the neighborhood of location i:

$$c_{ij} \begin{cases} \neq 0, & \forall j \in S_i \\ = 0, & \forall j \notin S_i. \end{cases} \tag{3.98}$$

Without loss of generality, the elements of the spatial weights matrix are typically row-standardized. That is, for a given i, $\sum_{j=1}^{N} c_{ij} = 1$.

Another way to define a spatial weights matrix is by spatial distances among sample locations. In the spatial weights matrix based on defined neighborhoods, explained earlier, the matrix elements are given either zero or nonzero values depending upon whether each element belongs to a defined neighborhood or not. Alternatively, the elements can be defined as the distance (d) between the two locations:

$$c_{ij} = d(i,j), \forall i, j. \tag{3.99}$$

The most commonly used specification test for the existence of spatial autocorrelation is Moran's I, which is a two-dimensional analog of the time-series autocorrelation (Moran, 1948, 1950a, b; Johnston and DiNardo, 1997). Moran's I is defined as follows:

$$I = (N/Z_0)(\hat{e}'W\hat{e}/\hat{e}'\hat{e})$$
$$\text{with} \quad Z_0 = \sum_i \sum_j c_{ij}. \tag{3.100}$$

where $\hat{e}$ is a vector of Ordinary Least Squares (OLS) residuals and Z_0 is a standardization factor that corresponds to the sum of weights for the nonzero cross-products.

Inference for Moran's I statistic is based on a normal approximation, using a standardized z-value which is obtained from the mean and variance of the statistic shown in Eq. 3.100 (Cliff and Ord, 1972, 1981). Moran's I statistic can be used for tests of the residuals in the 2SLS (2 Stage Least Squares) models as well as for tests of the generalized residuals in the Probit models (Anselin and Kelejian, 1997; Pinkse, 1998). Asymptotic normality of the Moran's I statistic in a large variety of regression models and conditions is provided by Pinkse (1998) and Kelejian and Prucha (1998).

In a standard outcome equation such as the first equation in Eq. 3.61, spatial dependence can be incorporated parametrically into the model using one of the following two ways. First, it can be incorporated as an additional regressor in the form of a spatially lagged dependent variable. Second, it can be incorporated into the error structure of the model. The former is called a spatial lag model while the latter is called a spatial error model (Anselin, 1998).

A spatial lag model, also called a spatial autoregressive model, is expressed as follows in the vector form:

$$y = \rho W y + X\beta + \varepsilon, \tag{3.101}$$

where y is the vector of outcome variables, for example, profit, ρ is a spatial autoregressive coefficient, W is a spatial weights matrix, and ε is a vector of residuals which is assumed to be iid normal with mean zero and variance σ^2. W is called a spatial lag operator.

A spatial error model is specified with a nonspherical error term in which off-diagonal elements of the covariance matrix capture the nature of spatial dependence. One way to express the spatial error model is through the spatial autoregressive error terms:

$$y = X\beta + \varepsilon$$
$$\text{and} \quad \varepsilon = \lambda W \varepsilon + u, \tag{3.102}$$

where u is a spherical error term.

Alternatively, spatial dependence can be incorporated in a nonparametric manner through simulation methods (Seo, 2011b, 2012a, 2015b; Efron 1979, 1981). Let's go back to the neighborhood definition before: R nonoverlapping neighborhoods with S_r denoting an individual neighborhood. Let's assume that the spatial neighborhood effect is zero outside the neighborhood S_r and nonzero within the neighborhood. The size of spatial neighborhood effect may vary from one neighborhood to another. The spatial weights matrix defined above in Eq. 3.98 is a special case of this neighborhood definition. That is, if the size of spatial neighborhood effect is assumed to be constant across the neighborhood, the spatial weights matrix in Eq. 3.98 captures this type of spatial dependence.

A researcher can model this form of neighborhood effect in a nonparametric way by spatially resampling from the neighborhoods. First, a researcher randomly samples one observation from each neighborhood S_r across the whole dataset S, which is denoted S_r^1. Then, the first sub-sample is composed of the following elements with size R:

$$\left\{ S_1^1, S_2^1, ..., S_r^1, ..., S_R^1 \right\}. \tag{3.103}$$

Second, one estimates a multinomial Logit probability for each alternative j for this first sub-sample and denotes it by P_j^1. Third, one repeats this procedure for a large number of times and denotes the k_{th} subsample and the B_{th} subsample as well as estimated subsample probabilities as follows:

$$\left\{ S_1^k, S_2^k, ..., S_r^k, ..., S_R^k \right\} \quad \text{and} \quad P_j^k$$
$$\left\{ S_1^B, S_2^B, ..., S_r^B, ..., S_R^B \right\} \quad \text{and} \quad P_j^B. \tag{3.104}$$

Finally, the researcher calculates the mean of the subsample probabilities for this alternative and denote it by $\breve{P}_j$:

$$\breve{P}_j = \frac{1}{B}\sum_{b=1}^{B} P_j^b, \ \forall j. \tag{3.105}$$

This probability takes care of spatial dependence in a nonparametric way. A wide range of parametric spatial dependence models can be approximated nonparametrically using the spatial resampling method, described above, by specifying the neighborhoods accordingly and sampling from the defined neighborhoods by employing proper sampling strategies.

In a variety of parametric spatial dependence model which has a continuous form of spatial dependence, for example, through a spatial weights matrix which has element-wise distances as its elements, a researcher can approximate it nonparametrically with a spatial resampling method by employing a sampling strategy, which is pertinent to the nature of spatial dependence in question (McFadden, 1999b; Bryman and Bell, 2015).

3.7 MODELING CHOICES FROM PANEL DATA

In some cases, repeated decisions and choices of individuals are available for a sustained period of time. Data availability may vary across the individuals. That is, for an individual decision maker, there may be no observation available in a specific year. In addition, a new alternative may be newly introduced in a certain year or one of the existing alternatives may be dropped out from the choice set of alternatives starting from a specific year. Besides the changes in choice decisions and outcomes across the years, characteristics of alternatives as well as characteristics of decision-makers can vary over time.

Panel data is the data structure that encompasses both changes of variables across time and changes of variables across space. In the microbehavioral econometric context, variables of interest are characteristics of each decision-maker as well as characteristics of each alternative in the choice set. In addition, geographic, social, market, and policy variables are entered into the panel data.

The Logit model explained in Section 3.2 can be applied to the panel data of choice decisions with minor modifications using the same theoretical framework. Let the profit function of individual n be written as follows, accommodating the panel data of individuals' choices (Train, 2003):

$$\pi_{njt}^* = Z_{njt}\beta_j + \varepsilon_{njt}, \forall j,t. \tag{3.106}$$

If ε_{njt} is Gumbel distributed, independent over n, j as before, but also independent over time t, then the probability of choosing alternative i can be expressed in the same way as a simple Logit formula:

$$P_{nit} = \frac{\exp(Z_{nit}\beta_i)}{\sum_j \exp(Z_{njt}\beta_j)}.$$ (3.107)

If the unobserved error terms that affect the individuals' choices are independent over the time period during which repeated choices are made, the Logit model developed for the cross-sectional data of individuals' choices in Section 3.2 can be extended to the panel data of individuals' serial choices with no major modifications.

Under this independence assumption across time-varying choices, repeated decisions by an individual are treated simply as if they are choice decisions made repeatedly during the single time period by the same individual or as if they are choice decisions made by other individuals in the same time period with different characteristics.

Further, the independence assumption over serial choices made by an individual over time takes a special meaning when an individual's choices are constant across time periods and characteristics of the explanatory variables remain the same as well. In this situation, recurring choices by an individual are all redundant. That is, these choices add no new information to the model. Therefore, it suffices to exclude these recurring choices from the analysis (Cameron and Trivedi, 2005).

The model in Eq. 3.106 can incorporate any dynamic changes in the observed variables, that is, changes in both choice decisions and explanatory variables over time (Adamowicz, 1994; Erdem, 1996; Train, 2003). State dependence of an individual's choices can be captured by the model in Eq. 3.106. That is, an individual's past choices can have influences on the choice of an individual at the current period, which can be modeled. In addition, a lagged response of an individual in making a choice in time period t to changes in observed explanatory variables that took place in time periods before t can be incorporated into the model.

The dynamics in the observed variables are incorporated into the model by specifying the dependent variable, for example, enterprise profit, in the current time period to be dependent upon the values of the explanatory variables observed in previous (or future) time periods. More formally, the dependent variable may be expressed as follows using the lagged values, denoted by W_{njt-1}, of the subset of the vector, denoted by Z_{njt}, of explanatory variables:

$$\pi_{njt}^* = Z_{njt}\beta_j + W_{njt-1}\zeta_j + \varepsilon_{njt}, \forall j,t. \tag{3.108}$$

An interesting theoretical outcome that arises from the independence assumption is that the above model—Eq. 3.108—is consistent (Train, 2003). In other words, an inclusion of a lagged dependent variable or a lagged explanatory variable into the model does not lead to inconsistent parameter estimates. And, this is because the unobserved error terms in the multinomial Logit model are assumed to be independent across time periods. Therefore, the lagged variables W_{njt-1} are uncorrelated with the error terms of the current time period ε_{njt} owing to this independence assumption of the error terms across time periods. Under this condition, consistency of parameter estimates is guaranteed (Casella and Berger, 2001; Wooldridge, 2010).

However, the assumption of independence of unobserved error terms across time periods is not guaranteed across the board. In many situations, there would be some unobserved factors which influence an individual's choices across the time periods that are considered by a researcher. In these situations, the Multinomial Logit model cannot be applied without major modifications. From a theoretical perspective, this is another weakness of the Multinomial Logit model, in addition to the fixed substitution patterns assumed that are embodied in the IIA hypothesis. More explicitly, the Multinomial Logit model cannot be applied directly to the panel data of choices when error terms in different time periods exhibit strong dependencies which are not possible to be controlled any other way.

In order to account for serial autocorrelations in unobserved factors, one should specify a more flexible choice model such as the Probit model or the mixed Logit model (Train, 2003). In the Probit model, the covariance matrix of the error terms should be specified to allow for correlations of the error terms across relevant time periods. With no regard to the complexity in the covariance matrix in a specific economic model, parameters of the choice model and probabilities can be estimated by employing an adequate simulation technique (Geweke, 1989, 1991; Hajivassiliou and McFadden, 1998; Keane, 1990, 1994; Train, 2003). From the practical standpoint of econometric modeling, a researcher is far better off by simplifying the covariance matrix as much as one can within the boundaries of economic theory.

Alternatively, the researcher can resort to the Mixed Logit model. One can specify the mixing distribution, $f(\beta)$ in Section 3.5, in a way that it incorporates serial autocorrelations in the error terms in different time periods. To be more specific, the variance matrix of the Normal distribution, that is, the mixing distribution, specified in Section 3.5 can be modified to reflect serial correlations across error terms. Parameters and probabilities are then estimated by employing an appropriate simulation method.

One advantage of the Mixed Logit model over the Probit model in modeling panel data of individuals' choices is that the covariance matrix of the error vector can be specified in a more flexible way. It doesn't have to be assumed a Normal distribution. In many economic situations, a Normal distribution may turn out to be less optimal, calling for an alternative error distribution including, but not limited to, a log-normal distribution or a triangular distribution.

3.8 MONTE CARLO EXPERIMENTS OF SELECTION BIAS CORRECTION METHODS

The present author introduced various selection bias correction methods in Sections 3.2 and 3.4 such as the Heckman's method, the Lee's method, the Dubin–McFadden method, and the Dahl's semi-parametric method. To a researcher, there remains the question of which method should be used in a specific application of the microbehavioral econometric method. This section discusses the Monte Carlo experiments to examine which of these methods perform better or worse when some form of selectivity does matter in microbehavioral models. The descriptions of this chapter are based on the paper by Bourguignon et al. (2004) who in turn replicated the simulation methods delineated in Schmertmann (1994).

To begin with, let's consider a selection and bias correction model with three alternatives in the choice set. With three alternatives to choose from, the model takes the following form:

$$\pi_1 \text{ is observed if and only if } \varepsilon_1 > 0.1 + z_2 + \varepsilon_2$$
$$\text{and} \quad \varepsilon_1 > 0.1 + z_3 + \varepsilon_3. \tag{3.109}$$

$$\pi_1 = 1 + x_1 + x_2 + h(\varepsilon_1, \varepsilon_2, \varepsilon_3) + N(0,16). \tag{3.110}$$

In the above, $\varepsilon_1, \varepsilon_2, \varepsilon_3$ are independently drawn from a Gumbel distribution; z_2, z_3 are independently normally distributed variables with mean zero and variance 16. x_1 is correlated with z_2 and z_3, and x_2 is correlated with z_2 and z_3 in the following manner:

$$x_i = r_{xz} * z_k + N\left(0, 16 * \left(1 - r_{xz}^2\right)\right). \tag{3.111}$$

The term $h(\varepsilon_1, \varepsilon_2, \varepsilon_3)$ is the mean of the residual of the equation of interest conditional on the selection. This will take various forms, reflecting the patterns of selection biases. By examining $h(\varepsilon_1, \varepsilon_2, \varepsilon_3)$, a researcher can write this term in correspondence with one of the assumptions that underlies one of the selection bias correction methods and test whether Monte-Carlo simulation results correspond to or violate the hypotheses underlying the various selection bias methods.

In this chapter, the present author examines the following three selection bias correction models, following the suggestion from Schmertmann (1994): the Lee model, the Dubin–McFadden model, and the Dubin–McFadden variant model. In each of these models, there are two different specifications: one in which the correlations among the alternatives (ρ_1, ρ_2, ρ_3) are the same and the other in which the correlations are assumed to have opposite signs.

Model 1: the Lee's model (Lee, 1983)

$$h(\varepsilon_1, \varepsilon_2, \varepsilon_3) = \rho \left[\Phi^{-1}(F_\varepsilon) + \frac{F_\varepsilon}{2\phi(\Phi^{-1}(F_\varepsilon))} \right] - k \tag{3.112}$$

with ρ, k being scalars and $F_\varepsilon = \dfrac{e^{-\varepsilon_1}}{e^{-\varepsilon_1} + e^{-\varepsilon_2} + e^{-\varepsilon_3}}$.

Model 2: the Dubin–McFadden model (Dubin and McFadden, 1984)

$$h(\varepsilon_1, \varepsilon_2, \varepsilon_3) = (\varepsilon_2 - \varepsilon_1, \varepsilon_3 - \varepsilon_1)\rho,$$
$$\text{with} \quad \rho' = (\rho_2, \rho_3). \tag{3.113}$$

Model 3: the Dubin–McFadden variant model in which the assumption that the correlations should sum up to zero is dropped (Bourguignon et al., 2004).

$$h(\varepsilon_1, \varepsilon_2, \varepsilon_3) = (\varepsilon_1, \varepsilon_2, \varepsilon_3)\rho - k,$$
$$\text{with} \quad \rho' = (\rho_1, \rho_2, \rho_3) \quad \text{and } k \text{ a scalar.} \tag{3.114}$$

To set up the Monte Carlo experiments, the number of steps in the following should be further specified:

1. In the three selection models, parameters ρ, k are chosen so that $E[h(\varepsilon_1, \varepsilon_2, \varepsilon_3)] \cong 0$, $Var[h(\varepsilon_1, \varepsilon_2, \varepsilon_3)] \cong 16$. Different values for $\rho = (\rho_1, \rho_2, \rho_3)$ allow for different correlation structure of the residual terms in choice and outcome equations. The variance calibration is set analogously to the variances of the other three terms in the outcome equation

in Eq. 3.110. This calibration ensures that about one fourth of the total variance in the outcome equation be due to selectivity in all models. The calibration of mean ensures that the noise in Eqs. 3.109 and 3.110 be centered.

2. In all models, r_{xz} is set to 0.9. This large correlation calibration, in addition to the substantial contribution of the selection bias correction term to the total variance of the outcome equation, makes sure that selection bias be salient, so that estimators from different selection methods can be contrasted. In other words, selection bias should be set to be sufficiently large for Monte Carlo simulation experiments to be intriguing.

3. As mentioned, because the Lee's model is based on the assumption that the correlations (ρ_1, ρ_2, ρ_3) are identical, that is, there is only one correlation parameter ρ, two versions of correlation assumption for each model are considered: one in which correlations are assumed to be identical and the other in which correlations are assumed to have opposite signs.

Putting together all the elements of the set-up for the Monte Carlo experiment, Table 3.1 summarizes the parameter values chosen for this Monte-Carlo experiment.

The authors add two additional components to the simulation experiments (Bourguignon et al., 2004). First, simulation experiments are designed with three different sample sizes in order to test the effects of sample size. For a large sample experiment, sample size is set at 5000. For a medium

Table 3.1 Parameters of the Monte Carlo experiments

Model	ρ	k
Experiment 1: three alternatives in the model		
LEE	3.02	0.05
DMF–a	(1.273, 1.273)	—
DMF–b	(2.205, −2.205)	—
DMF variant–a	(1.8, 1.8, 1.8)	3.117
DMF variant–b	(1.5417, 2.5124, −1.0278)	1.75
Experiment 2: five alternatives in the model		
LEE	4.72	−3.105
DMF–a	(0.7, 0.7, 0.7, 0.7)	—
DMF–b	(1.556, 1.556, −1.556, −1.556)	—
DMF variant–a	(1.4, 1.4, 1.4, 1.4)	4
DMF variant–b	(1.4336, 1.4336, 2.1504, −0.7168, −0.7168)	2.07

sample experiment, sample size is 500. For a small sample experiment, sample size is 50.

Second, the bottom panel of Table 3.1 also presents another set of design for the simulation experiment in which the number of alternatives in the choice set increases from three to five. This additional design is to check whether a larger number of alternatives to choose from would alter the performances of the selection bias correction methods. The five-alternative design can be set up with minor modifications from the case of a three alternative experiment described above:

$$
\begin{aligned}
x_1 &= r_{xz} * (z_1 + z_2) + N\left(0, 16 * \left(1 - r_{xz}^2\right)\right) \\
x_2 &= r_{xz} * (z_3 + z_4) + N\left(0, 16 * \left(1 - r_{xz}^2\right)\right).
\end{aligned}
\tag{3.115}
$$

To ensure that same variance decomposition as the three-alternative design simulation, the variance of z_1, z_2, z_3, z_4 is calibrated to be eight each, so that the sum of any two of these variables is 16.

To obtain the Monte Carlo results, the various simulation designs described so far of the following selection models are run: the Ordinary Least Squares (OLS) model without any form of selection bias correction, the Lee model, the Dubin–McFadden model, and the Dubin–McFadden variant model. Simulation results of the four models are compared based on the magnitudes of average bias and Root Mean Square Error (RMSE) calculated from each model experiment with 400 replications.

Major findings from the Monte-Carlo experiments are summarized as follows (Bourguignon et al., 2004):

1. Sample size has little effect on the magnitude of the bias, but the RMSE measure improves significantly when the size of sample is significantly large. More specifically, the RMSE falls significantly when sample size grows from 500 to 5000.
2. The OLS estimates, that is, the estimates from the model without any form of selection bias correction, are strongly biased in all cases. The estimates are significantly improved in terms of both biases and RMSE by employing any of the selection bias correction methods.
3. The Lee's method performs far better, both in terms of biases and RMSE, than the OLS model when correlations between η_1 and $\varepsilon_i's$ are assumed to be identical. When the correlations have opposite signs, the Lee's method leads to the estimates which are strongly biased.
4. The Dubin–McFaddden method and the Dubin–McFadden variant method, with or without the identical correlation assumption, are robust

and perform far better than the other models, that is, the Lee's method and the OLS method, in terms of both biases and RMSE. This means that when the information contained in the choice probability of each alternative is unique, it must be uniquely included in the selection bias correction model.

5. The Monte Carlo simulation experiments find one situation in which the Lee's method is preferable. In the simulation experiment of a small sample size with 50 observations, the estimates from the Lee's model are preferred in terms of biases and RMSE. This positive outcome holds, however, only for the simulation in which the correlations between η_1 and $\varepsilon_i's$ are assumed to be identical. When the correlations are assumed to have opposite signs, the Lee method results in a large bias, even though the RMSE remains the smallest.

6. Selection bias correction methods based on the Multinomial Logit model are quite robust to a change in the error assumption from a Gumbel distribution to a normality assumption of error distribution in the choice model. The sizes of the biases and RMSEs in the Dubin–McFadden method as well as in the Dubin–McFadden variant method are of the same order of magnitude to those that result from the corresponding selection bias correction methods based on the multinomial normal selection models. This means that a selection bias correction approach based on the Multinomial Logit model seems to be a reasonable alternative to that based on the multinomial normal models. This seems to be true even when the IIA hypothesis is severely at odds with a real choice situation.

7. The Monte Carlo simulation experiments with a five alternative model design, shown in the bottom panel of Table 3.1, lead to more or less same conclusions to those from the three alternative simulation experiments.

Interested readers are encouraged to verify the actual numbers of these simulation experiments documented in Bourguignon and coauthors (Bourguignon et al., 2004) and the preceding work by Schmertmann (1994).

In summary, the results from the Monte Carlo experiments inform us that (1) selection bias must be corrected when it is present; (2) correlation patterns are not uniform across the pairs of the alternatives in the model, therefore the Dubin–McFadden method or its variant should be preferred since it allows for heterogeneous patterns of correlations; (3) the Dubin–McFadden method is robust to the assumptions of the multinomial normal probability models and the IIA hypothesis.

As will be demonstrated in the upcoming chapters, applications of the selection bias correction methods to empirical data will shed further light on these theoretical findings from the Monte-Carlo experiments.

With this, the present author concludes the full description of the microbehavioral econometric methods both from the economic perspectives and from the statistical considerations. In the ensuing chapters that will cover empirical applications of the microbehavioral methods, readers will have further opportunities to review and reevaluate the economic and statistical aspects of the microbehavioral modeling framework presented up to this point in the contexts of actual field examples of environmental and natural resource enterprises.

Exercises

1. The Multinomial Logit model has limitations in capturing flexibly substitution patterns among the alternatives, known as the Independence of Irrelevant Alternatives hypothesis. Show that the mixed Logit model overcomes this limitation using the ratio of mixed Logit probabilities.

2. Referring to the Multinomial selection bias correction method proposed by Dubin and McFadden, provide an economic interpretation of the linearity condition in the context of natural resource managers. Write down the Dubin-McFadden selection bias correction term assuming that the linearity condition is violated. Write down the Dubin-McFadden selection bias correction term assuming that the linearity condition in Eq. 3.74 is changed to $\sum_{j=1}^{J} r_j = 1$.

REFERENCES

Adamowicz, W., 1994. Habit formation and variety seeking in a discrete choice model of recreation demand. J. Agric. Resour. Econ. 19, 19–31.

Agresti, A., 2013. Categorical Data Analysis, third ed. John Wiley & Sons, New Jersey.

Albert, J., Chib, S., 1993. Bayesian analysis of binary and polychotomous response data. J. Am. Stat. Assoc. 88, 669–679.

Allenby, G., Lenk, P., 1994. Modeling household purchase behavior with logistic normal regression. J. Amer. Statist. Assoc. 89, 1218–1231.

Andrews, D.K., 2001. Extreme estimators. Lecture Note. Yale University, New Haven.

Anselin, L., 1988. Spatial Econometrics: Methods and Models. Kluwer Academic Publishers, Dordrecht.

Anselin, L., 1998. Spatial Econometrics. Bruton Center, University of Texas at Dallas, Dallas, Texas.

Anselin, L., Kelejian, L.H., 1997. Testing for spatial error autocorrelation in the presence of endogenous regressors. Int. Reg. Sci. Rev. 20, 153–182.

Ben-Akiva, M., Bolduc, D., Bradley, M., 1993. Estimation of travel model choice models with randomly distributed values of time. Transport. Res. Rec. 1413, 88–97.

Berkson, J., 1944. Application of the logistic function to bio-assay. J. Am. Stat. Assoc. 39, 357–365.

Berkson, J., 1951. Why I prefer logits to probits. Biometrics 7, 327–339.

Beron, K.J., Vijberberg, W.P.M., 2004. Probit in a spatial context: a Monte Carlo approach. In: Anselin, L., Florax, R.J.G.M., Rey, S.J. (Eds.), Advances in Spatial Econometrics: Methodology, Tools and Applications. Springer-Verlag, Heidelberg, Germany, pp. 169–192.

Bliss, C.I., 1934a. The method of probits. Science 79, 38–39.

Bliss, C.I., 1934b. The method of probits. Science 79, 409–410.

Bourguignon, F., Fournier, M., Gurgand, M., 2004. Selection Bias Corrections Based on the Multinomial Logit Model: Monte-Carlo Comparisons. DELTA Working Paper No. 20, Département et Laboratoire d'Economie Théorique et Appliquée.(DELTA).

Boyd, J., Mellman, J., 1980. The effect of fuel economy standards on the U.S. automotive market: a hedonic demand analysis. Transp. Res. Part A Policy Pract 14, 367–378.

Bryman, A., Bell, E., 2015. Business Research Methods, fourth ed. Oxford University Press, Oxford.

Cameron, A.C., Trivedi, P.K., 2005. Microeconometrics: Methods and Applications. Cambridge University Press, Cambridge.

Cardell, S., Dunbar, F., 1980. Measuring the societal impacts of automobile downsizing. Transp. Res. Part A Policy Pract. 14, 423–434.

Case, A., 1992. Neighborhood influence and technological change. Reg. Sci. Urban Econ. 22, 491–508.

Casella, G., Berger, R.L., 2001. Statistical Inference, second ed. Duxbury Press, CA.

Chib, S., Greenberg, E., 1998. Analysis of multivariate Probit models. Biometrika 85, 347–361.

Chintagunta, P., Jain, D., Vilcassim, N., 1991. Investigating heterogeneity in brand preference in logit models for panel data. J. Market. Res. 28, 417–428.

Chipman, J., 1960. The foundations of utility. Econometrica 28, 193–224.

Chow, G.C., 1983. Econometrics. McGraw Hill Book Company, New York.

Cliff, A., Ord, J.K., 1972. Testing for spatial autocorrelation among regression residuals. Geogr. Anal. 4, 267–284.

Cliff, A., Ord, J.K., 1981. Spatial Processes: Models and Applications. Pion, London.

Cramer, J.S., 2003. Logit Models from Economics and Other Fields. Cambridge University Press, Cambridge, UK.

Cropper, M.L., Oates, W.E., 1992. Environmental economics: a survey. J. Econ. Lit. 30 (2), 675–740.

Dahl, G.B., 2002. Mobility and the returns to education: testing a Roy model with multiple markets. Econometrica 70, 2367–2420.

Debreu, G., 1960. Review of R.D. Luce individual choice behavior. Am. Econ. Rev. 50, 186–188.

Deschenes, O., Greenstone, M., 2007. The economic impacts of climate change: evidence from agricultural output and random fluctuations in weather. Am. Econ. Rev. 97, 354–385.

Deschenes, O., Greenstone, M., 2012. The economic impacts of climate change: evidence from agricultural output and random fluctuations in weather: reply. Am. Econ. Rev. 102, 3761–3773.

Dubin, J.A., McFadden, D.L., 1984. An econometric analysis of residential electric appliance holdings and consumption. Econometrica 52 (2), 345–362.

Efron, B., 1979. Bootstrap methods: another look at the jackknife. Ann. Stat. 7, 1–26.

Efron, B., 1981. Nonparametric estimates of standard error: the jackknife, the bootstrap and other methods. Biometrika 68, 589–599.

Engle, R.F., 1984. Wald, likelihood ratio, and Lagrange multiplier tests in econometrics. In: Griliches, Z., Intriligator, M.D. (Eds.), Handbook of Econometrics. North-Holland, Amsterdam.

Erdem, T., 1996. A dynamic analysis of market structure based on panel data. Market. Sci. 15, 359–378.

Fisher, F.M., 1966. The Identification Problem in Econometrics. McGraw-Hill, New York.

Freeman, III, A.M., Herriges, J.A., Cling, C.L., 2014. The Measurements of Environmental and Resource Values: Theory and Practice. RFF Press, New York.

Geweke, J., 1989. Bayesian inference in econometric models using Monte Carlo integration. Econometrica 57, 1317–1339.

Geweke, J., 1991. Efficient simulation from the multivariate normal and Student-t distributions subject to linear constraints. In: Keramidas, EM., (Ed.), Computer Science and Statistics: Proceedings of the Twenty-Third Symposium on the Interface, Fairfax: Interface Foundation of North America, Inc., pp. 571–578.

Granger, C.W.J., 1969. Investigating causal relations by econometric methods and cross-spectral methods. Econometrica 37, 424–438.

Greene, W.H., 2011. Econometric Analysis. Prentice Hall, New York.

Hajivassiliou, V., McFadden, D., 1998. The method of simulated scores for the estimation of LDV models. Econometrica 66, 863–896.

Hastings, N.A.J., Peacock, J.B., 1975. Statistical Distributions. Butterworth & Co, London.

Hausman, J.A., 1978. Specification tests in econometrics. Econometrica 46, 1251–1271.

Heckman, J., 1979. Sample selection bias as a specification error. Econometrica 47, 153–162.

Heckman, J., 2000. Microdata, heterogeneity and the evaluation of public policy. Nobel Prize Lecture for Economic Sciences. Stockholm University, Sweden.

Hilbe, J.M., 2009. Logistic Regression Models. Chapman & Hall/CRC Press, Florida.

Hogg, R.V., Craig, A., McKean, J.W., 2012. Introduction to Mathematical Statistics, seventh ed. Pearson, New York.

Johnston, J., DiNardo, J., 1997. Econometric Methods, fourth ed. McGraw-Hill, New York.

Kamakura, W.A., Russell, G., 1989. A probabilistic choice model for market segmentation and elasticity structure. J. Market. Res. 26, 379–390.

Keane, M., 1990. Four essays in empirical macro and labor economics. PhD Thesis, Brown University, Rhode Island.

Keane, M., 1994. A computationally practical simulation estimator for panel data. Econometrica 62, 95–116.

Kelejian, H., Prucha, I., 1998. A generalized spatial two stage least squares procedure for estimating a spatial autoregressive model with autoregressive disturbances. J. Real Estate Finance Econ. 17, 99–121.

Lee, L.F., 1983. Generalized econometric models with selectivity. Econometrica 51, 507–512.

Luce, D., 1959. Individual Choice Behavior. John Wiley and Sons, New York.

Maddala, G.S., 2001. Introduction to Econometrics, 3rd ed. Wiley.

Mandelbrot, B., 1963. The variation of certain speculative prices. J. Bus. 36 (4), 394–419.

Manski, C.F., 1995. Identification Problems in the Social Sciences. Harvard University Press, Cambridge, MA.

McFadden, D.L., 1974. Conditional logit analysis of qualitative choice behavior. In: Zarembka, P. (Ed.), Frontiers in Econometrics. Academic Press, New York, pp. 105–142.

McFadden, D.L., 1978. Modeling the choice of residential location. In: Karlqvist, A., Lundqvist, L., Snickars, F., Weibull, J. (Eds.), Spatial Interaction Theory and Residential Location. North Holland, Amsterdam.

McFadden, D.L., 1984. Econometric analysis of qualitative response models. Grilliches, Z., Intrilligator, M.D. (Eds.), Handbook of Econometrics, Vol. II, Elsevier Science Publishers, BV.

McFadden, D., 1999a. Chapter 1. Discrete response models. Lecture Note. University of California, Berkeley, CA.

McFadden, D., 1999b. Chapter 2. Sampling and selection. Lecture Note. University of California, Berkeley, CA.

McFadden, D., Train, K., 2000. Mixed MNL models for discrete response. J. Appl. Econom. 15, 447–470.

Mendelsohn, R., Nordhaus, W., Shaw, D., 1994. The impact of global warming on agriculture: a Ricardian analysis. Am. Econ. Rev. 84, 753–771.

Moran, P.A.P., 1948. The interpretation of statistical maps. Biometrika 35, 255–260.

Moran, P.A.P., 1950a. Notes on continuous stochastic phenomena. Biometrika 37, 17–23.

Moran, P.A.P., 1950b. A test for the serial dependence of residuals. Biometrika 37, 178–181.

Nordhaus, W., 2011. The economics of tail events with an application to climate change. Rev. Environ. Econ. Policy 5, 240–257.

Pinkse, J., 1998. Asymptotic properties of the Moran and related tests and a test for spatial correlation in probit models. Working Paper. Department of EconomicsUniversity of British Columbia, Vancouver, BC.

Schlenker, W., Hanemann, M., Fisher, A., 2006. The impact of global warming on U.S. agriculture: an econometric analysis of optimal growing conditions. Rev. Econ. Stat. 88 (1), 113–125.

Schlenker, W., Roberts, M., 2009. Nonlinear temperature effects indicate severe damages to crop yields under climate change. Proc. Natl. Acad. Sci. USA 106 (37), 15594–15598.

Schmertmann, C.P., 1994. Selectivity bias correction methods in polychotomous sample selection models. J. Econom. 60, 101–132.

Schuster, E.F., 1984. Classification of probability laws by tail behavior. J. Am. Stat. Assoc. 79 (388), 936–939.

Seo, S.N., 2010. A microeconometric analysis of adapting portfolios to climate change: adoption of agricultural systems in Latin America. Appl. Econ. Perspect. Policy 32, 489–514.

Seo, S.N., 2011a. An analysis of public adaptation to climate change using agricultural water schemes in South America. Ecol. Econ. 70, 825–834.

Seo, S.N., 2011b. A geographically scaled analysis of adaptation to climate change with spatial models using agricultural systems in Africa. J. Agri. Sci. 149, 437–449.

Seo, S.N., 2012a. Adaptation behaviors across ecosystems under global warming: a spatial microeconometric model of the rural economy in South America. Pap. Reg. Sci. 91, 849–871.

Seo, S.N., 2012b. Decision making under climate risks: an analysis of sub-Saharan farmers' adaptation behaviors. Wea. Climate Soc. 4, 285–299.

Seo, S.N., 2015a. Micro-Behavioral Economics of Global Warming: Modeling Adaptation Strategies in Agricultural and Natural Resource Enterprises. Springer, Cham, Switzerland.

Seo, S.N., 2015b. Modeling farmer adaptations to climate change in South America: a microbehavioral econometric perspective. Environ. Ecol. Stat. 23 (1), 1–21.

Seo, S.N., Mendelsohn, R., 2008. Measuring impacts and adaptations to climate change: a structural Ricardian model of African livestock management. Agri. Econ. 38, 151–165.

Train, K., 2003. Discrete Choice Methods With Simulation. Cambridge University Press, Cambridge.

Train, K., McFadden, D., Ben-Akiva, M., 1987. The demand for local telephone service: a fully discrete model of residential calling patterns and service choice. Rand J. Econ. 18, 109–123.

Weitzman, M.L., 2009. On modeling and interpreting the economics of catastrophic climate change. Rev. Econ. Stat. 91, 1–19.

White, H., 1980. A heteroscedasticity-consistent covariance matrix estimator and a direct test for heteroscedasticity. Econometrica 48, 817–838.

Wooldridge, J.M., 2010. Econometric Analysis of Cross Section and Panel Data. MIT Press, Boston, MA.

Wu, D., 1973. Alternative tests of independence between stochastic regressors and disturbances. Econometrica 41, 733–750.

CHAPTER 4

Application of the Microbehavioral Econometric Methods to Microdecisions Under Global Warming

This chapter provides an application of the microbehavioral econometric methods introduced in the previous two chapters to one of the most salient environmental and natural resource problems today. The application focus of this chapter is agricultural and natural resource systems in South America in which individual managers make decisions conditioning on climatic factors and changes in climate in the future. Relying on the microlevel household data obtained from rural household surveys across seven countries in South America, this chapter highlights various aspects of the microbehavioral econometric methods explained in the previous two chapters.

As the Earth has warmed gradually throughout the 20th century and early 21st century, many scientists and citizens are concerned about a rapidly rising Carbon Dioxide concentration in the atmosphere due to anthropogenic sources (Keeling et al., 2005; Hansen et al., 2006; Le Treut et al., 2007; Blunden and Arndt, 2014). Among the many areas of concern in the early days of global warming literature, agriculture received the most attention when it comes to how harmful climatic changes and global warming would be to human societies (IPCC 1990; Adams et al., 1990; Rosenzweig and Parry, 1994; Mendelsohn et al., 1994). The Intergovernmental Panel on Climate Change (IPCC) reported that agricultural and crop damages will account for one third of the total market and nonmarket damage in the United States caused by climatic changes (Cline, 1992; Pearce et al., 1996). In the early literature, a prevalent assumption was—early evidence also showed—that global warming will hit hard agriculture and crop productions in low-latitude developing countries where agricultural damage is assumed or predicted to be twice as large as the damage expected in temperate developed countries (Reilly et al., 1996; Mendelsohn et al., 2006).

In the past decade and a half, climate researchers have endeavored to measure the impact of climatic changes and global warming in the low-latitude developing regions. Broadly speaking, one of the following three methodological approaches has been taken (Seo, 2015a,b). The first approach is a hedonic (econometric) approach which examines the variation of agricultural land value or profit across a range of climate zones, which is known in the literature as the Ricardian model (Mendelsohn et al., 2001; Seo et al., 2005; Schlenker et al., 2005; Kurukulasuriya et al., 2006; Seo and Mendelsohn, 2008a; Sanghi and Mendelsohn 2008; Seo et al., 2009). The second approach is an agroeconomic approach which combines the agronomic experiments of the impact of the elevated Carbon Dioxide level on major staple crops such as wheat, maize, rice, and soybeans with a national agricultural sector model of concern (Adams et al., 1999; Rosenzweig and Hillel, 1998; Butt et al., 2005; Hillel and Rosenzweig, 2010). The third approach is a microlevel portfolio adaptation approach which models an individual manager's adaptation of farm portfolios and land values for different portfolios of agriculture at the microlevel conditional on adoption of one of the portfolios (Seo, 2006, 2010b, 2011a, 2015b). This method was called the G-MAP model abbreviated for the Geographically scaled Microeconometric model of Adapting Portfolios in response to climatic changes (Seo, 2010b, 2011b). This third approach is, in fact, built upon the microbehavioral econometric methods introduced in the previous two chapters.

In this chapter, the present author applies the battery of microbehavioral econometric methods to the rural farm household data collected through individual farm household surveys across seven countries in South America by the World Bank and Yale University (Seo and Mendelsohn, 2008a). Data on net income, land value, and other farm decisions are coupled with a high resolution climatology database, future global climate change scenarios, and soils and geography data (New et al., 2002; FAO 2003). This Chapter assumes for the purposes of predictions of farm behaviors and outcomes that the climate change predictions by two of the most-widely used global climate models would unfold by the middle of this century: the Goddard Institute for Space Studies (GISS) ER model and the United Kingdom Meteorology Office (UKMO) HadCM3 model (Gordon et al., 2000; Schmidt et al., 2005).

The map of Latin America is given in Fig. 4.1, with sampled household locations marked with solid black circles. Colored countries are the seven countries where sample data are collected through rural household surveys while gray-colored (and italicized in small letters) countries are those not included in the surveys. The surveyed countries cover both the Southern Cone and the Andean regions. From the Southern cone region of South America,

Figure 4.1 *Geography of Latin America and sampled household locations.*

Brazil, Argentina, Uruguay, and Chile are included in the rural surveys and sample data. From the Andean region of South America, Ecuador, Colombia, and Venezuela are included in the rural surveys and sample data.

The primary objective of this Chapter is to show how microbehavioral statistical methods are applied to today's environmental and natural resource problems in the real world which call for wide-ranging policy dialogues. What the application of this Chapter will provide for the dialogues is a comprehensive analysis on the impact of climate change on agriculture in low-latitude developing regions and how rural farmers can adapt to climatic changes, which has been considered one of the most challenging tasks in the literature of global warming and climate change (Easterling et al., 2007; Dinar and Mendelsohn, 2012; Seo, 2013b, 2014c).

4.1 A THEORY OF THE MICROBEHAVIORAL MODEL OF AGRICULTURAL SYSTEMS

Across South America, conditioned on climate, soils, and geography, a farmer maximizes the profit by engaging in a variety of farming activities, input or output related, with a long-term perspective. In South America, the equatorial line cuts through Ecuador, Colombia, and Venezuela in the Andean region. These countries are influenced by tropical climates but also conditioned by high Andes mountain ranges. The Amazon Basin is dominated by tropical rainforests interspersed with rivers and lakes. There are various types of deserts including the Atacama Desert in Chile. There are highland grasslands in Colombia and Venezuela called the Llanos while there are lowland grasslands in the Cerrado in Brazil and the Pampas grasslands in Uruguay and Argentina. In the southernmost parts of Chile and Argentina, the ecosystems are a cryosphere, that is, frozen lands (Matthews, 1983; Mata and Campos et al., 2001; Seo, 2012a).

A farmer chooses a farm portfolio and a set of inputs of production to achieve the highest profit in the long-term given the lands s/he manages. Land rent is equal to the net revenue earned on the land in a given year (Ricardo, 1817). It captures all revenues and costs from all the activities performed on the land including grains, vegetables, fruits, and animals. The profits in the long-term can be captured as the land value which is the discounted present value of the stream of yearly land rents earned in the future (Fisher, 1906; Mendelsohn et al., 1994). In a formal notation,

$$V_t = \int_{k=0}^{\infty} \pi_{t+k} e^{-r_{t+k} k} dk \tag{4.1}$$

where V_t is land value at time t, π is land rent, and r_{t+k} is a variable discount rate between time t and $t + k$.

Let a farmer choose one portfolio from the following three agricultural systems (portfolios) that are defined to be mutually exclusive and exhaustive: a specialized crop system (system 1), a mixed system of crops and livestock (system 2), and a specialized livestock system (system 3). The farmer's choice problem is to choose the system that yields the highest expected long-term profit, that is, the land value when that system is chosen.

Let j denote a portfolio (system) and suppose the observed long-term profit of the system j as well as the latent long-term profit, that is, in the sense that the land value of only a chosen system is observable, of the system j can be written as the sum of an observable component and an unobservable component in the following form:

$$
\begin{aligned}
V_j &= X\beta_j + \mu_j \\
V_j^* &= Z\gamma_j + \varepsilon_j, \quad j = 1, 2, \ldots, J.
\end{aligned}
\tag{4.2}
$$

The Z is a vector of all explanatory variables that are relevant to all alternatives, which includes climate normals such as temperature normals and precipitation normals; soil characteristics and geographical conditions; and socioeconomic characteristics of individual farm households such as gender, age, number of household members, accessibility to various markets, schooling, cultural variables, etc. X is a vector of explanatory variables that are pertinent only to alternative j.

Assuming an independently and identically distributed (iid) Gumbel distribution of the error, the probability (P) of choosing system 1 is succinctly written as a Logit (McFadden, 1974, 1984):

$$
P_1 = \frac{\exp(Z\gamma_1)}{\displaystyle\sum_{j=1}^{J} \exp(Z\gamma_j)}.
\tag{4.3}
$$

After constructing a log-likelihood function or a simulated log-likelihood function in the case of a spatial Logit modeling, the parameters are estimated by a Maximum Likelihood (ML) method. The maximization is done through a nonlinear optimization technique such as the Newton-Raphson method.

Given the choice of an agricultural system, a farmer makes numerous decisions on inputs, practices, and land uses in order to maximize the long-term profit from the land s/he manages and the system of agriculture s/he chose. A conditional (long-term) profit function for system 1 can be expressed without selection bias as follows by correcting for the selection behavior (Heckman, 1979):

$$V_1 = X\beta_1 + \sigma_1 \sum_{\substack{j=1 \\ j \neq 1}}^{J} \rho_j \cdot \left(\frac{P_j \cdot \ln P_j}{1 - P_j} + \ln P_1 \right) + \varphi_1. \tag{4.4}$$

Note that the above equation is different from the first equation in Eq. 4.2 above. That is, a direct estimation of the first equation of Eq. 4.2 which had been a common practice of applied economists and statisticians before James Heckman leads to biased estimates of the parameters (Heckman, 2000).

The second term on the right-hand side is the selection bias correction term while φ_1 is the white noise error term. From a number of methods that are available for the selection bias correction when there are more than two alternatives in the choice set such as the Lee's, the Dahl's, and the Dubin–McFadden's method (Lee, 1983; Dubin and McFadden, 1984; Schmertmann, 1994), Eq. 4.4 employs the Dubin–McFadden selection bias correction method since it out-performs the other methods due to a severe correlation assumption imposed by the other methods, as explained in detail in the previous chapter (Schmertmann, 1994; Bourguignon et al., 2004).

In Eq. 4.4, σ_1 is the standard deviation of the error term in the (uncorrected) profit function for agricultural system 1 (the first equation in Eq. 4.2 above) and ρ_j is the correlation coefficient between the error term in the choice equation for system j and the error term in the (uncorrected) profit equation of agricultural system 1. The Dubin–McFadden method assumes the linearity condition that the correlation coefficients sum up across the alternatives in the choice set to zero, as explained in Chapter 3 (Dubin and McFadden, 1984).

The model in Eq. 4.2 is identified by excluding $J - 1$ identification variables from the set of explanatory variables in the choice equations with J being the total number of alternatives in the choice set, that is, three in our case (Fisher, 1966; Johnston and DiNardo 1997). This analysis uses elevation and a flat terrain dummy for identification variables, which will be further justified in the empirical section, after a number of sensitivity tests in empirical applications (Seo and Mendelsohn, 2008b; Seo, 2010b, 2011b).

Expected profit in the long-term (land value) is then expressed as the weighted average of the potential land values from different agricultural systems estimated through Eq. 4.4 in which the weights are choice probabilities of the corresponding alternatives estimated in the first stage of the model, that is, Eq. 4.3:

$$EV = \sum_{j=1}^{J} P_j \cdot V_j. \tag{4.5}$$

The impact of a climatic change is measured as the difference between the expected land value in Eq. 4.5 under the current climate and that under the future climate. In the microbehavioral econometric model described above, namely the G-MAP model (Seo, 2010b, 2015b), the impact of a climatic change on choice probabilities (Eq. 4.3), on unbiased land values of the different systems (Eq. 4.4), and on the expected land value of the farm (Eq. 4.5) are measured simultaneously. Uncertainties in the mean and variance estimates of these quantitative variables are obtained by estimating standard errors through bootstrap methods (Efron, 1979, 1981).

4.2 DATA AND SOURCES

The data used for the applications of the microbehavioral models in this Chapter come from various sources. The primary data, that is, microlevel behavioral data, come from the South American farm household surveys which were collected as part of the World Bank project on climate change and rural income in Latin America (Seo and Mendelsohn, 2008a). Participating countries were Argentina, Brazil, Uruguay, and Chile from the Southern Cone region and Ecuador, Colombia, and Venezuela from the Andean region. Regional and sub-regional efforts were coordinated by regional partner organizations including the PROCISUR (the Cooperative Program for the Development of Agricultural Technology in the Southern Cone), the IICA (the Inter-American Institute for Cooperation on Agriculture), and the PROCIANDINO (the Cooperative Agricultural Research and Technology Transfer Program for the Andean Subregion).

For sampling, a number of clusters from each country were chosen in a way to represent the wide range of climate, ecosystems, and agricultural activities of the country. Random sampling was done within each cluster. Through face-to-face interviews, detailed data on each household's characteristics, crop activities, livestock activities, market conditions, and land values during the Jul. 2003–Jun. 2004 period were recorded. In each country, household surveys were conducted by a group of participating scientists who were members of the national agricultural organizations of the corresponding country.

Climate data of the South American countries included in the surveys are available from various sources at varied spatial resolutions. Broadly, these data are obtained and constructed based on the ground weather stations or satellite observations of climate conditions (Mendelsohn et al., 2007). For the latter, climate data derived from the satellites operated by the US Department of Defense with the Special Sensor Microwave/Imager (SSMI) are one of the climate data sources used in the past empirical applications (Basist et al., 1998; Mendelsohn et al., 2007; Seo and Mendelsohn, 2008a; Seo, 2013a). These satellites rotate the Earth and measures climate variables at each location twice per day at 6 am and 6 pm.

Many other satellites are now operated by the NASA (National Aeronautics and Space Administration) and other agencies including Aqua, Terra, Landsat, GRACE (The Gravity Recovery And Climate Experiment), CloudSat, and ICEsat (NASA, 2007, 2015). These satellites are equipped with special sensors such as AIRS (Atmospheric Infrared Sounder) and MODIS (Moderate Resolution Imaging Spectroradiometer). Other frequently discussed satellites in the climate change literature include the satellites run by the University of Alabama at Huntsville and those run by the Remote Sensing Systems in California (UAH 2015; REMSS, 2015).

Analyses in this chapter rely on the high resolution climatology data constructed by the Climate Research Unit (CRU) which provides monthly climate normals for the period from 1961 to 1990 at a 10 arc-minute resolution based on more than 16,000 weather stations across the world (New et al., 2002; Seo, 2015b). A 10 arc-minute resolution is approximately 1/36th times finer than a 1 degree cell resolution. The CRU data were the primary climate source data in one of the recent Intergovernmental Panel on Climate Change (IPCC)'s assessment reports and have been continuously updated since then (IPCC, 2007).

From the high resolution climatology data set, monthly temperature normals and monthly precipitation normals are averaged to construct seasonal temperature normals and precipitation normals. In the Southern Hemisphere, summer temperature is constructed as the average of Dec., Jan., and Feb. temperature. In the Northern Hemisphere, it is defined as the average of Jun., Jul., and Aug. temperature. Winter temperature in the

Southern Hemisphere is defined to be the average of temperatures of the summer months in the Northern Hemisphere. Seasonal precipitations are defined using the same method.

In addition, the CRU data provide indicators of climate risk such as the Coefficient of Variation in Precipitation (CVP) which measures the variability of precipitation for the 30-year period at the high resolution grid cell level. Variability is a conventional measure of risk in economic studies (Zilberman, 1998; Fabozzi et al., 2009). In the climate literature, climate risk is expressed often in terms of variability of a climate variable. Again, the measure of variability in the climate literature is expressed as a climate normal. That is, it is a measure of variability in a climate variable for a long period of time, for example, 30 years. Put different, it is not a measure of variability in a climate variable for a short duration of time, for example, 2 or 3 years. For this reason, these risk measures can be called a climate risk normal (Seo, 2012c, 2014c).

A fluctuation in annual precipitation level has long been known to be a key factor in the yearly fluctuations of crop yields (Udry, 1995; Rosenzweig et al., 2001; Kazianga and Udry, 2006). Climate researchers revealed that the degree of precipitation variability across the years in certain regions has been changing in a multidecadal time frame due to greenhouse warming or simply due to weather events such as El Nino, La Nina, Atlantic Multi-decadal Oscillation, and Pacific Decadal Oscillation (Ropelewski and Halpert, 1987; Curtis et al., 2001; Hulme et al., 2001; Shanahan et al., 2009).

In the climate literature, a focus has been shifted over the past decade or so from changes in climate mean normals to changes in climate risk normals. Climate scientists have increasingly emphasized the changes in the variability of climate variables, that is, climate risk normals (Tebaldi et al., 2007; Hansen et al., 2012). In addition, climate scientists have gradually shifted the emphasis from gradual changes in global average temperature to extreme events and disasters that are associated with weather realizations and/or climatic shifts (Lenton et al., 2008; IPCC, 2012; NRC, 2013; Titley et al., 2016).

Another measure of climate risk provided by the CRU data set is Diurnal Temperature Range (DTR). Again, monthly DTRs are provided for the 30-year period from 1961 to 1990, which has been continuously updated. The DTR is the range between daily maximum temperature and daily minimum temperature. An increase in the DTR is understood to be one aspect of a higher climate risk. If daily maximum temperature increases, the DTR would increase, ceteris paribus. If daily minimum temperature decreases, the DTR would again increase, ceteris paribus. This range is a meaningful variable that influences agriculture and food productions (Easterling et al., 2000, 2007; Seo, 2012c, 2014b).

Future climate change scenarios are obtained from the following two gridded Atmospheric Oceanic General Circulation Model (AOGCM) predictions: the GISS (Goddard Institute for Space Studies) ModelE-R and the UKMO (United Kingdom Meteorology Office) HadCM3 (Hadley Coupled Model version 3) (Gordon et al., 2000; Schmidt et al., 2005). These models have been used for the Intergovernmental Panel on Climate Change (IPCC) assessment reports and are available to the public at the Data Distribution Center of the IPCC (IPCC, 2007).

For both models, this Chapter relies on an A2 emissions scenario in order to capture the impacts of a high emissions and a severe climate change scenario. The IPCC associates this high emissions and severe climate change scenario with rapid and regionally divergent economic growth patterns which are projected to be achieved through extensive uses of fossil fuels throughout the 21st century (Nakicenovic et al., 2000). The climate change projections for the middle of this century, specifically the period of 2040–69 for the UKMO model and the period of 2046–65 for the GISS model, are used.

Soils data of farmlands are obtained from the Food and Agriculture Organization (FAO)'s dominant soil map of the world CD-ROM which provides the distributions of the dominant soil types for the entire global land surface (FAO 2003). The data set reports percentages of 116 dominant soil types, which are further grouped into 26 great soil groups. Also, soil texture (sandy, clay, mixed soils) and soil terrain information (flat, medium, steep terrain) are provided by the FAO data set at the 0.5 degree latitude by 0.5 degree longitude grid cell resolution.

Elevation data are from the Global Multi-resolution Terrain Elevation Data 2010 (GMTED2010) dataset developed by the United States Geological Survey (USGS) and the National Geospatial-Intelligence Agency (NGA). The source data of the GMTED2010 for the present study is the NGA's SRTM (Shuttle Radar Topology Mission) data which are provided at 1 arc-second resolution and they are aggregated at 7.5 arc-second pixels (Danielson and Gesch, 2011). The GMTED2010 superseded the Global 30 Arc-Second Elevation (GTOPO30) data set also developed by the USGS as the high resolution elevation data set for global studies.

4.3 DESCRIPTIVE STATISTICS OF SAMPLE DATA

In Table 4.1, the number of farms in the sample data that chose each of the three agricultural systems is presented for each country where household surveys were collected. A farm is classified into one of the three systems based on the direct answers given by the farm to the two questions: whether the farm owns any livestock and whether it owns any cropland.

In South America, farmers grow a large variety of cereals, oil seeds, vegetables/tubercles, and specialty crops (Baethgen, 1997; Mata and Campos et al., 2001). Livestock in South America are an important source of income and livelihoods as Argentina and Brazil are the world's largest exporters of beef cattle and Argentina is the world's largest consumer of beef cattle per capita (Steiger, 2006; Nin et al., 2007). In Latin American countries, pastureland is four (eg, Brazil) to eight (eg, Argentina) times larger than the size of croplands (Baethgen, 1997; Seo, 2012b). About two thirds of farms in South America own some species of livestock and the fraction of a specialized livestock enterprise is especially high in the continent in comparison to Sub-Saharan countries (Seo, 2010a,b).

As shown in Table 4.1, across the entire sample, 48% of the farms are a mixed crops–livestock system, 37% are a crops–only system, and 16% are a livestock–only system. The adoption rates of the three systems are varied across the seven countries. A livestock–only farm is most frequently practiced in Argentina (25%), Uruguay (26%), and Venezuela (27%). These countries are where the largest grasslands in South America are located: the Llanos highland grasslands and the Pampas grasslands. A crops–only farm is most often practiced in Ecuador (60%), followed by Argentina and

Table 4.1 Adoptions of agricultural systems in South America

	Number of farms			Percentage of farms		
	Crops-only	Crops-livestock	Livestock-only	Crops-only	Crops-livestock	Livestock-only
Argentina	153	117	91	42%	32%	25%
Brazil	206	377	63	32%	58%	10%
Chile	120	209	37	33%	57%	10%
Colombia	115	111	61	40%	39%	21%
Ecuador	111	73	1	60%	39%	1%
Uruguay	20	56	28	19%	54%	27%
Venezuela	61	68	48	34%	38%	27%
Total	786	1011	329	37%	48%	15%

Table 4.2 Descriptive statistics of explanatory variables by agricultural portfolio

Variables	A specialized crop portfolio	A mixed crop-livestock portfolio	A specialized livestock portfolio
Summer temperature (°C)	21.7	22.0	22.9
Summer precipitation (mm)	125.9	123.1	135.1
Winter temperature (°C)	16.5	16.6	16.8
Winter precipitation (mm)	72.1	87.2	65.3
Summer CVP (%)	82.1	78.1	64.3
Winter CVP (%)	98.1	94.5	99.7
Dominantly Phaeozems (0/1)	0.09	0.06	0.06
Dominantly Lithosols (0/1)	0.14	0.13	0.08
Dominantly Fluvisols (0/1)	0.12	0.02	0.09
Dominantly Luvisols (0/1)	0.13	0.18	0.15
Dominantly Andosols (0/1)	0.08	0.11	0.05
Altitude (m above sea level)	791.3	600.5	395.9
Flat terrain (0/1)	0.06	0.09	0.12
Clay soils (0/1)	0.20	0.18	0.12
Number of household members (n)	4.6	4.9	4.6
Age of head (n)	51.0	52.7	53.7
Number of years in schooling (n)	9.1	8.0	10.4
Computer ownership (0/1)	0.27	0.21	0.24
Land is privately owned (0/1)	0.75	0.78	0.03
Farming is primary occupation (0/1)	0.85	0.82	0.67
Argentina (0/1)	0.22	0.17	0.36
Chile (0/1)	0.15	0.21	0.11
Venezuela (0/1)	0.08	0.07	0.15
Ecuador (0/1)	0.14	0.07	0.00
Colombia (0/1)	0.15	0.11	0.19

Colombia. A mixed crops-livestock farm is most frequently practiced in Brazil (58%), Chile (57%), and Uruguay (54%). In Uruguay, a specialized crop system is chosen least frequently.

For each of the agricultural portfolios, climate, soils, geography, markets, and household characteristics are summarized in Table 4.2. Summer temperature is 1.2°C higher in a livestock-only system than in a crops-only system. Summer precipitation is 10 mm/month higher in a livestock-only system than in a crops-only system. Winter precipitation is 22 mm/month higher in a crops-livestock system than in the other systems. Across the three systems, precipitation variability expressed as a CVP is much lower in South America than in Sub-Saharan Africa where summer CVP far exceeds 200% (Seo, 2014b). Summer CVP is much lower in a livestock-only farm while it is higher in a crops–livestock system. Winter CVP is slightly lower in a mixed crops–livestock system.

Distinct geographical footprints of the three agricultural portfolios are evident. A livestock-only farm tends to be located in a flat terrain more often than a mixed crops–livestock farm which tends to be located in a flat terrain more often than a crops-only farm. Average elevation of farms is also much lower in a livestock-only system (395 m above sea level) and a crops–livestock system (600 m) than a crops-only system (712 m).

The table shows the percentage of farms in each agricultural system that is located on each major soil type. Major soil types are Phaeozems, Fluvisols, Luvisols, Andosols, and Lithosols which are found to be most common in South American farms. In Phaeozems and Fluvisols, a crops-only system is more often adopted. Phaeozems are fertile dark soils for agriculture rich in organic matter while Fluvisols are formed by river actions which are often suitable for crops and vegetables. In Luvisols and Andosols, a mixed crops–livestock system is more often chosen. Luvisols are washed-out soils, for example, by flooding. Andosols are dark soils found in volcanic areas. Both of these soils are less fertile for crops. Lithosols are not favored for a livestock-only, which are shallow soils in steep slopes (Driessen et al., 2001). In clay soils, it is less likely that a livestock-only system is adopted; it is just painful for animals to move around on muddy soils.

Across the three agricultural portfolios, socioeconomic characteristics of the sample households are varied. In the mixed system, the number of household members is slightly larger than in the other systems. In the livestock-only system, age of the head is larger and the number of years in schooling is also larger. When the primary occupation of the household is agriculture, the farm is more likely to be a crops-only system. When the land is privately owned, the farm is not likely to be a livestock-only farm. About three quarters of the farms in either a crops-only system or a crops–livestock system own the lands they manage.

Other than the variables in Table 4.2 which are entered into the models in the subsequent sections of this Chapter, variables such as gender, electricity provision, distance to input and output markets, distance to coasts, and frequency of extension visits are found to be significant factors elsewhere and tested for sensitivity analyses (Seo, 2010b, 2011b, 2012c).

4.4 APPLICATIONS OF THE MICROBEHAVIORAL ECONOMETRIC METHODS

This section presents the results from the applications of the microbehavioral econometric methods to the South American data described above. In the first stage, a Multinomial Logit model is run in Table 4.3 to explain adoptions of agricultural systems by individual farmers. Against the base case of a livestock-only system, parameter estimates for the other two systems, relative to the base case, are presented: a crops–only and a mixed system. That is to say, the parameters of the livestock-only system are set as the baseline, setting all estimates of this system to zeros. This is because the adoption probabilities of the three portfolios must add up to one, hence only two sets of parameters can be identified. According to the Wald test statistic and its P-value (<0.0001), the choice model is highly significant.

All estimates of the climate variables are significant either at 5% level or at 10% level with an exception of summer temperature in the crops–livestock system. Winter climate normals, both temperature normals and precipitation normals, are highly significant for the mixed system, implying the importance of a nongrowing season, that is, of crops, for the mixed system because of the livestock in the mix of the portfolio. Summer CVP is significant and positive in the crops–only system. Summer CVP is high in the Andes Mountain range along Chile where a specialized crop system is frequently adopted (Seo, 2014b).

Some of the dominant soil types are shown to be significant explanatory variables. Soils Phaeozems and Fluvisols are significant at 5% level. If the dominant soil type of the farmland is Phaeozems, a farmer chooses more often a crops–only system, as soils Phaeozems are fertile organic soils for crops. A farmer chooses less often a crops–livestock system under the dominant Fluvisols soil type of the farmland. Fluvisols are formed by river actions and often preferred for grasses and tree products (Driessen et al., 2001). In higher altitudes, a farmer is less likely to adopt a livestock-only system. That is, animal enterprises are more common in a flat terrain, which is also the case in Sub-Saharan Africa (Seo, 2011b).

The Logit model shows that household social and economic characteristics play a significant role in which agricultural and natural resource portfolio is adopted by rural households. The older the head of the household, the more likely s/he is to choose a livestock-only system. The more educated a farmer is, the more probable s/he is to adopt a specialized livestock system. These estimates of household characteristics indicate that animal

Table 4.3 A multinomial logit choice model of farm portfolios

	A crops-only system		A crops-livestock system	
	Estimates	P value of Chi-Square	Estimates	P value of Chi-Square
Intercept	−5.61	0.001	−1.62	0.32
Summer temperature	0.47	0.004	0.033	0.83
Sum temp × 2	−0.015	0.000	−0.0026	0.52
Summer precipitation	−0.010	0.03	−0.009	0.05
Sum prec × 2	0.000025	0.04	0.000018	0.14
Winter temperature	0.22	0.01	0.35	<0.0001
Win temp × 2	−0.0019	0.33	−0.0064	0.002
Winter precipitation	0.011	0.08	0.012	0.06
Win prec × 2	−0.0000002	0.99	−0.000005	0.81
Summer CVP	0.015	0.003	0.005	0.28
Winter CVP	0.006	0.17	0.006	0.12
Dominantly Phaeozems	0.81	0.02	0.46	0.17
Dominantly Lithosols	0.23	0.55	0.31	0.41
Dominantly Fluvisols	0.26	0.42	−1.65	<0.0001
Dominantly Luvisols	−0.39	0.15	0.00028	0.99
Dominantly Andosols	−0.55	0.31	0.18	0.72
Elevation (meters)	0.0012	<.0001	0.0009	<0.0001
Flat (0/1)	−0.036	0.90	0.11	0.68
Clay (0/1)	−0.084	0.80	−0.33	0.32
Number of household members	−0.010	0.78	0.046	0.19
Age of head	−0.028	<.0001	−0.02	0.001
Years of schooling	−0.065	0.000	−0.097	<0.0001
Computer (0/1)	0.64	0.002	0.46	0.02
Farming is primary occupation	0.98	<.0001	0.69	<0.0001
Argentina and Uruguay (0/1)	0.19	0.68	−0.03	0.94
Chile (0/1)	−2.33	0.001	−0.43	0.48
Venezuela (0/1)	−1.04	0.004	−1.59	<0.0001
Ecuador (0/1)	14.63	0.96	13.73	0.96
Colombia (0/1)	−1.64	<.0001	−1.58	<0.0001

Summary statistics

N	2134
Wald statistic	915.3 (P < 0.0001)

systems are quite often commercially managed for profits in South America, that is, instead of household consumptions. These household specific patterns are not found in Sub-Saharan Africa where small holders in arid and semi-arid zones heavily rely on ruminant animals such as goats and sheep (Seo, 2011b, 2012c).

If a farm owns a computer(s), it is most likely to choose a specialized crop system. If a household's primary occupation is reported to be farming, the household is most likely to choose a specialized crops system and least likely to choose a specialized livestock system. The "primary occupation" variable captures nonagricultural activities as well as agricultural marketing activities especially with regard to a variety of specialty crops that are performed in rural households (Lanjouw and Lanjouw, 2001).

The five country dummy variables are intended to capture country-specific policy factors as well as differences in culture and language. Brazil is set as the base case and Argentina and Uruguay are grouped as one. Other than Brazil where Portuguese is spoken officially, Spanish is spoken in the other countries. Against the baseline case of Brazil, Venezuelan and Colombian farms are more likely to own a livestock-only portfolio because in part of the highland grasslands, that is, the Llanos located in the two countries. A Chilean farm less frequently chooses a crops-only system than a Brazilian farm.

Based on the estimated model in Table 4.3, the impact of a climatic change on adoption probabilities of the three agricultural portfolios is calculated in Table 4.4 by altering the value of one of the climatic variables marginally. In the baseline climate condition, 36% of the farms is estimated to adopt a crops-only system, 49% of the farms a crops-livestock system, and 15% of the farms a livestock-only system. By increasing seasonal temperatures, that is, both summer temperature and winter temperature, by 1°C, changes in adoption probabilities of the three agricultural systems from the

Table 4.4 Changes in adoption probabilities of agricultural portfolios due to marginal climate changes

	Baseline climate adoption probabilities	Changes due to +1°C temperature increase	Changes due to +1% increase in precipitation
A crops-only system	35.8%	−1.5%	0.06%
A crops-livestock system	48.9%	1.6%	−0.01%
A livestock-only system	15.2%	−0.02%	−0.04%

baseline probabilities are calculated for each rural household and averaged across the entire sample households. An increase in seasonal temperatures, that is, both summer temperature and winter temperature, by 1°C is estimated to cause an 1.6% increase in the adoption probability of a mixed crops-livestock system. On the other hand, the same change in seasonal temperatures is estimated to cause the adoption probability of a crops-only enterprise to fall by 1.5%. Adoption probability of a livestock-only system is also estimated to fall, but only slightly.

At this point, it is worthwhile to put these results from the microbehavioral econometric model into context. In particular, a microbehavioral researcher has an opportunity here to directly compare the results from the microbehavioral models with those from physically-based models. That an individual's adoption probability of a crops-only portfolio is to fall if temperature were to increase was first reported in the microbehavioral studies of African agriculture (Seo, 2010a, 2011b, 2014a). This finding has been reconfirmed in the microbehavioral studies of South American agriculture (Seo, 2010b, 2013a, 2015b).

These findings from the microbehavioral models are in line with the agroeconomic studies that reported significant losses of yields of major grains due to temperature increase (Adams et al., 1990; Rosenzweig and Parry, 1994; Rosenzweig and Hillel, 1998; Reilly et al., 1996; Parry et al., 2004). Agronomic crop simulation models applied to the South American crop regions and major grains such as maize, wheat, rice, and other crops reported similar losses (Baethgen, 1997; Magrin et al., 1997, 2007). These reductions in the yields of major grains would occur despite fertilization effects of increased Carbon Dioxide which have been confirmed by agronomic studies and field experiments on crops such as the FACE (Free Air CO_2 Enrichment) experiments (Tubiello and Ewert, 2002; Ainsworth and Long, 2005; Tubiello et al., 2007; Seo, 2015a).

The finding that adoption of the mixed crops-livestock system increases in a hotter climate was first reported in an African study (Seo and Mendelsohn, 2008b; Seo, 2010a). The authors reported an increase in adoptions of small ruminants such as goats and sheep in hotter and arid zones of Africa. Analogously to the agronomic crop simulation models, animal productivity studies in relation to weather and climate factors have been developed historically by a separate group of academic communities (Johnson, 1965; Hahn, 1999). The animal science literature seems to imply that major livestock such as beef cattle, dairy cattle, sheep, pigs, and goats are more heat tolerant than major staple grains (Hahn, 1981; Hahn et al., 2009). This literature also indicates that there are many management options current-ly applied by livestock managers to deal with weather related constraints such as barns, water-spray, shades, air-conditioning, among other things (Hahn, 1981; Mader and Davis, 2004).

The finding that a mixed portfolio of crops and livestock is preferred to a crops-only portfolio in a hotter climate can be understood as a di-versification strategy of a portfolio in order to reduce the risk in portfolio return (Seo, 2014a). A hotter climate is associated with a higher climate risk such as precipitation variability and temperature variability (Seo, 2012c). A higher climate risk, that is, variability, leads to a higher risk in portfolio return. The portfolio risk can be reduced by holding negatively correlated assets in the occurrence of a shock, economic or natural (Markowitz, 1952; Modigliani and Pogue, 1974). A farmer who is risk averse will choose a portfolio with a lower risk among the portfolios with the same expected returns (Arrow, 1971; Zilberman, 1998).

From the microbehavioral perspectives, these results highlight the key strength of microbehavioral models. That is, both agronomic studies and animal productivity studies have inherent shortcomings that behavioral re-sponses cannot be adequately accounted for. An agronomic study of corn is incapable of capturing a farmer's switch from corn to, say, millet or sor-ghum. An animal productivity study of cattle is incapable of a livestock manager's decision to switch to, say, sheep. Further, behavioral responses such as diversification, hedging, and forward-looking cannot be explained through these physically-based scientific methods.

In Table 4.4, changes in adoption probabilities of the three portfolios due to a marginal increase in seasonal precipitation normals are presented. An increase of precipitation normals, both summer precipitation and winter precipitation, by 1% is estimated to lead to an increase in the adoption prob-ability of a crops-only portfolio by 0.05%. This can be ascribed, in part, to beneficial effects of increased precipitation on a variety of crops especially during the growing seasons, which has been well documented in agro-nomic literature (Reilly et al., 1996; Gitay et al., 2001; Magrin et al., 2007; Hillel and Rosenzweig, 2010).

On the other hand, precipitation increase leads to a decrease in adop-tions of livestock systems, both a crops-livestock portfolio and a livestock-only portfolio. The decrease is large in the livestock-only portfolio, −0.04%. The evidence that farmers avoid livestock enterprises in a humid climate zone has been strong in Sub-Saharan studies of climate change and agriculture (Seo and Mendelsohn, 2008b; Seo, 2010a, 2011b, 2014a). A primary reason for farmers' unwillingness to raise animals in humid conditions is thought to be associated with a higher rate of occurrence and prevalence of a variety of livestock diseases under a high rainfall climate regime (USAHA 2008; Fox et al., 2012). In Africa, Nagana (*Trypanosomiasis*) disease, commonly called sleeping sickness, spread by Tsetse flies kills millions of cattle in lowland humid zones of Sub-Saharan Africa in bad years (Ford and Katondo, 1977). Genome scientists recently completed the complete recording of the entire genome of the Tsetse flies, which is believed to be a significant progress in developing a cure/prevention for the Nagana disease (Aksoy et al., 2014).

There are more than a few animals that are often raised by rural households across the world. Animals that are favored by rural households are varied across arid zones. In Africa, farmers favored goats and chickens in lowland humid zones over sheep and cattle which are favored in arid agroecological zones (Seo and Mendelsohn, 2008b). In South America, sheep are found to be adopted more frequently in arid zones (Seo et al., 2010). In Australia, the number of cattle and sheep managed by Australian farmers vastly increase in hot and arid zones of the country, especially so for sheep (Seo, 2015d). In India, a monsoon climate which is characterized by extremely heavy rainfall in the monsoon season and extremely low rainfall in the nonmonsoon season makes rural Indian households depend heavily on goats (Seo, 2016). Indian farmers get quick cash by selling goats, for which reason goats are often called an ATM machine for Indian farmers.

Having chosen a farm portfolio, a farmer will make an array of decisions with regards to inputs, outputs, and various farming practices in order to maximize the profit from the land in a long-term horizon. An estimation of the profit (land value) function of a specific system must address the problem of selection bias (Heckman, 1979). Using the Dubin-McFadden selection bias correction method developed for a multinomial choice situation, a system-wise land value function is estimated in Table 4.5 for each system of agriculture (Dubin and McFadden, 1984). To identify the choice and land value model, all the explanatory variables used in the multinomial choice model in Table 4.3 are entered in the set of land value regressions in Table 4.5 except for the two identification variables: elevation and a dummy for a flat terrain (Fisher 1966; Johnston and DiNardo, 1997). All three land value regressions are highly significant according to the F-statistics for the model significances. Adjusted R-squares are presented in the table.

One of the most salient features of Table 4.5 is that the estimated Dubin-McFadden selection bias correction terms are all large which are also significant in all three land value regressions. The capacity for selection bias

Table 4.5 System-wise land value regressions with selection bias corrections

	A crops-only system		A crops-livestock system		A livestock-only system	
	HC[a]		HC		HC	
	Estimate	P-value	Estimate	P-value	Estimate	P-value
Intercept	7397.4	0.01	42.06	0.97	11080	0.005
Summer temperature	260.4	0.27	283.64	0.20	−668.2	0.04
Sum temp × 2	−6.05	0.34	−2.4	0.70	29.2	0.001
Summer precipitation	−0.84	0.8	10.3	0.01	17.3	0.03
Sum prec × 2	−0.0081	0.39	−0.021	0.08	−0.051	0.016
Winter temperature	9.09	0.94	−135.24	0.13	−363.1	0.002
Win temp × 2	−3.19	0.26	−3.52	0.18	−4.2	0.19
Winter precipitation	−5.31	0.41	−4.49	0.22	−27.8	0.001
Win prec × 2	0.0087	0.60	−0.0013	0.90	0.012	0.40
Summer CVP	−10.59	0.15	2.04	0.75	−63.35	<.0001
Winter CVP	−4.60	0.28	−6.85	0.0002	−31.87	<.0001
Dominantly Phaeozems	682.03	0.11	−713.9	0.02	−847.4	0.012
Dominantly Lithosols	1136.3	0.008	−184.4	0.54	1361.2	0.004
Dominantly Fluvisols	−2152.3	0.005	−331.8	0.76	−1803.4	0.03
Dominantly Luvisols	129.1	0.69	−339.9	0.21	827.9	0.05
Dominantly Andosols	569.2	0.35	437.6	0.34	91.4	0.84
Clay soils	−1343.9	<.0001	−326.7	0.24	−1178.0	0.005
Age of head	−14.8	0.10	12.4	0.10	43.4	<.0001
Years of schooling	−61.5	0.05	22.6	0.32	54.7	0.15
Computer ownership	−355.7	0.15	59.6	0.78	−1264.6	<.0001
Number of household members	159.9	0.006	23.9	0.43	−12.6	0.79
Farming is primary occupation	−470.6	0.22	−440.7	0.08	−1893.4	<.0001
Argentina and Uruguay	−1441.1	0.004	−2777.8	<.0001	−3387.9	<.0001
Chile	−310.4	0.77	−2323.2	0.02	4215.6	0.0006
Venezuela	−2135.7	0.002	523.9	0.23	1859.2	0.01

Table 4.5 System-wise land value regressions with selection bias corrections (*cont.*)

	A crops-only system		A crops-livestock system		A livestock-only system	
	Estimate	HC[a] P-value	Estimate	HC P-value	Estimate	HC P-value
Ecuador	−1225.2	0.012	−910.9	0.18		
Colombia	231.0	0.66	2160.2	<.0001	3275.9	<.0001
DM[b] crops-only			−1706.8	0.15	−6262.4	0.0002
DM[b] mixed	3349.1	0.02			4170.3	0.01
DM[b] livestock-only	−1987.1	0.07	1731.9	0.03		
Summary statistics						
N	685		934		291	
Adj Rsq	0.10		0.24		0.51	

[a]HC means Heteroscedasticity-Consistent.
[b]DM means Dubin-McFadden selection bias correction.

corrections is unique in the microbehavioral models. That is, physically-based models and nonmicrobehavioral econometric models are not capable of accounting for selection biases.

The land value of a crops-only system is estimated to be lower in a farm where a livestock-only system is adopted but to be higher in a farm where a mixed system is adopted. Put differently, a factor that increases the choice of a livestock-only system decreases the land value of a crops-only system while a factor that increases the choice of a mixed system increases the land value of a crops-only system. The land value of a mixed system is estimated to be higher in a farm where a livestock-only system is adopted but to be lower in a farm where a crops-only system is adopted. The land value of a livestock-only farm is estimated to be lower in a farm where a crops-only system is adopted but to be higher in a farm that adopted a crops-livestock system.

The estimates of the signs and magnitudes of selection biases are one of the finest empirical results that microbehavioral econometric models can bring out (Seo, 2014a). The large magnitudes of these estimates shown in the table mean that statistical or experimental models that attempt to quantify the impact of a climatic change on crop yields and net revenues must heed to selection behaviors of individual managers, without which final estimates will be more often than not severely biased (Jones and

Kiniry, 1986; Williams et al., 1989; Auffhammer et al., 2006; Deschenes and Greenstone, 2007; Schlenker and Roberts, 2009; Welch et al., 2010; Lobell et al., 2011).

Another aspect of the estimated selection bias correction terms in Table 4.5 is that the estimated correlation parameters in each of the land value regressions have opposite signs across selections of different portfolios. These patterns give another justification for the use of the Dubin-McFadden method over the Lee's method which assumes all correlation parameters to have the same sign. In fact, the Lee's method proposes only one selection bias correction term. Due to this rigid assumption with regard to the patterns of correlation parameters, as explained in Chapter 3, the Dubin-McFadden method out-performs the Lee's method or the semi-parametric method in selection bias correction models (Schmertmann, 1994; Dahl, 2002; Bourguignon et al., 2004).

Many of the estimates of seasonal climate mean normals are significant at 5% level, especially in the mixed portfolio and the livestock-only portfolio. Indicators of climate risk normals, that is, seasonal CVPs, are significant. In the land value regression of the mixed portfolio, summer precipitation and winter CVP are significant. The higher the winter rainfall variability (CVP), the lower the land value of the mixed portfolio. In the land value regression of the livestock-only portfolio, both summer and winter climate variables are significant, so are seasonal rainfall variability variables (seasonal CVPs). The higher the summer CVP, the lower the land value of the livestock-only portfolio. The higher the winter CVP, the lower the land value of the livestock-only portfolio. It is notable that the land value of the mixed portfolio is relatively more resilient to variations in seasonal CVPs (rainfall variability) than that of the specialized livestock portfolio. These sensitivity estimates are by and large consistent with those found in Sub-Saharan Africa where even stronger responses are recorded (Seo, 2012c).

Soils, geologic, and geographic variables all play an important role in the determination of land values of agricultural systems. If the dominant soils of the farmland is Phaeozems, the land value of the mixed crops-livestock portfolio is lower. The land value of the livestock-only portfolio is also lower in the dominant soils of Phaeozems. However, in the crops-only portfolio, the land value is not lower in the Phaeozems soils. Soils Phaeozems are fertile organic black soils suitable for growing crops. As such, farmers more frequently opt for a crops-only portfolio than the other portfolios, as we can see in Table 4.3.

In the dominant soils of Fluvisols, the land value of the crops-only portfolio is lower, so is that of the livestock-only portfolio. In the dominant Lithosols which are shallow soils, the land value of a crops-only is higher, so is the land value of a livestock-only. Under the dominant Luvisols which are washed-out soils found commonly in the regions with distinct alternating heavily wet and severely dry seasons, the land value of the livestock-only portfolio is higher. As such, farmers are less likely to choose a crops-only or a mixed portfolio, given dominant Luvisols. Given clay soils, the land values of the specialized portfolios are lower, both the crops-only portfolio and the livestock-only portfolio.

For the crops-only portfolio, land value is lower when the farmer is older. For the livestock-only portfolio, on the other hand, land value is higher when the farmer is older. As such, older farmers are more likely to choose a livestock-only portfolio than the other portfolios. For the crops-only portfolio, land value is lower if the farmer is more educated. For the livestock-only portfolio, land value is higher if the farmer has more years of schooling, that is, more educated. This means that an educated farmer is more likely to choose a livestock-only portfolio than a crops-only portfolio. The signs of these parameter estimates unravel intriguing contrasts to those behaviors of farmers found in Sub-Sahara in which more experience and education tend to motivate farmers to favor crops (Schultz, 2004; Seo, 2011b, 2014a).

The land value of a livestock-only portfolio is lower in the rural household that owns a computer(s) than in the rural household that does not own a computer. For a crops-only portfolio, land value is higher when there are more members in the family. For a livestock-only portfolio, land value is lower if there are more members in the family. In the farms where a primary occupation is farming, land value is lower in the livestock-only portfolio and the mixed portfolio. This means farmers will more likely choose a crops-only portfolio, which was indeed the case in Table 4.3.

Against the baseline case of Brazil, land value for a crops-only portfolio is lower in Argentina, Venezuela and Ecuador. However, the land value of a livestock-only portfolio is higher in Chile, Venezuela, and Colombia while it is lower in Argentina, against the base case of Brazil. The land value of a mixed crops-livestock portfolio is lower in Argentina and Chile, but is higher in Colombia, relative to the base case of Brazil.

Given the estimated conditional land value models and the parameter estimates in Table 4.5, the impact of a marginal shift in a climate variable on the land value of each of the agricultural portfolios can be calculated by altering the corresponding climate variable by a marginal amount

Table 4.6 Changes in system-wise land values due to marginal climatic changes

	Baseline land value ($/ha)	Changes due to +1°C temperature increase	Changes due to +1% precipitation increase
A crops-only system	2418	−204	−6
A crops-livestock mixed system	1641	−105	+1
A livestock-only system	1058	+42	−8

(Table 4.6). The baseline land value, given the current climate condition, is estimated to be 2418 $/ha for the crops-only portfolio, 1640 $/ha for the mixed portfolio, and 1058 $/ha for the livestock-only portfolio. If seasonal temperature normals, both summer and winter normals, are altered by +1°C, land value decreases by 204 $/ha in a crops-only portfolio, decreases by 104 $/ha in a mixed portfolio, but increases by 42 $/ha in a livestock-only portfolio. What these estimates tell us is that, although all three portfolios would suffer from marginal temperature increases, livestock systems cope better with marginal temperature changes.

If seasonal precipitation normals, both summer and winter normals, are altered by +1%, land value decreases in a crops-only portfolio by −5 $/ha of farmland and decreases by −8 $/ha in a livestock-only portfolio. In contrast, the land value of a mixed portfolio increases by +1 $/ha. This means that the livestock-only portfolio is the most vulnerable to a precipitation increase among the three portfolios.

4.5 FUTURE CLIMATE SIMULATIONS

The results described in the previous section show that both choices of agricultural portfolios and land values conditional on the choices of portfolios are sensitive to climatic changes that have materialized historically. Therefore, future climatic changes and global warming will lead to changes in individuals' behavioral decisions and the economic outcomes of such decisions. Microbehavioral econometric models such as the G-MAP model (Geographically-scaled Microeconometric model of Adapting Portfolios in response to climatic changes) have the built-in capacity for predicting the changes in these microbehavioral variables if climate and other variables are altered in the future owing to, for example, anthropogenic global warming.

The realizations of changes in individuals' behaviors will depend on how the future climate will turn out to be. Climate scientists make predictions of future climates based on a complex computer simulation model called an AOGCM (Atmospheric Oceanic General Circulation Model) (IPCC, 2014; Le Treut et al., 2007). Because of a very large computing capacity and a highly complex programming called for a climate projection in the far future, there are only a limited number of institutions in the world that can build an AOGCM model to make such a projection. The selected AOGCM models used in the recent CMIP5 (Climate Model Intercomparison Project 5) project are summarized in Table 4.7 (Taylor et al., 2012).

Table 4.7 Selected CMIP5 (climate model intercomparison project 5) climate models

Modeling center	Institute ID	Model name
Canadian Center for Climate Modeling and Analysis	CCCMA	CanESM2 CanCM4 CanAM4
National Center for Atmospheric Research	NCAR	CCSM4
Centro Euro-Mediterraneo per I Cambiamenti Climatici	CMCC	CMCC-CESM CMCC-CM CMCC-CMS
Centre National de Recherches Météorologiques/Centre Européen de Recherche et Formation Avancée en Calcul Scientifique	CNRM-CERFACS	CNRM-CM5 CNRM-CM5-2
Commonwealth Scientific and Industrial Research Organization	CSIRO-QCCCE	CSIRO-Mk3.6.0
NOAA Geophysical Fluid Dynamics Laboratory	NOAA GFDL	GFDL-CM3 GFDL-ESM2G GFDL-HIRAM-C180
NASA Goddard Institute for Space Studies	NASA GISS	GISS-E2-H GISS-E2-R
Met Office Hadley Centre	MOHC	HadCM3 HadGEM2-CC HadGEM2-ES HadGEM2-A
Atmosphere and Ocean Research Institute (The University of Tokyo), National Institute for Environmental Studies, and Japan Agency for Marine-Earth Science and Technology	MIROC	MIROC4h MIROC5
Meteorological Research Institute	MRI	MRI-AGCM3.2H MRI-CGCM3 MRI-ESM1

To project the climates in a far future, scientists need to assume what the future would look like besides climate, in the aspects of, most notably, economic growth, national economic structures, population changes, and technological changes. It is of course a near impossible task to predict with precision the future world in 100 years or more. Climate scientists from the Intergovernmental Panel on Climate Change (IPCC), the international body of scientists who is assembled by the United Nations to report on climate change, have taken a scenario (storyline) approach in hypothesizing possible future paths of the world (Nakicenovic et al., 2000). The IPCC scientists make a number of scenarios (storylines) of the future world without much concern on which scenario (storyline) is more likely or less likely to come to pass. These scenarios are called "emissions scenarios."

As described in the Special Report on Emissions Scenarios (SRES) by the IPCC, the four storyline (scenario) families proposed by the IPCC are as follows (Nakicenovic et al., 2000):

1. A1 storyline and scenario family:

   It describes a future world of very rapid economic growth, global population that peaks in mid-century and declines thereafter, and the rapid introduction of new and more efficient technologies. Major underlying themes are convergence among regions, capacity building, and increased cultural and social interactions, with a substantial reduction in regional differences in per capita income.

2. A2 storyline and scenario family:

   It describes a very heterogeneous world. The underlying theme is self-reliance and preservation of local identities. Fertility patterns across regions converge very slowly, which results in continuously increasing global population. Economic development is primarily regionally oriented and per capita economic growth and technological changes are more fragmented and slower than in other storylines.

3. B1 storyline and scenario family:

   It describes a convergent world with the same global population that peaks in mid-century and declines thereafter, as in the A1 storyline, but with rapid changes in economic structures toward a service and information economy, with reductions in material intensity, and the introduction of clean and resource-efficient technologies. The emphasis is on global solutions to economic, social, and environmental sustainability, including improved equity, but without additional climate initiatives.

4. B2 storyline and scenario family:

   It describes a world in which the emphasis is on local solutions to economic, social, and environmental sustainability. It is a world with continuously increasing global population at a rate lower than A2, intermediate levels of economic development, and less rapid and more diverse technological change than in the B1 and A1 storylines. While the scenario is also oriented toward environmental protection and social equity, it focuses on local and regional levels.

Each scenario family is further divided into finer scenarios. For example, in the A1 scenario family, there are three refined scenarios depending on the alternative directions of technological developments in the energy system: A1F1, A1T, and A1B. The A1F1 scenario assumes a rapid economic growth with intensive uses of fossil fuels; The A1T scenario assumes a rapid economic growth with reliance on nonfossil energy sources; The A1B assumes a rapid economic growth with a balance across all sources of energy production.

Recently, the IPCC scientists moved away from the SRES scenario approach to an RCP scenario approach (IPCC, 2014). The RCP stands for Representative Concentration Pathways. The RCP approach rids scientists of the burdens of the descriptions of the future worlds through economic growth, regional changes, technological changes, population changes, and social behaviors that characterized the SRES scenarios. Instead, the RCP approach relies on possible CO_2 concentration scenarios: a low concentration scenario, a middle concentration scenario, and a high concentration scenario.

From the array of the AOGCM models and storylines that are available, this Chapter relies on two most widely used climate models: the UKMO (United Kingdom Met Office) HadCM3 (Hadley Coupled Model version 3) model and the GISS (Goddard Institute of Space Studies) E-R (ModelE-R) model (Gordon et al., 2000; Schmidt et al., 2005). For both models, the A2 storyline is applied for the ensuing analysis in this Chapter in order to reflect a high emissions growth scenario due to a rapid economic growth relying heavily on exhaustion of fossil fuels (Nakicenovic et al., 2000).

The time frame that the present author is concerned about is the middle of this century, about 50 years from now. Therefore, the present author relies on the projections from these models for the middle of this century, specifically the period of 2040–69 for the UKMO model and the period of 2046–65 for the GISS model.

The selected climate models' projections of future climates are shown in Table 4.8. Note that these climate projections are made by the climate scientists from the corresponding institutions at a grid-cell level across almost the entire globe. The grid-cell size varies from one AOGCM model to

Table 4.8 AOGCM Models' climate projections by the middle of this century

	Summer season		Winter season	
	Summer temperature normals (°C)	Summer precipitation normals (mm/mo)	Winter temperature normals (°C)	Winter precipitation normals (mm/mo)
Baseline climate normals	17.4	125.9	12.3	77.4
ΔUKMO HadCM3 A2 Scenario	+2.5	−5.9	+2.3	−4.8
ΔGISS ER A2 scenario	+2.0	+6.2	+1.5	+0.2

another. The summary results shown in Table 4.8 are a summary of projections of climatic changes at spatial locations where farm households who were interviewed were located.

By the middle of this century, the UKMO model predicts about 2.4°C increase in seasonal temperature normals and about 5 mm decrease in seasonal monthly precipitation normals. The predicted change in summer temperature is slightly larger than that in winter temperature. Summer precipitation is predicted to decrease by 6 mm/month and winter precipitation is predicted to decrease by 5 mm/month. The UKMO scenario is, in short, a hotter and drier climate scenario by the middle of this century.

The GISS model predicts a smaller degree of temperature increase and an increase in summer precipitation by 6 mm per month. Summer temperature is predicted to increase by about 2°C and winter temperature by 1.5°C. Summer precipitation is predicted to increase by 6 mm/month while winter precipitation is predicted to increase by 0.2 mm per month. Again, the predicted changes in summer season climate variables are larger than the predicted changes in winter season climate variables. The GISS scenario is a mildly hotter and wetter climate scenario by the middle of this century.

It is notable from Table 4.8 that predictions of climate change are varied across the range of AOGCM models that are widely reported. Especially, predictions of seasonal rainfall changes often have opposite signs among the models in which the range of predictions exceeds 200% of the current rainfall in some cases (Seo et al., 2005). This is the uncertainty with regards to climate change which has been unresolved since the first report

Table 4.9 Changes in adoption probabilities of agricultural portfolios under climatic changes by mid-century

	A crops-only system	A crops-livestock system	A livestock-only system
Baseline probabilities	35.9%	48.9%	15.2%
Changes due to GISS ER A2 Scenario	−3.3%	+2.1%	+1.3%
95% confidence intervals of expected changes	(−3.5%, −3.1%)	(+1.9%, +2.2%)	(+1.1%, +1.4%)

by the IPCC in early 1990s (IPCC, 1990). This uncertainty is even further magnified across the variety of scenarios or storylines (A1, A2, B1, B2, and so on) of the AOGCMs. Moreover, the uncertainty with regards to future climate changes becomes even larger, the further the time period we are interested in predicting the climate.

If the predicted changes in seasonal climate normals by the above AOGCMs were to be realized over time, changes in behaviors and profits from various agricultural and natural resource enterprises are expected to occur, as the microbehavioral model outcomes shown in the previous section demonstrate. These changes in choice decisions and resultant profits can be calculated, as explained in the theory section, by the changes in the dependent variables in the choice model and the conditional land value models in response to the changes in climate variables which are entered as explanatory variables in these microbehavioral models.

Changes in adoption probabilities of the three agricultural and natural resource portfolios are presented in Table 4.9. If the future climate comes to pass by the middle of this century according to the GISS ER model's A2 scenario, there is a substantial decrease in a crops-only portfolio, a decrease of 3.3% points from the baseline. The 95% confidence interval of the expected change is (−3.5% points, −3.1% points).

The decrease in adoption of a crops-only portfolio is offset by the increases in adoptions of both a crops–livestock portfolio and a livestock-only portfolio. The choice probability of a mixed crops–livestock portfolio is predicted to increase by 2.1% points and that of a livestock–only portfolio to increase by 1.3%. The increases in the choices of livestock systems, both specialized and diversified portfolios, indicate a higher resilience of these systems in the changing climates.

Assuming that the same climate change scenario would unfold over time, changes in the land value for each of the three portfolios are calculated

Table 4.10 Changes in conditional land values of agricultural portfolios under climatic changes by mid-century

	A crops-only system	A crops-livestock system	A livestock-only system
Baseline land value ($/ha)	2418.6	1640.9	1058.4
Absolute changes due to GISS ER scenario	−230.4	−57.7	+629.2
Percentage changes due to GISS ER scenario	−9.5%	−3.5%	+59.5%
95% Confidence intervals of expected changes due to GISS ER scenario	(−247.3, −213.4)	(−73.1, −42.3)	(+559.6, +698.8)

in Table 4.10. Land value of a crops-only portfolio is predicted to fall by 230 $/ha, a decrease of 9.5% from the baseline land value. Land value of a mixed crops-livestock portfolio is predicted to decline as well but by a much smaller amount. It would fall by 58 $/ha, a decrease of 3.5% from the baseline land value. Land value of a livestock-only portfolio is predicted to go in an opposite direction. It is predicted to increase by 629 $/ha, an increase of 59.5% from the baseline land value.

The predicted changes in the land values of the three enterprises underlie the changes in adoption probabilities shown in Table 4.9. As the mixed portfolio and the livestock-only portfolio perform more profitably under a changed climate relative to the specialized crop portfolio, more rural managers choose the former portfolios and fewer managers choose the specialized crops portfolio under the hypothesized climate regime, that is, that projected by the GISS, by the middle of this century.

The expected land value of a rural household is calculated as the sum of adoption probability of each portfolio multiplied by conditional land value of that portfolio across the three agricultural and natural resource portfolios. The baseline expected land value at the baseline climate is estimated to be 1857 $/ha of land. Under the GISS E-R model, the expected land value is predicted to fall by 13 $/ha, a decrease of only 0.7% by the middle of this century.

The change in the expected land value shown in Table 4.11 occurs due to both changes in adoption probabilities of agricultural portfolios and changes in conditional land values caused by climatic changes according to the GISS model. What is most salient is the small magnitude in the change

Table 4.11 Changes in the expected land value under climatic changes by mid-century

	GISS E-R climate regime		UKMO HadCM3 climate regime	
	Absolute changes ($/ha)	Percentage changes (%)	Absolute changes ($/ha)	Percentage changes (%)
Baseline expected land value	1857.2		1857.2	
Changes due to GISS ER A2 Scenario	−13.3	−0.7%	−62.4	−3.4%
95% Confidence interval ($/ha)	(−25.9, −0.8)		(−80.7, −44.0)	

in the expected land value in comparison with the changes in the land values predicted for each of the agricultural systems in Table 4.10. That is, although a crops-only portfolio is predicted to fall almost by 10% in the land value, the change in the expected land value is negligible.

This is because rural managers can switch to more profitable portfolios under the changed condition such as the mixed portfolio and the livestock-only portfolio. Rural managers are not too dumb to stick headlong to the traditional portfolio even though the climate has been shifted away. This is superbly captured in the microbehavioral econometric models (Seo, 2014a, 2015a).

From another angle, these results from the microbehavioral models unravel a serious shortcoming of the climate change impact studies that focus on selected major grains or crops (Rosenzweig and Parry, 1994; Auffhammer et al., 2006; Schlenker and Roberts, 2009; Welch et al., 2010; Lobell et al., 2011). These studies predicted a large devastating loss on agriculture, with some damage estimates being as large as an 85% loss in crop yields in a high-end climate change scenario. These predictions, however, overlook the possibility of noncropping systems such as a mixed crops-livestock system and a livestock-only system that can increase under a changed climate condition, as shown in this chapter. In other words, microbehavioral econometric models can capture and explicitly quantify these behavioral changes of all kinds that could happen owing to shifts in external conditions such as climate.

Under the UKMO HadCM3 model's A2 scenario, the expected land value is predicted to decrease more substantially by 62 $/ha, which is 3.4%

decrease from the baseline current expected land value. The larger decrease in the expected land value under this scenario is predicted to occur because seasonal temperature increases are higher with a 2.4°C increase and seasonal precipitations do not increase but decrease by about 5 mm per month by the middle of this century (Table 4.8).

4.6 DESCRIPTION OF POLICY IMPLICATIONS

This chapter begins applications of the microbehavioral econometric methods to the environmental and natural resource problems that global communities are concerned about. This chapter provided one example of a complete analysis of a microbehavioral econometric model applied to address the questions of global warming and climatic changes that face low-latitude developing countries. Agricultural and natural resource portfolios that are held by individual managers across the full range of climate and ecological zones in South America are modeled based on the rural household surveys collected from seven countries in the continent. Many capabilities of the applied model for addressing critical questions with regards to global warming are highlighted throughout this chapter.

In the next three chapters, the present author will continue to provide applied works of the microbehavioral econometric methods in the areas of global climatic, environmental, and natural changes. In the process, the readers will have the opportunities to revisit and view from alternative angles the models and results presented in this chapter.

The problem of global warming is one of the many important environmental and natural resource policy issues that the current generation of researchers are struggling to find solutions (Tietenberg and Lewis, 2014). In contrast to many other environmental and natural resource questions, global warming is distinct as a global public good (Nordhaus, 1994). Scientific and policy efforts to address the problems of global warming, unlike other issues, have taken from the beginning the global platform through global organizations and global negotiation roundtables (IPCC 1990; UNFCCC 1998).

What policy relevance do microbehavioral models hold? First of all, microbehavioral models are well suited for examinations of behavioral changes in response to changes in external conditions (Seo, 2006, 2014a). In the global climate change literature, the research in this area is referred to as adaptation literature (Mendelsohn, 2000, 2012; Hanemann, 2000; Smit et al., 2001; Adger et al., 2007; UNFCCC 2011; Seo, 2015c). The study of adaptation is one of the most important research areas, if not the most, in the global warming literature. The microbehavioral models show, by examining individual managers' behaviors, which adaptation strategies are effective and how they should be implemented in response to a variety of potential climate change scenarios.

The analysis in this chapter provides evidence that rural managers adapted to a hotter climate by switching from a crops-only portfolio to a mixed portfolio and a livestock-only portfolio. This, however, does not mean that all the farms will adapt in the same way (Seo, 2014a). Adaptation strategies will differ across the farms given the current and future climates, soils, geographic, and market conditions. Some rural managers may find it more desirable to switch from a mixed system to a crops-only system.

Beyond the global climate change literature, the study of individuals' behavioral changes owing to changes in external factors is an essential area of research in numerous policy analyses. The present author will provide a review of some of these policy analyses in environmental issues, natural resource uses, energy policy, transportation policy, agricultural subsidies in Chapters 7 and 8 of this book.

Second, microbehavioral econometric models provide a quantitative estimate of the value of an adaptation strategy (Seo, 2010b, 2015b). An adaptation measure would be taken in an endeavor to reduce the damage expected from climatic changes or to gain the benefit from such changes. A crops-only portfolio farm would suffer by almost 10% of the current land value, on average, but it can minimize the loss by switching to a mixed portfolio farm. The total net benefit of adaptation will be considered by a rural manager in making a decision on an adaptation strategy which will certainly cost a certain amount of investment dollars.

Third, microbehavioral models have the capacity of providing quantitative estimates of vulnerabilities and resilience of different enterprises that are in the choice set of a decision-maker. That is, enterprise-wise estimates of damages from climatic changes can be provided (Seo, 2010b, 2015b). This informs policy-makers of which enterprise is most vulnerable to external changes and which enterprise is least vulnerable. Policy efforts can then be directed to the most vulnerable enterprises and how they can adapt. This chapter's analysis shows that a specialized crop system is the most vulnerable system to changes in the climatic system.

Fourth, microbehavioral econometric models can provide the total impact of climatic changes on the whole array of enterprises after embedding the full variety of adaptation activities. Many nonmicrobehavioral impact studies of climate change fail to account for behavioral changes while many other studies take into account only a partial set of adaptation measures (Seo, 2013b). These studies tend to report a high damage from climatic changes on agriculture. However, the true impact of climate change cannot be measured without accounting for a full array of adaptation measures and strategies (Seo, 2015a).

Before closing this chapter, the present author hopes to make additional comments on policy-relevant aspects of the microbehavioral models introduced in this chapter that are not well addressed by the models in this chapter but will be the focus of the ensuring chapters of this book. First, there is a great diversity of agricultural and natural resource portfolios that rural residents manage in South America or any other developing countries (Seo, 2012a). This chapter classifies the multitude of rural portfolios into a specialized crop portfolio, a specialized livestock portfolio, and a mixed portfolio. Each of these portfolios is again composed of a variety of sub-portfolios. For example, a crops-only portfolio contains major grains, vegetables, beans, root (tuber) crops and vegetables, specialty crops, and tree products. Also, a livestock-only portfolio contains large ruminant animals such as cattle and smaller ruminant and nonruminant animals such as goats, sheep, pigs, turkeys, beehives, and chickens. From a statistical viewpoint, there is little difficulty involved in building a microbehavioral model with a larger number of portfolios as alternatives in the choice set of the model, taking into account a great variety of subportfolios. The question of which classification of the portfolios, that is, which choice set of distinct portfolios, should be preferred is an economic question, which is the main theme in the next two chapters.

Second, an individual manager's decisions in managing agricultural and natural resource enterprises are driven by private incentives, that is, personal benefits. There may exist externalities in individuals' decisions (Pigou, 1920; Coase, 1960). In the context of the model in this chapter, growing trees are reported to have public benefits because, among other things, forests sink, that is, absorb, carbon dioxide present in the atmosphere (Ainsworth and Long, 2005; Houghton, 2008). Growing crops are known to have external environmental effects because crop agriculture leads, among other things, to water pollution and food chain contaminations by applications of fertilizers and pesticides (Zilberman, 1998). Similarly, livestock management is known to emit methane, one of the potent greenhouse gases, through the processes of enteric fermentation and manure (US EPA, 2006, 2011). Livestock management also leads to increased grasslands which sink carbon dioxide (Scurlock and Hall, 1998; Denman et al., 2007). Individual managers' decisions are made without considerations of these external effects, whether positive or negative.

Therefore, future decisions of individuals will be shifted if environmental policies are to be designed and implemented in order to internalize some of these external effects. For example, carbon credits may be given to forest owners based on the amount of carbon emissions absorbed by the trees (UNFCCC 1998). This will increase people's adoption of forest management relative to the estimates presented in this Chapter. If grasslands can be managed well to serve as carbon sink, carbon credits can be given to livestock management. This again will increase adoption of animal husbandry in comparison with the estimates presented in this chapter.

Third, the results of the microbehavioral econometric models presented in this chapter point to meaningful areas of technological innovations. When it comes to climate change debates, a major breakthrough technology such as nuclear fusion or a carbon-capture-storage has been most often a focal point (IEA, 2013; ITER, 2015; Lawrence Livermore National Laboratory, 2015). Technologies that would be most meaningful at the microdecision-maker level have been gravely overlooked, the point which microbehavioral models have highlighted. One example is a methane reduction technology. Given that grasslands are carbon sinks as well as carbon storage, an increased livestock production will simultaneously have carbon-reducing effects if methane emissions from cattle and other animals can be reduced or captured and reused. Some technologies already exist (US EPA, 2006), but meaningful research efforts can be directed to advance these technologies further. A significant reduction in methane emissions from cattle and other ruminants may be possible through dietary changes, feed additives, or capture inside feedlots.

Another example of potential technological innovations is the development of technologies to prevent and cure animal diseases such as Nagana, Cattle Tick, Blue Tongue (Ford and Katondo, 1977; White et al., 2003; Fox et al., 2012). A recent development in the animal genetics is a good example which fully coded the genomes of Tsetse flies, the carriers of the Nagana disease (Trypanosomiasis) commonly called sleeping sickness (Aksoy et al., 2014). In each year, millions of cattle die of this disease in Africa in a bad year. A reduction in cattle fatalities through innovations in the prevention and cure of animal diseases can increase the productivity of livestock management per unit area of lands.

A further increase in the yields of grains is highly anticipated to be achieved through many on-going crop variety improvement programs worldwide. The so-called Green Revolution has been successful in enhancing crop yields especially in South Asian countries but also in South America (Evenson and Gollin, 2003; World Bank, 2009). Additionally, an increase in the grain yields can be achieved through effective grain disease and insect treatments, for example, wheat rust, and weed managements (Porter et al., 1991; Sutherst, 1991; Ziska, 2003). An increase in the yields of grains means that a smaller area of land is needed to produce the same amount of grains.

Fourth, many governments offer different kinds of subsidies to agricultural farmers, of which a crop insurance and subsidy program accounts for a dominant portion of agricultural subsidies (Barry et al., 2000; Sumner and Zulauf, 2012). For example, in the fiscal year 2013, the US crop insurance program accounted for about 63% of the total budgeted outlays of the United States Department of Agriculture (USDA) for crop subsidy. Since the early 1990s, the US federal crop insurance program has expanded immensely. During this time period, the number of crops separately insured has grown from about 50 crops to more than 300 crops while the size of insured farmlands has increased from about 101 million acres in 1990 to 272 million acres to in 2007 (Sumner and Zulauf, 2012). The crop insurance and subsidy program is expected to expand even further under the Agricultural Act of 2014, the so called 2014 Farm Bill (Goodwin and Smith, 2014).

To finance the program, taxpayers subsidize much of the federal crop insurance program. Across the crop insurance programs, US taxpayers cover 60% of the premium costs. In addition, taxpayers subsidize the federal government's reimbursement of the private crop insurance companies' administrative and operating costs which amounts to about 22–24% of total premiums. Further, taxpayers subsidize a significant share of the government payments that go directly to farmers in the event of a yield or revenue loss (Shields, 2013). According to the Risk Management Agency of the United States Department of Agriculture (USDA), the total cost to taxpayers has increased significantly from 3.1 billion USD in 2001 to 14 billion USD in 2012 (USDA RMA, 2015).

With the availability of the extensive crop insurance programs that are subsidized by taxpayers, farmers will have less incentive to switch agricultural systems or crops that they manage in a new climatic system. This will lead to a larger loss of the yield of a grain than those predicted by scientists. A moral hazard problem inherent in the crop insurance and subsidy program will be further exacerbated under the warming climate. That is, climatic changes will lead to reduced yields as well as more variable yields, but farmers will not adapt to these changes since losses are covered by taxpayers. This will turn out to be a hindrance for a farmer who needs to make a switch from crops to livestock management.

With this, the present chapter is concluded. As mentioned before, this chapter will serve as the foundation chapter for the ensuring chapters that are directed to applications of the microbehavioral econometric methods. This means that we will revisit many of the topics discussed in this chapter in the rest of this book with alternative perspectives and with a focus on each of these topics.

Exercises

1. In the conditional land value regressions in Table 4.5, write down mathematically each of the selection bias correction terms as the product of a correlation parameter and a variance parameter of the uncorrected regression. Provide an interpretation of each of the selection bias correction terms using the estimated numbers in Table 4.5.

2. The changes in the expected land value under the two climate scenarios are estimated in Table 4.11. Write down mathematically the expected land value function for each rural household. Explain, using the estimates in Table 4.9 and 4.10, the reasons why farm j can still benefit from a climatic change even if it is predicted to suffer from a large loss in a certain system, for example, a crops-only portfolio.

REFERENCES

Adams, R., Rosenzweig, C., Peart, R.M., Ritchie, J.T., McCarl, B.A., Glyer, J.D., Curry, R.B., Jones, J.W., Boote, K.J., Allen, L.H., 1990. Global climate change and US agriculture. Nature 345, 219–224.

Adams, R., McCarl B.A., Segerson, K., Rosenzweig, C., Bryant, K., Dixon, B.L., Conner, R., Evenson, R.E., Ojima, D., 1999. The economic effects of climate change on US agriculture. In: Mendelsohn, R., Neumann, J. (Eds.), The Impact of Climate Change on the United States Economy. Cambridge University Press, Cambridge.

Adger, W.N., Agrawala, S., Mirza, M.M.Q., Conde, C., O'Brien, K., Pulhin, J., Pulwarty, R., Smit, B., Takahashi, K., 2007. Assessment of adaptation practices, options, constraints and capacity. In: Parry, M.L., Canziani, O.F., Palutikof, J.P., van der Linden, P.J., Hanson, C.E. (Eds.), Climate change 2007: Impacts, Adaptation and Vulnerability. Contribution of Working Group II to the Fourth Assessment Report of the Intergovernmental Panel on Climate Change. Cambridge University Press, Cambridge, UK.

Ainsworth, E.A., Long, S.P., 2005. What have we learned from 15 years of free-air CO_2 enrichment (FACE)? A meta-analytic review of the responses of photosynthesis, canopy properties and plant production to rising CO_2. New Phytol. 165, 351–371.

Aksoy, S., Attardo, G., et al., 2014. Genome sequence of the Tsetse fly (Glossina morsitans): vector of African Trypanosomiasis. Science 344 (6182), 380–386.

Arrow, K.J., 1971. Essays in the Theory of Risk Bearing. Markham Publishing Co, Chicago.

Auffhammer, M., Ramaathan, V., Vincent, J.R., 2006. Integrated model shows that atmospheric brown clouds and greenhouse gases have reduced rice harvests in India. Proc. Nat. Acad. Sci. USA 103, 19668–19672.

Baethgen, W.E., 1997. Vulnerability of agricultural sector of Latin America to climate change. Clim. Res. 9, 1–7.

Barry, P.J., Elllinger, P.N., Baker, C.B., Hopkin, J.A., 2000. Financial Management in Agriculture, sixth ed. Interstate Publishers, Illinois, USA.

Basist, A., Peterson, N., Peterson, T., Williams, C., 1998. Using the special sensor microwave imager to monitor land surface temperature, wetness, and snow cover. J. App. Meteorol. 37, 888–911.

Blunden, J., Arndt, D.S. (Eds.), 2015. State of the Climate in 2014. Bull. Am. Meteorol. Soc. 96 (7), S1–S238.

Bourguignon, F., Fournier, M., Gurgand, M., 2004. Selection Bias Corrections Based on the Multinomial Logit Model: Monte-Carlo Comparisons. DELTA Working Paper No. 20, Département et Laboratoire d'Economie Théorique et Appliquée (DELTA).

Butt, T.A., McCarl, B.A., Angerer, J., Dyke, P.T., Stuth, J.W., 2005. The economic and food security implications of climate change in Mali. Clim. Change 68, 355–378.

Cline, W., 1992. The Economics of Global Warming. Institute of International Economics, Washington DC.

Coase, R., 1960. The problem of social cost. J. Law Econ. 3, 1–44.

Curtis, S., Adler, R.F., Huffman, G.J., Nelkin, E., Bolvin, D., 2001. Evolution of tropical and extratropical precipitation anomalies during the 1997 to 1999 ENSO cycle. Int. J. Meteorol. 21, 961–971.

Dahl, G.B., 2002. Mobility and the returns to education: testing a Roy model with multiple markets. Econometrica 70, 2367–2420.

Danielson, J.J., Gesch, D.B., 2011. Global multi-resolution terrain elevation data 2010 (GMTED2010). US Geo-logical Survey Open-File Report 2011–1073, 26 p.

Denman, K.L., Brasseur, G., Chidthaisong, A., Ciais, P., Cox, P.M., Dickinson, R.E., Hauglustaine, D., Heinze, C., Holland, E., Jacob, D., Lohmann, U., Ramachandran, S., da Silva Dias, P.L., Wofsy, S.C., Zhang, X., 2007. Couplings between changes in the climate system and biogeochemistry. In: Solomon, S., Qin, D., Manning, M., Chen, Z., Marquis, M., Averyt, K.B., Tignor, M., Miller, H.L. (Eds.), Climate Change 2007, the Physical Science Basis. Contribution of Working Group I to the Fourth Assessment Report of the Intergovernmental Panel on Climate Change. Cambridge University Press, Cambridge.

Deschenes, O., Greenstone, M., 2007. The economic impacts of climate change: evidence from agricultural output and random fluctuations in weather. Am. Econ. Rev. 97, 354–385.

Dinar, A., Mendelsohn, R. (Eds.), 2012. Handbook of Climate Change and Agriculture. Edward Elgar, London.

Driessen, P., Deckers, J., Nachtergaele, F., 2001. Lecture notes on the major soils of the world. Food and Agriculture Organization, Rome.

Dubin, J.A., McFadden, D.L., 1984. An econometric analysis of residential electric appliance holdings and consumption. Econometrica 52 (2), 345–362.

Easterling, D.R., Evans, J.L., Groisman, P.Y., Karl, T.R., Kunkel, K.E., Ambenje, P., 2000. Observed variability and trends in extreme climate events: a brief review. Bull. Am. Meteorol. Soc. 81, 417–425.

Easterling, W.E., Aggarwal, P.K., Batima, P., Brander, K.M., Erda, L., Howden, S.M., Kirilenko, A., Morton, J., Soussana, J.-F., Schmidhuber, J., Tubiello, F.N., 2007. In: Parry, M.L., Canziani, O.F., Palutikof, J.P., van der Linden, P.J., Hanson, C.E., (Eds.). Food, Fibre and Forest Products. Climate Change 2007 Impacts, Adaptation and Vulnerability. Contribution of working group II to the fourth assessment report of the intergovernmental panel on climate change. Cambridge University Press, Cambridge.

Efron, B., 1979. Bootstrap methods: Another look at the Jackknife. Ann. Stat. 7, 1–26.

Efron, B., 1981. Nonparametric estimates of standard error: the jackknife, the bootstrap and other methods. Biometrika 68, 589–599.

Evenson, R., Gollin, D., 2003. Assessing the impact of the Green Revolution 1960-2000. Science 300, 758–762.

Fabozzi, F.J., Modigliani, F.G., Jones, F.J., 2009. Foundations of Financial Markets and Institutions, fourth ed. Prentice Hall, New York.

Fisher, I., 1906. The nature of capital and income. Macmillan, New York.

Fisher, F.M., 1966. The identification problem in econometrics. McGraw-Hill, New York.

Food and Agriculture Organization (FAO), 2003. The digital soil map of the world (DSMW) CD-ROM. Rome.

Ford, J., Katondo, K., 1977. Maps of tsetse fly (Glossina) distribution in Africa. Bull. Animal Health Prod. Afr. 15, 187–193.

Fox, N.J., Marion, G., Davidson, R.S., White, P.C.L., Hutchings, M.R., 2012. Livestock Helminths in a changing climate: approaches and restrictions to meaningful predictions. Animals 2, 93–107.

Gitay, H., Brwon, S., Easterling, W., Jallow, B., 2001. Ecosystems and their goods and services. In: McCarthy, J.J. et al. (Ed.), Climate Change 2001, Impacts, Adaptations, and Vulnerabilities. Cambridge University Press, Cambridge, pp. 237–342.

Goodwin, B.K., Smith, V.K., 2014. Theme overview: the 2014 farm bill—an economic welfare disaster or triumph? Choices 29 (3), 1–4.

Gordon, C., Cooper, C., Senior, C.A., Banks, H.T., Gregory, J.M., Johns, T.C., Mitchell, J.F.B., Wood, R.A., 2000. The simulation of SST, sea ice extents and ocean heat transports in a version of the Hadley Centre coupled model without flux adjustments. Clim. Dyn. 16, 147–168.

Hahn, G.L., 1981. Housing and management to reduce climate impacts on livestock. J. Animal Sci. 52, 175–186.

Hahn, G.L., 1999. Dynamic responses of cattle to thermal heat loads. J. Animal Sci. 77, 10–20.

Hahn, G.L., Gaughan, J.B., Mader, T.L., Eigenberg, R.A., 2009. In: DeShazer, J.A., (Eds.) Livestock Energetics and Thermal Environmental Management. Chapter 5 Thermal Indices and Their Applications for Livestock Environments. St. Joseph, Mich., American Society of Agricultural and Biological Engineers, pp. 113–130.

Hanemann, W.M., 2000. Adaptation and its management. Clim. Change 45, 511–581.

Hansen, J., Sato, M., Reudy, R., Lo, K., Lea, D.W., Medina-Elizade, M., 2006. Global temperature change. Proc. Nat. Acad. Sci. USA 103, 14288–14293.

Hansen, J., Sato, M., Reudy, R., 2012. Perception of climate change. Proc. Nat. Acad. Sci. USA 109, E2415–E2423.

Heckman, J., 1979. Sample selection bias as a specification error. Econometrica 47, 153–162.

Heckman, J., 2000. Microdata, Heterogeneity and the Evaluation of Public Policy. Nobel Prize Lecture for Economic Sciences. Stockholm University, Sweden.

Hillel, D., Rosenzweig, C. (Eds.), 2010. Handbook of Climate Change and Agroecosystems: Impacts, Adaptation and Mitigation. Imperial College Press, London.

Houghton, R.A., 2008. Carbon flux to the atmosphere from land-use changes: 1850–2005. In: Trends: A compendium of data on global change. Carbon Dioxide Information Analysis Center, Oak Ridge National Laboratory, US Department of Energy, Oak Ridge, TN, USA.

Hulme, M., Doherty, R.M., Ngara, T., New, M.G., Lister, D., 2001. African climate change: 1900–2100. Clim. Res. 17, 145–168.

International Energy Agency (IEA), 2013. Technology roadmap: carbon capture and storage. IEA, France.

Intergovernmental Panel on Climate Change (IPCC), (1990). Climate Change: The IPCC Scientific Assessment, Cambridge University Press, Cambridge.

IPCC, 2007. Climate Change 2007: the Physical Science Basis, the Fourth Assessment Report. Cambridge University Press, Cambridge.

IPCC, 2012. Managing the risks of extreme events and disasters to advance climate change adaptation. A special report of working groups I and II of the Intergovernmental Panel on Climate Change. Cambridge University Press, Cambridge.

IPCC, 2014. Climate Change 2014, The Physical Science Basis, the Fourth Assessment Report. Cambridge University Press, Cambridge.

ITER, 2015. ITER: the world's largest Tokamak. Available at https://www.iter.org/mach.

Jones, C.A., Kiniry, J.R., 1986. CERES-Maize: A Stimulation Model of Maize Growth and Development. Texas A&M University Press, College Station, Texas.

Johnson, H.D., 1965. Response of animals to heat. Meteorol. Mono. 6, 109–122.

Johnston, J., Dinardo, J., 1997. Econometric methods, fourth ed. McGraw-Hill, New York.

Kazianga, H., Udry, C., 2006. Consumption smoothing? Livestock, insurance, and drought in rural Burkina Faso. J. Dev. Econ. 79, 413–446.

Keeling, C.D., Piper, S.C., Bacastow, R.B., Wahlen, M., Whorf, T.P., Heimann, M., Meijer, H.A., 2005. Atmospheric CO_2 and $^{13}CO_2$ exchange with the terrestrial biosphere and oceans from 1978 to 2000, Observations and carbon cycle implications. In: Ehleringer, J.R., Cerling, T.E., Dearing, M.D. (Eds.), A History of Atmospheric CO_2 and its Effects on Plants, Animals, and Ecosystems. SpringerVerlag, New York, pp. 83–113.

Kurukulasuriya, P., Mendelsohn, R., Hassan, R., Benhin, J., Diop, M., Eid, H.M., Fosu, K.Y., Gbetibouo, G., Jain, S., Mahamadou, A., El-Marsafawy, S., Ouda, S., Ouedraogo, M., Sène, I., Maddision, D., Seo, N., Dinar, A., 2006. Will African agriculture survive climate change? World Bank Econ. Rev. 20, 367–388.

Lanjouw, J.O., Lanjouw, P., 2001. The rural non-farm sector: issues and evidence from developing countries. Agric. Econ. 26 (1), 1–23.

Lawrence Livermore National Laboratory, 2015. How NIF works. Available at https://lasers.llnl.gov/about/how-nif-works.

Lee, L.F., 1983. Generalized econometric models with selectivity. Econometrica 51, 507–512.

Le Treut, H., Somerville, R., Cubasch, U., Ding, Y., Mauritzen, C., Mokssit, A., Peterson, T., Prather, M., 2007. Historical overview of climate change. In: Solomon S, Qin D, Manning M, Chen Z, Marquis M, Averyt KB, Tignor M, Miller HL (Eds.), Climate Change 2007, the physical science basis. Contribution of working group I to the fourth assessment report of the intergovenmental panel on climate change. Cambridge University Press, Cambridge.

Lenton, T.M., Held, H., Kriegler, E., Hall, J.W., Lucht, W., Rahmstorf, S., Schellnhuber, H.J., 2008. Tipping elements in the earth's climate system. Proc. Nat. Acad. Sci. USA 105, 1786–1793.

Lobell, D., Schlenker, W., Costa-Roberts, J., 2011. Climate trends and global crop production since 1980. Science 333, 616–620.

Mader, T.L., Davis, M.S., 2004. Effect of management strategies on reducing heat stress of feedlot cattle: feed and water intake. J. Animal Sci. 82, 3077–3087.

Magrin, G.O., Travasso, M.I., Díaz, R.A., Rodríguez, R.O., 1997. Vulnerability of the agricultural systems of Argentina to climate change. Clim. Res. 9, 31–36.

Magrin, G., Garcia, C.G., Choque, D.C., Gimenez, J.C., Moreno, A.R., Nagy, G.J., Nobre, C., Villamizar, A., 2007. Latin America. In: Parry, M.L., Canziani, O.F., Palutikof, J.P., van der Linden, P.J., Hanson, C.E. (Eds.), Climate Change 2007, Impacts, Adaptation, and Vulnerability: Contribution of Working Group II to the Fourth Assessment Report of the Intergovernmental Panel on Climate Change. Cambridge University Press, Cambridge, pp. 581–615.

Markowitz, H., 1952. Portfolio selection. J. Fin. 7, 77–91.

Mata, L.J., Campos, M., et al., 2001. Latin America. In: Climate Change 2001 impacts, adaptation, vulnerability—Contribution of Working Group II to the Third Assessment Report of the Intergovernmental Panel on Climate Change, Cambridge University Press, Cambridge,

Matthews, E., 1983. Global vegetation and land use: new high-resolution data bases for climate studies. J. Clim. App. Meteorol. 22 (3), 474–487.

McFadden, D.L., 1974. Conditional logit analysis of qualitative choice behavior. In: Zarembka, P. (Ed.), Frontiers in Econometrics. Academic, New York, pp. 105–142.

McFadden, D.L., 1984. Econometric analysis of qualitative response models. In: Grilliches, Z., Intrilligator, M.D., (Eds.) Handbook of Econometrics, Vol. II, Elsevier Science Publishers BV, Amsterdam.

Mendelsohn, R., 2000. Efficient adaptation to climate change. Clim. Change 45, 583–600.

Mendelsohn, R., 2012. The economics of adaptation to climate change in developing countries. Clim. Change Econo. 3, 1–21.

Mendelsohn, R., Nordhaus, W., Shaw, D., 1994. The impact of global warming on agriculture: a Ricardian analysis. Am. Econo. Rev. 84, 753–771.

Mendelsohn, R., Dinar, A., Sanghi, A., 2001. The effect of development on the climate sensitivity of agriculture. Environ. Dev. Econo. 6, 85–101.

Mendelsohn, R., Dinar, A., Williams, L., 2006. The distributional impact of climate change on rich and poor countries. Environ. Dev. Econo. 11, 1–20.

Mendelsohn, R., Kurukulasuriya, P., Basist, A., Kogan, F., Williams, C., 2007. Measuring climate change impacts with satellite versus weather station data. Clim. Change 81, 71–83.

Modigliani, F., Pogue, G.A., 1974. An introduction to risk and return: concepts and evidence. Finan. Anal. J. 30, 68–80.

National Aeronautics and Space Administration (NASA), 2007. Our changing planet: the view from space. Cambridge University Press, Cambridge.

NASA, 2015. Taking a global perspective on Earth's climate. Available at http://climate.nasa.gov/nasa_role/.

Nakicenovic, N., Davidson, O., Davis, G., Grübler, A., Kram, T., La Rovere, E.L., Metz, B., Morita, T., Pepper, W., Pitcher, H., Sankovski, A., Shukla, P., Swart, R., Watson, R., Dadi, Z., 2000. Emissions Scenarios, A Special Report of Working Group III of the Intergovernmental Panel on Climate Change. IPCC, Geneva.

National Research Council (NRC), 2013. Abrupt impacts of climate change: anticipating surprises. The National Academies Press, Washington DC.

New, M., Lister, D., Hulme, M., Makin, I., 2002. A high-resolution data set of surface climate over global land areas. Clim. Res. 21, 1–25.

Nin, A., Ehui, S., Benin, S., 2007. Livestock productivity in developing countries: an assessment. In: Evenson, R., Pingali, P. (Eds.) Handbook of Agricultural Economics, vol. 3. North Holland, Oxford, UK, 2467–2532.

Nordhaus, W.D., 1994. Managing the global commons: the economics of climate change. MIT Press, Cambridge, MA.

Parry, M.L., Rosenzweig, C.P., Iglesias, A., Livermore, M., Fischer, G., 2004. Effects of climate change on global food production under SRES emissions and socioeconomic scenarios. Global Environ. Change 14, 53–67.

Pearce, D.W., et al., 1996. The social costs of climate change: greenhouse damage and the benefits of control. In: Climate Change 1995 Economic and Social Dimensions of Climate Change. IPCC. Cambridge University Press, Cambridge. 183–224.

Pigou, A.C., 1920. Economics of Welfare. Macmillan and Co, London.

Porter, J.H., Parry, M.L., Carter, T.R., 1991. The potential effects of climatic change on agricultural insect pests. Agric. Forest Meteorol. 57, 221–240.

Remote Sensing Systems (REMSS), 2015. Climate Analysis. Santa Rosa, California. http://www.remss.com/research/climate

Reilly, J., et al., 1996. Agriculture in a changing climate: impacts and adaptations. In: Climate Change 1995 Impacts, Adaptations, and Mitigation of Climate Change. IPCC. Cambridge University Press, Cambridge, 427–468.

Ricardo, D., 1817. On the principles of political economy and taxation. John Murray, London, England.

Ropelewski, C.F., Halpert, M.S., 1987. Global and regional precipitation patterns associated with the El Nino/Southern Oscillation. Monthly Weather Rev. 115, 1606–1626.

Rosenzweig, C., Parry, M., 1994. Potential impact of climate change on world food supply. Nature 367, 133–138.

Rosenzweig, C., Hillel, D., 1998. Climate Change and the Global Harvest: Potential Impacts of the Greenhouse Effect on Agriculture. Oxford University Press, Oxford, United Kingdom, 324.

Rosenzweig, C., Iglesias, A., Yang, X.B., Epstein, P.R., Chivian, E., 2001. Climate change and extreme weather events: implications for food production, plant diseases, and pests. Global Change Hum. Health 2 (2), 90–104.

Sanghi, A., Mendelsohn, R., 2008. The impacts of global warming on farmers in Brazil and India. Global Environ. Change 18, 655–665.

Schlenker, W., Hanemann, M., Fisher, A., 2005. Will US agriculture really benefit from global warming? Accounting for irrigation in the hedonic approach. Am. Econo. Rev. 95, 395–406.

Schlenker, W., Roberts, M., 2009. Nonlinear temperature effects indicate severe damages to crop yields under climate change. Proc. Nat. Acad. Sci. USA 106(37), 15594–15598.

Schmertmann, C.P., 1994. Selectivity bias correction methods in polychotomous sample selection models. J. Econo. 60, 101–132.

Schmidt, G.A., et al., 2005. Present day atmospheric simulations using GISS ModelE: comparison to in-situ, satellite and reanalysis data. J. Clim. 19, 153–192.

Schultz, T.P., 2004. Evidence of returns to schooling in Africa from household surveys: monitoring and restructuring the market for education. J. Afr. Econo. 13 (2), 95–148.

Seo, S.N., 2006. Modeling farmer responses to climate change: climate change impacts and adaptations in livestock management in Africa. PhD Dissertation, Yale University, New Haven.

Seo, S.N., 2010a. Is an integrated farm more resilient against climate change?: a microeconometric analysis of portfolio diversification in African agriculture? Food Policy 35, 32–40.

Seo, S.N., 2010b. A microeconometric analysis of adapting portfolios to climate change: adoption of agricultural systems in Latin America. App. Econo. Perspec. Policy 32, 489–514.

Seo, S.N., 2011a. An analysis of public adaptation to climate change using agricultural water schemes in South America. Ecol. Econo. 70, 825–834.

Seo, S.N., 2011b. A geographically scaled analysis of adaptation to climate change with spatial models using agricultural systems in Africa. J. Agric. Sci. 149, 437–449.

Seo, S.N., 2012a. Adapting natural resource enterprises under global warming in South America: a mixed logit analysis. Econ. J. Latin Am. Caribbean Econo. Assoc. 12, 111–135.

Seo, S.N., 2012b. Adaptation behaviors across ecosystems under global warming: a spatial microeconometric model of the rural economy in South America. Papers Reg. Sci. 91, 849–871.

Seo, S.N., 2012c. Decision making under climate risks: an analysis of sub-Saharan farmers' adaptation behaviors. Weather Clim. Soc. 4, 285–299.

Seo, S.N., 2013a. Refining spatial resolution and spillovers of a microeconometric model of adapting portfolios to climate change. Mitig. Adap. Strat. Global Change 18, 1019–1034.

Seo, S.N., 2013b. An essay on the impact of climate change on US agriculture: weather fluctuations, climatic shifts, and adaptation strategies. Clim. Change 121, 115–124.

Seo, S.N., 2014a. Evaluation of Agro-Ecological Zone methods for the study of climate change with micro farming decisions in sub-Saharan Africa. Eur. J. Agron. 52, 157–165.

Seo, S.N., 2014b. Coupling climate risks, eco-systems, anthropogenic decisions using South American and Sub-Saharan farming activities. Meteorol. App. 21, 848–858.

Seo, S.N., 2014c. Adapting sensibly when global warming turns the field brown or blue: A comment on the 2014 IPCC Report. Econo. Affairs 34, 399–401.

Seo, S.N., 2015a. Micro-behavioral Economics of Global Warming: Modeling Adaptation Strategies in Agricultural and Natural Resource Enterprises. Springer, Cham, Switzerland.

Seo, S.N., 2015b. Modeling farmer adaptations to climate change in South America: a micro-behavioral economic perspective. Environ. Ecol. Stat. 23, 1–21. doi: 10.1007/s10651-015-0320-0.

Seo, S.N., 2015c. Adaptation to global warming as an optimal transition process to a green-house world. Econ. Affairs 35, 272–284.

Seo, S.N., 2015d. Adapting to extreme climate changes: raising animals in hot and arid eco-systems in Australia. Int. J. Biometeorol. 59, 541–550.

Seo, S.N., 2016. Untold tales of goats in deadly Indian monsoons: adapt or rain-retreat under global warming? J. Extr. Events 3. doi: 0.1142/2345737616500019.

Seo, S.N., Mendelsohn, R., Munasinghe, M., 2005. Climate change and agriculture in Sri Lanka: A Ricardian valuation. Environ. Dev. Econo. 10, 581–596.

Seo, S.N., Mendelsohn, R., 2008a. Measuring impacts and adaptations to climate change: a structural Ricardian model of African livestock management. Agric. Econ. 38, 151–165.

Seo, S.N., Mendelsohn, R., 2008b. A Ricardian analysis of the impact of climate change impacts on South American farms. Chil. J. Agric. Res. 68, 69–79.

Seo, S.N., Mendelsohn, R., Dinar, A., Hassan, R., Kurukulasuriya, P., 2009. A Ricardian analysis of the distribution of climate change impacts on agriculture across Agro-Ecological Zones in Africa. Environ. Res. Econo. 43, 313–332.

Seo, S.N., McCarl, B., Mendelsohn, R., 2010. From beef cattle to sheep under global warming? An analysis of adaptation by livestock species choice in South America. Ecol. Econo. 69, 2486–2494.

Shanahan, T.M., Overpeck, J.T., Anchukaitis, K.J., Beck, J.W., Cole, J.E., Dettman, D.L., Peck, J.A., Scholz, C.A., King, J.W., 2009. Atlantic forcing of persistent drought in West Africa. Science 324, 377–380.

Shields, D.A., 2013. Federal crop insurance: background. Congressional Research Service. R40532. US Congress, Washington DC.

Smit, B., Pilifosova, O., et al., 2001. Adaptation to climate change in the context of sustain-able development and equity. In: McCarthy, J.J., Canzianni, O.F., Leary, N.A., Dokken, D.J., White, KS., (Eds.), Climate Change 2001 Impacts, Adaptation, and Vulnerability—Contribution of Working Group II to the Third Assessment Report of the Intergovern-mental Panel on Climate Change. Cambridge University Press, Cambridge. 1000 pp.

Steiger, C., 2006. Modern beef production in Brazil and Argentina. Choices 21, 105–110.

Sumner, D.A., Zulauf, C., 2012. Economic & environmental effects of agricultural insur-ance programs. The Council on Food, Agricultural & Resource Economics (C-FARE), Washington DC.

Scurlock, J.M.O., Hall, D.O., 1998. The global carbon sink: a grassland perspective. Global Change Biol. 4, 229–233.

Sutherst, R.W., 1991. Pest risk analysis and the greenhouse effect. Rev. Agric. Entomol. 79, 1177–1187.

Taylor, K.E., Stouffer, R.J., Meehl, G.A., 2012. An overview of CMIP5 and the experiment design. Bull. Am. Meteorol. Soc. 93, 485–498.

Tebaldi, C., Hayhoe, K., Arblaster, J.M., Meehl, G.E., 2007. Going to the extremes: an inter-comparison of model-simulated historical and future changes in extreme events. Clim. Change 82, 233–234.

Tietenberg, T., Lewis, L., 2014. Environmental & Natural Resource Economics. Prentice Hall, New York.

Titley, D.W., Hegerl, G., Jacobs, K.L., Mote, P.W., Paciorek, C.J., Shepherd, J.M., Shepherd, T.G., Sobel, A.H., Walsh, J., Zwiers, F.W., Thomas, K., Everett, L., Purcell, Gaskins, R., Markovich, E., 2016. Attribution of Extreme Weather Events in the Context of Climate Change. National Academies of Sciences, Engineering, and Medicine. National Acad-emies Press, Washington, DC.

Tubiello, F.N., Ewert, F., 2002. Simulating the effects of elevated CO_2 on crops: approaches and applications for climate change. Eur. J. Agro. 18, 57–74.

Tubiello, F.N., Amthor, J.A., Boote, K.J., Donatelli, M., Easterling, W., Fischer, G., Gifford, R.M., Howden, M., Reilly, J., Rosenzweig, C., 2007. Crop response to elevated CO_2 and world food supply. Eur. J. Agro. 26, 215–223.

University of Alabama in Huntsville (UAH), 2015. Global temperature report. Earth System Science Center, UAH. Available at http://nsstc.uah.edu/climate/.

Udry, C., 1995. Risk and saving in Northern Nigeria. Am. Econo. Rev. 85, 1287–1300.

United States Animal Health Association (USAHA), 2008. Foreign animal diseases-the gray book. Committee on Foreign and Emerging Diseases of the USAHA, MO.

United Nations Framework Convention on Climate Change (UNFCCC), 1998. Kyoto Protocol to the United Nations Framework Convention on Climate Change. UNFCCC, Geneva.

United Nations Framework Convention on Climate Change (UNFCCC), 2011. Report of the transitional committee for the design of Green Climate Fund. UNFCCC, Geneva.

US Department of Agriculture, Risk Management Agency, 2015. Costs and Outlays of Crop Insurance Program. http://www.rma.usda.gov/aboutrma/budget/costsoutlays.html.

United States Environmental Protection Agency (US EPA), 2006. Global mitigation of non-CO_2 greenhouse gases. US EPA, Washington DC.

United States Environmental Protection Agency (US EPA), 2011. Inventory of US greenhouse gas emissions and sinks: 1990–2009. US EPA, Washington DC.

Welch, J.R., Vincent, J.R., Auffhammer, M., Moya, P.F., Dobermann, A., Dawe, D., 2010. Rice yields in tropical/subtropical Asia exhibit large but opposing sensitivities to minimum and maximum temperatures. Proc. Nat. Acad. Sci. USA 107, 14562–14567.

White, N., Sutherst, R.W., Hall, N., Whish-Wilson, P., 2003. The vulnerability of the Australian beef industry to impacts of the Cattle Tick (Boophilus microplus) under climate change. Clim. Change 61, 157–190.

Williams, J.R., Jones, C.A., Kiniry, J.R., Spaniel, D.A., 1989. The EPIC crop growth model. Trans. Am. Soc. Agric. Eng. 32, 497–511.

World Bank, 2009. Awakening Africa's Sleeping Giant: Prospects for Commercial Agriculture in the Guinea Savannah Zone and Beyond. World Bank and FAO, Washington DC.

Zilberman D., 1998. Agricultural and Environmental Policies: Economics of Production, Technology, Risk, Agriculture and the Environment. The State University of New York - Oswego, NY.

Ziska, L.H., 2003. Evaluation of yield loss in field-grown sorghum from a C3 and C4 weed as a function of increasing atmospheric carbon dioxide. Weed Sci. 51, 914–918.

CHAPTER 5

Modeling Microbehavioral Decisions: Modeling the Whole System Versus the Subsystems

In this second chapter on applications of the microbehavioral econometric methods, the present author sheds a different perspective in interpreting the results from the microbehavioral econometric models presented in the previous chapter. The author compares the microbehavioral model introduced in Chapter 4 with another economic model which has been the precursor of the microbehavioral models (Seo, 2010b). The comparison will yield deeper insights on modeling adaptation behaviors as well as the underlying motives and psychologies that are entailed in adapting to external climate changes.

The harbinger economic methodology was named the Ricardian model and is also often called a hedonic method (Mendelsohn et al., 1994). Since its publication at the American Economic Review more than two decades ago, this methodology has had the most powerful influences on the discussions of global warming. It was a highly innovative publication presented in a provocative manner that argued that the Ricardian model captures the full range of substitution behaviors by farmers in response to climatic shifts (Mendelshon, 2000, 2012; Hanemann, 2000). The paper challenged a conventional wisdom in that it found that the impact of climate change on the US agriculture may be positive, that is, beneficial if a full variety of adaptations are taken into account and climate change turns out to be mild.

In any case, the paper has had the most powerful influences on thinking about global warming and economy. The h-index of a set of papers is defined as the maximum number for which holds that there are h papers each of which is cited at least h times. The h-core is the set of papers that are cited h times or more. A Scopus search on "climate change" or "global warming", limited to "economics, econometrics and finance" yields the list of h-core for climate economics papers. The Ricardian paper tops the all-time list of papers in this area, as of Aug. 2015 (H-core of climate economics. Available at http://economicsofclimate.blogspot.co.uk/2014/08/the-h-core-of-climate-economics.html.).

The purpose of this chapter is to compare the microbehavioral econometric methods introduced in this book with the Ricardian model using the same empirical data. The present author will run the Ricardian analysis in this chapter using the same household survey data used in the previous chapter. For the purpose of comparison, all the aspects of the models will be kept the same such as explanatory variables in the model, functional specifications, seasonal specifications, dependent variables, error assumptions.

By the end of this chapter, the readers will be led to the bottom lines of making economic decisions given external circumstances, risks, and uncertainties. This topic has been the intense focus of behavioral finance and economics for many decades, challenging one of the central tenets of economics (von Neumann and Morgenstern 1947; Fama, 1970; Kahneman and Tversky, 1979; Shiller, 1981, 2003, 2005, 2014). This Chapter shows that psychological and behavioral dimensions will lead to diverging estimates between the Ricardian models and the microbehavioral models. In other words, two models will converge as psychological and behavioral aspects in adaptation decisions become smaller (Seo, 2015b)

5.1 A THEORY OF THE RICARDIAN MODEL FOR CAPTURING ADAPTATION BEHAVIORS

The authors of the Ricardian analysis—Robert Mendelsohn, William Nordhaus, Daigee Shaw—introduced for the first time a full range of adaptations into the analysis of the impact of climate change. Although the subject matter was agriculture, their analysis was the first impact model in any climate change literature with a full range of adaptation behaviors accounted for. The Ricardian model differed starkly from the other models which lacked capacities to model behavioral changes therefore treated them only marginally (IPCC 1990, Adams et al., 1990; Rosenzweig and Parry, 1994).

Before its publication, researchers relied on a "production function approach" in estimating the impact of climate change on agriculture. In this approach, researchers take an underlying production function (eg, of a grain) and estimate impacts of climatic changes by altering one of the input variables such as temperature, precipitation, and carbon dioxide levels. The production function is most often obtained from carefully calibrated crop yield simulation models such as CERES-Maize, CERES-Wheat, or SOYGRO (Jones and Kiniry, 1986; Williams et al., 1989). These studies often predicted severe yield reductions of major grains such as wheat, maize, and rice due to expected global warming (Mendelsohn et al., 1994).

The authors of the Ricardian model pointed out that these agronomic studies have an inherent bias, called the "dumb farmer scenario," because these studies "omit a variety of adaptations that farmers customarily make in response to changing economic and environmental conditions." Adaptations cited in the article were changes in fertilizer application, irrigation, or cultivars; introduction of completely new crops; technological changes; changes in land use from farming to livestock, grasslands, or forestry; conversion to cities, retirement homes, campsites, or many uses of lands for industrial activities. The authors concluded that, with no or little adaptations taken into account, agronomic models will overestimate the damage of global warming on agriculture (Mendelsohn et al., 1994).

The Ricardian model was developed to measure the impact of climate change on agriculture taking into account a full range of adaptations that farmers can make in response to external changes in climate. In the model, a farmer is assumed to maximize the profit from a variety of farming activities, taking climate, soils, and geographic factors as given. S/he would decide on a farm portfolio, a set of production inputs, and a vector of farming practices in order to achieve the highest profit on the given land. Let π_{it} is the profit earned by farm i and year t per unit land, which is expressed as total revenue minus total cost:

$$\pi_{it} = \sum_{j=1}^{J} p_{jt} \cdot y_{itj}(C_{it}, E_{it}, M_{it}) - TC_{it}(C_{it}, E_{it}, M_{it}) \qquad (5.1)$$

where subscript j denotes a crop, y denotes yield of a crop, p denotes market price of a crop, TC denotes total cost, C is a vector of climate variables, E a vector of soils and geographic factors, and M a vector of household and social factors.

Land rent is determined by the net income earned on the land, that is, π_{it}^* where the superscript denotes the maximized value from Eq. 5.1 (Ricardo, 1817). Land value is the capital value of the land, that is, the present value of the stream of net incomes earned in the future on the land. With ρ_t being the discount rate at time t, land value is expressed as follows (Fisher, 1906, 1930):

$$V_i = \int_{t=0}^{\infty} \pi_{it}^* \cdot e^{-\rho_t t} dt. \qquad (5.2)$$

Land value is then expressed as a reduced-form model of exogenous variables (Wooldridge, 2010; Greene, 2011):

$$V_i = f(C_{it}, E_{it}, M_{it}). \tag{5.3}$$

The Ricardian model estimates Eq. 5.3 by specifying a functional form and assuming an error term, which will be explained in the empirical section of this chapter. In estimating this equation, the authors used two weighting methods: crop-revenue weights and crop-land weights. This is because the original Ricardian model was applied to the land value data at the US county level. That is, the land value data did not come from an individual household level. Therefore, there was the need to account for nonspherical error terms due to differences in land sizes of US counties as well as differences in land uses across different counties in the US (Deschenes and Greenstone, 2007). That is, some counties are primarily agricultural counties while others are primarily urban counties.

The impact of a climatic change on agriculture is then estimated as the difference in V_i before and after the change, given all other things remain unchanged:

$$\Delta V_i = V_i(C_1) - V_i(C_0). \tag{5.4}$$

The Ricardian analysis has been applied widely to study agriculture and climate change in different parts of the world: Canada (Reinsborough, 2003), Sri Lanka (Seo et al., 2005; Kurukulasuriya and Ajwad, 2007), Africa (Seo et al., 2009; Deressa and Hassan, 2009; Kala et al., 2012), South America (Seo and Mendelsohn, 2008b), India (Kumar and Parikh, 2001; Sanghi and Mendelsohn, 2008), Mexico (Mendelsohn et al., 2010). China (Wang et al., 2009), and US (Schlenker et al., 2005; Kelly et al., 2005; Masseti and Mendelsohn, 2011).

As Mendelsohn, Nordhaus, and Shaw argued, the Ricardian model can capture changes in land uses from one to another, thereby a full range of possible uses of the lands. This means all farming practices, input combinations, variety improvements, and land uses are captured in the Ricardian analysis (Evenson and Gollin, 2003; World Bank, 2009). In this sense, the Ricardian model and the microbehavioral econometric model described in the previous chapter, that is, the G-MAP model, are identical. That is, a farmer is assumed to choose land uses and all other farming practices in order to maximize the profit from the land as external conditions are altered.

Further, the Ricardian model is apt for capturing microbehavioral decisions across a great array of ecosystems or ecological zones (Adams et al., 1990; Seo 2010c, Seo, 2012a,b, 2014a; Kala et al., 2012). For example, it captures all agro-ecological zones of Africa: humid forest zones, subhumid zones, moist savannah zones, semiarid zones, arid zones, and deserts. In tandem with changes of ecosystems, natural resource activities are varied: grains, vegetables/tubers, tree products, animals.

However, there is one salient feature that differentiates the two models: adaptation strategies are implicit in the Ricardian analysis while adaptation strategies are made explicit in the microbehavioral model. In the microbehavioral model, researchers are enabled to estimate adaptation behaviors directly such as choice of an agricultural and natural resource portfolio and thereby predict the changes in adaptation behaviors as climate conditions are shifted (Seo, 2006; Seo and Mendelsohn, 2008a).

From a policy standpoint, microbehavioral methods such as the G-MAP model add much to the literature in that adaptation strategies can be described, modeled, and predicted based on climate conditions. Empirical results from the microbehavioral models can be fed into an environmental policy platform, for example, on which adaptation strategies are most pertinent to support and how much adaptation strategies can help rural managers in coping with changing conditions.

From a modeling perspective, microbehavioral methods presented throughout this book are inevitably tied to the Ricardian analysis. This is because the former is developed in an endeavor to reveal what is inside the Ricardian analysis. For example, the microbehavioral model introduced in the previous chapter contains the three agricultural portfolios: a specialized crop system, a specialized livestock system, and a mixed crops-livestock system. In the Ricardian model, these portfolios are implicitly included, not explicitly, as if in a black box of an airplane. We would never know what is inside the black box until the plane is crashed and should be opened.

Will the two methods lead to the same conclusion in terms of the final consequence of a change in an external condition? Put differently, will the two methods result in the same damage estimate from climate change? The analyses of this chapter will provide some answers to this question empirically. The present author will put together the results from the Ricardian model and the results from the microbehavioral model applied to the same data using same specifications and assumptions applied to the two models. All the parameters of the models will be kept the same across the two models.

5.2 DATA AND DESCRIPTIVE STATISTICS

For the purpose of a direct comparison of the two methodologies, the same data used in the previous chapter for the application of the microbehavioral econometric methods are used in this Chapter for the application of the Ricardian analysis. A brief summary of the data and their sources, though, would be warranted in the particular contexts of the application of the Ricardian model.

Unlike the seminal Ricardian paper which relied on county-level data in the single country, that is, the US, the data this Chapter utilizes is household data drawn from the seven South American countries: some of them are Andean region countries while the others are Southern Cone countries (Seo and Mendelsohn, 2008b). Reported activities and values by the rural households are for the time period covering from July 2003 to June 2004. A group of scientists from each country who belong to one of the national agricultural centers conducted interviews with the farmers.

As explained in the previous chapter, climate data are a set of seasonal climate normals constructed from the high resolution climatology dataset constructed by the Climate Research Unit (CRU) at a 10 arc-minute resolution based on more than 16,000 weather stations in the world (New et al., 2002; Mendelsohn et al., 2007; Seo, 2013a). The 10 arc-minute resolution climatology divides an one degree grid cell into 36 smaller grid cells. The present author constructed, from monthly climate normals, seasonal temperature normals and precipitation normals. To account for opposite Hemispheres, summer and winter months are defined differently in the two Hemispheres. Seasonal Coefficients of Variation in Precipitation (CVP) capture the degree of climate risk, that is, precipitation variability from year to year for a 30-year period (Ropelewski and Halpert, 1987; Hansen et al., 2012; NRC, 2013; Seo, 2012c, 2013b, 2014b).

Simulations of the future climate changes are based on the two climate models: the GISS (Goddard Institute for Space Studies) ModelE-R model and the UKMO (United Kingdom Meteorology Office) HadCM3 (Hadley Coupled Model version 3) model (Gordon et al., 2000; Schmidt et al., 2005). For both models, future projections with an A2 emissions scenario by the middle of this century by the Intergovernmental Panel on Climate Change are employed (Nakicenovic et al., 2000).

Soils and geography data are from the Food and Agriculture Organization (FAO) of the United Nations (FAO, 2003). This chapter uses dominant soil types, soil texture, and terrain topography which are provided by the FAO data set at the grid cell level with the size of 0.5 degree longitude by 0.5 degree latitude. High resolution elevation data, aggregated at 7.5 arc-second pixels, are obtained from the Global Multi-resolution Terrain Elevation Data 2010 (GMTED2010) data set developed by the United States Geological Survey (USGS) and the National Geospatial-Intelligence Agency (NGA) (Danielson and Gesch, 2011).

Descriptive statistics of the variables used in this chapter for the Ricardian model are summarized in Table 5.1. Of the total sampled households, Brazilian sample accounts for 30%, Argentina and Uruguay 22%, Chile 17%,

Table 5.1 Descriptive statistics of the sample

Variables	Mean	Standard deviation
Summer temperature (°C)	21.99	5.11
Summer precipitation (mm)	125.82	90.70
Winter temperature (°C)	16.58	7.68
Winter precipitation (mm)	78.28	72.57
Summer CVP (%)	77.49	50.06
Winter CVP (%)	96.51	48.58
Phaeozems (0/1)	0.07	0.25
Lithosols (0/1)	0.13	0.33
Fluvisols (0/1)	0.07	0.25
Luvisols (0/1)	0.16	0.36
Andosols (0/1)	0.09	0.28
Elevation (meter above sea level)	642.80	724.97
Flat (0/1)	0.08	0.28
Clay (0/1)	0.17	0.38
Household size (number of family members)	4.72	2.30
Age (n)	52.30	12.33
Education (number of years in schooling)	8.78	5.01
Computer (0/1)	0.24	0.42
Land privately owned (0/1)	0.65	0.48
Primary occupation is farming (0/1)	0.80	0.40
Argentina and Uruguay (0/1)	0.22	
Chile (0/1)	0.17	
Venezuela (0/1)	0.08	
Ecuador (0/1)	0.09	
Colombia (0/1)	0.14	
Land value ($/ha)	1840.31	

Ecuador 9%, Colombia 14%, and Venezuela 8%. In the whole sample, land value per hectare of land was, on average, 1,840 US$.

Summer temperature is about 22°C with standard deviation of 5.1 degrees. Winter temperature is on average 16.6°C. Summer precipitation is on average 126 mm per month while winter precipitation is on average 78 mm per month. Note that South America's precipitation is far larger than that of Sub-Saharan countries while average temperature is also far colder in South America than in Sub-Sahara (Seo, 2012c). Precipitation variation across the continent in the sampled locations is very high in both summer and winter.

Summer CVP is 77%, on average, while winter CVP is 97%, on average. This means that precipitation fluctuation from year to year is larger in the winter season than in the summer season. In South and Central America, yearly precipitation fluctuation is by and large determined by El Nino Southern Oscillation (ENSO) that alternates often multidecadally (Ropelewski and Halpert, 1987; Curtis et al., 2001). In many parts of the world, an El Nino/La Nina cycle is a primary cause of a multidecadal swing in rainfall amount (Seo, 2014b, c).

In many other places of the world, however, climate risk is caused by other events. In Sub-Saharan Africa, a multi-decadal fluctuation in yearly precipitation is associated with the Atlantic Multi-decadal Oscillation (AMO) (Janowiak, 1988; Hulme et al., 2001; Shanahan et al., 2009; Seo, 2012c). In India and Bangladesh, the monsoon climate dominates the weather risk (IPCC, 2014; Seo, 2016).

The means and standard deviations of the dominant soil types which are defined as dummy variables are presented: Phaeozems, Lithosols, Fluvisols, Luvisols, and Andosols. Luvisols is the dominant soil type for 16% of the farms in the sample, Lithosols for 13%, Andosols for 9%, Phaeozems for 7%, and Fluvisols for 7%. Other geographic variables are elevation, clay soils, and flat terrain. Farms are located on average at 642 m above sea level. 8% of the farms are located on flat terrain while 17% of the farms on clay soils.

Household and farmer characteristics of the sample are described in Table 5.1. About 65% of the farmers in the sample reported that they privately own their lands. Farming is a primary occupation for 80% of the farms in the sample. About a quarter of the farms has at least one computer. Each household has about 5 members in the family. Average age of the farmers is 52 years and an average farmer has about 9 years of schooling, that is, completion of a middle school.

5.3 EMPIRICAL RESULTS FROM THE RICARDIAN ANALYSIS

The present author applies a Ricardian model explained in Section 5.1 to the South American household data, the results of which are presented in Table 5.2 and 5.4. The dependent variable is land value per hectare

Table 5.2 A Ricardian model applied to South America

Explanatory variables	Parameter estimate	Heteroscedasticity consistent P-value
Intercept	−875.7	0.44
Summer temperature (°C)	566.2	<.0001
Summer temperature squared	−12.7	<.0001
Summer precipitation (mm/month)	4.71	0.08
Summer precipitation squared	−0.011	0.08
Winter temperature (°C)	−107.61	0.04
Winter temperature squared	−0.98	0.46
Winter precipitation (mm/month)	−4.47	0.16
Winter precipitation squared	0.006	0.44
Summer Coefficient of Variation in Precipitation (%)	6.8	0.01
Winter Coefficient of Variation in Precipitation (%)	−6.6	0.001
Phaeozems (dummy)	649.9	0.01
Lithosols (dummy)	533.4	0.02
Fluvisols (dummy)	242.3	0.37
Luvisols (dummy)	−487.4	0.003
Andosols (dummy)	123.9	0.68
Elevation (meter above sea level)	0.49	0.000
Flat terrain (dummy)	36.5	0.81
Clay soils (dummy)	−629.1	0.001
Household size (number of family members)	−7.5	0.09
Age (number)	−8.9	0.46
Education (number of years in schooling)	187.9	0.14
Computer (dummy)	25.9	0.27
Privately owned (dummy)	−99.4	0.50
Primary occupation (dummy)	−2193.4	<.0001
Argentina and Uruguay (dummy)	−3176.8	<.0001
Chile (dummy)	−245.4	0.25
Venezuela (dummy)	−349.12	0.17
Ecuador (dummy)	1003.1	0.000

Summary Statistics

Number of Observations = 1920, Adj Rsq = 0.17

of farmland. Summer and winter season climate normals variables, both temperature and precipitation, are entered in a quadratic functional form, following the norm in the Ricardian tradition (Sanghi and Mendelsohn, 2008; Seo and Mendelsohn, 2008b). Summer and winter CVPs are entered linearly into the model. Other explanatory variables are soils, geographic variables, household characteristics, and country dummies.

The Ricardian model in Table 5.2 has the following form and assumptions:

$$V_i = \alpha + \sum_{k=\text{seasons}} (\beta_{1k} C_{ik} + \beta_{2k} C_{ik}^2) + \sum_{k=\text{seasons}} \gamma_k CVP_{ik}$$
$$+ \sum_j \kappa_j G_{ij} + \sum_l \nu_l H_{il} + \varepsilon_i \tag{5.5}$$

where all the variables are as defined in the theory section and the last term on the right is the error term which is assumed to be independently and identically Normal distributed.

The parameters of Eq. 5.5 are estimated conventionally by one of the extreme estimators such as an Ordinary Least Squares regression or a Generalized Methods of Moments (Greene, 2011). By using the White estimator, heteroscedastic error variances can be accommodated into the model (White, 1980; Johnston and DiNardo, 1997).

The estimated model using the Least Squares method in Table 5.2 has Adjusted Rsq of 0.17. The F-test of model significance strongly rejects the hypothesis that the model is not significant. Estimates of all climate normals and climate risk normals are significant at least at 10% level of significance except for winter precipitation variables according to the heteroscedasticity-consistent standard errors and P-values.

Estimates of the summer temperature normals variables show a hill-shaped response, indicating that a "very" high summer temperature is harmful to agriculture. The same is true of the winter temperature normals variables. Estimates of summer precipitation normals variables also show a hill-shaped response, indicating that a "very" high rainfall, which can lead, among other things, to the problem of livestock diseases (Ford and Katondo, 1977; Fox et al., 2012), is not good for agricultural activities as a whole. This relationship does not hold for winter precipitation.

Estimates of the climate risk normals reveal noticeable patterns. An increase in summer Coefficient of Variation in Precipitation (CVP) is beneficial for agriculture. In other words, land value is higher in the areas where summer CVP is higher. This is reversed in winter CVP. That is, land value is lower in the areas where winter CVP is higher. This may mean that farmers find it harder to adapt to a large winter rainfall swing than a large summer rainfall swing. That is, the combination of cold temperature and rainfall fluctuation is harder to cope with.

Differences in seasonal CVPs across South America are determined by and large by alternations of El Nino and La Nina that originate in the Northeast Pacific Ocean (Ropelewski and Halpert, 1987; Seo, 2014b). However, seasonal CVPs, that is, climate risk normals, are much lower in South America in comparison with Sub-Sahara (Seo, 2012c).

In the fertile black organic soils such as Phaeozems and the shallow soils in steeply-sloped locations such as Lithosols, land value is higher per unit land while it is lower in Luvisols, washed-out soils most likely found on flood-prone zones (Driessen et al., 2001). A farmland on higher altitude has a higher land value per hectare of land than a farmland on lower altitude. In clay soils, land value is lower than elsewhere, that is, nonclay soils. Soils and geographic factors explain a large portion of the variation of land value across the continent. For example, land value in Phaeozems soils is on average 650 US$ higher than land value in the other soils, per hectare of farmland. Land value in Luvisols soils in on average 430 US$ lower than land value in the other soils, per hectare of farmland.

Among the household-related explanatory variables, household size and a primary occupation are significant factors according to the model in Table 5.2 while age, education, computer ownership, gender, private ownership are not significant. The larger the number of family members, the lower the land value per hectare of land. Land value is significantly lower in a farm where primary occupation is reported to be farming. Households with nonfarming income tend to be richer, therefore they seem to own a higher quality land (Lanjouw and Lanjouw, 2001).

Of the country dummies, Argentina/Uruguay and Ecuador estimates are highly significant. Against the base case of the Brazilian farmland, land value of Argentina/Uruguay is much lower, on average. On the other hand, the land value of Ecuador is much higher, on average. This may be attributed to high reliance on specialty crop farming in Ecuador.

Based on the estimated parameters, the present author calculates the marginal effects of climatic changes in Table 5.3. From the baseline land value of 1838 $/ha, if the temperature is increased by 1°C across the seasons, land value falls by 147$/ha of land, an 8% decrease in the land value. According to this model, the impact of temperature increase is quite large on agriculture, confirming the literature of climate change and agriculture

Table 5.3 Marginal effects of climate changes from the Ricardian Model

	Scenarios	Mean change	% change	Lower 95% confidence interval	Upper 95% confidence interval
Ricardian Model	Baseline ($/ha)	1838.1			
	Change due to + 1°C temperature increase	−147.2	−8.0%	−153.5	−140.9
	Change due to + 1% precipitation increase	−1.5	−0.08%	−1.6	−1.3
Ricardian Model with spatial resampling	Baseline ($/ha)	2184.4			
	Change due to + 1°C temperature increase	−157.2	−7.2%	−161.3	−153.2
	Change due to + 1% precipitation increase	−1.9	−0.09%	−2.4	−1.3

(Reilly et al., 1996; Gitay et al., 2001; Easterling et al., 2007; Baethgen, 1997; Magrin et al., 1997, 2005, 2007).

A one percent increase in precipitation across the seasons is predicted to decrease the land value by 1.5 $/ha, a decrease of 0.08% from the baseline. Put differently, a 10% increase in precipitation would decrease the land value by only 0.8%. Precipitation effects are minute in contrast to the agronomic literature which is abundant with the evidence of severe yield losses in dry seasons and large yield gains during high rainfall seasons (Reilly et al., 1996; Rosenzweig et al., 2001).

In the seminal Ricardian paper, US county-level land values are regressed against climate normals and other variables. To account for county-level differences, the authors introduced two weighting schemes: crop-revenue weights and cropland weights (Mendelsohn et al., 1994). These weights address the fact that some counties are major food baskets of the country while other counties are suburban areas where farming is marginal but can be directed to high-value specialty crops. These weighting schemes were debated and adopted selectively by the subsequent authors in the literature (Schlenker et al., 2005; Deschenes and Greenstone, 2007, 2012; Fisher et al., 2012).

The weighting schemes introduced by the Ricardian paper are seen as an approach to account for spatial characteristics of the spatial data. Being county-level data, the authors cared little of spatial correlation of spatial data, with Schlenker and coauthors being the exception (Schlenker et al., 2006). In the microlevel data such as the one used in this chapter and throughout this book, spatial correlations of microlevel data, for example, land values, must be addressed (Anselin, 1988).

Spatial correlations in the microbehavioral data arise from spatial spillover or neighborhood effects (Case, 1992; Anselin, 1998). Neighborhood effects can be present in adoption of a new technology, or a new practice, or a new variety of crop because a neighborhood or a village may have a unique history or a value system that affects individuals' decisions within the neighborhood (Case, 1992). Spatial spillover can be present in such cases as development of a new technique or new information that spread slowly from the source to the other areas in a concentric manner (Anselin, 1998).

To capture spatial spillover and neighborhood effects, the present author run a Ricardian model with spatial resampling based on defined neighborhoods in Table 5.4. Spatial resampling is done as follows (Seo, 2011):

Step 1: Neighborhoods are defined. In the current analysis, neighborhoods are defined at the level of 2nd administrative division, that is, districts of a country. The first administrative division is a province in the country.

Step 2: One household is selected from each defined neighborhood by random sampling, which is repeated for all defined neighborhoods.

Step 3: A Ricardian regression shown in Table 5.2 is run for the resampled data.

Step 4: Based on the estimated regression parameters, marginal effects are calculated in the same manner as Table 5.3.

Step 5: The procedures in steps 2, 3, and 4 are repeated a large number of times.

Step 6: Spatial parameter estimates are calculated as averages of the Ricardian parameter estimates. Standard error estimates of the parameters are obtained from the parameter estimates from the bootstrap runs (Efron, 1979, 1981). Marginal effects are calculated as averages of the Ricardian marginal effects from the resample data.

In Table 5.4, a Ricardian model with spatial resampling based on defined neighborhoods is presented. There are 481 defined neighborhoods and 200

Table 5.4 A spatial Ricardian Model with spatial resampling based on defined neighborhoods

Variables	Mean	Std
Intercept	1140.51	1454.59
Summer temperature (°C)	482.80	134.89
Summer temperature squared	−9.43	3.52
Summer precipitation (mm/month)	12.75	3.34
Summer precipitation squared	−0.03	0.01
Winter temperature (°C)	−178.67	58.86
Winter temperature squared	−1.12	1.43
Winter precipitation (mm/month)	−7.01	3.16
Winter precipitation squared	0.002	0.01
Summer Coefficient of Variation in Precipitation (%)	5.79	3.56
Winter Coefficient of Variation in Precipitation (%)	−10.30	2.10
Phaeozems (dummy)	954.76	217.49
Lithosols (dummy)	601.10	262.56
Fluvisols (dummy)	496.04	304.00
Luvisols (dummy)	376.92	196.52
Andosols (dummy)	185.44	333.98
Elevation (meter above sea level)	0.32	0.11
Flat terrain (dummy)	628.04	118.02
Clay soils (dummy)	−795.41	194.84
Household size (number of family members)	0.06	30.13
Age (number)	−13.37	5.64
Education (number of years in schooling)	−24.49	18.27
Computer (dummy)	515.40	197.54
Privately owned (dummy)	−396.51	227.18
Primary occupation (dummy)	−2761.62	264.85
Argentina and Uruguay (dummy)	−2616.53	406.81
Chile (dummy)	487.43	304.92
Venezuela (dummy)	94.43	279.84
Ecuador (dummy)	1740.06	246.11
Summary Statistics		

Number of defined neighborhoods = 481, Number of bootstrap regressions = 200

bootstrap samples from each of which the Ricardian regression is run. The means and standard deviations of the parameters calculated from the 200 Ricardian regressions are presented.

Commensurate with the Ricardian model regression in Table 5.2, land value has a hill shaped response to summer temperature as well as to winter temperature. Land value has a hill shaped response to summer precipitation, but a U shaped response to winter precipitation. Summer CVP has a positive parameter estimate while winter CVP has a negative parameter estimate. The latter is significant at the 5% level.

Limited to the significant parameter estimates based on the standard error estimates, land value is higher in soils Phaeozems or Lithosols. The higher the elevation, the higher is the land value. Land value is higher in flat terrains. Land value is much lower in clay soils.

From the household characteristics, age and primary occupation are significant estimates. The older the head of the farm, the lower is the land value. The land value is lower in the farm where primary occupation is farming.

Against the base case of Brazil, Argentina/Uruguay farms have lower land values, on average. The farms in Ecuador have higher land values on average against the Brazilian farms. Land values in the other countries are not significantly different from the Brazil's.

The effects of marginal climate changes are calculated from the spatial Ricardian model's parameter estimates, which are shown at the bottom panel of Table 5.3. The baseline land value is slightly higher in the spatial Ricardian model. The change in land value from an 1°C increase in temperature is the decrease by 7.2% in land value, which is slightly smaller than the marginal temperature effect from the Ricardian model.

The change in land value from the spatial Ricardian model due to an 1% increase in precipitation is 0.09% loss in the land value, which is close to the estimated marginal effect from the Ricardian model.

5.4 FUTURE CLIMATE SIMULATIONS FROM THE RICARDIAN MODEL

As described in detail in the previous chapter, the impacts of future climatic changes are calculated using the estimated Ricardian and spatial Ricardian relationships in Tables 4.2, 4.4 by assuming a number of climate scenarios. To directly compare the results from this chapter with those from the microbehavioral models introduced in Chapter 4, the present author relies on the same climate models: The UKMO (United Kingdom Meteorology Office) HadCM3 (Hadley Coupled Model version 3) model and the GISS (Goddard Institute for Space Studies) E-R (ModelE-R) model (Gordon et al., 2000; Schmidt et al., 2005). Again, for both models, A2 storyline is applied in order to capture a high emissions growth scenario (Nakicenovic et al., 2000). The time frame for future simulations is also maintained from the previous chapter to the middle of this century, about 50 years from now.

The two climate models were already explained in the previous chapter. To briefly sum up, the UKMO model predicts about 2.4°C increase in temperature normals. The predicted temperature change is slightly larger in the summer season than in the winter season. The UKMO model predicts about 5 mm decrease in seasonal precipitations, both summer and winter.

The GISS model forecasts a slightly smaller degree of temperature increase than the UKMO model. Summer temperature is predicted to increase by about 2°C and winter temperature to increase by 1.6°C. Again, the changes in summer season climate variables are larger than the changes in winter season climate variables. The GISS model predicts an increase in summer precipitation by 6 mm per month while no major changes are predicted for winter precipitation.

Given these climate models' predictions, the impacts on land value are calculated in Table 5.5 by altering values of climate variables accordingly. Based on the parameter estimates from the Ricardian model presented in Table 5.2, land value is predicted to fall by 22.2% if the UKMO scenario comes to pass. If the GISS is materialized, the impact on land value amounts to 14.2% decrease.

The decrease in the land value under the GISS scenario is smaller because of a smaller temperature increase and a rainfall increase during the summer growing season predicted by this scenario.

Table 5.5 The impacts on land value under climate scenarios by the middle of this century

	Ricardian Model		Spatial Ricardian Model	
	Absolute change	% change	Absolute change	% change
Baseline land value ($/ha)	1838.14		2194.38	
Change due to ΔUKMO HadCM3 Scenario ($/ha)	−408.77	−22.2%	−446.94	−20.4%
95% Confidence Interval	(−429.3, −388.3)		(−459.2, −434.7)	
Change due to ΔGISS ER Scenario ($/ha)	−261.28	−14.2%	−232.48	−10.6%
95% Confidence Interval	(−274.6, −248.0)		(−242.4, −222.6)	

If instead the parameter estimates from the Ricardian model with spatial resampling are used for climate simulations, land value is predicted to fall by 20.4% under the UKMO scenario but to fall only by 10.6% under the GISS scenario. Again, the damage from climate change is much smaller under the GISS scenario, only half of the damage expected under the UKMO scenario.

A comparison of the Ricardian model's damage predictions with the spatial Ricardian model's damage predictions reveals two novel findings. First, the predicted damages are smaller in the spatial Ricardian model. Expected damage is 2% smaller under the UKMO scenario and 4% smaller under the GISS scenario. Second, the gap between the Ricardian damage estimate and the spatial Ricardian damage estimate becomes larger in the GISS scenario, a milder climate change scenario.

This means that spatial correlation, more specifically spatial neighborhood effects, accounts for some of the damage estimate in the Ricardian model. That is, it can be ascribed to uncorrected spatial correlation rather than to the effect of climate. When spatial neighborhood effects are controlled, predicted damages given climate model predictions would be smaller (Seo, 2010b, 2015b).

5.5 RICARDIAN MODEL VERSUS THE MICROBEHAVIORAL MODEL

Having examined the empirical results from the microbehavioral models. that is, the G-MAP model, in the previous chapter and the empirical results from the Ricardian model in the present chapter, we are in a vantage point to appreciate the two modeling approaches and evaluate them comparatively (Seo, 2015b).

The two methodologies are founded on the same principle of individual behaviors, namely, a long-term profit maximization motive of an individual manager. Both methodologies are capable of capturing the full range of adaptation measures that individuals customarily take to cope with climatic changes.

The defining feature that distinguishes the two behaviorally based methodologies is that choices of adaptation strategies are explicitly modeled in the microbehavioral models while they are implicitly included into the model, that is, hidden in the model, in the Ricardian approach. Consequently, the microbehavioral modelers can estimate portfolio-specific response functions while the Ricardian modelers can provide a single overarching response function to changes in the climate system.

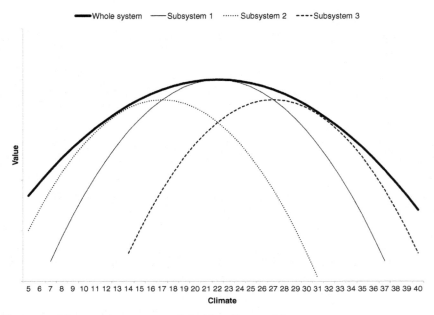

Figure 5.1 *The complex structure of the Ricardian model.*

Note that the microbehavioral models, for example, the G–MAP model, emerged quite naturally from the solid foundation laid by the Ricardian model (Seo and Mendelsohn, 2008b). The Ricardian modelers customarily assumed that there are underlying response functions that support the overarching response function. The microbehavioral models were developed in the process of uncovering these underlying response functions explicitly (Seo, 2006, 2010b).

This point is illustrated in Fig. 5.1. In the figure, there is one overarching response function which is supported by the three underlying response functions. The Ricardian model estimates the "envelop" response function which traces the best profit outcomes given the climate conditions.

The microbehavioral model is developed to make explicit the underlying subsystem response functions. Each subsystem has its own response function. But, the peak climate upon which each subsystem reaches the highest value differs from one subsystem to another. In the lower end climate zone, the value of subsystem is higher than those from the others. As the climate variable increases, the value of subsystem 1 is dominated by the value of subsystem 2 at some climate point which again is dominated by the value of subsystem 3 at some climate point. This means an individual manager will switch from subsystem 1 to subsystem 2 at one climate point, and then from subsystem 2 to subsystem 3 at another climate point.

The previous chapter showed the empirical results from the microbehavioral model on choices of agricultural and natural resource systems by individual managers. Individuals' choices are explained by an empirical model, that is, a spatial Multinomial Logit model, given the climate and natural conditions. Changes in the choices owing to climatic changes are then predicted based on the empirical model estimates and a set of climate models. These choices and changes in these choices are in the Ricardian model, but only in an implicit way.

The microbehavioral models have the capacity to reveal varied sensitivities of natural resource systems to climate factors while the Ricardian model does not. The land value function for each system of natural resources is estimated separately but in an unbiased way due to selectivity. In the microbehavioral model shown in the previous chapter, there were three agricultural and natural resource systems, for each of which the impacts of climatic change are presented. Again, the conditional land value functions are what is inside the black box in the Ricardian model.

Both the Ricardian model and the microbehavioral model such as the G-MAP model are capable of measuring the quantitative estimate of the impact of climate change on agriculture. The damage estimate from the Ricardian model is shown above in Table 5.5 while the damage estimate from the G-MAP model is shown in Table 4.11 in Chapter 4. Do the two methods come to the same conclusion with regards to the expected damage from global warming?

A closer examination of Table 5.5 in the current chapter and Table 4.11 in the previous chapter reveals that the two methodologies result in significantly different damage estimates, despite that the same data and the same climate models were employed for both models. The spatial Ricardian model with neighborhood effects predicts an 11% reduction in land value, given the GISS model. By contrast, the microbehavioral model predicts only a 0.7% reduction in land value, given the GISS model. Under the UKMO model, the spatial Ricardian model predicts a 20.2% loss in the land value while the microbehavioral model predicts a 3.4% loss in the land value.

The gap between the estimates from the two modeling approaches remains significant subject to a number of sensitivity analyses by the present author. In other words, the microbehavioral model such as the G-MAP model consistently predicts a smaller damage than the Ricardian model.

The critical question that this chapter poses is why the two modeling approaches yield different damage estimates despite the same behavioral assumptions, model specifications, and empirical data (Seo, 2015b). It is an important empirical question for applied statisticians and econometricians, but also a highly policy relevant question to ask why the microbehavioral model underpredicts the damage, or equivalently why the Ricardian model always overpredicts the damage from global warming.

The primary reason that the impact estimates from the two methods diverge lies in behavioral and psychological aspects of an individual's decisions as well as behavioral assumptions of the Ricardian model (Kahneman and Tversky, 1979; Shiller, 2003). While the microbehavioral models such as the G-MAP estimate choice decisions explicitly, choices and changes in choices are assumed in the Ricardian model. The latter assumes that an agricultural and natural resource portfolio in one climate regime can be transformed efficiently into another portfolio in another climate regime by adjustments of inputs, outputs, and numerous practices of farm productions if climate were to be shifted from one regime to another.

Let's consider the system of crops-only. In this system, there are a large number of possible portfolios a farmer can choose from. For example, a farmer may choose a maize-only portfolio given the climate, soils, and other conditions. Let's say that s/he transforms the maize-only system into a millet-only portfolio because of the change in a climate regime. As assumed in the Ricardian model, the farmer will find the transformation necessary and feasible and make the actual transition. There is little transformation cost involved because the array of inputs, outputs, and farm practices are by and large identical in the two distinct portfolios.

Now, let's consider the system of maize-only. But, this time a farmer decides to switch from a maize-only portfolio to a sheep-only portfolio. In this transformation, the farmer will be more reluctant to make it because the inputs, outputs, numerous practices, and markets to sell are mostly distinct in the two systems. The farmer will not make the transition due to psychological and behavioral reasons, for example, s/he is not familiar with the new system. Secondly, there is large sunk cost involved in the transition. That is, new facilities, managements, marketing routes should be all newly employed.

In the second type of transformation, a transformation will still take place as the Ricardian model implies. However, the rate and speed of transformation will likely diverge from the rate and speed of transformation assumed in the Ricardian model. The microbehavioral model, on the other hand, directly estimates adoptions of portfolios by the farmers, therefore can correctly approximate the transformation process.

If there is large cost, psychological cost as well as economic cost, required for the transformation, an actual transition from one portfolio to another will take place in a slower pace than the rates implied in the Ricardian model. The damage from the Ricardian model will turn out to be larger than that from the microbehavioral model due to the faster rates of adaptation transitions than those that are actually needed and took place.

From another perspective, a transformation of natural resource portfolio into another portfolio which is very different will entail a large capital cost. In the today's agricultural and natural resource portfolios that rural managers hold, this cost is sunk cost. Sunk cost is different from the concept of transition cost (Kelly et al., 2005). The latter is incurred mostly after sunk cost is run out. That is, the sunk cost was incurred at the point of transition and is not any more important in today's decisions of a rural manager. He makes yearly decisions to maximize the expected profit, given the sunk cost (von Neumann and Morgenstern 1947). The sunk cost turns out to be pivotal to an individual manager only at the time of deciding whether to enter into a quite new enterprise (Kahnemann and Tversky, 1984). If sunk cost is large and uncertainty is high, especially a small-scale farmer will behave in a risk-averse manner, that is, cautious of entering into a new enterprise (Arrow, 1971; Zilberman 1998).

With the sunk cost factored in, the value of the land at time t can be defined as the present value of the stream of future net incomes and sunk cost with time-varying discount rates:

$$V_t = \sum_{k=0}^{\infty} \frac{\pi_{t+k} + \Omega_{t+s}}{(1+\rho_{t+k})^k},$$
(5.6)

where π_{t+k} is net income at time $t+s$, Ω_{t+s} is sunk cost at time $t+s$ at which a transformation of system occurs and ρ_{t+k} is the discount rate from time t to time $t+k$.

If the transformation from one enterprise to another is customarily expected by a rural manager and the nature of the transformation is well understood by her/him, s/he can expect the sunk cost correctly. Market forces interact to set the sunk cost through demand and supply reactions. For example, a farm is accustomed to making changes in a variety of farm practices across major grains, that is, within the crops-only system.

If, however, a rural manager is not accustomed to making a specific change and the nature of the enterprise into which s/he is entering is not comprehended well, sunk cost will tend to be large and s/he will not be able to correctly anticipate the sunk cost through the market. This is the case for the transition of a crops-only system to a livestock-only system (Hahn, 1981; Hahn et al., 2009; Mader and Davis, 2004; Mader et al., 2009; Nin et al., 2007). In this case, the realized land value would drift away from the true land value in Eq. 5.6:

$$V_{t,observed} \approx V_{t,true}. \tag{5.7}$$

The microbehavioral econometric models such as the G-MAP, the problem of sunk cost is dealt with effectively by modeling behavioral changes explicitly. Since the conditional land value function is estimated for the crops-only system only, there is no problem of capital sunk cost since the estimated function traces only a large variety of crop portfolios. The same is true of the livestock-only system or the mixed system.

Further, sunk cost is fully embedded in the individual's decision to switch from one enterprise to another. That is, it is realized through switching behaviors which are observed and used as a basis for the microbehavioral models. Transitions of enterprises are fully captured by the G-MAP model.

The primary reason that the damage estimate of the Ricardian model diverges from that of the microbehavioral models is because the microbehavioral models can pinpoint the efficient transition times from one enterprise to another and at the same time account directly for the sunk costs of transitions.

Let's say both the Ricardian modeler and the microbehavioral modeler are examining the whole system in which a large number of distinct subsystems and the transition from one subsystem to another incurs large sunk cost. The Ricardian model yields a substantially larger damage estimate than the G-MAP model owing to sunk costs. If sunk cost of transformation from one subsystem to another is negligible and well understood by managers, the damage estimates from the two methodologies will converge. The larger the sunk costs, the larger the gap between the two estimates.

5.6 ADDITIONAL INSIGHTS AND UPSHOTS

This chapter has dealt with an import issue in econometric models: the whole system and the subsystems. In the econometrics literature, this topic is somewhat related with the structural breaks, although not the same, but largely overlooked in the literature (Chow, 1960; Andrews, 1993, 2003; Johnston and DiNardo, 1997). This chapter provides an insightful analysis on the topic by way of the microbehavioral modeling framework outlined in Chapter 2. The analysis in this chapter is applicable to any kind of a set of distinct systems.

The analyses in this chapter utilized the two well-established empirical models in applied economics: the Ricardian model and the microbehavioral econometric model. In the applied literature, the microbehavioral models, that is, the G–MAP model, stemmed from the foundation of the Ricardian analysis in the literature on climate change (Mendelsohn et al., 1994; Seo and Mendelsohn, 2008a, Seo, 2010a,b). The former emerged in the middle of contentious debates around the Ricardian model in the process of resolving the debates (Seo, 2015a).

Both methodologies are founded upon the same economic rationale of an individual who makes decisions to maximize the profit in a long-term horizon. In the microbehavioral models, choice decisions are explicitly modeled based upon actual observed decisions obtained from surveys (McFadden, 1974). Then, the conditional land value function is estimated separately for each of the chosen system after correcting for selection biases (Heckman 1979; Dubin and McFadden, 1984; Bourguignon et al., 2004). These statistical procedures make it possible for a modeler to control sunk costs and account for sunk costs.

The direct comparison of the results from the Ricardian model in this chapter with the results from the G–MAP model in the previous chapter reveals that the two methodologies result in significantly different damage estimates from climate change. For example, the spatial Ricardian model with neighborhood effects results in 11% loss of land value if the GISS scenario comes to be realized, but the microbehavioral model results in less than 1% loss of land value under the same model.

The sunk costs of transformations of systems, that is, adaptations, are what differentiate the two models in terms of damage estimates. The larger the sunk costs, the larger the gap between the Ricardian model damage estimate and the G–MAP model damage estimate. The smaller the sunk costs, the smaller the gap between the two estimates. The two estimates will converge when sunk costs become negligible.

The problem of sunk cost is pervasive in the econometric studies of economic activities beyond the literature on the analysis of the impact of climate change on agriculture. Agroeconomic studies based on crop simulation models cannot resolve the problems of sunk costs in farmers' behaviors

(Adams et al., 1990; Rosenzweig and Parry, 1994; Magrin et al., 1997; Parry et al., 2004; Butt et al., 2005). Econometric studies that focused on a specific grain of major importance to a national economy are not generally concerned about the sunk costs which only matter in the long-term management of resources (Auffhammer et al. 2006; Schlenker and Roberts, 2009; Welch et al., 2010; Lobell et al., 2011). Agronomic experiments or the FACE (Free Air Carbon Enrichment) experiments are not concerned about the sunk cost as these experiments are not keen to modeling changes of anthropogenic behaviors, that is, adaptation behaviors (Ainsworth and Long, 2005; Tubiello and Ewert, 2002; Tubiello et al., 2007). Notwithstanding, when it comes to modeling, planning and building adaptation strategies, sunk cost is a vital element.

Exercises

1. From Eq. 5.5 in this chapter, define the two weighting schemes used in the Ricardian method: cropland weight and crop-revenue weight. Discuss the strengths and weaknesses of each weighting scheme in comparison to the other. Rewrite Eq. 5.5 by embedding the weighting schemes into the equation. From the rewritten equations, write down the vector formulas for the weighted OLS estimates of the climate parameters.

2. Write down the formula for land value assuming that the land bound by a contract and a government regulation must be used for the current use in the future without changes in it. Write down the formula for land value again assuming that the land should be converted from the current use to an alternative use in the $(i)th$ period from now, and again to another use in the $(i + j)th$ period from now onward. For the land value formulas, define carefully a number of different discount rates. Also for the land value formulas, make use of three different sizes of sunk cost: negligible, substantial, and huge.

REFERENCES

Adams, R., Rosenzweig, C., Peart, R.M., Ritchie, J.T., McCarl, B.A., Glyer, J.D., Curry, R.B., Jones, J.W., Boote, K.J., Allen, L.H., 1990. Global climate change and US agriculture. Nature 345, 219–224.

Ainsworth, E.A., Long, S.P., 2005. What have we learned from 15 years of free-air CO_2 enrichment (FACE)? A meta-analytic review of the responses of photosynthesis, canopy properties and plant production to rising CO_2. New Phytol. 165, 351–371.

Andrews, D., 1993. Tests for parameter instability and structural change with unknown change point. Econometrica 61 (4), 821–856.

Andrews, D., 2003. Tests for parameter instability and structural change with unknown change point: a corrigendum. Econometrica 71 (1), 395–397.

Anselin, L., 1988. Spatial econometrics: methods and models. Kluwer Academic Publishers, Dordrecht.

Anselin, L., 1998. Spatial econometrics. Bruton Center, University of Texas at Dallas. Dallas, Texas.

Arrow, K.J., 1971. Essays in the Theory of Risk Bearing. Markham Publishing Co, Chicago.

Auffhammer, M., Ramaathan, V., Vincent, J.R., 2006. Integrated model shows that atmospheric brown clouds and greenhouse gases have reduced rice harvests in India. Proc. Nat. Acad. Sci. USA 103, 19668–19672.

Baethgen, W.E., 1997. Vulnerability of agricultural sector of Latin America to climate change. Clim. Res. 9, 1–7.

Bourguignon, F., Fournier, M., Gurgand, M., 2004. Selection Bias Corrections Based on the Multinomial Logit Model: Monte-Carlo Comparisons. DELTA Working Paper No. 20, Département et Laboratoire d'Economie Théorique et Appliquée.(DELTA).

Butt, T.A., McCarl, B.A., Angerer, J., Dyke, P.T., Stuth, J.W., 2005. The economic and food security implications of climate change in Mali. Clim. Change 68, 355–378.

Case, A., 1992. Neighborhood influence and technological change. Reg. Sci. Urban Econ. 22, 491–508.

Chow, G.C., 1960. Tests of equality between sets of coefficients in two linear regressions. Econometrica 28 (3), 591–605.

Curtis, S., Adler, R.F., Huffman, G.J., Nelkin, E., Bolvin, D., 2001. Evolution of tropical and extratropical precipitation anomalies during the 1997 to 1999 ENSO cycle. Int. J. Climatol. 21, 961–971.

Danielson, J.J., Gesch, D.B., 2011. Global multi-resolution terrain elevation data 2010 (GMTED2010). US Geological Survey Open-File Report 2011-1073, 26 p.

Deressa, T.T., Hassan, R.M., 2009. Economic impact of climate change on crop production in Ethiopia: evidence from cross-section measures. J. Afr. Econo. 18 (4), 529–554.

Deschenes, O., Greenstone, M., 2007. The economic impacts of climate change: evidence from agricultural output and random fluctuations in weather. Am. Econo. Rev. 97, 354–385.

Deschenes, O., Greenstone, M., 2012. The economic impacts of climate change: evidence from agricultural output and random fluctuations in weather: Reply. Am. Econo. Rev. 102, 3761–3773.

Driessen, P., Deckers, J., Nachtergaele, F., 2001. Lecture Notes on the Major Soils of the World. Food and Agriculture Organization, Rome.

Dubin, J.A., McFadden, D.L., 1984. An econometric analysis of residential electric appliance holdings and consumption. Econometrica 52 (2), 345–362.

Easterling, W.E., Aggarwal, P.K., Batima, P., Brander, K.M., Erda, L., Howden, S.M., Kirilenko, A., Morton, J., Soussana, J.-F., Schmidhuber, J., Tubiello, F.N., 2007. Food, fibre and forest products. Climate change 2007: impacts, adaptation and vulnerability. In: Parry, M.L., Canziani, O.F., Palutikof, J.P., van der Linden, P.J., Hanson, C.E. (Eds.), Contribution of Working Group II to the Fourth Assessment Report of the Intergovernmental Panel on Climate Change. Cambridge University Press, Cambridge.

Efron, B., 1979. Bootstrap methods: another look at the Jackknife. Ann. Stat. 7, 1–26.

Efron, B., 1981. Nonparametric estimates of standard error: the jackknife, the bootstrap and other methods. Biometrika 68, 589–599.

Evenson, R., Gollin, D., 2003. Assessing the impact of the Green Revolution 1960-2000. Science 300, 758–762.

Fama, E.F., 1970. Efficient capital markets: a review of empirical work. J. Finance 25 (2), 383–417.

Fisher, I., 1906. The Nature of Capital and Income. Macmillan, New York.

Fisher, I., 1930. The Theory of Interest. Macmillan, New York.

Fisher, A.C., Hanemann, W.M., Roberts, M.J., Schlenker, W., 2012. The economic impacts of climate change: evidence from agricultural output and random fluctuations in weather: comment. Am. Econo. Rev. 102, 3749–3760.

Food and Agriculture Organization (FAO), 2003. The digital soil map of the world (DSMW) CD-ROM. Rome.

Ford, J., Katondo, K., 1977. Maps of tsetse fly (Glossina) distribution in Africa. Bull. Animal Health Prod. Afr. 15, 187–193.

Fox, N.J., Marion, G., Davidson, R.S., White, P.C.L., Hutchings, M.R., 2012. Livestock Helminths in a changing climate: approaches and restrictions to meaningful predictions. Animals 2, 93–107.

Gitay, H., Brwon, S., Easterling, W., Jallow, B., 2001. Ecosystems and their goods and services. In: McCarthy et al., (Ed.), Climate Change 2001: Impacts, Adaptations, and Vulnerabilities. Cambridge University Press, Cambridge, pp. 237–342.

Gordon, C., Cooper, C., Senior, C.A., Banks, H.T., Gregory, J.M., Johns, T.C., Mitchell, J.F.B., Wood, R.A., 2000. The simulation of SST, sea ice extents and ocean heat transports in a version of the Hadley Centre coupled model without flux adjustments. Clim. Dyn. 16, 147–168.

Greene, W.H., 2011. Econometric Analysis. Prentice Hall, New York.

Hanemann, W.M., 2000. Adaptation and its management. Clim. Change 45, 511–581.

Hahn, G.L., 1981. Housing and management to reduce climate impacts on livestock. J. Animal Sci. 52, 175–186.

Hahn, G.L., Gaughan, J.B., Mader, T.L., Eigenberg, R.A., 2009. Chapter 5: Thermal Indices and Their Applications for Livestock Environments. In: DeShazer, J.A. (Ed.), Livestock Energetics and Thermal Environmental Management. American Society of Agricultural and Biological Engineers, St. Joseph, Mich, pp. 113–130.

Hansen, J., Sato, M., Reudy, R., 2012. Perception of climate change. Proc. Nat. Acad. Sci. USA 109, E2415–E2423.

Heckman, J., 1979. Sample selection bias as a specification error. Econometrica 47, 153–162.

Hulme, M., Doherty, R.M., Ngara, T., New, M.G., Lister, D., 2001. African climate change: 1900–2100. Clim. Res. 17, 145–168.

Intergovernmental Panel on Climate Change (IPCC), 1990. Climate Change: The IPCC Scientific Assessment. Cambridge University Press, Cambridge.

IPCC, 2014. Climate Change 2014 the Physical Science Basis, the Fourth Assessment Report. Cambridge University Press, Cambridge.

Janowiak, J.E., 1988. An investigation of interannual rainfall variability in Africa. J. Clim. 1, 240–255.

Jones, C.A., Kiniry, J.R., 1986. CERES-Maize: A Stimulation Model of Maize Growth and Development. Texas A&M University Press, College Station, Texas.

Johnston, J., Dinardo, J., 1997. Econometric Methods, fourth ed. McGraw-Hill, New York.

Kahneman, D., Tversky, A., 1979. Prospect theory: an analysis of decision under risk. Econometrica 47, 263–291.

Kahneman, D., Tversky, A., 1984. Choices, values and frames. Am. Psychol. 39 (4), 341–350.

Kala, N., Kurukulasuriya, P., Mendelsohn, R., 2012. The impact of climate change on Agro-Ecological Zones: evidence from Africa. Environ. Dev. Econo. 17, 663–687.

Kelly, D.L., Kolstad, C.D., Mitchell, G.T., 2005. Adjustment costs from environmental change. J. Environ. Econo. Manage. 50, 468–495.

Kumar, K.S.K., Parikh, J., 2001. Indian agriculture and climate sensitivity. Global Environ. Change 11, 147–154.

Kurukulasuriya, P., Ajwad, M.I., 2007. Application of the Ricardian technique to estimate the impact of climate change on smallholder farming in Sri Lanka. Clim. Change 81, 39–59.

Lanjouw, J.O., Lanjouw, P., 2001. The rural non-farm sector: issues and evidence from developing countries. Agric. Econo. 26 (1), 1–23.

Lobell, D., Schlenker, W., Costa-Roberts, J., 2011. Climate trends and global crop production since 1980. Science 333, 616–620.

Mader, T.L., Davis, M.S., 2004. Effect of management strategies on reducing heat stress of feedlot cattle: feed and water intake. J. Animal Sci. 82, 3077–3087.

Mader, T.L., Frank, K.L., Harrington, J.A., Hahn, G.L., Nienaber, J.A., 2009. Potential climate change effects on warm-season livestock production in the Great Plains. Clim. Change 97, 529–541.

Magrin, G.O., Travasso, M.I., Díaz, R.A., Rodríguez, R.O., 1997. Vulnerability of the agricultural systems of Argentina to climate change. Clim. Res. 9, 31–36.

Magrin, G.O., Travasso, M.I., Rodriguez, G.R., 2005. Changes in climate and crop production during the 20th century in Argentina. Clim. Change 72, 229–249.

Magrin, G., Garcia, C.G., Choque, D.C., Gimenez, J.C., Moreno, A.R., Nagy, G.J., Nobre, C., Villamizar, A., 2007. Latin America. In: Parry, M.L., Canziani, O.F., Palutikof, J.P., van der Linden, P.J., Hanson, C.E. (Eds.), Climate change 2007: impacts, adaptation, and vulnerability: contribution of working group II to the fourth assessment report of the intergovernmental panel on climate change. Cambridge University Press, Cambridge, pp. 581–615.

Masseti, E., Mendelsohn, R., 2011. Estimating Ricardian models with panel data. Clim. Change Econo. 2, 301–319.

McFadden, D.L., 1974. Conditional logit analysis of qualitative choice behavior. In: Zarembka, P. (Ed.), Frontiers in Econometrics. Academic, New York, pp. 105–142.

Mendelshon, R., 2000. Efficient adaptation to climate change. Clim. Change 45, 583–600.

Mendelsohn, R., 2012. The economics of adaptation to climate change in developing countries. Clim. Change Econo. 3, 1–21.

Mendelsohn, R., Nordhaus, W., Shaw, D., 1994. The impact of global warming on agriculture: a Ricardian analysis. Am. Econo. Rev. 84, 753–771.

Mendelsohn, R., Kurukulasuriya, P., Basist, A., Kogan, F., Williams, C., 2007. Measuring climate change impacts with satellite versus weather station data. Clim. Change 81, 71–83.

Mendelsohn, R., Arellano-Gonzalez, J., Christensen, P., 2010. A Ricardian analysis of Mexican farms. Environ. Dev. Econo. 15, 153–171.

Nakicenovic, N., Davidson, O., Davis, G., Grübler, A., Kram, T., La Rovere, E.L., Metz, B., Morita, T., Pepper, W., Pitcher, H., Sankovski, A., Shukla, P., Swart, R., Watson, R., Dadi, Z., 2000. Emissions Scenarios, A Special Report of Working Group III of the Intergovernmental Panel on Climate Change. IPCC, Geneva.

National Research Council (NRC), 2013. Abrupt Impacts of Climate Change: Anticipating Surprises. The National Academies Press, Washington DC.

New, M., Lister, D., Hulme, M., Makin, I., 2002. A high-resolution data set of surface climate over global land areas. Clim. Res. 21, 1–25.

Nin, A., Ehui, S., Benin, S., 2007. Livestock productivity in developing countries: an assessment. Evenson, R., Pingali, P. (Eds.), Handbook of Agricultural Economics, vol. 3, North Holland, Oxford, UK, pp. 2467–2532.

Parry, M.L., Rosenzweig, C.P., Iglesias, A., Livermore, M., Fischer, G., 2004. Effects of climate change on global food production under SRES emissions and socioeconomic scenarios. Global Environ. Change 14, 53–67.

Reilly, J., et al., 1996. Agriculture in a changing climate: impacts and adaptations. In: Climate Change 1995 Impacts, Adaptations, and Mitigation of Climate Change. IPCC. Cambridge University Press, Cambridge, pp. 427–468.

Reinsborough, M.J., 2003. A Ricardian model of climate change in Canada. Can. J. Econo. 36, 21–40.

Ricardo, D., 1817. On the Principles of Political Economy and Taxation. John Murray, London.

Ropelewski, C.F., Halpert, M.S., 1987. Global and regional precipitation patterns associated with the El Nino/Southern Oscillation. Monthly Weather Rev. 115, 1606–1626.

Rosenzweig, C., Parry, M., 1994. Potential impact of climate change on world food supply. Nature 367, 133–138.

Rosenzweig, C., Iglesias, A., Yang, X.B., Epstein, P.R., Chivian, E., 2001. Climate change and extreme weather events: implications for food production, plant diseases, and pests. Global Change Hum Health 2 (2), 90–104.

Sanghi, A., Mendelsohn, R., 2008. The impacts of global warming on farmers in Brazil and India. Global Environ. Change 18, 655–665.

Schenkler, W., Hanemann, M., Fisher, A., 2005. Will US agriculture really benefit from global warming? Accounting for irrigation in the hedonic approach. Am. Econo. Rev. 95, 395–406.

Schenkler, W., Hanemann, M., Fisher, A., 2006. The impact of global warming on U.S. agriculture: an econometric analysis of optimal growing conditions. Rev. Econ. Stat. 88 (1), 113–125.

Schlenker, W., Roberts, M., 2009. Nonlinear temperature effects indicate severe damages to crop yields under climate change. Proc. Nat. Acad. Sci. 106 (37), 15594–15598.

Schmidt, G.A., et al., 2005. Present day atmospheric simulations using GISS ModelE: comparison to in-situ, satellite and reanalysis data. J. Climate 19, 153–192.

Seo, S.N., 2006. Modeling Farmer Responses to Climate Change: Climate Change Impacts and Adaptations in Livestock Management in Africa. PhD Dissertation, Yale University, New Haven.

Seo, S.N., 2010a. Is an integrated farm more resilient against climate change?: a microeconometric analysis of portfolio diversification in African agriculture? Food Policy 35, 32–40.

Seo, S.N., 2010b. A microeconometric analysis of adapting portfolios to climate change: adoption of agricultural systems in Latin America. Appl. Econ. Perspect. Policy 32, 489–514.

Seo, S.N., 2010c. Managing forests, livestock, and crops under global warming: a microeconometric analysis of land use changes in Africa. Aust. J. Agric. Resour. Econ. 54 (2), 239–258.

Seo, S.N., 2011. An analysis of public adaptation to climate change using agricultural water schemes in South America. Ecol. Econ. 70, 825–834.

Seo, S.N., 2012a. Adapting natural resource enterprises under global warming in South America: a mixed logit analysis. Econ. J. Lat. Am. Caribb. Econ. Assoc. 12, 111–135.

Seo, S.N., 2012b. Adaptation behaviors across ecosystems under global warming: a spatial microeconometric model of the rural economy in South America. Papers Reg. Sci. 91, 849–871.

Seo, S.N., 2012c. Decision making under climate risks: an analysis of sub-Saharan farmers' adaptation behaviors. Weather Clim. Soc. 4, 285–299.

Seo, S.N., 2013a. Refining spatial resolution and spillovers of a microeconometric model of adapting portfolios to climate change. Mitig. Adap. Strat. Global Change 18, 1019–1034.

Seo, S.N., 2013b. An essay on the impact of climate change on US agriculture: weather fluctuations, climatic shifts, and adaptation strategies. Clim. Change 121, 115–124.

Seo, S.N., 2014a. Evaluation of Agro-Ecological Zone methods for the study of climate change with micro farming decisions in sub-Saharan Africa. Eur. J. Agron. 52, 157–165.

Seo, S.N., 2014b. Coupling climate risks, eco-systems, anthropogenic decisions using South American and Sub-Saharan farming activities. Meteorol. App. 21, 848–858.

Seo, S.N., 2014c. Adapting to extreme climates: raising animals in hot and arid ecosystems in Australia. Int. J. Biometeorol. 59, 541–550. doi: 10.1007/s00484-014-0867-8.

Seo, S.N., 2015a. Micro-behavioral Economics of Global Warming: Modeling Adaptation Strategies in Agricultural and Natural Resource Enterprises. Springer, Cham, Switzerland.

Seo, S.N., 2015b. Modeling farmer adaptations to climate change in South America: a micro-behavioral economic perspective. Environ. Ecol. Stat. 23 (1), 1–21.

Seo, S.N., 2016. Untold tales of goats in deadly Indian monsoons: adapt or rain-retreat under global warming? J Extreme Events 3. doi: 10.1142/S2345737616500019.

Seo, S.N., Mendelsohn, R., Munasinghe, M., 2005. Climate change and agriculture in Sri Lanka: A Ricardian valuation. Environ. Dev. Econo. 10, 581–196.

Seo, S.N., Mendelsohn, R., 2008a. Measuring impacts and adaptations to climate change: a structural Ricardian model of African livestock management. Agric. Econo. 38, 151–165.

Seo, S.N., Mendelsohn, R., 2008b. A Ricardian analysis of the impact of climate change impacts on South American farms. Chil. J. Agric. Res. 68, 69–79.

Seo, S.N., Mendelsohn, R., Dinar, A., Hassan, R., Kurukulasuriya, P., 2009. A Ricardian analysis of the distribution of climate change impacts on agriculture across Agro-Ecological Zones in Africa. Environ. Res. Econo. 43, 313–332.

Shanahan, T.M., Overpeck, J.T., Anchukaitis, K.J., Beck, J.W., Cole, J.E., Dettman, D.L., Peck, J.A., Scholz, C.A., King, J.W., 2009. Atlantic forcing of persistent drought in West Africa. Science 324, 377–380.

Shiller, R.J., 1981. Do stock prices move too much to be justified by subsequent changes in dividends? Am. Econo. Rev. 71 (3), 421–436.

Shiller, R.J., 2003. From efficient markets theory to behavioral finance. J. Econo. Perspect. 17, 83–104.

Shiller, R.J., 2005. Irrational Exuberance, second ed. Princeton University Press, Princeton, NJ.

Shiller, R.J., 2014. Speculative asset prices. Am. Econo. Rev. 104 (6), 1486–1517.

Tubiello, F.N., Ewert, F., 2002. Simulating the effects of elevated CO_2 on crops: approaches and applications for climate change. Eur. J. Agron. 18, 57–74.

Tubiello, F.N., Amthor, J.A., Boote, K.J., Donatelli, M., Easterling, W., Fischer, G., Gifford, R.M., Howden, M., Reilly, J., Rosenzweig, C., 2007. Crop response to elevated CO_2 and world food supply. Eur. J. Agron. 26, 215–223.

von Neumann, J., Morgenstern, O., 1947. Theory of Games and Economic Behavior, second ed. Princeton University Press, Princeton, NJ.

Wang, J., Mendelsohn, R., Dinar, A., Huang, J., Rozelle, S., Zhang, L., 2009. The impacts of climate change on China's agriculture. Agric. Econo. 40, 323–337.

Welch, J.R., Vincent, J.R., Auffhammer, M., Moya, P.F., Dobermann, A., Dawe, D., 2010. Rice yields in tropical/subtropical Asia exhibit large but opposing sensitivities to minimum and maximum temperatures. Proc. Nat. Acad. Sci. USA 107, 14562–14567.

White, H., 1980. A heteroskedasticity-consistent covariance matrix estimator and a direct test for heteroskedasticity. Econometrica 48 (4), 817–838.

Williams, J.R., Jones, C.A., Kiniry, J.R., Spaniel, D.A., 1989. The EPIC crop growth model. Trans. Am. Soc. Agric. Eng. 32, 497–511.

Wooldridge, J.M., 2010. Econometric Analysis of Cross Section and Panel Data. MIT Press, Boston, MA.

World Bank, 2009. Awakening Africa's Sleeping Giant: Prospects for Commercial Agriculture in the Guinea Savannah Zone and Beyond. World Bank and FAO, Washington, DC.

Zilberman, D., 1998. Agricultural and Environmental Policies: Economics of Production, Technology, Risk, Agriculture, and the Environment. The State University of New York-Oswego, New York.

CHAPTER 6

Modeling a Complex Structure in Microbehavioral Methods in Tandem With Changes in Global Ecosystems

Chapters 4 and 5 were devoted to applications of the microbehavioral methods to agricultural and natural resource enterprises in South America faced with climatic challenges. In Chapter 5, the present author provided a comparison of the microbehavioral econometric methods with the Ricardian method. This chapter continues the discussions of the applied aspects of the microbehavioral methods in two directions. In the first direction, the present author examines changes in ecosystems and ecological zones under climatic changes that underlie changes in microbehavioral decisions. This chapter will establish a microbehavioral model with the link between the former and the latter.

In the second direction, in combination with the coupling of the two components, the present author looks into the structure of the microbehavioral model. A complex structure of the model will be built and applied, against a simple structure of the model.

To compare the results from this chapter with the results from the models in Chapters 4 and 5, the present author relies on the same data used in previous chapters: household surveys, climate data, soils, and climate models. Additional data are discussed on ecosystems and ecological zones of South America.

6.1 CHANGES IN NATURAL SYSTEMS CAUSED BY ANTHROPOGENIC INTERVENTIONS

Let's begin this chapter with the description of the range of ecosystems that exist today in South America. South America prides itself of a great diversity of ecological zones and biodiversity. The continent is home to the Amazon rainforest, the world's largest pluvial forest, which covers 7.5 million km^2 of land area (Mata et al., 2001; World Resources, 2005). The forest cover of the continent is varied in type and shape (Matthews, 1983). Grasslands and pasturelands are vast resources across the continent. Pasturelands are as much as eight times larger than croplands in major countries (Baethgen, 1997). The Pampas lowland grasslands stretch across Argentina, Uruguay, and Southern Brazil whereas the Llanos highland grasslands spread across Colombia and Venezuela. Desert ecosystems are existent in, for example, the Atacama Desert in Chilean highlands which is known as the driest place on Earth. The Andes Mountains provide the highland mountain ecosystems that are distinct from the lowlands' ecosystems, including the glaciers such as the Zongo glacier in Bolivia and the Antisana glacier in Ecuador (Rabatel et al., 2013). There are remarkably influential river basins such as the Amazon Basin and the Orinoco Basin that flow across multiple countries (WWF, 2014). There are landlocked countries such as Paraguay and Bolivia. There are oil-rich natural reserves including the Yasuni National Park in Ecuador. Latin America is known as home to some of the Earth's greatest biodiversity concentrations which are critical for global biodiversity (Global Biodiversity Outlook, 2010).

An early effort to classify the diverse ecosystems of the continent, as a component of a global study, was made by Matthews who classified them into major land covers/vegetations. Her classification was based on the collection of then existing studies on land uses and the NASA (National Aeronautic and Space Administration) satellite imageries. Major land covers are determined at the resolution of a degree cell which is the size of 1 degree latitude by 1 degree longitude (Matthews, 1983). She adopted the international system of classification and mapping of vegetation provided by the United Nations' Educational, Scientific, and Cultural Organization (UNESCO, 1973).

The variety of ecosystems of Latin America is broadly classified into major land covers: grasslands, shrub lands, meadow, woodlands, forests, deserts, and water bodies such as coastal zones, rivers, and lakes. Each of these major land covers is further divided into multiple minor land covers (UNESCO, 1973).

Latin America is the continent with the largest forest coverage in the world with about half of the continent covered by the dense forests (WRI, 2005). There are many types of forests which vary in physiological, apparent, seasonal, and geographical characteristics: a xeromorphic forest/woodland, a tropical/subtropical evergreen seasonal broad-leaved forest, a subtropical needle-leaved forest, a tropical/subtropical drought deciduous forest, a cold-deciduous forest with evergreens, a subtropical evergreen rainforest, a temperate/subpolar evergreen rainforest, and a tropical evergreen rainforest.

In less dense tree areas, there are various types of woodlands: an evergreen broad-leaved sclerophyllous woodland, an evergreen needle-leaved woodland, a tropical/subtropical drought woodland. Sclerophylls are trees with hard and thick leaves. It comes from the Greek words "skleros" (hard) and "phyllon" (leaf). An example is Ficus, commonly called a fig tree in Oceania or a banyan tree in South Asia (UNESCO, 1973). There are various types of shrublands: an evergreen broad-leaved shrubland, a drought deciduous shrubland, a xeromorphic shrubland. Xerophyte is any plant adapted to life in a dry habitat by means of mechanisms, both internal and external, to prevent water loss or store available water. It comes from the Greek words "xero" (dry) and "phuton" (plant) (UNESCO, 1973).

Various types of grasslands are classified further by the height of grasslands as well as different covers of grasslands: a tall/medium/short grassland with <10% woody cover, a tall/medium/short grassland with shrub cover, a tall/medium/short grassland with 10–40% woody cover, a tall grassland with no woody cover, a medium grassland with no woody cover, and a short grassland with no woody cover.

In less dense areas of grasslands, there are meadows which are open areas composed primarily of grasslands and forb formations which are open areas composed primarily of wildflowers such as clover, milkweed, etc. In the areas where grasses and flowers are absent most of the time during the year, the landscape turns to desert zones.

Besides these primarily terrestrial ecosystems, there are water-based ecosystems such as lakes, rivers, and coastal zones which are classified into a water body. In addition, there are salt flats as well as glaciers and icesheets.

These diverse ecosystems are dispersed across South America (Seo, 2012a, 2015a). Tropical rainforests are spread across northern Brazil and the Andean countries in the Amazon Basin. Eastern provinces of Brazil are covered with grasslands with smaller (<10%) or larger (>10% and <40%) woody covers and xeromorphic forests. Western and southern parts of Brazil, including the Cerrado, are covered by various types of forests such as xeromorphic forests, tropical/subtropical drought deciduous forests, seasonal forests, and evergreen forests.

Uruguay is dominantly small/medium/tall grasslands with shrub cover. The northern provinces of Argentina are covered by tall grasslands. The predominant areas of Argentina are covered by drought deciduous shrub lands. There exist meadows and deserts in the southern edges of Argentina.

The Andes Mountains stretch prominently from north to south as well as from west to east of the continent and provide the highland mountain ecosystems that are distinct from the lowlands' ecosystems. In the highlands of Colombia and Venezuela, there exist grasslands with <10% woody cover, called the Llanos, and tropical/subtropical drought deciduous forests.

Southern provinces of Peru are dominantly meadows with no woody cover. Northern provinces of Chile, including the ecosystems of the Atacama Desert, are meadows with no woody cover and xeromorphic shrub lands. The middle parts of Chile are dominantly xeromorphic forests and subtropical and temperate evergreen rainforests. Southern provinces of Chile are covered by temperate evergreen rainforests and cold deciduous forests.

Major vegetations in Paraguay and Bolivia, two landlocked countries in the continent, are xeromorphic forests, tropical/subtropical seasonal forests, subtropical evergreen forests, and evergreen needle-leaved woodlands.

There are well-known desert zones which are dispersed across South America: the Atacama Desert in Chile, the Sechura Desert in Peru, the La Guajira Desert in Colombia and Venezuela, and the Patagonian Desert and the Monte Desert in Argentina (WWF, 2014).

Along the coastal areas of the continent which enclose the entire continent from all sides, water ecosystems are dominant, for example, oceans. The same is true of the major river basins such as the Amazon Basin and the Orinoco River Basin where water-based ecosystems such as rivers, reservoirs, and lakes are dominant. There are salt flats such as the Salinas Grandes in Argentina (WWF, 2014). High mountain peaks are covered with glaciers and icesheets which are mentioned previously (Rabatel et al., 2013).

Another way to classify the ecological zones of South America that has been widely used by agricultural researchers is the concept of agro-ecological zones (AEZ) (FAO, 1978; Dudal, 1980; FAO/IIASA, 2012). The AEZ method classifies the ecosystems into six AEZs based on the concept of the length of growing periods (LGP) for crops: humid forest, subhumid, moist savannah, semiarid, arid zones, and deserts. The AEZ classification system is a reasonable way to capture productive croplands, but less so for other systems such as animal system and forestry system (Seo et al., 2009; Seo, 2014a).

The characteristics and distributions of these ecosystems are expected to undergo significant changes if global climatic changes would unfold as climate scientists have predicted (Le Treut et al., 2007; IPCC, 2014). Changes in climatic variables such as temperature, precipitation, carbon dioxide concentration all will directly influence the functions and distributions of these ecosystems (Schlesinger, 1997; Denman et al., 2007). Indirectly, changes in the climatic variables also lead to changes in growth and distributions of weeds, insects, and plant diseases through which the ecosystems are affected

(Porter et al., 1991; Sutherst, 1991; Ziska, 2003). Further, occurrences and prevalence of animal diseases are sensitive to changes in climatic variables, which then affect ecosystem characteristics and land uses by people (Ford and Katondo, 1977; Fox et al., 2012).

The review of the decades-long FACE (free air CO_2 enrichment) experiments that are conducted in the field conditions finds that a doubling of CO_2 concentration in the atmosphere leads to an increase in soybean (legumes) yield by 24%, an increase in sorghum yield by 40% under no other stress, an increase in cotton yield by 42%, an increase in rice yield by 10%, an increase in wheat yield by 17%, and an increase in maize yield by around 6% (Ainsworth and Long, 2005; Seo, 2015a). The agronomic experiments which are conducted in the laboratory environments by controlling the factors that affect growth find by and large similar conclusions (Tubiello and Ewert, 2002; Tubiello et al., 2007).

The same review of the FACE experiments and other studies reports changes in tree productivities and distributions (Joyce et al., 1995; Sohngen and Mendelsohn, 1998). Tree height would increase by about 5% and shrub height would increase by about 25% under the doubling of carbon dioxide concentration in the atmosphere. It means taller trees and higher shrubs under the elevated CO_2 world.

At the same time, the review reports that the leaf area index (LAI) would increase by about 20% for the trees and 10% for the grasses under the elevated CO_2 condition, which means a larger canopy for a tree and a large leaf area for grasses. See also Campbell et al., (2000) and Shaw et al., (2002) for grassland productions under elevated CO_2 condition. The dry matter production (DMP) is reported to increase by about 30% for the trees under the elevated CO_2 conditions, which means thicker trees, that is, a larger diameter of a tree, say, at the breast height (DBH) in biometric terms (Ainsworth and Long, 2005).

6.2 NATURAL RESOURCE ENTERPRISES ACROSS ECOSYSTEMS OF SOUTH AMERICA

Across the multitude of ecosystems in South America, people manage agricultural and natural resource enterprises in varied ways. At present, about a third of the total land area in South America is utilized for agricultural lands (World Resources, 2005). A large number of crops are planted across the continent: major cereals planted are wheat, maize, barley, rice, oats, sorghum, millet; major oil seeds planted are soybeans, peanuts, sunflowers; major vegetables/tubercles planted are potatoes and cassavas; specialty crops include cotton, tobacco, tea, coffee, sugar canes, and sugar beets (Mata et al., 2001; Magrin et al., 2007). In each of these crops, there can be multiple genetic varieties (World Bank, 2009).

The continent is famed for its vast grasslands: the Pampas and the Llanos. As such, pasturelands which are used mainly for livestock management are eight times larger than the croplands in Argentina and four times larger in Brazil and elsewhere (Baethgen, 1997). Consequently, animal husbandry is an important part of agriculture in South America (Nin et al., 2007). A specialized livestock system is adopted by about 20% of rural households in the continent while it is adopted by only 5% of rural households in Sub-Saharan Africa (Seo, 2010b, 2011). Argentina and Brazil are one of the world's largest beef cattle exporters and consumers of beef per head annually (Steiger, 2006). Major animals that are raised by South American farmers are beef cattle, dairy cattle, chickens, pigs, goats, and sheep (Seo et al., 2010).

The continent has the largest land area in the world covered by forests, with 48% of the total land area being covered by forests, defined by >40% forest coverage (World Resources, 2005). The income earned from forest activities may account for more than 20% of the rural income in South and Central America (Vedeld et al., 2007). People manage tree plantations either for the sale of timber products, or nontimber products, or even because of various government subsidies and international aids (Peters et al., 1989). Most common trees reported by the rural households who responded to the household surveys are as numerous as palm, cashew, cacao, mango, pineapple, citrus, banana, shea nut, apple, Kola, peach, almond, prune, apricot, avocado, cherry, hickory, eucalyptus, lemon, and Brazil nuts (Seo, 2012a). Latin America is the largest emitter of carbon dioxide generated from land use changes, accounting for around 70% of the total world emissions of CO_2 due to land use changes, which arise mostly from deforestation (Houghton, 2008).

This chapter will build a microbehavioral econometric model which couples microbehavioral decisions with ecosystem characteristics. For this purpose, based on the rural portfolios of the natural resource products such as crops, animals, and forests, we can define the seven natural resource intensive enterprises, as already introduced in Chapter 2.

Diversified (mixed) enterprises are as follows:

Enterprise 1: crops–livestock;
Enterprise 2: crops–forests;
Enterprise 3: crops–livestock–forests;
Enterprise 7: livestock–forests;

Specialized enterprises are as follows:

Enterprise 4: livestock-only;

Enterprise 5: forests-only;

Enterprise 6: crops-only.

There is a livestock–forests enterprise in South America, but only a small percentage of farms adopted this enterprise. So, the livestock–forests enterprise will be dropped from the ensuing analysis. Methodologically, there is no additional difficulty in including this enterprise into the microbehavioral model if this enterprise is adopted by a significant number of rural households in another part of the world.

The seven natural resource enterprise classification presents a more complex structure of the microbehavioral model than the three agricultural system classification used in Chapter 4: crops-only, livestock-only, and crops–livestock. In the three agricultural system classification used in Chapter 4, the crops-only system is inclusive of a crops-only enterprise, a forests-only enterprise, and a crops–forests enterprise. Similarly, the crops–livestock agricultural system is inclusive of a crops–livestock enterprise, a livestock–forest enterprise, and a crops–livestock–forests enterprise.

The seven natural resource enterprise classification shows that the microbehavioral model can be built to accommodate an increasing structural complexity of the model. By way of a simile, the three agricultural system model can be understood as the house with three rooms while the seven natural resource system as the house of the same size and appearance but with seven rooms.

Where in each of the ecosystems is each of these natural resource enterprises favored by rural households in South America? The microbehavioral economic models have paid a great deal of attention on this linkage and how it would be shifted if a global climate alteration would occur (Seo, 2012b, 2014a). This is the second aspect of the model built in this chapter. That is, let alone the present author constructs a microbehavioral model with a complex structure, the present author connects this complex structure with the ecosystems.

The distributions of rural enterprises across the major land covers in South America are summarized in Table 6.1 (Seo, 2012b). First, a livestock-only enterprise accounts for 49% of the total households in the tall/medium/short grasslands with shrub cover, a dominant land cover around Uruguay, while only 24% of the households choose a crops-only enterprise there. A large portion of the Pampas Plain has this type of ecosystem. Similarly, in the tall/medium/short grasslands with <10% wood cover, a livestock-only enterprise is chosen by

Table 6.1 Individuals' adoptions of natural resource enterprises across ecosystems (fraction)

	A crops–livestock enterprise	A crops–forests enterprise	A crops–livestock–forests enterprise	A livestock-only enterprise	A forests-only enterprise	A crops-only enterprise
Tall/medium/short grassland, <10% woody cover	0.09	0.20	0.04	0.41	0.04	0.22
Tall/medium/short grassland, shrub cover	0.15	0.07	0.04	0.49	0.01	0.24
Tall/medium/short grassland, 10–40% woody cover	0.23	0.08	0.29	0.22	0.01	0.18
Tall grassland, no woody cover	0.24	0.06	0.02	0.12	0	0.57
Xeromorphic shrubland/dwarf shrubland	0.20	0.11	0.02	0.31	0.01	0.37
Meadow, short grassland, no woody cover	0.43	0.05	0.04	0.14	0	0.35
Xeromorphic forest/woodland	0.35	0.04	0.11	0.19	0.01	0.31
Trop/subtropical evergreen seasonal broad-leaved forest	0.23	0.04	0.58	0	0.12	0.04
Cold-deciduous forest, with evergreens	0	0.69	0.08	0	0	0.23
Subtropical evergreen rainforest	0.20	0.10	0.02	0.20	0	0.49
Temperate/subpolar evergreen rainforest	0.88	0	0	0.09	0	0.03
Tropical evergreen rainforest	0.26	0.09	0.12	0.16	0.004	0.37
Tropical/subtropical drought–deciduous forest	0.35	0.04	0.08	0.12	0.004	0.41
Water (coast, river, lake)	0.25	0.20	0.18	0.18	0.03	0.16

41% of the households. This ecosystem is dominant in the highland grasslands, the Llanos in Colombia and Venezuela.

For the crops-only enterprise, tall grasslands with no woody cover, subtropical evergreen forests, tropical/subtropical drought–deciduous forests are favored zones. The crops-only enterprise is chosen by 57, 49, and 41%, respectively, by the rural households located in each of these ecosystems.

The crops–livestock enterprise is most often adopted in temperate rainforests, meadow/short grasslands with no woody cover, xeromorphic forests, and temperate drought–deciduous forests. In xeromorphic forests/woodlands, the crops–livestock enterprise is preferred to the crops-only enterprise by 35–31% whereas the livestock-only is chosen by 19% of farms.

The crops–forests enterprise is adopted most often in the tropical rainforests, the coastal/lake/river ecosystems, and cold-deciduous evergreen forests. The forests-only enterprise is most frequent, in the number of households that adopted, near the water body such as oceans, rivers, and lakes. The forests-only enterprise is also adopted most often in the tropical/subtropical seasonal forests.

The crops–livestock–forests enterprise, the most diversified enterprise of all, is most favored, in order, by tropical/subtropical seasonal forests, tall/medium/short grasslands with substantial (10–40%) woody cover, and tropical rainforests. These are all ecosystems with a substantial forest coverage.

The distributions of agricultural and natural resource enterprises across major land covers at the present time summarized in Table 6.1 are conditioned on climate variables which determine the distributions of the ecosystems. Therefore, future changes in the climate system will lead to changes in the present distributions of these enterprises motivated by changes in ecosystem productivities and distributions (Gitay et al., 2001; Fischlin et al., 2007).

6.3 A THEORY OF THE MICROBEHAVIORAL MODEL OF NATURAL RESOURCE ENTERPRISES

A natural resource manager chooses a portfolio of natural resources he/she manages given climatic, geologic, and geographic conditions. The portfolio of her/his choice can be a specialized portfolio or a diversified (mixed) portfolio. He/she chooses only one of the six enterprises identified in the previous section in order to earn the highest return in the long-term horizon. Conditional on the choice of one of these natural resource enterprises, he/she will decide on the levels of inputs and outputs to maximize the profit in the long-term (Seo, 2010b, 2015b).

Let the observed long-term profit (π) from enterprise 1 and the latent long-term profit (π^*) from enterprise j (with $j = 1, 2, \ldots, 6$) for an individual manager n be written as a function of exogenous factors as follows (Dubin and McFadden, 1984; Bourguignon et al., 2004):

$$\pi_{n1} = X_n \beta_1 + \varphi_{n1}, \tag{6.1}$$

$$\pi_{nj}^* = Z_n \gamma_j + \eta_{nj}. \tag{6.2}$$

The two error terms in the aforementioned equations are, as before, assumed parametrically in the following manner:

$$\begin{aligned} E(\varphi_{n1} \mid X_n, Z_n) &= 0, \\ \mathrm{Var}(\varphi_{n1} \mid X_n, Z_n) &= \sigma^2. \end{aligned} \tag{6.3}$$

In the aforementioned equations, the vector Z represents the set of exogenous variables that are pertinent to all six natural resource enterprises such as climate variables, soils, geology, geography, household characteristics, and country fixed effects. The vector X contains the determinants of the profit of enterprise 1, that is, the crops–livestock enterprise. The two vectors of explanatory variables Z, X need not be identical.

Although the latent profit for enterprise 1 is existent in all rural farms, the profit for enterprise 1 is observed only if it is chosen by an individual manager from the available enterprises, which occurs when (For simplicity, from now on we will drop the subscript indicating an individual manager as far as there is no risk of confusion):

$$\pi_1^* > \pi_k^*, \forall k \neq 1. \tag{6.4}$$

Applying the spatial resampling method from the predefined neighborhoods as explained in Chapter 3, it is assumed that $\eta_{nj}'s$ are identically and independently Gumbel distributed (McFadden, 1984; Case, 1992; Seo, 2011). That is, with the cumulative distribution function F,

$$\begin{aligned} \eta_n &= (\eta_{n1}, \eta_{n2}, \ldots, \eta_{n6}), \\ F(\eta_{nj}) &= \exp(-e^{-\eta_{nj}}). \end{aligned} \tag{6.5}$$

Under this assumption, the probability of natural resource enterprise m to be adopted by an individual resource manager is written in a simple form as a Logit (McFadden, 1974):

$$P_m = \text{Prob}(\text{enterprise } m) = e^{Z\gamma_m} \cdot \left(\sum_{k=1}^{K=6} e^{Z\gamma_k} \right)^{-1}. \tag{6.6}$$

As explained in the previous chapters, the parameters are estimated by constructing the log-likelihood function using the Logit probabilities and maximizing it with a nonlinear optimization technique.

The choice equations are identified nonparametrically from the conditional outcome equations that follow by a set of soils and geographic variables (Fisher, 1966; Johnston and DiNardo, 1997). The identification variables are explained in detail in the empirical section.

Having chosen the enterprise 1, the manager chooses the bundle of inputs and outputs to maximize the long-term profit from the enterprise. The direct estimation of Eq. (6.1) will lead to selection bias (Heckman, 1979). Of the variety of selection bias correction methods in a polychotomous choice setting, the Dubin–McFadden method is superior to other methods such as the Lee's or the semiparametric Dahl's method (Dubin and McFadden, 1984; Schmertman, 1994; Bourguignon et al., 2004). This is because the Dubin–McFadden method allows for a more flexible correlation structure among the parameters unlike the other methods (Lee, 1983; Dahl, 2002).

Let $\upsilon_j = \text{corr}(\varphi_1, \eta_j)$ and assume the linearity condition proposed by Dubin and McFadden explained in Chapters 2 and 3. The conditional long-term profit function for enterprise m shown in Eq. (6.1) can be estimated consistently after correcting for selection biases as follows, with the second term on the right-hand side being the selection bias correction term:

$$\pi_m = X\xi_m + \sum_{j \neq m}^{J} \tau_j \cdot \left[\frac{P_j \cdot \ln P_j}{1 - P_j} + \ln P_m \right] + \delta_m, \tag{6.7}$$

$$\text{with} \quad \tau_j = \sigma \upsilon_j.$$

The parameters to be estimated are ξ_m, τ_j. The error term in the aforementioned equation is assumed to be a white noise term. In each of the conditional land value equations estimated, there will be $J - 1$ selection bias correction terms. The parameter estimates of $J - 1$ selection bias correction terms, that is, τ_j, reveal the signs of correlations υ_j. The choice probabilities and the conditional profit functions for the other enterprises are estimated in the same manner.

The expected long-term profit for each household is constructed by summing across the six natural resource enterprises the product of the choice probability of an enterprise and the enterprise's conditional profit, given the current climate C_0:

$$\Pi_n(C_0) = \sum_{j=1}^{J} P_j(C_0) \cdot \pi_j(C_0). \tag{6.8}$$

If climate were to be shifted from C_0 to C_1, the change in welfare ($\Delta\Pi$) for each household resulting from the change in climate can be measured as the difference in the expected profit before and after the change. The uncertainty around the estimate of welfare change is measured by a 95% confidence interval using the estimate of the bootstrap standard error (Efron, 1981; Seo and Mendelsohn, 2008a).

6.4 DATA, SOURCES, AND DESCRIPTIVE STATISTICS

Again, to compare the results from this chapter directly with the results from Chapters 4 and 5, this chapter employs the same data used in the previous two chapters. Each of these three chapters develops a microbehavioral model with a different level of structural complexity which is again linked to a classification of ecosystems.

The primary new empirical data of this chapter are those on an individual household's adoption of one of the seven natural resource enterprises. From the household data collected in South America by the World Bank project described in the previous chapters, each household is assigned to one of the seven natural resource enterprises based on the examination of the full portfolio that each household manages (Seo and Mendelsohn, 2008b). For example, if the household is found to manage maize and wheat only, it is classified as a crops-only enterprise. Similarly, if the household is found to manage both maize and sheep, it is assigned to a crops–livestock enterprise.

With little change from the previous chapters, climate data are applied to the model in this chapter (New et al., 2002). The same goes for the climate prediction data from the global climate models (Gordon et al., 2000; Schmidt et al., 2005).

Soils, topography, geology, and geography data all remain unchanged from the ways they are used in the previous chapters. These variables come from the FAO soil data and the most refined USGS/NGA elevation data (FAO, 2003; Danielson and Gesch, 2011).

Table 6.2 summarizes the distributions of the six natural resource enterprises within each of the seven surveyed countries. A specialized crop enterprise is adopted most often in Ecuador probably because of heavy

Table 6.2 Observed distributions of natural resource enterprises by individuals' adoptions

	A crops–livestock enterprise	A crops–forests enterprise	A crops–livestock–forests enterprise	A livestock-only enterprise	A forests-only enterprise	A crops-only enterprise	All enterprises
Argentina	0.28	0.09	0.04	0.25	NR	0.34	1
Brazil	0.21	0.11	0.31	0.14	0.021	0.22	1
Chile	0.57	0.01	NR	0.09	0.003	0.33	1
Colombia	0.29	0.13	0.05	0.25	0.003	0.28	1
Ecuador	0.18	0.05	0.05	0.05	0.004	0.66	1
Uruguay	0.18	0.01	0.01	0.63	NR	0.18	1
Venezuela	0.32	0.04	NR	0.25	NR	0.39	1

Note: NR stands for "Not Reported".

rainfall along the Equator and high elevation. This enterprise is adopted by about a third of the rural households in Argentina and Venezuela. A specialized livestock enterprise is adopted most frequently in Uruguay, Argentina, and Venezuela where major grasslands are located such as the Pampas and the Llanos. A specialized forestry is rare but found in Brazil where 2.1% of rural households adopted this enterprise. A crops–livestock enterprise is most common in Chile, probably because of a higher interannual rainfall variability in the mountains. A crops–forests enterprise is most common in Colombia and Brazil most likely because most of the Amazon rainforests belong to these countries. It is notable that a crops–livestock–forests enterprise is chosen in Brazil by more than 30% of the households.

6.5 EMPIRICAL RESULTS FROM THE MICROBEHAVIORAL MODEL OF NATURAL RESOURCE ENTERPRISES

Taking the multitude of ecological zones (or ecosystems) explained previously as given, natural resource intensive enterprises are practiced across the continent. The following statistics on the regional economy are useful for understanding the natural resource intensive enterprises in the region. The percentage of the economically active population that agriculture employs is in the range of 30–40% in Latin America while it reaches up to 60% in the high Andean regions (Baethgen, 1997; Mata et al., 2001). On agricultural lands, a great diversity of grains, oil seeds, vegetables, root crops, and other specialty crops are raised. In addition, livestock management is performed broadly in a commercial and a noncommercial manner. Argentina is the world's largest consumer of beef per person and Argentina and Brazil are one of the world's largest exporters of cattle (Steiger, 2006). Besides the income earned from a large variety of crops and animals managed by farmers, forest income is another indispensable component of the regional economy, from which about 20% of the rural income is generated (Peters et al., 1989; Vedeld et al., 2007).

Of the six natural resource intensive enterprises defined in the previous section (Seo, 2012a), the survey of individual rural households in South America reveals that a crops-only enterprise accounts for 33% of rural households in the sample, a crops–livestock enterprise 30%, a crops–forests enterprise 8%, a crops–livestock–forests enterprise 10%, a forests-only enterprise <1%, and a livestock-only enterprise 19%.

A multinomial Logit model is estimated in Table 6.3 for the choices of the six natural resource enterprises by individual households. In order to

Table 6.3 A multinomial Logit model of choices of natural resource enterprises

Variables	A crops–livestock enterprise		A crops–forests enterprise		A crops–livestock–forests enterprise	
	Estimate	P value	Estimate	P value	Estimate	P value
Intercept	3.82	0.002	−2.54	0.31	−7.78	0.03
Summer temperature	−0.243	0.07	0.075	0.76	−0.017	0.96
Summer temperature sq	0.007	0.04	−0.0006	0.92	0.0007	0.93
Summer precipitation	0.0057	0.12	0.019	0.004	0.019	0.02
Summer precipitation sq	−0.00002	0.01	−0.000033	0.01	−0.00003	0.05
Winter temperature	−0.027	0.70	−0.37	0.002	0.105	0.55
Winter temperature sq	−0.00086	0.64	0.007	0.01	−0.001	0.78
Winter precipitation	−0.0034	0.44	0.00062	0.94	0.0098	0.42
Winter precipitation sq	5.64E-06	0.67	−1.95E-06	0.94	−0.00006	0.26
Summer CVP (%)	−0.0107	0.001	0.029	0.001	0.033	0.006
Winter CVP (%)	0.00037	0.89	−0.0069	0.14	−0.0078	0.13
Soils Phaeozems (dummy)	−1.19	<.0001	−2.12	0.001	−1.52	0.03
Lithosols (dummy)	−0.85	0.005	−0.85	0.17	−0.258	0.67
Fluvisols (dummy)	−2.095	<.0001	0.48	0.29	−0.307	0.66
Luvisols (dummy)	0.114	0.60	0.081	0.83	0.25	0.54
Andosols (dummy)	0.154	0.66	1.36	0.02	1.37	0.05
Elevation (km above sea level)	−0.00046	0.000	−0.00048	0.07	−0.00005	0.88
Flat (dummy)	0.065	0.81	0.17	0.69	0.607	0.16
Clay (dummy)	0.257	0.33	0.10	0.82	0.106	0.85
Household size (n)	0.054	0.07	−0.007	0.89	0.15	0.001
Age (n)	0.011	0.04	0.032	0.001	0.009	0.34
Education (n)	−0.011	0.49	0.108	<.0001	0.015	0.59
Computer (dummy)	−0.24	0.15	−0.093	0.73	−0.098	0.76

(Continued)

Table 6.3 A multinomial Logit model of choices of natural resource enterprises (cont.)

Variables	A crops–livestock enterprise		A crops–forests enterprise		A crops–livestock–forests enterprise	
	Estimate	P value	Estimate	P value	Estimate	P value
Primary farmer (dummy)	−0.35	0.06	−0.34	0.25	0.27	0.49
Argentina (dummy)	−1.019	0.01	−2.38	0.000	−0.14	0.84
Chile (dummy)	1.54	0.005	−8.10	<.0001	−6.95	0.003
Venezuela (dummy)	−0.97	0.001	−18.026	0.99	−18.37	0.99
Ecuador (dummy)	−1.85	<.0001	−2.83	<.0001	−2.53	<.0001
Colombia (dummy)	0.017	0.96	0.104	0.85	−0.41	0.53

Variables	A livestock-only enterprise		A forests-only enterprise	
	Estimate	P value	Estimate	P value
Intercept	5.85	0.001	−155.11	0.03
Summer temperature	−0.55	0.001	10.86	0.05
Summer temperature sq	0.016	<.0001	−0.23	0.05
Summer precipitation	0.012	0.005	0.17	0.01
Summer precipitation sq	−0.000028	0.01	−0.0004	0.009
Winter temperature	−0.258	0.002	−0.38	0.72
Winter temperature sq	0.0019	0.35	0.012	0.66
Winter precipitation	0.0074	0.22	0.088	0.09
Winter precipitation sq	−0.000023	0.29	−0.00024	0.15
Summer CVP (%)	−0.0039	0.45	0.11	0.04
Winter CVP (%)	0.00075	0.83	0.056	0.02
Soils Phaeozems (dummy)	−0.75	0.01	−17.80	0.99
Lithosols (dummy)	0.47	0.19	−16.63	0.99
Fluvisols (dummy)	−0.107	0.75	−11.94	0.99

Luvisols (dummy)	0.47	0.07	2.13	0.18
Andosols (dummy)	0.84	0.12	−1.25	0.99
Elevation (km above sea level)	−0.0014	<.0001	−0.007	0.003
Flat (dummy)	0.032	0.91	−23.14	0.98
Clay (dummy)	−0.64	0.05	0.41	0.74
Household size (n)	−0.006	0.86	−0.10	0.47
Age (n)	0.03	<.0001	0.04	0.08
Education (n)	0.077	<.0001	0.051	0.49
Computer (dummy)	−0.45	0.01	0.72	0.33
Primary farmer (dummy)	−1.06	<.0001	0.81	0.46
Argentina (dummy)	−1.226	0.005	−16.67	0.98
Chile (dummy)	−1.64	0.01	−9.79	0.32
Venezuela (dummy)	0.11	0.74	−15.05	0.99
Ecuador (dummy)	−20.56	0.99	−19.29	0.98
Colombia (dummy)	1.008	0.01	0.11	0.96

Note: Likelihood ratio statistics = 926.6 (P-value < 0.0001).

compare the results in this chapter directly with those in Chapters 4 and 5, the present author maintained the model specifications used in the previous chapters. That is, the specifications of seasonal climate variables, temperature normals and precipitation normals, a quadratic functional form for a climate normal variable, seasonal climate risk variables, soils, household characteristics, and country dummies are all entered in the same manner.

Parameters are identified only for the five enterprises against the crops-only enterprise which serves as the base case. The Likelihood Ratio test statistic indicates that the model is highly significant, with P value <0.0001. The P-values of many climatic variables are significant at 5 or 10% level, indicating that climate is a significant determinant of individuals' choices of natural resource enterprises. Both climate mean normals and climate risk normals, that is, coefficients of variation in precipitation (CVPs), are significant.

Many of the soils, geology, and topography variables are significant. In the Phaeozems which are dark fertile soils (Driessen et al., 2001), a crops-only enterprise is most often chosen. In the Fluvisols which are formed by river actions, a crops–livestock enterprise is less likely to be chosen. In the Andosols which are found in volcanic areas, a crops–forests and a crops–livestock–forests are chosen more frequently. In the Lithosols which are found in steep mountainous regions, a crops–livestock enterprise is less often adopted.

In clay soils which make roaming and grazing difficult for animals, a livestock-only enterprise is not preferred. The higher the altitude, the less frequently are a livestock-only, a crops–livestock, and a forests-only enterprise selected.

Household socio-economic characteristics are significant factors in how natural resource enterprises are chosen by rural households. The larger the number of household members, the more likely is a crops–livestock–forests enterprise chosen. This may be due to additional labor forces available for livestock herding or picking forest products or flexibility in labor allocations to various activities (Seo, 2011). The older the head of the household, the more likely is he/she to choose a crops–livestock, a crops–forests, or a livestock-only. The more educated the head is, the more likely is he/she to choose a livestock-only or a crops–forests enterprise.

When the farm has a computer, it is less likely to choose a livestock-only enterprise. When the head of the farm is primarily a farmer, he/she is less likely to choose a livestock-only enterprise. This implies that a livestock-only enterprise is more likely to have a nonfarm income.

These estimates of household characteristics are in accordance with those from the microbehavioral models explained in Chapters 4 and 5.

These estimates also lay a solid foundation for a more complex model of microbehaviors in managing natural resources that this chapter hopes to deliver.

Further, these patterns in the estimates of household variables reveal striking contrasts between Sub-Sahara and South America. In South America, age, experience, and education all are estimated to help rural households to move away from crops to noncrop enterprises such as animal husbandry and forestry. In Sub-Sahara, by contrast, age, experience, and education all motivate farmers to move into a variety of crop portfolios (Seo, 2011, 2014a).

One factor that explains this contrast seems to be foreign development aids which are directed heavily toward to crop productivity improvements in Sub-Saharan countries (Byerlee and Eicher, 1997; World Development Report, 2008; World Bank, 2009). In addition, national agricultural agencies direct their extension services mostly to a variety of crop programs, overlooking the livestock sector especially in Africa (Seo, 2010a, 2011). The lesson from these results from the microbehavioral models is that a well-thought-out development aid approach should be inclusive of all natural resource enterprises in the region of concern.

Country dummy variables are intended to capture country-specific factors such as culture, language, history, and policy interventions that are not captured by the other explanatory variables. For example, in the sampled countries, Spanish is spoken officially except in Brazil whose official language is Portuguese. Against the base case of Brazil, a crops–livestock enterprise is least likely to be chosen in Ecuador but more likely in Chile. Against Brazil, a livestock-only enterprise is more likely in Colombia to be adopted by natural resource managers. A crops–forests enterprise is more likely in Brazil against the other countries. A crops–livestock–forests enterprise is less likely in Chile and Ecuador against Brazil where this enterprise is most frequently chosen.

From the estimated parameters shown in Table 6.3, adoption probabilities of the six enterprises are calculated for each household by multiplying the estimated parameters to the observed values of the corresponding variables at the household level. For each enterprise, adoption probabilities across all the rural households which are situated across the entire range of temperature normals are plotted. A box plot is drawn for each enterprise, which shows, for each temperature point or precipitation point, mean, median, 95% confidence interval, minimum, and maximum of the estimated choice probabilities.

The distributions of the crops–only enterprise across climate normals are shown in Fig. 6.1. For the temperature normals, adoption probability increases initially at cold temperature zones, fluctuates at temperate zones before it declines in hot temperature zones. Again, the crops–only enterprise is shown to be vulnerable to high temperatures (Adams et al., 1990; Rosenzweig and Parry, 1994; Reilly et al., 1996; Schlenker and Roberts 2009).

For the range of precipitation normals, adoption probability of the crops–only enterprise is shown to decline steadily as average annual monthly precipitation increases up to about 200 mm/month. Almost all farms in

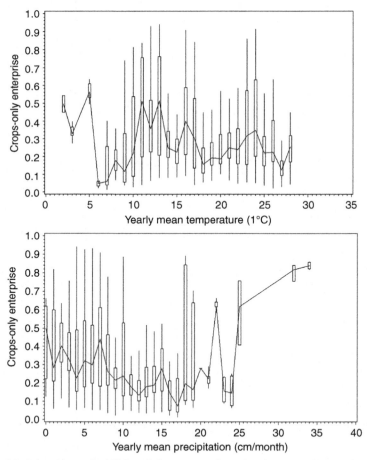

Figure 6.1 *Adoption probabilities of the crops-only enterprise across temperature normals (top) and precipitation normals (bottom).*

the sample belong to the rainfall zones with less than 200 mm/month. The decrease in adoption of this enterprise in higher rainfall zones can be attributed to decoupling of forest-related activities from the crops-only system. In much higher rainfall zones, the probability of adopting this enterprise seems to increase.

The distributions of the livestock-related enterprises are shown in Fig. 6.2 across the range of temperature normals: a livestock-only, a crops–livestock, and a crops–livestock–forests enterprise. The distribution of a livestock-only enterprise shows that adoption probability is increasing as average temperature gets warmer. However, it does have a fluctuating pattern as well. At the range from 12 to 18°C, adoption probability increases

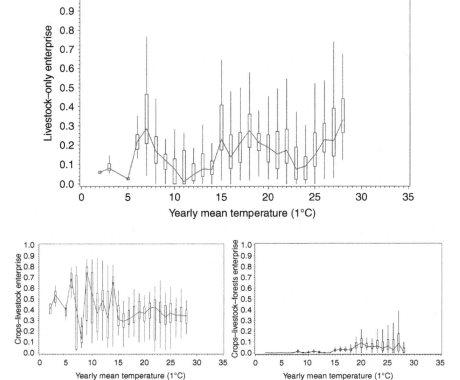

Figure 6.2 *Adoption probabilities of the livestock-related enterprises across temperature normals (counter-clockwise livestock-only, crops–livestock, crops–livestock–forests).*

as temperature increases. Also at the temperature range from 25°C, adoption probability increases as normal temperature gets warmer. These results indicate a higher resilience of animal enterprises than crop enterprises to a hotter climate (Seo and Mendelsohn, 2008a; Seo, 2010a,b).

The distribution of adoption probabilities of the crops–livestock enterprise shows that adoption probability is quite stable across the entire average temperature range, albeit with ups and downs in adoption probabilities, which is a strong indication that the crops–livestock enterprise is resilient to the variation in average temperature.

The distribution of adoption probabilities of a crops–livestock–forests enterprise, the most diversified enterprise of all, shows an increasing trend of adoption as normal temperature increases. In hotter zones, rural managers adapt by diversifying into crops, livestock, and forests. What this indicates is that behavioral responses through diversification are one of the most effective measures adopted by farmers to cope with a hotter and more risky climate regime (Seo, 2012c, 2014a).

In Fig. 6.3, the distributions of the livestock-related enterprises are drawn across the range of precipitation normals. The distribution of adoption probabilities of a livestock-only enterprise shows a stable distribution until 200 mm/month, after which adoption probability falls as average precipitation further increases.

Adoption probability of a crops–livestock enterprise shows a hill shape response function. That is, adoption probability increases initially in low precipitation zones as precipitation increases. When annual precipitation per month exceeds 160 mm/month, adoption probability of crops–livestock enterprise falls at a fast rate.

Adoption probability of a crops–livestock–forests enterprise, the most diversified enterprise of all, also shows a linear increasing trend with precipitation increase, albeit the slope of increase is steeper. The distribution is a strong indication that the combinations of crops and forest products that are suitable in high rainfall zones make this enterprise remain competitive in such conditions.

The distributions of forest-related enterprises are shown in Fig. 6.4. For the crops–forests enterprise, adoption probability increases as normal temperature becomes warmer. For this enterprise, adoption probability exhibits a linearly increasing trend across the precipitation range. These distributions indicate that a warmer and wetter climate regime may benefit forest-related enterprises such as the crops–forests enterprise and the forests-only enterprise (Seo, 2010c, 2012a,b).

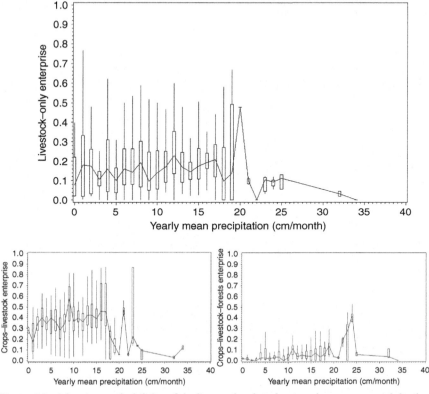

Figure 6.3 *Adoption probabilities of the livestock-related enterprises across precipitation normals (counter-clockwise livestock-only, crops–livestock, crops–livestock–forests).*

Due to a limited number of rural farms that chose the forest-only enterprise, it is hard to tell a trend in the adoption of forests-only enterprise, other than the concentration of this enterprise at around 18°C. Hence, the distributions of this enterprise are not included in the box plot figures shown in Figs. 6.1–6.4.

Based on the estimated model parameters in Table 6.3, changes in choice probabilities of the six enterprises due to shifts in climate variables marginally are calculated and presented in Table 6.4. The baseline adoption probability for the crops-only enterprise is about 30%, for the livestock-only about 20%, for the crops–livestock enterprise about 37%, for the crops–forests about 7%, for the crops–livestock–forests about 5%, and for the forests-only less than 1%.

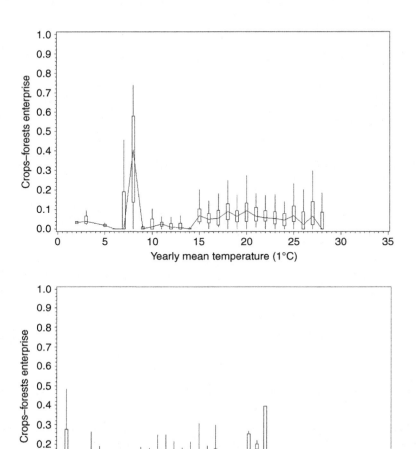

Figure 6.4 *Adoption probabilities of the crops–forests enterprise across temperature normals (top) and precipitation normals (bottom).*

When temperature normals are increased by 1°C, the probability of choosing a crops-only enterprise is predicted to fall by 0.3% points and a crops–forests enterprise to fall by 0.5% points. A forests-only enterprise would also fall by 0.07% point.

On the other hand, the livestock-only enterprise choice is predicted to increase by 0.4% points and the crops–livestock enterprise to increase by 0.32% points. The crops–livestock–forests enterprise also increases by 0.2% points. These marginal effects show that the livestock-related

Table 6.4 Marginal effects of climate shifts on choices of natural resource enterprises

	Baseline (%)	Change due to temperature increase by +1°C (%)	Change due to precipitation increase by +1% (%)
A crops–livestock enterprise	37.2	0.3	−0.16
A crops–forests enterprise	6.8	−0.5	0.04
A crops–livestock–forests enterprise	5.1	0.2	0.04
A livestock-only enterprise	20.4	0.4	0.05
A forests-only enterprise	0.8	−0.07	0.03
A crops-only enterprise	29.8	−0.3	0.001

enterprises and the mixed enterprises are more resilient to a hotter climate than crop enterprises (Seo, 2010b, 2012c).

When rainfall is altered upward by 1%, the crops–livestock enterprise is projected to fall by 0.16% points. The enterprises with forests in the portfolio, that is, the crops–forests, crops–livestock–forests, and forests-only enterprises are all projected to increase due probably to beneficial effects of increased rainfall on trees (Seo, 2010c). The livestock-only enterprise is predicted to increase due most likely to an increase in pasturelands under increased rainfall. There is little change at the margin in the crops-only enterprise.

Changes in climate normals such as seasonal temperature normals and precipitation normals may influence changes in climate risk normals, that is, the seasonal CVPs (Hansen et al., 2006, 2012; Ropelewski and Halpert 1987; Curtis et al., 2001). If that is the case, some of the "indirect" effects of changes in climate normals are absorbed by the coefficients in the seasonal CVPs in the model shown in Table 6.3. Notwithstanding, the present author focuses on changes in climate mean normals because the exact relationships between climate mean normals and climate risk normals are not available yet. Further, changes in climate risk indicators such as the CVP due to global warming are not established yet (Tebaldi et al., 2007; IPCC, 2012; NRC, 2013).

Conditional on the choice of one of the six enterprises, the present author estimates in Table 6.5 the land value (per hectare) of each chosen enterprise by the same set of explanatory variables entered in the choice model in Table 6.3. Due to a limited number of sample households for the

Table 6.5 Enterprise-specific land value regressions

	A crops–livestock enterprise		A crops–forests enterprise		A crops–livestock–forests enterprise	
	Estimate	P-value	Estimate	P-value	Estimate	P-value
Intercept	893.4	0.60	9514.2	0.15	−5086.5	0.64
Summer temperature (°C)	−68.9	0.68	−34.1	0.96	−206.1	0.88
Summer temperature sq	5.66	0.21	4.5	0.79	13.6	0.66
Summer precipitation (mm/month)	11.6	0.03	−28.7	0.11	34.04	0.11
Summer precipitation sq	−0.027	0.10	0.055	0.08	−0.06	0.05
Winter temperature (°C)	69.5	0.46	−386.7	0.09	−99.8	0.86
Winter temperature sq	−8.34	0.00	2.9	0.56	−8.26	0.52
Winter precipitation (mm/month)	2.52	0.62	−13.1	0.64	30.04	0.29
Winter precipitation sq	−0.0053	0.62	0.11	0.42	−0.24	0.11
Summer CVP (%)	2.02	0.77	−36.7	0.19	7.40	0.81
Winter CVP (%)	−2.23	0.22	−0.76	0.94	−4.25	0.69
Soils Phaeozems (dummy)	−111.7	0.89				
Lithosols (dummy)	955.1	0.18				
Fluvisols (dummy)	−1298.8	0.34				
Luvisols (dummy)	70.94	0.83				
Andosols (dummy)	714.8	0.08				
Clay (dummy)	−920.2	0.03	−1612.0	0.14	−647.4	0.70
Age (n)	−1.32	0.90			−3.28	0.87
Education (n)	−34.8	0.32			−182.3	0.04
Household size (n)	79.7	0.17			196.8	0.05
Computer (dummy)	73.0	0.74			2475.8	0.00
Primary farmer (dummy)	−390.9	0.21			−504.4	0.65
Argentina (dummy)	−2052.8	0.01	−3164.6	0.00	−4482.6	0.00

(Continued)

	A livestock-only enterprise		A forests-only enterprise		A crops-only enterprise	
	Estimate	P-value	Estimate	P-value	Estimate	P-value
Intercept	3405.6	0.24	5523.4	0.68	−2619.5	0.41
Summer temperature (°C)	−100.4	0.75	1773.3	0.20	886.0	0.00
Summer temperature sq	8.44	0.27	−41.9	0.19	−19.4	0.00
Summer precipitation (mm/month)	5.34	0.55	41.1	0.06	9.8	0.05
Summer precipitation sq	−0.03	0.17	0.01	0.34	−0.02	0.07
Winter temperature (°C)	−221.8	0.14	−3645.6	0.04	−176.8	0.18
Winter temperature sq	−1.87	0.55	95.1	0.04	1.15	0.72
Chile (dummy)	−1916.0	0.14	258.9	0.95	−2942.8	0.60
Venezuela (dummy)	712.1	0.45	2287.1	0.17	−1107.3	0.46
Ecuador (dummy)	−1391.6	0.23	963.6	0.22	3198.4	0.00
Colombia (dummy)	1467.2	0.02	−3098.6	0.13	−781.7	0.71
M_1					−11682.0	0.01
M_2	−6529.8	0.01	1702.4	0.46		
M_3	2949.1	0.10	−3294.3	0.03	−1054.5	0.76
M_4	1477.4	0.19	8269.5	0.00	16968.0	0.00
M_5	3558.1	0.01				
M_6	−1775.4	0.30	−3179.1	0.02	−4252.8	0.01

Summary Statistics

	A livestock-only enterprise		A forests-only enterprise		A crops-only enterprise	
N	742		147		103	
P value for F	<.0001		<.0001		<.0001	
Adj-Rsq	0.27		0.31		0.46	

Table 6.5 Enterprise-specific land value regressions (cont.)

	A livestock-only enterprise		A forests-only enterprise		A crops-only enterprise	
	Estimate	P-value	Estimate	P-value	Estimate	P-value
Winter precipitation (mm/month)	8.08	0.15	−34.3	0.01	−7.57	0.32
Winter precipitation sq	−0.03	0.00	0.07	0.15	−0.005	0.78
Summer CVP (%)	−30.7	0.00			12.5	0.21
Winter CVP (%)	−13.4	0.00			−13.9	0.00
Soils Phaeozems (dummy)					530.1	0.35
Lithosols (dummy)					1361.8	0.03
Fluvisols (dummy)					−338.5	0.69
Luvisols (dummy)					−66.7	0.84
Andosols (dummy)					412.7	0.54
Clay (dummy)	−1341.3	0.00			−1163.2	0.01
Age (n)	38.0	0.00			−26.4	0.00
Education (n)	75.4	0.04			−27.3	0.45
Household size (n)	−55.9	0.22			204.8	0.00
Computer (dummy)	−544.1	0.01			−397.3	0.19
Primary farmer (dummy)	−1201.9	0.00			−206.2	0.63
Argentina (dummy)	−3944.5	000			−1812.4	0.01
Chile (dummy)	−3551.6	0.00			−3673.8	0.09
Venezuela (dummy)	−333.7	0.61			−2442.2	0.00
Ecuador (dummy)						
Colombia (dummy)	1432.6	0.01			779.5	0.13
M_1	1060.1	0.33	−1,7101.0	0.06	−1836.6	0.34
M_2	1128.8	0.46	−7383.5	0.06	−2538.3	0.17

M_3	597.1	0.76	25184.0	0.06	8519.1	0.00
M_4	375.7	0.76			−1551.2	0.19
M_5	−4681.4	0.00			−2058.4	0.24
M_6						

Summary Statistics

N	420		15		638	
P value for F	<.0001		0.07		<.0001	
Adj-Rsq	0.39		0.91		0.12	

forests-only enterprise, a parsimonious specification is used for this enterprise. The six regressions are highly significant according to the F statistics. Many climate variables are significant at 10% level.

To identify the choice model non-parametrically from the conditional land value regressions, the present author dropped five explanatory variables from the conditional land value regressions: flat terrain, elevation, and some soil variables.

Selection bias correction terms, denoted as M_1, M_2, M_3, M_4, M_5, and M_6 in the table, are entered into the regressions following the Dubin–McFadden procedure. Here the numbers 1–6 mean a selection bias correction term for, in order, choice of a crops–livestock enterprise, choice of a crops–forests enterprise, choice of a crops–livestock–forests enterprise, choice of a livestock-only enterprise, choice of a forests-only enterprise, and choice of a crops-only enterprise.

Estimates of the selection bias correction terms are large and significant, implying that any estimate of the impact of climate change on natural resource enterprises will be biased in a severe way without correcting for the selectivity. Some of these estimates are positive whereas others are negative, which means that the Dubin–McFadden correction method would be superior to the other selection correction methods which assume the same correlation coefficient, therefore the same sign, among the related terms of alternatives (Dubin and McFadden, 1984; Schmertman, 1994; Bourguignon et al., 2004).

The selectivity correction terms are interpreted as follows. The land value of a livestock-only enterprise is lower at the households where a crops-only enterprise is chosen. The land value of a crops-only enterprise is higher at the households where a crops–livestock–forests enterprise is chosen. The land value of a crops–forests enterprise is higher at the households where a forests-only enterprise is chosen, but lower at the households where a crops-only is chosen. The land value of a crops–livestock enterprise is lower at the households where a crops–forests enterprise is chosen, but higher at the households where a forests-only enterprise is chosen.

For climate normals variables, the land value function of the crops-only enterprise is hill-shaped against summer temperature while that of the crops–livestock enterprise is hill-shaped against the winter temperature. This means a very high summer temperature normals is harmful to the crops-only enterprise and a very high winter temperature normals is harmful to the crops–livestock enterprise.

Against summer precipitation, the land value function of the crops-only enterprise is hill-shaped while that of the crops–livestock–forests enterprise is U-shaped. Against winter precipitation, the land value function of the livestock-only enterprise is hill-shaped. That is, a very high summer precipitation is harmful for the crops-only enterprise and a very high winter precipitation is harmful for the livestock-only enterprise.

Climate risk normals are significant factors that determine variations of enterprise-specific land values. When climate risk is high, specialized systems are shown to have lower land values. More specifically, when the winter CVP is higher, the land value of a crops-only enterprise is lower, so is that of a livestock-only enterprise. Similarly, if summer CVP is higher, the land value of a livestock-only enterprise is lower. This means a specialized enterprise, either in crops or livestock, which is most often managed commercially for profit, is adopted more often in low climate risk zones by South American farmers. The results show that these specialized enterprises warily take climate risks into account when they locate their enterprises.

Some but not all soils, topographic, and geologic variables are estimated to be significant in the determination of land values. When the estimate of a soil variable is far from being significant, the present author dropped it from the final regressions of minority enterprises, for example, the forests-only, because of the statistical collinearity concern especially in the small sample enterprises. In soils Lithosols which are most common in steep mountainous regions, the land value of a crops-only enterprise is higher. A high-value livestock enterprise tends to be located in flat terrains, as a large scale livestock operation is difficult in steep high elevation terrains. The land value of a crops-only enterprise is estimated to be lower in clay soils, probably because clay soils are not ideal for the growth of the crops favored by specialized crop enterprises. In the clay soils, the land value is also lower for a livestock-only, so is for a crops–livestock enterprise.

Of the household and socio-economic characteristics, some parameter estimates are significant at 5% level. The more educated the head of a household, the higher the land value of a livestock-only enterprise. The older the head of a household, the higher the land value of a livestock-only enterprise but the lower the land value of a crops-only enterprise. When the household head engages in farming as her/his primary occupation, then the land value of that farm is lower in the case of a livestock-only enterprise. In the households with more than one computer, the land value is lower in the case of a livestock-only enterprise, but higher in the case of a crops–livestock–forests enterprise. The larger the number of family members, the higher the land value of a crops-only enterprise.

Finally, country dummy variables are entered as control variables by leaving out Brazil as the base case. Against the base case of Brazil, land value in Argentina is lower especially for a livestock-only and a crops–livestock–forests enterprise. In Colombia, the land value is higher for the livestock systems: a crops–livestock, a crops–livestock–forests, and a livestock-only. In Venezuela, the land value for a crops-only is lower. In Chile, the land value for a crops-only is lower than that in Brazil, so is the land value of a livestock-only.

From the estimated parameters in Table 6.5, changes in the land value of each of the six enterprises in response to a marginal change in temperature normals or precipitation normals are calculated in Table 6.6. An increase in temperature normals by 1°C is predicted to decrease the land value by more than 105 $ ha^{-1} for a crops-only enterprise, but to increase the land value of a livestock-only enterprise by 12 $ ha^{-1}. The decrease in land value for the crops–livestock enterprise is predicted to be 16 $ ha^{-1} whereas the increase

Table 6.6 Marginal effects of climate change on enterprise land values ($ ha^{-1})

		Absolute changes		% Changes	
	Baseline land value ($ ha^{-1})	Changes due to temperature increase by +1°C ($ ha^{-1})	Changes due to precipitation increase by +1% ($ ha^{-1})	Changes due to temperature increase by +1°C ($ ha^{-1})	Changes due to precipitation increase by +1% ($ ha^{-1})
A crops–livestock enterprise	1621	−16	+2	−1.0%	0.1%
A crops–forests enterprise	2349	−114	+1	−4.9%	0.0%
A crops–livestock–forests enterprise	2020	+27	−4	1.3%	−0.2%
A livestock-only enterprise	1169	+12	−7	1.0%	−0.6%
A forests-only enterprise	1512	−203	+56	−13.4%	3.7%
A crops-only enterprise	2408	−104	−2	−4.3%	−0.1%

in the land value for a crops–livestock–forests enterprise is to be 27 $ ha^{-1}. The land value is predicted to fall significantly for a crops–forests, so is the land value for a forests-only enterprise.

In percentage terms, the decrease of the crops-only land value amounts to 4.3%, the decrease of the crops–forests land value 5%, and the decrease of the forests-only land value 13%. The increase in the livestock-only land value is 1% and the increase in the crops–livestock–forests land value is 1.3%.

If precipitation should increase by 1% from the baseline, land value is predicted to increase for a forests-only enterprise by 56 $ ha^{-1} (+3.7%). The land value is predicted to fall in a crops-only enterprise by 3 $ ha^{-1} (−0.1%) and in a livestock-only by 7.6 $ ha^{-1} (−0.6%). The land value is predicted to increase for the crops–livestock enterprise by 3 $ ha^{-1} (+0.1%) whereas that of the crops–livestock–forests enterprise is to fall by 4 $ ha^{-1} (−0.2%).

6.6 FUTURE SIMULATIONS WITH CLIMATE CHANGE SCENARIOS

Given the current sensitivities of the natural resource enterprises to climate conditions as explained in the previous section, future changes in climate conditions will affect natural resource managers in terms of both individuals' choices of enterprises and profits earned from the enterprises. To simulate the changes in choice decisions and profit outcomes, the same climate change predictions from the two Atmospheric Oceanic General Circulation Models (AOGCMs) which are used in Chapters 4 and 5 are assumed to manifest by the middle of this century: the UKMO (United Kingdom Meteorology Office) HadCM3 (Hadley center Coupled Model version 3) model and the GISS (Goddard Institute of Space Studies) ER (ModelE-R) model (Gordon et al., 2000; Schmidt et al., 2005). Same with the previous chapters, an A2 emissions scenario is assumed to capture a high economic growth and emissions growth storyline (Nakicenovic et al., 2000).

As described in detail in Chapter 4, the UKMO scenario tells a hotter and more arid storyline whereas the GISS scenario tells a milder and wetter storyline. By the middle of this century, the UKMO model predicts about a 2.4°C increase in temperature and about 13 mm/month decrease in summer precipitation. The GISS model predicts a slightly smaller degree of temperature increase, that is, an increase of 2.0°C, and an increase in summer precipitation by 8 mm/month.

The impacts of the assumed changes in climate on individuals' choices of natural resource enterprises are calculated in Table 6.7. Under the

Table 6.7 Impacts of climate change on adoption probabilities of natural resource enterprises by 2060

	Baseline (%)	Change due to UKMO HadCM3 (%)	Change due to GISS ER (%)
A crops–livestock enterprise	37.2	+0.9	−0.2
A crops–forests enterprise	6.8	−1.2	−0.7
A crops–livestock–forests enterprise	5.1	+0.1	+0.5
A livestock-only enterprise	20.4	+1.8	+2.0
A forests-only enterprise	0.8	−0.5	+0.01
A crops-only enterprise	29.8	−1.1	−1.6

UKMO scenario, a livestock-only enterprise is expected to increase by 1.8% points and a crops–livestock enterprise to increase by 0.9% points. A crops–livestock–forests enterprise is also expected to increase by 0.1%. On the other hand, a crops-only enterprise is expected to decrease by 1.06% points whereas a crops–forests enterprise is predicted to fall by 1.2% and a forests-only enterprise to fall by 0.5%.

Note that a hotter and drier climate scenario from the UKMO model is pushing individuals away from enterprises based on forests or crops to enterprises based on livestock. In a hotter and drier future, animal husbandry seems to have relative advantage against crop agriculture and forestry because grasslands can still be abundant and of high quality under such a condition (Seo and Mendelsohn, 2008a; Seo, 2010a, 2014a, 2015d).

If, on the other hand, a milder and wetter GISS scenario should come to fruition, a livestock-only enterprise is predicted to increase by 2% points and a crops–livestock–forests enterprise to increase by 0.5% points. A crops-only enterprise is projected to decrease by 1.6%. In this wetter scenario, a crops–livestock enterprise turns out to decrease by 0.2% while a forests-only enterprise turns out to increase slightly. A crops–forests enterprise is predicted to decrease but only by 0.7% points.

In Table 6.8, the impact of climatic change on the land value of each of the six enterprises is calculated under each of the assumed scenarios. If the GISS scenario should be materialized, a large decrease in the land value of a crops-only enterprise by 200 $ ha^{-1} is predicted to occur. This amounts to 8.3% loss of the land value from the baseline land value of this enterprise. By contrast, a livestock-only enterprise would gain largely, the land value of

Table 6.8 Impacts of climate change on enterprise land values ($ ha^{-1}) by 2060

		Absolute changes		Percentage changes	
	Baseline	Change due to UKMO HadCM3	Change due to GISS ER	Change due to UKMO HadCM3 (%)	Change due to GISS ER (%)
A crops–livestock enterprise	1621.4	−111.6	18.0	−6.9	1.1
A crops–forests enterprise	2349.2	−34.2	−28.9	−1.5	−1.2
A crops–livestock-forests enterprise	2021.0	−219.0	157.4	−10.8	7.8
A livestock-only enterprise	1169.1	64.6	103.9	5.5	8.9
A forests-only enterprise	1512.6	−527.6	26.7	−34.9	1.8
A crops-only enterprise	2408.3	−298.5	−198.8	−12.4	−8.3

which is predicted to increase by 8.9%. A crops–livestock–forests enterprise is predicted to gain by 7.8% of the land value.

The impacts on the land values of the other enterprises are more muted. A crops–livestock enterprise would gain the land value by 1.1% and a forests–only enterprise would gain by 1.7%. The land value of a crops–forests enterprise is predicted to fall by 1.2%.

If the more severe UKMO scenario should come to fruition, the changes in the land values of enterprises would turn out to be larger. The land value of a crops-only enterprise is predicted to decrease by as much as 299 $ ha^{-1}, 12.4% from the baseline land value. A crops–livestock–forests enterprise is expected to decrease in the land value by 10.8%. The land value of a crops–livestock enterprise is predicted to fall by 6.9%. The land value of the crops–forests enterprise would decrease by 1.5% whereas the land value of the forests-only enterprise would decrease by 35%. On the other hand, the land value of a livestock-only enterprise is predicted to increase by 5.5%.

When all components of the model are put together, what is the total impact of climate change on agriculture and natural resource enterprises? If changes in choices of natural resource enterprises and changes in conditional

Table 6.9 Total impact of climate change on expected land values ($ ha^{-1}) by 2060

		Change due to UKMO HadCM3	Change due to GISS ER
Baseline	1801		
Absolute changes		−111	−33
% Changes		−6.2%	−1.9%
95% Confidence interval		(−129, −94)	(−47, −20)

enterprise land values are all accounted for, what is the change in the expected land value? In the microbehavioral model, the total impact estimate would capture a full array of adaptation behaviors that will be employed by natural resource managers.

In Table 6.9, the total damage is calculated by allowing for the changes in choices of natural resource enterprises and the enterprise-specific changes in land values that are caused by climate alterations by the middle of this century predicted by the two climate models. With the UKMO scenario that unfolds by the middle of this century, the expected land value is predicted to fall by 6.2%, about 111 $ ha^{-1}, from the baseline land value of 1801 $ ha^{-1}. The 95% confidence interval ranges from 95 to 129 $ ha^{-1}.

With the milder GISS scenario that unfolds by the middle of this century, the expected land value is predicted to decline by 1.9%, 34 $ ha^{-1}, from the baseline. In the GISS scenario, the harmful effects of climate change on crops are mostly offset by the beneficial effects of climate change on grasslands and animals, resulting in only a minor change in the expected land value in five decades.

6.7 FURTHER INSIGHTS ON STRUCTURAL COMPLEXITY AND ECOSYSTEM CHANGES

This chapter presents a complex structure of the microbehavioral econometric methods. This is achieved by coupling changes in ecosystems with changes in behavioral decisions in the context of global climatic changes and natural resource enterprises. The literature on ecosystems or ecological changes conditioned and caused by changes in climatic conditions is reviewed, which is then applied to understand ecological changes that would occur in South America (Schlesinger, 1997; Ainsworth and Long, 2005; Denman et al., 2007). Aligning with the ecosystem sciences, the present author defines seven natural resource enterprises: a crops–livestock, a crops–forests, a livestock–forests, a crops–livestock–forests, a livestock–only, a forests–only, and a crops–only enterprise.

The empirical results are revealing and capture many of the novel aspects of the microbehavioral model developed in this chapter. As has been emphasized in previous chapters, rural managers are shown to adapt to climatic shifts by switching from one to another natural resource enterprise. For example, when the GISS scenario unfolds by the middle of this century, they will choose less frequently a crops-only enterprise, so will a crops-forests enterprise. Instead, they will switch to a livestock-only as well as a crops–livestock–forests enterprise in order to cope with the changed climate conditions predicted by the GISS model. Thereby, a dominant enterprise in South America will change from a crops-only enterprise to, for example, a livestock enterprise at some point in the future.

The effects of global warming will be felt differently by the natural resource enterprises. With the GISS scenario materializing by the middle of this century, a crops-only enterprise will lose the value of land by 8.3%, taking into account all the adaptive changes the enterprise would make. However, a livestock-only enterprise will gain in land value under the GISS scenario by 8.9%, again taking into account all adaptive changes it would make. A crops–livestock–forests enterprise will also gain largely by 7.8% from the baseline land value. A crops–livestock enterprise is expected to gain by 1% in land value. A forests-only enterprise is expected to gain by 1.8%, but a crops–forests enterprise to lose by 1.2%.

A qualification in interpreting the results presented in this chapter for policy interventions is that a new variety of crops, livestock species, or trees that are more resilient to climatic shifts or animal diseases may be developed in the near future in a similar manner that the Green Revolution has accomplished high-yield varieties of crops (Ruttan, 2002; Evenson and Gollin, 2003; World Bank, 2009; James, 2012; Aksoy et al., 2014). Although the microbehavioral model of this chapter is capable of capturing the effects of such changes, it does not capture unforeseen advancements, that is, those entirely unknown to us now. Unexpected discoveries and breakthroughs will surely motivate these enterprises significantly, especially in the far future.

From the perspectives of the microbehavioral modeling, this chapter showcases a number of novel aspects. First, this chapter presents a more complex structure of microbehavioral decisions by natural resource managers. From a single-room structure in Chapter 5, the present author moved on to show a three-room structure with the three agricultural system model in Chapter 4. This chapter goes further from the three-room structure to the six-room structure. In the process, an increasingly more complex structure of the microbehavioral econometric model has been developed.

Second, microbehavioral decisions are explicitly coupled with changes in ecosystems due to external factors, that is, climate change (Seo, 2014a,b). This chapter provides a succinct but broad review of the literature on ecosystems and changes of ecological zones in South America due to climate change. Based on the literature, the choice set of the microbehavioral model is calibrated.

Third, this chapter provides a conceptual framework and analysis on measuring the impact of global warming on natural resource enterprises, which has been a central debate of global warming impacts from the very beginning of the climate change literature (IPCC, 1990; Adams et al., 1990; Nordhaus, 1994; Pearce et al., 1996; Seo, 2013, 2014c). The model is inclusive of all natural resource-related enterprises that would be hit by global warming. Nonetheless, this analysis is exclusive of the impacts that would occur primarily through the ocean-based ecosystems. There will be additional changes that are incurred from climate change through sea level rises, hurricane damages, and marine ecosystems (Yohe and Schlesinger, 1998; Ng and Mendelsohn, 2006; Nordhaus, 2010; Seo, 2014c).

Exercises

1. Referring to the literature on natural resource managements of Sub-Saharan Africa, provide the portfolio of natural resources of the entire continent by including at least 50 crop varieties, 20 animal species, and 30 forest-related varieties. Assuming that you are a microbehavioral econometric modeler, define the choice set of a natural resource manager in Sub-Sahara based on the portfolio of natural resource products you provided.
2. An alternative way to model the choice of a portfolio by a natural resource manager is a nested Logit model which was already introduced in Chapter 3. Making use of the choice set defined previously, write down the nested Logit model along with key assumptions of the model. Derive the choice probability of an individual natural resource portfolio from the nested Logit model. Explain the estimation procedure of your model.

REFERENCES

Adams, R., Rosenzweig, C., Peart, R.M., Ritchie, J.T., McCarl, B.A., Glyer, J.D., Curry, R.B., Jones, J.W., Boote, K.J., Allen, L.H., 1990. Global climate change and US agriculture. Nature 345, 219–224.

Ainsworth, E.A., Long, S.P., 2005. What have we learned from 15 years of free-air CO_2 enrichment (FACE)? A meta-analytic review of the responses of photosynthesis, canopy properties and plant production to rising CO_2. New Phytol. 165, 351–371.

Aksoy, S., Attardo, G., et al., 2014. Genome sequence of the Tsetse fly (Glossina morsitans): vector of African trypanosomiasis. Science 344 (6182), 380–386.

Baethgen, W.E., 1997. Vulnerability of agricultural sector of Latin America to climate change. Clim. Res. 9, 1–7.

Bourguignon, F., Fournier, M., Gurgand, M., 2004. Selection bias corrections based on the multinomial logit model: Monte-Carlo comparisons. DELTA Working Paper No. 20, Département et Laboratoire d'Economie Théorique et Appliquée (DELTA).

Byerlee, D., Eicher, C.K., 1997. Africa's Emerging Maize Revolution. Lynne Rienner Publishers Inc., USA.

Campbell, B.D., Stafford Smith, D.M., Ash, A.J., Fuhrer, J., Gifford, R.M., Hiernaux, P., Howden, S.M., Jones, M.B., Ludwig, J.A., Manderscheid, R., Morgan, J.A., Newton, P.C.D., Nösberger, J., Owensby, C.E., Soussana, J.F., Tuba, Z., ZuoZhong, C, 2000. A synthesis of recent global change research on pasture and rangeland production: reduced uncertainties and their management implications. Agric. Ecosyst. Environ. 82, 39–55.

Case, A., 1992. Neighborhood influence and technological change. Reg. Sci. Urban Econ. 22, 491–508.

Curtis, S., Adler, R.F., Huffman, G.J., Nelkin, E., Bolvin, D., 2001. Evolution of tropical and extratropical precipitation anomalies during the 1997 to 1999 ENSO cycle. Int. J. Climatol. 21, 961–971.

Dahl, G.B., 2002. Mobility and the returns to education: testing a Roy model with multiple markets. Econometrica 70, 2367–2420.

Danielson, J.J., Gesch, D.B., 2011. Global multi-resolution terrain elevation data 2010 (GMTED2010). U.S. Geological Survey Open-File Report 2011-1073, 26 p.

Denman, K.L., Brasseur, G., Chidthaisong, A., Ciais, P., Cox, P.M., Dickinson, R.E., Hauglustaine, D., Heinze, C., Holland, E., Jacob, D., Lohmann, U., Ramachandran, S., da Silva Dias, P.L., Wofsy, S.C., Zhang, X., 2007. Couplings between changes in the climate system and biogeochemistry. Climate Change 2007 The Physical Science Basis. Cambridge University Press, Cambridge and New York, NY, pp. 499–587.

Driessen, P., Deckers, J., Nachtergaele S F., 2001. Lecture Notes on the Major Soils of the World. Food and Agriculture Organization (FAO), Rome.

Dubin, J.A., McFadden, D.L., 1984. An econometric analysis of residential electric appliance holdings and consumption. Econometrica 52 (2), 345–362.

Dudal, R., 1980. Soil-related Constraints to Agricultural Development in the Tropics. International Rice Research Institute, Los Banos.

Efron, B., 1981. Nonparametric estimates of standard error: the jackknife, the bootstrap and other methods. Biometrika 68, 589–599.

Evenson, R., Gollin, D., 2003. Assessing the impact of the green revolution 1960–2000. Science 300, 758–762.

FAO, 2003. The Digital Soil Map of the World (DSMW) CD-ROM. Italy. Rome. Available in: http://www.fao.org/AG/agl/agll/dsmw.stm Accessed: March 2004.

Fischlin, A., Midgley, G.F., Price, J.T., Leemans, R., Gopal, B., Turley, C., Rounsevell, M.D.A., Dube, O.P., Tarazona, J., Velichko, A.A., 2007. Ecosystems, their properties, goods, and services. In: Parry, M.L., Canziani, O.F., Palutikof, J.P., van der Linden, P.J., Hanson, C.E. (Eds.), Climate Change 2007: Impacts, Adaptation and Vulnerability. Contribution of Working Group II to the Fourth Assessment Report of the Intergovernmental Panel on Climate Change. Cambridge University Press, Cambridge.

Fisher, F.M., 1966. The Identification Problem in Econometrics. McGraw-Hill, New York.

Food and Agriculture Organization (FAO), 1978. Report on Agro-Ecological Zones: Volume 1. Methodology and Results for Africa, Rome.

Food and Agriculture Organization (FAO)/International Institute of Applied Systems Analysis (IIASA), 2012. Global Agro-ecological Zones (GAEZ v3. 0) Model Documentation. FAO, Rome.

Ford, J., Katondo, K.M., 1977. Maps of tsetse fly (Glossina) distribution in Africa, 1973, according to subgeneric groups on a scale of 1: 5000000. Bull. Anim. Health Prod. Afr. 15, 187–193.

Fox, N.J., Marion, G., Davidson, R.S., White, P.C.L., Hutchings, M.R., 2012. Livestock helminths in a changing climate: approaches and restrictions to meaningful predictions. Animals 2, 93–107.

Gitay, H., Brwon, S., Easterling W, Jallow, B., 2001. Ecosystems and their Goods and Services. In: McCarthy et al (Ed.), Climate Change 2001: Impacts, Adaptations, and Vulnerabilities. Cambridge University Press, Cambridge, pp. 237–342.

Gordon, C., Cooper, C., Senior, C.A., Banks, H.T., Gregory, J.M., Johns, T.C., Mitchell, J.F.B., Wood, R.A., 2000. The simulation of SST, sea ice extents and ocean heat transports in a version of the Hadley Centre coupled model without flux adjustments. Clim. Dyn. 16, 147–168.

Hansen, J., Sato, M., Reudy, R., Lo, K., Lea, D.W., Medina-Elizade, M., 2006. Global temperature change. Proc. Natl. Acad. Sci. USA 103, 14288–14293.

Hansen, J., Sato, M., Reudy, R., 2012. Perception of climate change. Proc. Natl. Acad. Sci. USA 109, E2415–E2423.

Heckman, J., 1979. Sample selection bias as a specification error. Econometrica 47, 153–162.

Houghton, R.A., 2008. Carbon flux to the atmosphere from land-use changes: 1850-2005. Trends: A Compendium of Data on Global Change. Carbon Dioxide Information Analysis Center, Oak Ridge National Laboratory, US Department of Energy, Oak Ridge, TN, USA.

Intergovernmental Panel on Climate Change (IPCC), 1990. Climate Change: The IPCC Scientific Assessment. Cambridge University Press, Cambridge.

IPCC, 2012. Managing the Risks of Extreme Events and Disasters to Advance Climate Change Adaptation. A Special Report of Working Groups I and II of the Intergovernmental Panel on Climate Change. Cambridge University Press, Cambridge.

IPCC, 2014. Climate Change 2014: The Physical Science Basis, The Fifth Assessment Report of the IPCC. Cambridge University Press, Cambridge.

James, C., 2012. Global Status of Commercialized Biotech/GM Crops: 2012. ISAAA (The International Service for the Acquisition of Agri-biotech Applications) Brief No. 44. ISAAA, Ithaca, NY.

Johnston, J., Dinardo, J., 1997. Econometric Methods, fourth ed. McGraw-Hill, New York.

Joyce, L.A., Mills, J.R., Heath, L.S., McGuire, A.D., Haynes, R.W., Birdsey, R.A., 1995. Forest sector impacts from changes in forest productivity under climate change. J. Biogeogr. 22, 703–713.

Le Treut, H., Somerville, R., Cubasch, U., Ding, Y., Mauritzen, C., Mokssit, A., Peterson, T., Prather, M., 2007. Historical overview of climate change. Climate Change 2007 Cambridge University Press, Cambridge, New York.

Lee, L.F., 1983. Generalized econometric models with selectivity. Econometrica 51, 507–512.

Magrin, G., Garcia, C.G., Choque, D.C., Gimenez, J.C., Moreno, A.R., Nagy, G.J., Nobre, C., Villamizar, A., 2007. Latin America. In: Parry, M.L., Canziani, O.F., Palutikof, J.P., van der Linden, P.J., Hanson, C.E. (Eds.), Climate Change 2007: Impacts, Adaptation, and Vulnerability: Contribution of Working Group II to the Fourth Assessment Report of the Intergovernmental Panel on Climate Change. Cambridge University Press, Cambridge, pp. 581–615.

Mata, L.J., Campos, M., et al., 2001. Latin America. Climate Change 2001: Impacts, Adaptation, Vulnerability—Contribution of Working Group II to the Third Assessment Report of the Intergovernmental Panel on Climate Change Cambridge University Press, Cambridge.

Matthews, E., 1983. Global vegetation and land use: new high-resolution data bases for climate studies. J. Clim. Appl. Meteorol. 22, 474–487, Available from: http://data.giss.nasa.gov/landuse/vegeem.html.

McFadden, D.L., 1974. Conditional logit analysis of qualitative choice behavior. In: Zarembka, P. (Ed.), Frontiers in Econometrics. Academic Press, New York, pp. 105–142.

McFadden, D.L., 1984. Econometric analysis of qualitative response models. Grilliches, Z., Intrilligator, M.D. (Eds.), Handbook of Econometrics, Volume II, Elsevier Science Publishers BV, Amsterdam.

Nakicenovic, N., Davidson, O., Davis, G., Grübler, A., Kram, T., La Rovere, E.L., Metz, B., Morita, T., Pepper, W., Pitcher, H., Sankovski, A., Shukla, P., Swart, R., Watson, R., Dadi, Z., 2000. Emissions Scenarios, A Special Report of Working Group III of the Intergovernmental Panel on Climate Change. IPCC, Geneva.

National Research Council (NRC), 2013. Abrupt Impacts of Climate Change: Anticipating Surprises. The National Academies Press, Washington DC.

New, M., Lister, D., Hulme, M., Makin, I., 2002. A high-resolution data set of surface climate over global land areas. Clim. Res. 21, 1–25.

Ng, W.S., Mendelsohn, R., 2006. The economic impact of sea-level rise on nonmarket lands in Singapore. Ambio 35, 289–296.

Nin, A., Ehui, S., Benin, S., 2007. Livestock productivity in developing countries: an assessment. Evenson, R., Pingali, P. (Eds.), Handbook of Agricultural Economics, vol. 3, North Holland, Oxford, UK, pp. 2467–2532.

Nordhaus, W., 1994. Managing the Global Commons. The MIT Press, Cambridge, MA.

Nordhaus, W., 2010. The Economics of Hurricanes and Implications of Global Warming. Clim. Change Econ. 1, 1–24.

Pearce, D., Cline, W.R., Achanta, A., Fankhauser, S., Pachauri, R., Tol, R., Vellinga, P., 1996. The social costs of climate change: greenhouse damage and benefits of control. In: Bruce, J., Lee, H., Haites, E. (Eds.), Climate Change 1995: Economic and Social Dimensions of Climate Change. Cambridge University Press, Cambridge.

Peters, C.M., Gentry, A.W., Mendelsohn, R.O., 1989. Valuation of an Amazonian rainforest. Nature 339 (6227), 655–656.

Porter, J.H., Parry, M.L., Carter, T.R., 1991. The potential effects of climatic change on agricultural insect pests. Agric. Forest Meteorol. 57, 221–240.

Rabatel, A., Francou, B., Soruco, A., Gomez, J., Caceres, B., Ceballos, J.L., Basantes, R., Buille, M., Sicart, J.E., Huggel, C., Scheel, M., Lejeune, Y., Arnaud, Y., Collet, M., Condom, T., Consoli, G., Favier, V., Jomelli, V., Galarraga, R., Ginot, P., Maisincho, L., Mendoza, J., Menegoz, M., Ramirez, E., Ribstein, P., Suarez, W., Villacis, M., Wagnon, P., 2013. Current state of glaciers in the tropical Andes: a multi-century perspective on glacier evolution and climate change. The Cryosphere 7, 81–102.

Reilly, J., Baethgen, W., Chege, F., Van de Geijn, S., Enda, L., Iglesias, A., Kenny, G., Patterson, D., Rogasik, J., Rotter, R., Rosenzweig, C., Sombroek, W., Westbrook, J., 1996. Agriculture in a changing climate: impacts and adaptations. In: Watson, R., Zinyowera, M., Moss, R., Dokken, D. (Eds.), Climate Change 1995: Impacts, Adaptations, and Mitigation of Climate Change. Intergovernmental Panel on Climate Change (IPCC). Cambridge University Press, Cambridge.

Ropelewski, C.F., Halpert, M.S., 1987. Global and regional precipitation patterns associated with the El Nino/Southern Oscillation. Mon. Weather Rev. 115, 1606–1626.

Rosenzweig, C., Parry, M., 1994. Potential impact of climate change on world food supply. Nature 367, 133–138.

Ruttan, V.W., 2002. Productivity growth in world agriculture: sources and constraints. J. Econ. Perspect. 16, 161–184.

Schlenker, W., Roberts, M., 2009. Nonlinear temperature effects indicate severe damages to crop yields under climate change. Proc. Natl. Acad. Sci. USA 106 (37), 15594–15598.

Schlesinger, W.H., 1997. Biogeochemistry: An Analysis of Global Change, second ed. Academic Press, San Diego.

Schmertman, C.P., 1994. Selectivity bias correction methods in polychotomous sample selection methods. J. Econ. 60, 101–132.

Schmidt, G.A., Ruedy, R., Hansen, J.E., Aleinov, I., Bell, N., Bauer, M., Bauer, S., Cairns, B., Canuto, V., Cheng, Y., DelGenio, A., Faluvegi, G., Friend, A.D., Hall, T.M., Hu, Y., Kelley, M., Kiang, N.Y., Koch, D., Lacis, A.A., Lerner, J., Lo, K.K., Miller, R.L., Nazarenko, L., Oinas, V., Perlwitz, J., Rind, D., Romanou, A., Russell, G.L., Sato, M., Shindell, D.T., Stone, P.H., Sun, S., Tausnev, N., Thresher, D., Yao, M.S., 2005. Present day atmospheric simulations using GISS ModelE: comparison to in-situ, satellite and reanalysis data. J. Clim. 19, 153–192.

Secretariat of the Convention on Biological Diversity (2010) Global Biodiversity Outlook 3. Montréal, 94 pages.

Seo, S.N., 2010a. Is an integrated farm more resilient against climate change?: a microeconometric analysis of portfolio diversification in African agriculture? Food Pol. 35, 32–40.

Seo, S.N., 2010b. A microeconometric analysis of adapting portfolios to climate change: adoption of agricultural systems in Latin America. Appl. Econ. Perspect. Policy 32, 489–514.

Seo, S.N., 2010c. Managing forests, livestock, and crops under global warming: a microeconometric analysis of land use changes in Africa. Austral. J. Agric. Resour. Econ. 54 (2), 239–258.

Seo, S.N., 2011. A geographically scaled analysis of adaptation to climate change with spatial models using agricultural systems in Africa. J. Agric. Sci. 149, 437–449.

Seo, S.N., 2012a. Adapting natural resource enterprises under global warming in South America: a mixed logit analysis. Economia 12, 111–135.

Seo, S.N., 2012b. Adaptation behaviors across ecosystems under global warming: a spatial microeconometric model of the rural economy in South America. Pap. Reg. Sci. 91, 849–871.

Seo, S.N., 2012c. Decision making under climate risks: an analysis of sub-Saharan farmers' adaptation behaviors. Weather, Clim. Soc. 4, 285–299.

Seo, S.N., 2013. An essay on the impact of climate change on US agriculture: weather fluctuations, climatic shifts, and adaptation strategies. Clim. Change 121, 115–124.

Seo, S.N., 2014a. Evaluation of agro-ecological zone methods for the study of climate change with micro farming decisions in sub-Saharan Africa. Eur. J. Agron. 52, 157–165.

Seo, S.N., 2014b. Coupling climate risks, eco-systems, anthropogenic decisions using South American and Sub-Saharan farming activities. Meteorol. Appl. 21, 848–858.

Seo, S.N., 2014c. Adapting sensibly when global warming turns the field brown or blue: a comment on the 2014 IPCC Report. Econ. Affairs 34, 399–401.

Seo, S.N., 2015a. Micro-behavioral Economics of Global Warming: Modeling Adaptation Strategies in Agricultural and Natural Resource Enterprises. Springer, Cham.

Seo, S.N., 2015b. Modeling farmer adaptations to climate change in South America: a microbehavioral economic perspective. Environ. Ecol. Stat. 23 (1), 1–21.

Seo, S.N., 2015d. Adapting to extreme climate changes: raising animals in hot and arid ecosystems in Australia. Int. J. Biometeorol. 59, 541–550.

Seo, S.N., Mendelsohn, R., 2008a. Measuring impacts and adaptations to climate change: a structural Ricardian model of African livestock management. Agric. Econ. 38, 151–165.

Seo, S.N., Mendelsohn, R., 2008b. A Ricardian analysis of the impact of climate change impacts on South American farms. Chil. J. Agric. Res. 68, 69–79.

Seo, S.N., Mendelsohn, R., Dinar, A., Hassan, R., Kurukulasuriya, P., 2009. A Ricardian analysis of the distribution of climate change impacts on agriculture across agro-ecological zones in Africa. Environ. Resour. Econ. 43, 313–332.

Seo, S.N., McCarl, B., Mendelsohn, R., 2010. From beef cattle to sheep under global warming? An analysis of adaptation by livestock species choice in South America. Ecol. Econ. 69, 2486–2494.

Shaw, M.R., Zavaleta, E.S., Chiariello, N.R., Cleland, E.E., Mooney, H.A., Field, C.B., 2002. Grassland responses to global environmental changes suppressed by elevated CO_2. Science 298, 1987–1990.

Sohngen, B., Mendelsohn, R., 1998. Valuing the impact of large-scale ecological change in a market: the effect of climate change on US timber. Am. Econ. Rev. 88, 686–710.

Steiger, C., 2006. Modern beef production in Brazil and Argentina. Choices 21, 105–110.

Sutherst, R.W., 1991. Pest risk analysis and the greenhouse effect. Rev. Agric. Entomol. 79, 1177–1187.

Tebaldi, C., Hayhoe, K., Arblaster, J.M., Meehl, G.E., 2007. Going to the extremes: an intercomparison of model-simulated historical and future changes in extreme events. Clim. Change 79, 185–211.

Tubiello, F.N., Ewert, F., 2002. Simulating the effects of elevated CO_2 on crops: approaches and applications for climate change. Eur. J. Agron. 18, 57–74.

Tubiello, F.N., Amthor, J.A., Boote, K.J., Donatelli, M., Easterling, W., Fischer, G., Gifford, R.M., Howden, M., Reilly, J., Rosenzweig, C., 2007. Crop response to elevated CO_2 and world food supply. Eur. J. Agron. 26, 215–223.

United Nations Education, Scientific and Cultural Organization (UNESCO), 1973. The International Classification and Mapping of Vegetation. UNESCO, Paris.

Vedeld, P., Angelsen, A., Bojø, J., Sjaastad, E., Kobugabe, G.K., 2007. Forest environmental incomes and the rural poor. Forest Pol. Econ. 9, 869–879.

World Bank., 2009. Awakening Africa's Sleeping Giant: Prospects for Commercial Agriculture in the Guinea Savannah Zone and Beyond. World Bank and FAO, Washington DC.

World Development Report, 2008. World Development Report 2008: Agriculture for Development. World Bank, Washington.

World Resources Institute (WRI), 2005. World Resources 2005: The Wealth of the Poor: Managing Ecosystems to Fight Poverty. WRI, Washington, DC.

World Wildlife Fund (WWF) (2014) Ecoregion. Encyclopedia of Earth, Washington DC. Available from http://www.eoearth.org/view/article/51cbed7a7896bb431f692731.

Yohe, G.W., Schlesinger, M.E., 1998. Sea level change: the expected economic cost of protection or abandonment in the United States. Clim. Change 38, 337–342.

Ziska, L.H., 2003. Evaluation of yield loss in field-grown sorghum from a C3 and C4 weed as a function of increasing atmospheric carbon dioxide. Weed Sci. 51, 914–918.

CHAPTER 7

Modeling Risk, Perceptions, and Uncertainties With Microbehavioral Methods

In modeling microbehavioral decisions of individuals in order to cope with environmental and natural changes, a researcher must carefully examine the unique characteristics of the changes with which he/she is concerned. One of the prominent features of environmental and natural changes is that the changes often turn out to be a high risk event, or disruptive, or irreversible (IPCC, 2012; National Research Council, 2013; Titley et al., 2016). This chapter describes these types of events and explains how microbehavioral econometric models can capture these events.

The present author relates microbehavioral modeling approaches for these types of events in environmental and natural problems with the concepts of financial managements and instruments developed in the financial sectors in the presence of high risk and uncertainties in the financial markets. All the financial securities are available to environmental or natural resource managers, for example, equities, bonds, commodity trades, futures, options, insurance, and subsidy (Barry et al., 2000; Fabozzi et al., 2009).

Financial economists have long been deeply engaged in modeling a rare but high risk event such as the great crash in 1930, the dotcom bubble burst in 2000, or the global real estate bubble burst in 2008 (Galbraith, 1954; Shiller, 2000, 2005). Financial decisions in the presence of riskiness in investment returns have long been a subject of great interests and debates to the economists (Markowitz, 1952; Tobin, 1958; Sharpe, 1964; Fama, 1970; Arrow, 1971; Arrow and Fisher, 1974; Black and Scholes, 1973; Kahneman and Tversky, 1979; Shiller, 1981, 2004; Geanakoplos, 2010). These events in financial markets will be explained in the contexts of the high risk and high uncertainty events in natural resource and environmental sectors.

Most, if not all, financial assets and instruments are available to natural resource and environmental managers and the concepts and instruments in financial markets, as will be shown, apply well to environmental and natural resource sectors. Individual managers of environmental and natural resources rely on these financial instruments and similar instruments to cope with risk and uncertainties (Udry, 1995; Zilberman, 1998; Wright, 2011; Sumner and Zulauf, 2012). However, more fundamentally, managing risk and uncertainties in environmental and natural resource sectors cannot be accomplished without close linkages to broader financial markets and the economy.

7.1 MEASURES OF RISK

In Chapter 2, the present author already introduced the measures of environmental/natural risk—climate risk more specifically—that can be entered as explanatory variables into a microbehavioral model. They are coefficient of variation in precipitation (CVP), diurnal temperature range (DTR), and monsoon variability index (MVI). Let us begin this chapter by reviewing these measures and adding additional measures of climate risk, which will serve well as a platform for the discussions to come in this chapter.

Climate risk measures are different from climate normals such as a temperature normal and a precipitation normal. A temperature normal is a 30-year average of annual temperature while a precipitation normal is a 30-year average of annual precipitation. An increase in greenhouse gases is projected to alter both climate normals and climate risks (Keeling et al., 2005; Hansen et al., 2006, 2012; IPCC, 2012). Natural resource managers are found to adapt to changes in both climate normals and climate risks (Seo, 2012c, 2014b).

The CVP is a measure of rainfall dispersion that does not depend on the unit of measurement and can be defined as follows with PR_{kj} being monthly precipitation in month j and year k and $\bar{R}_j$ being 30-year average rainfall for month j:

$$\mathrm{CVP}_j = \breve{\sigma}_j / \bar{R}_j \tag{7.1}$$

$$\text{where } \breve{\sigma}_j = \sqrt{\sum_{k=1}^{K} (PR_{kj} - \bar{R}_j)^2 \Big/ (K-1)}.$$

The CVP is a measure of variability of precipitation in a given location in a specific season from one year to another. It is different from precipitation normals in a given location in a specific season which has been known to affect natural resources in various ways, for example, directly through productivity changes and indirectly through diseases, weeds, and pests (Mendelsohn et al., 1994; Reilly et al., 1996; Gitay et al., 2001; Ford and Katondo, 1977; Ziska, 2003; Hahn et al., 2009; Fox et al., 2012; Aksoy and Attardo, 2014). A higher CVP location is a higher risk zone where asset returns are more uncertain and more variable.

Average monthly DTR for the 30-year period, DTR normals, can be measured by averaging the 30-year monthly DTR data. The DTR captures temperature variability in a given location which will be altered if maximum temperature or minimum temperature were to be changed (Easterling et al., 2000; Tebaldi et al., 2007; United States Environmental Protection Agency, 2014). Let TE_{max} be daily maximum temperature, TE_{min} daily minimum temperature, j day, m month, and k year. Then, the DTR for month m is defined as follows:

$$\text{DTR}_m = \frac{\sum_{k=1}^{K} \sum_{j=1}^{J} (\text{TE}_{k,m,j,\max} - \text{TE}_{k,m,j,\min})}{J \star K} \tag{7.2}$$

where J = number of days per month, K = 30 years.

The MVI is intended to identify the unique characteristics of the monsoon climate system. The monsoon climate system dominates climate and weather characteristics in some regions, for example, India (Meehl and Hu, 2006; Goswami et al., 2006; IPCC, 2014). First, based on the 40-year period (from 1971 to 2010) monthly weather data, the present author calculates the ratio of monsoon season total rainfall (PR_t^M) to nonmonsoon season total rainfall (PR_t^{NM}) for each year (t). The coefficient of variation in this monsoon rainfall ratio for the 40-year period is defined to be the MVI:

$$\Sigma = \sigma^M(\Phi_t)/\bar{\Phi}$$

$$\text{with } \Phi_t = \frac{PR_t^M}{PR_t^{NM}} \cdot \tag{7.3}$$

The MVI (Σ) is a unit-independent measure of variability in the ratio Φ_t where σ^M is the standard deviation in the 40-year data of the ratio. The key point is that the MVI is not a measure for one single year. It is a measure of variability for over 40-year time period.

In Chapter 2, the present author described that these measures of climate risk are found to vary across different ecosystems or ecological zones.

Fig. 7.1 shows the distributions of the CVP and DTR across the agro-ecological zones of the lowlands of Sub-Sahara (Seo, 2012c). In the lowland semiarid zones, the CVP is as high as 230% whereas it is as low as 70% in the lowland humid forest zones. The CVP is also high in the dry savannah zones whereas it is also low in subhumid zones.

In Fig. 7.1, temperature variability and risk is also seen in the DTR distribution across the agro-ecological zones. The DTR is as high as 13°C in the lowland semiarid zones and the lowland dry savannah zones. It is as low as 8°C in the lowland humid forest zones and 10°C in the lowland subhumid zones (Seo, 2012c).

The distribution of the MVI across the Indian States and Territories was described in Chapter 2. As shown in Fig. 7.2, the MVI varies from as low as 0.7 in Punjab to as high as 3.4 in Gangetic West Bengal and Jharkhand. The MVI is also low in the States of Haryana and West Rajasthan close to which the capital city New Delhi is located. East Madhya Pradesh and Bihar are also with large MVIs (Seo, 2016).

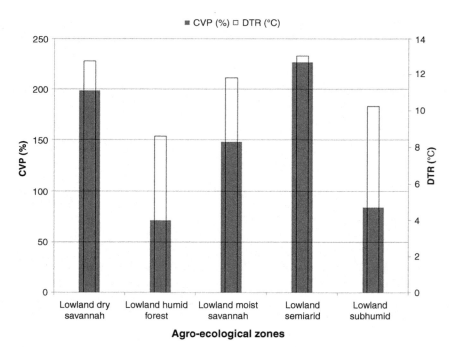

Figure 7.1 *The distributions of measures of climate risk across agro-ecological zones.*

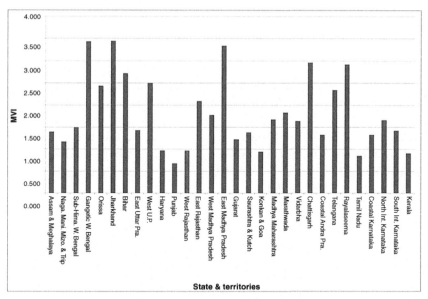

Figure 7.2 *The distribution of MVI across Indian States and Territories.*

7.2 RISK AND RETURN IN THE PORTFOLIO THEORY

Microbehavioral modelers attempt to explain individuals' responses to changes in risks that arise from various causes including climatic changes. An individual manager makes decisions in changed circumstances considering changes in risks and returns in the new situations. Research efforts to model an individual's decisions given the risky nature of decisions are deeply rooted in financial economics. The financial economics literature is filled with the studies of investor behaviors faced with different types of risks and uncertainties attached to different investment possibilities. So, this literature is seamlessly related to the microbehavioral econometric modeling efforts in environmental and natural resource enterprises.

The financial economics literature began with theories of capital, income, interest rates, inflation, and the great crash in the early 20th century by Irving Fisher and others (Fisher, 1906, 1930; Keynes, 1936). The theory of an individual's investment behaviors is first formally formulated by Markowitz (1952). He examined what constitutes the best portfolio of an investor, given the returns and risks of various possible portfolios he/she can own. His portfolio theory states the simple rule that the best portfolio is the one which earns her the highest return among the portfolios with the same risk, that is, variability in returns. Alternatively, the best portfolio is the one which has the lowest risk among the portfolios with the same average return.

In Fig. 7.3, basic concepts of the modern portfolio theory which originated from Markowitz are depicted. Six portfolios dotted on the hyperbola are as follows, each of which is plotted on the plane of expected annual return and standard deviation of annual return. These return and risk data are drawn from actual historical data of the US assets compiled by Robert Shiller with broad categories of stocks, bonds, oil, and cash (Shiller, 2008):

Portfolio 1: 100% bonds;
Portfolio 2: 9% oil, 27% stocks, 64% bonds;
Portfolio 3: 10% oil, 40% stocks, 45% bonds, 5% cash;
Portfolio 4: 15% oil, 53% stocks, 32% bonds;
Portfolio 5: 21% oil, 79% stocks;
Portfolio 6: 28% oil, 115% stocks, −44% bonds.

The top portion of the hyperbola is called the efficient portfolio frontier because all other portfolios inside the hyperbola are dominated by the portfolios on this curve, that is, on the top portion of the hyperbola (Markowitz, 1952, 1959). For example, portfolio 1 (100% bonds) is

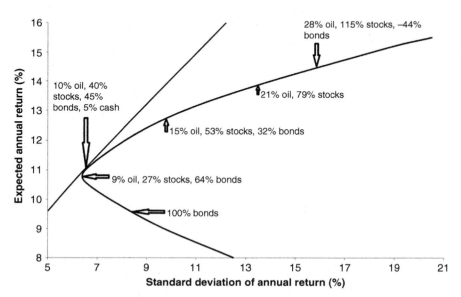

Figure 7.3 *Modern portfolio theory: risks and returns of portfolios.*

dominated by portfolio 4 (15% oil, 53% stocks, 32% bonds) since the latter's return is greater than the former's while the risk (standard deviation of annual return) is the same in the two portfolios.

The straight line from the vertical intercept is called the capital allocation line (CAL) which is a tangent line to the efficient portfolio frontier. The CAL has a vertical intercept which is the rate of return from a risk-free asset. The tangent point is called a tangency portfolio. On this tangent line, that is, the capital allocation line, an investor makes a trade-off between risk and return (Tobin, 1958).

The portfolio risk is lowered if an investor chooses a portfolio of financial assets whose returns are negatively correlated (Modigliani and Pogue, 1974). A portfolio with a single asset is exposed to a high risk since economic shocks would occur from any of the dimensions of the economy. A portfolio of more than one assets is less risky than a portfolio of a single asset unless their returns are perfectly positively correlated. A portfolio composed of assets whose returns are negatively correlated assets is less risky than a portfolio of assets whose returns are positively correlated.

Markowitz's portfolio theory was further developed in a way to explain the price of a portfolio of capital assets as risk premium (Sharpe, 1964; Ross, 1976).

$$E(R_i) = R_F + \beta_i \cdot (E(R_M) - R_F) \tag{7.4}$$

where $E(R_i)$ is expected return of the portfolio of capital assets i, $E(R_M)$ is expected return of a market portfolio, R_F is the risk-free rate of interest, and β_i is a relative measure of risk.

In the risk premium form,

$$E(R_i) - R_F = \beta_i \cdot (E(R_M) - R_F), \tag{7.5}$$

where the left-hand side is risk premium and the right-hand side is called the market premium.

Applying the concepts of the financial economics literature to modeling individuals' behaviors in agricultural and natural resource enterprises, a shock and variability to these enterprises would occur from any of many sources in various aspects, one of which is an environmental or climatic shift. The three risk measures introduced previously, that is, the CVP, DTR, and MVI capture shocks and risks to agricultural and natural resource enterprises. These indicators measure average shocks occurring to specific individuals for a long period of time, for example, 30 years.

To an individual manager, each of these shocks would occur from different directions to the portfolio owned by her/him. In other words, each of these risk indicators has its own unique characteristics from the others. That means each of these shocks will influence various portfolios of different individuals in a dissimilar way. Further, even the same portfolios owned by different individuals will be affected differently by changes in any of these climate risk indicators.

Which portfolios of agricultural and resource managers are less risky than the other portfolios or which ones are more risky than the others? This can be examined empirically. The present author introduced more than one classification of natural resource enterprises in this book. Let's consider the following three enterprises: a crops-only enterprise, a livestock-only enterprise, and a crops–livestock enterprise. In Table 7.1, average of CVP normals and average DTR normals are presented for each of the three enterprises in Sub-Saharan Africa (Seo, 2012c). It is noticeable that the rainfall variability expressed as average CVP normals is much higher in the mixed crops–livestock portfolio than the other two specialized portfolios. The CVP is 16% higher in the mixed enterprise: about 142% for the specialized crop enterprise and the specialized livestock enterprise versus 158% for the mixed enterprise.

This means that agricultural and natural resource managers choose to diversify through the mixed enterprise in high rainfall risk zones. A diversified portfolio of crops and livestock is more effective in reducing the risk in returns from rainfall variability than a specialized crop portfolio or a specialized livestock enterprise. The manager of the diversified portfolio would make a trade-off between reduced risk in returns and lower return. She may choose a lower risk and a lower return enterprise.

In the lower CVP zones, a farmer chooses a specialized crop enterprise over a mixed enterprise because reduced risk from a mixed enterprise is not enough to offset a higher return from a crops-only enterprise. She chooses a higher return and a higher risk enterprise.

Table 7.1 Climate risks and agricultural and resource enterprises in Sub-Saharan Africa

	Number of farms	Average CVP normals (%)	Average DTR normals (°C)
A crops-only enterprise	2880	141.78	11.87
A crops–livestock enterprise	4309	158.06	12.43
A livestock-only enterprise	444	142.94	12.73

Even in the bread basket of the United States such as Iowa, rainfall varies a great deal year by year. In the State, maize yield falls often by more than 20% from the average yield in a severe drought year and far exceeds the average yield in a favorable rainfall year (Rosenzweig et al., 2001; Seo, 2013). If net income from livestock is negatively correlated with net income from maize, then the mixed portfolio of livestock and maize will reduce the risk in the returns from this enterprise. A farmer will choose the specialized maize enterprise if the reduced net income from the mixed portfolio is too large to justify the reduced risk.

This is one of the most salient findings in the literature on adaptation to climatic changes in the future. What it means is that an increase in rainfall risk and variability due to global warming and climatic changes will place farmers better suited to adopt a mixed crops–livestock portfolio in an effort to coping with climatic changes (Seo, 2010a,b). Further, it means that the damage of climate change on those who adapt by switching to this mixed portfolio will be smaller than the owners of the other specialized portfolios who do not switch.

The average of DTR normals, another risk variable shown in Table 7.1, is somewhat higher in the livestock-only portfolio than in the crops-only portfolio by about 0.9°C . This may be due to higher resilience of raised animals than crops to daily temperature variability. It is notable that the average of DTR normals in the mixed portfolio is "lower" than that in the specialized livestock portfolio.

It means that an increase in temperature variability, that is, the DTR normals, does not necessarily mean a higher risk in returns which would force farmers to diversify into both crops and livestock. It means that higher temperature variability is harmful to crops relative to livestock.

Raising livestock in farms is often understood as a form of saving in rural areas of poor regions (Udry, 1995; Fafchamps et al., 1998; Kazianga and Udry, 2006). In contrast to crops and vegetables, animals do not decay quickly. A farmer in poor regions would sell a variety of crops, vegetables, and fruits upon harvests and invest the revenue into buying cows. Cows are not perishable in a matter of days and months, but also endure the drought and heat better in a bad weather year. Further, a cow earns interests similar to the capital in developed countries, indeed quite a high interest in some cases (Rosenzweig and Wolpin, 1993). For example, a high quality dairy cow may produce 20 L of milk every day. Once in a while, a cow will give birth to an offspring, a calf (bull, heifer, steer).

The discussions up to now lead us to ask how a microbehavioral modeler should specify the choice set, that is, the whole set of a agricultural and natural resource portfolios, given the varied return and risk characteristics of the possible portfolios? There is no doubt that there is more than one way to define the choice set in any problem the modeler is attempting to address. However, there is often the best way to define the choice set emerging from the existing literature.

For the current example of agricultural and natural resources, literature shows that a variety of crops, a variety of animals, and a variety of fruits/vegetables can be uniquely identified. Put differently, each of these enterprises exhibit unique characteristics different from the others, including the unique return-and-risk characteristics in response to natural fluctuations. For example, many inputs of productions from each of these enterprises do not overlap with the inputs employed in the other enterprises. That is, a tractor and other machineries are needed for cropping, feedlots and pastures are for livestock management, and forestry tools including sawmills are needed for forest enterprises.

The following enterprises can be defined as the choice set of the model given a proper context, which has been already introduced in the previous chapters (Seo, 2010c, 2012a, b):

Enterprise 1: crops-only,
Enterprise 2: livestock-only,
Enterprise 3: fruits/vegetables-only,
Enterprise 4: crops–livestock,
Enterprise 5: crops–fruits/vegetables,
Enterprise 6: livestock–fruits/vegetables,
Enterprise 7: crops–livestock–fruits/vegetables.

7.3 ATTITUDES TOWARD RISK

What does the modern portfolio theory tell us about an individual's attitudes toward risk in investment returns? According to Arrow and Pratt, people's different attitudes toward risk can be defined to be risk averse, risk-loving, or risk neutral (Pratt, 1964; Arrow, 1971). One is said to be risk averse if, "starting from a position of certainty, one is not willing to take a bet which is actuarially fair" (Arrow, 1971). Similarly, one is said to be risk-loving if, starting from a position of certainty, one is willing to take a bet which is actuarially unfair.

Arrow and Pratt introduced two measures of risk aversion based on the von Neumann and Morgenstern's expected utility theory: an absolute measure of risk aversion and a relative measure of risk aversion (von Neumann and Morgenstern, 1947; Mas–Colell et al., 1995). An absolute measure of risk aversion (RA_A) is defined as

$$RA_A = \frac{u''(w)}{u'(w)}, \tag{7.6}$$

where w is wealth, $u(\cdot)$ is von Neumann–Morgenstern expected utility function which is bounded and twice differentiable, u' is marginal utility of wealth, u'' is the rate of change in the marginal utility of wealth.

The coefficient of the absolute measure of risk aversion tells us how much the odds of winning have to be affected to induce a risk-averse individual to take a constant-sum gamble. It is positive for a risk-averse individual. As the amount of gamble increases, a higher probability of winning is needed for an individual to be indifferent between gambling and certainty (Zilberman, 1998).

A relative measure of risk aversion (RA_R) is a measure of risk proportional to the level of wealth. It can be understood to be the elasticity of risk aversion:

$$RA_R = \frac{u''(w)}{u'(w)} \cdot w = RA_A(w) \cdot w. \tag{7.7}$$

The higher the relative measure of risk aversion, the higher must be the odds of winning for the individual to be indifferent, given a share of wealth at stake in the gamble.

An actuarially fair bet is, in the rational expectation theory, one with expected value of a bet is zero. A bet is actuarially fair even if there is a very high probability of a large loss if there is a smaller probability of a very large gain. The risk in this bet is the weighted average of possible outcomes from the bet weighted by the probabilities of each outcome to occur.

If an individual is risk averse, he/she will reject an actuarially fair bet with a higher risk if there is another actuarially fair alternative bet with a lower risk. So, the modern portfolio theory is assuming a risk-averse individual. This is because it assumes that a portfolio with a lower risk will be preferred by an individual if all the portfolios yield the same expected return.

If an individual investor is risk-loving, he/she will choose a portfolio with a significantly higher risk if it yields a slightly higher expected return. That is, the investor is willing to take a high risk even for a small increase in expected return. If an individual is risk-neutral, he/she is indifferent to the portfolios with different levels of risk if all of them yield the same expected return.

If an individual is risk averse, it is possible that he/she chooses a portfolio with a slightly lower expected return if it contains significantly lower risk than the other portfolios. A risk-averse natural resource manager can choose a diversified crops–livestock portfolio over a specialized crop portfolio if the former has a lower risk even if the former yields a slightly lower expected return in the long-term than the latter, which is what we saw in the previous section.

Of course, a risk-averse natural resource manager can choose a diversified crops–livestock portfolio if it has a lower risk but at the same time it yields a higher expected return in the long-term, in comparison with the other portfolios such as the crops-only system or the livestock-only system. As shown in Fig. 7.3, a portfolio with a higher return and a lower risk dominates a portfolio with a lower return and a higher risk.

If, on the other hand, an agricultural and natural resource manager is risk neutral, he/she will choose a mixed crops–livestock portfolio if it yields a higher expected return in the long-term regardless of the magnitudes of risks involved in the potential alternatives in the choice set.

The keyword here is "long-term". It is repeated "gambles" for many years to come, that is, more than 30 years of gamble in the context of climate literature (Gibbons, 1992). In a one-time-and-done gamble, an individual is more likely to show a risk-averse attitude due to various reasons (Kahneman and Tversky, 1984). As the bet is repeated many times, an individual is more likely to exhibit a risk-neutral or even a risk-loving attitude in one specific bet.

To be more specific, let an individual be forced to choose one from the two portfolios in a one-time-and-done bet: (1) a portfolio with expected return of 5% and the risk (standard deviation) of 2%; (2) a portfolio with expected return of 5% and the risk of 4%. A risk-averse individual is certain to choose the first portfolio over the second portfolio.

Now, suppose that the game is repeated 100 times and he/she is forced to choose from the following portfolios: (1) a portfolio with expected return of 5% and the risk of 2% in a one-time bet; (2) a portfolio with expected return of 6% and the risk of 4% in a one-time bet. In this repeated game, many people with a risk-averse attitude will choose portfolio 2 over portfolio 1, knowing that he/she can recover the loss, should that happen, in the 99 games that ensue.

The risk in the return in the game with 100 repetitions is lower than the risk in the return involved in one-time game. Mathematically, the risk in the return in this gamble with 100 repetitions is the risk in the return in one-time gamble divided by square root of the number of repetitions (Hogg et al., 2012).

From another perspective, an individual's attitudes toward risk may depend upon other economic and social factors such as endowment of wealth, size of land, years of schooling, gender, age, and field experiences, leading to heterogeneous choices of natural resource enterprises (Seo, 2011b, 2015b). Studies in African farms show that small farms and large farms exhibit different income responses to climatic changes (Seo and Mendelsohn, 2008c). Small household farms and large commercial farms in African animal husbandry hold portfolios that are structurally different. That is, small household farms rely more heavily on small ruminants such as goats and sheep (Seo and Mendelsohn, 2008a).

7.4 FUTURES AND OPTIONS

Another way to hedge against the risk from a bad weather year such as a severe drought year is transactions in futures markets (Working, 1953, 1962). A farmer can sell a grain in a futures market upon harvests instead of selling at a spot market. In the spot market, that is, in the absence of the futures market, the price of the grain hits the bottom due to a high supply during the harvest time while the price of the grain hits the peak in the month just before the following year's harvest because of a low supply. In the spot market, the price of the grain will also fluctuate across the years in the same manner. That is, the price will hit a trough during the harvest time of a good weather year and will reach a peak during the month just before the harvest time of a bad weather year. In the absence of futures markets, risk in return is high due to intraannual and interannual weather fluctuations.

A farmer can sell the grain in the futures market instead in order to avoid selling the grain at the lowest price during the harvest time. A farmer sells a futures contract which is purchased by a consumer. The futures market is formed because a futures contract benefits both a producer and a consumer. In other words, it is Pareto welfare improving to both parties and the society (Fudenberg and Tirole, 1991). A farmer benefits because she can avoid selling the grain at a low price during the period of high supply and a consumer benefits because she can buy the grain at a lower price during the period of low supply (Barry et al., 2000; Fabozzi et al., 2009).

A futures contract is structured as follows: a seller will deliver one unit of a certain grain (x) at price F_x on a designated date to a purchaser. Let's assume that a farmer sells one bushel of maize produced in a good weather year to a consumer 12 months later in a bad weather year. Let's suppose that the market interest rate is r and the storage cost of the grain for one year which a farmer must pay is c_x, expressed as a fraction of the spot market price. Let the dividend, that is, any income earned from holding the grain, from holding x for 1 year be d_x, expressed as a function of the spot market price. Then, the futures price is determined as follows given the spot price of the grain P_x (Fabozzi et al., 2009):

$$F_x = P_x + P_x(r + c_x - d_x). \tag{7.8}$$

Eq. (7.8) is called the intertemporal no-arbitrage condition. That is, in the condition expressed in Eq. (7.8), a seller is indifferent between selling at the spot price and selling at the futures price. In addition, a buyer is indifferent between buying in the spot market and buying in the futures market.

In Fig. 7.4, the trajectory of the futures price of corn (with the symbol ZC) traded at the Chicago Board Of Trade (CBOT) exchange with the delivery date of July 15, 2015 is shown (Bloomberg Business, 2015). The price is dollars per 5000 bushels of corn. The figure shows the 5 year trajectory of the futures contract. In the three years leading up to the delivery date, there is a yearly pattern of a price peak in planting time followed by a price trough in harvest time, reflecting the farming cycle. In addition,

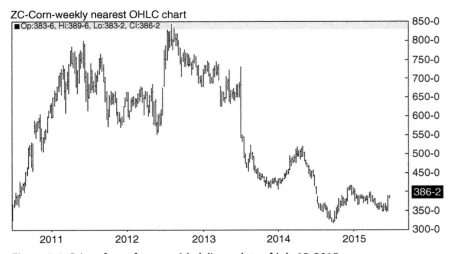

Figure 7.4 *Price of corn futures with delivery date of July 15, 2015.*

the closer the trade date is to the delivery date, the smaller the fluctuations of the futures price, reflecting the reduced storage cost and the interest payment by the delivery date.

With the availability of futures markets, a farmer is less vulnerable to climate risk, for example, annual rainfall variability than he/she is in the absence of futures markets. This is because a farmer can sell some of the harvest during the good weather year in the futures market with delivery date in the bad weather year. By doing this, she can reap the benefits of a higher price during the good weather year because of not selling everything immediately after a harvest and increase the earning for the bad weather year.

Note that this spreading of risk across the years through futures markets is untenable if weather realizations are truly random, that is, cannot be anticipated by farmers at all. However, some, though not all, of the factors that determine the yearly weather, for example, an El Nino/La Nina oscillation and an Atlantic Multidecadal Oscillation, are already known to have a trend or a cycle, which makes it possible for farmers to anticipate rainfall fluctuations at some level of certainty.

Futures markets are not established in Sub-Saharan countries, with the South African Futures Exchange (Safex) being the sole exception (South Africa Futures Exchange, 2015). However, behavioral responses to annual weather risk by farmers and natural resource managers in Sub-Sahara have been known well by researchers. Farmers in Sub-Saharan Africa are found to store major grains in order to consume it during the bad weather year (Udry, 1995; Kazianga and Udry, 2006). Purchasing animals with the revenue earned from a good weather year can be understood as a form of saving, as mentioned before, which bears occasional interests—in the form of milk and bullock labor—and potential earning for the bad weather year through selling one of the animals owned (Rosenzweig and Wolpin, 1993; Fafchamps et al., 1998). When farmers can store harvests of agricultural goods, the market price of an agricultural good is not determined by the harvest (production) in a single year, but by the total supply to the market (Wright, 2011).

A futures contract is one of many financial derivatives. It is called a derivative because the futures price of the underlying item, for example, wheat, is not determined by the item itself, but by the promise of the delivery of the item at a future date. In other words, the value of it is derived from an underlying asset, that is, a contract. Futures and forwards are widely used financial derivatives in agricultural markets. Indeed, these derivatives originated historically from transactions in rice markets in Asia (Shiller, 2004). Futures and forwards are the same financial instrument except that futures is a standardized market that removes a counter-party risk whereas a forwards contract is signed directly between the two parties of a contract.

Another financial derivative that is widely utilized by natural resource managers is options. An option is a contact that specifies the right for the option to buy or sell a financial asset at a specified price in a future date (Fabozzi et al., 2009). A contract which specifies the right for the option to buy an asset is called a call option and a contract which specifies the right for the option to sell an asset is called a put option. If an option can be exercised in the date specified in the contract only, it is called an American option. If an option can be exercised anytime before the specified date after the purchase, it is called a European option.

In the context of agricultural and natural resource enterprises, options play an important role. If an individual suspects that there is a natural gas reservoir under a certain piece of land, he/she may buy a call option. She buys an option instead of buying the land directly since she can decide not to exercise the option if the market price is below the price specified in the option contract. If the market price is higher than the option price, then she will exercise the option and purchase the land at a lower price than the market price at the exercise date. As this example demonstrates, an option's contract is Pareto welfare improving: it benefits both the buyer and the seller (Fudenberg and Tirole, 1991).

An example of a put option is the right for the option to sell an item at a specified price at a specified date. In the times during which property value is highly volatile with repeated bubbles, a property owner may purchase a put option for the sale of the property, by which she can ensure herself the specified price in the event of a drastic fall in the property price. In a property market crash, a put option of property sale would safeguard a property owner from going into a foreclosure (Shiller, 2005, 2009).

How is the price of an option (to buy or sell something in a future date) determined? Let T be the time to exercise, σ^2 the variance of one-time price change of an asset, ρ risk-free interest rate, and $\psi(\cdot)$ the standard normal cumulative distribution function. Further, let P_{stock} be the current stock price and $P_{exercise}$ be exercise (strike) price of an option. Then, according to the Black–Scholes model, the fair market value (price) of a call option is determined as follows (Black and Scholes, 1973; Fabozzi et al., 2009):

$$P_C = P_{stock} \cdot \psi(q_1) - P_{exercise} \cdot \psi(q_2),$$

where

$$q_1 = \frac{\ln\left(\dfrac{P_{stock}}{P_{exercise}}\right) + \rho T + \sigma^2 \cdot \left(\dfrac{T}{2}\right)}{\sigma\sqrt{T}}, \tag{7.9}$$

$$q_2 = \frac{\ln\left(\dfrac{P_{stock}}{P_{exercise}}\right) + \rho T - \sigma^2 \cdot \left(\dfrac{T}{2}\right)}{\sigma\sqrt{T}}.$$

Note from Eq. 7.9 that the larger the volatility in the price of the asset, σ^2, of concern, the higher the price of the call option. Given the exercise price, the higher the stock price, the higher is the price of a call option. Given the stock price, the higher the exercise price, the lower the price of a call option. The price of a call option becomes larger as the time to exercise T becomes larger.

How should an economist or an environmental scientist capture the futures and options markets in explaining individuals' behaviors in natural resources and environmental fields? The researcher should incorporate the individuals' behaviors taken in preparation for bad times as well as for good times into the microbehavioral model. In an extreme drought year, for example, a farmer may not suffer as much as what the models which do not incorporate futures and options behaviors indicate because of hedging against a bad year through storage facility, selling or buying in futures markets, selling or buying options, and investments into alternative assets such as animal husbandry and others.

How can a researcher achieve this in the microbehavioral econometric models? One strategy that was suggested in the literature is that lagged responses are explicitly modeled (Deschenes and Greenstone, 2007, 2012; Wooldridge, 2010). That is, this year's net revenue by an individual enterprise can be modeled to depend upon the weather of this year, but also those of the previous years. Alternatively, this year's weather can be modeled to influence not only this year's net revenue but also the net revenues in the following years:

$$y_{it} = \alpha_c + \alpha_t + \sum_{k=0}^{2} \beta_k f(x_{i,t-k}) + \sum_{j=1}^{J} r_j g(z_{jit}) + \varepsilon_{it} \tag{7.10}$$

where y_{it} is net revenue at time t of farm i; $x_{it}, x_{it-1}, x_{it-2}$ are weather at time $t, t-1, t-2$ respectively; z_{jit} is nonclimate variable; α_c a county fixed effect; α_t a year fixed effect; and ε_{it} is an iid normal error term.

In this model, farm profit at the current period is determined by the weather realizations in the current year as well as in the past years which affected the harvests in the past years. The underlying mechanism is that a farmer can store the harvests in the past years and sell them this year or he/she can lock in past harvests through futures/forwards contracts with the delivery date in the current year.

However, the distributed lag model in Eq. (7.10) has a limited capacity in capturing forward-looking behaviors through futures/forwards/options markets because it cannot capture adaptation strategies to a long-term climatic shift as well as their effects on the changes in the long-term profit due to such a climatic shift (Seo, 2012c, 2013).

To be more specific, in the class of distributed lag model as shown in Eq. (7.10), there are no climate normals included in the model. As explained throughout this book, climate normals include temperature normals, precipitation normals, temperature variability normals, and precipitation variability normals, each of which is defined to be a 30-year average of a yearly weather variable of concern. The distributed lag model does not capture adaptive responses to climate normals, some of which responses are taking place through futures and options contracts.

In addition, the distributed lag model does not contain the measure of the long-term profitability of the land, but rather focuses on yearly farm profits. In the advanced economy such as the United States, a yearly farm profit results from agricultural sales in that year including sales through futures and options with the delivery (exercise) dates set in that year. On the other hand, for a farmer to make a variety of farm decisions such as land use changes, input changes, changes in loans, and changes in sales arrangements which obviously influences yearly farm profits, the long-term profitability of the land will be a primary criterion for her decisions.

Another approach in the climate change literature is that a researcher can learn directly from the long-term profitability of the land (Mendelsohn et al., 1994, Seo and Mendelsohn 2008b). Land rent in a year is the net income earned from the land in that year (Ricardo, 1817). Land value is the value of land capital, that is, the present value of the stream of future net incomes earned on that land using time-dependent discount rates r_t (Fisher, 1906):

$$LV_{it} = \int_{t=0}^{\infty} y_{it} e^{-r_t t} dt. \qquad (7.11)$$

The land value captures the net revenue outcomes from all the economic activities that can be performed on the land now and in the future, which makes it an ideal measure of climate change and global warming studies. Like a climate normal which is a 30-year average of a weather variable, land value in Eq. (7.11) captures the long-term productivity of the land after all necessary adjustments.

As a farmer adapts to a change in climate system, the value of the land would be also changed as it calls for changes in land uses, a variety of farming practices, and purchases and sales arrangements. For example, a farmer may cope with a climatic shift by transforming the land with a major grain at present to the pastures or the lands with vegetables and fruit products (Seo, 2015a). In this way, land value would capture changes in farming and financial activities on the land that would take place now and at some points in the future (Mendelsohn et al., 1994; Mendelsohn 2000; Seo, 2014a, 2015b).

7.5 INSURANCE AND SUBSIDY

Insurance is a financial instrument for hedging against a low probability high risk event, or put differently, an unexpected catastrophic event such as a house fire, a car accident, a certain disease, accidental death, a hurricane disaster, etc. Under an insurance contract, the insured will pay regularly a small premium and, in exchange for the premium, the insurer will pay a loss if a specified contingency should arise (Fabozzi et al., 2009).

For the insured, it is welfare improving to purchase a specific insurance, for example, a housefire insurance, if the expected damage payment by the insurer exceeds the premium. The insurer is able to pay for the damage by pooling the risks from a large group of individuals who are faced with similar risks. The law of large numbers ensures that if individual risks are independent, a housefire will break out to only a small fraction of the whole group of individuals at one time interval in time, making it possible for the insurance company to pay the losses or claims expenses made by the insured individuals and companies.

Any insurance program is vulnerable to the two behavioral issues and must be designed in a way to overcome or at least limit these perverse behaviors: moral hazard and adverse selection. Moral hazard is said to occur when an insurance policy holder behaves in such a way that increases the probability of the occurrence of an event which is insured in order to receive the indemnity payment. Adverse selection occurs when an insurance policy attracts only individuals or corporations that have a higher probability of a loss than average individuals. This occurs because the insurance company does not have the full knowledge of the individuals who are potential insurance buyers. This is one of the situations with asymmetric information.

In environmental and natural resource managements, insurance is one of the most important financial contracts for many managers. In the United States, crop insurance which is probably the most widely purchased insurance policy in natural resource sectors has evolved into the most important crop subsidy program over the past two decades (Barry et al., 2000; Sumner and Zulauf, 2012). The modern crop insurance program in the United States can be dated to the Crop Insurance Reform Act of 1994 and the creation of the Risk Management Agency (RMA) in 1995 to administer the Federal Crop Insurance Corporation (FCIC) which was formed in 1938. In the fiscal year 2013, the crop insurance program accounted for about 63% of the total budgeted outlays of the United States Department of Agriculture (USDA) for crop subsidy (Sumner and Zulauf, 2012).

Since the early 1990s, the federal crop insurance program in the United States has expanded immensely, as summarized in Table 7.2. The table is modified by the present author from Sumner and Zulauf (2012). During this period, the number of crops separately insured has grown from about 50 crops to more than 300 crops. The number of insured acres has increased from about 101 million acres in 1990 to 272 million acres in 2008. Four crops—corn, cotton, soybeans, and wheat—account for more than two-thirds of the incurred acres. Total liabilities have increased from US$12 billion to US$114 billion whereas total indemnity has grown from about US$1 billion

Table 7.2 Profile of the US crop insurance program

Year	Total policies sold (million)	Buy-up policies sold (million)	Net acres insured (million)	Total liability ($ billion)	Total premium ($ billion)	Total indemnity ($ billion)
1990	0.89	0.89	101.4	12.83	0.84	0.97
1995	2.03	0.86	220.5	23.73	1.54	1.57
2000	1.32	1.01	206.5	34.44	2.54	2.59
2005	1.19	1.05	245.9	44.26	3.95	2.37
2006	1.15	1.03	242.2	49.92	4.58	3.5
2007	1.14	1.02	271.6	67.34	6.56	3.55
2008	1.15	1.03	272.3	89.9	9.85	8.68
2009	1.17	1.08	264.8	79.57	8.95	5.23
2010	1.14	1.06	256.2	78.1	7.59	4.25
2011	1.15	1.07	265.3	114.07	11.95	10.71

in 1990 to US$11 billion in 2011. Total premium has grown from less than US$1 billion to US$12 billion in 2011. The US crop subsidy program is expected to expand further under the Agricultural Act of 2014, the so-called 2014 Farm Bill (Goodwin and Smith, 2014).

Crop insurance policies in the United States are sold and serviced by 16 private insurance companies from which a farmer can purchase one of these policies (Barry et al., 2000). An insurance policy guarantees the insured farmer an insurance damage (indemnity) payment when a loss occurs in excess of insurance deductible. That is, indemnity payment equals the difference between the assessed damage from the event and the deductible.

Crop insurance is a multiperil insurance in that it covers a range of natural events such as severe drought, heavy and intense rainfall, heat stress, frost, fire, earthquakes, insects, etc. (Sumner and Zulauf, 2012; Wright, 2014). A crop insurance policy can be written either yield-based or revenue-based. A yield-based insurance policy provides a damage payment for a yield loss whereas a revenue-based insurance policy provides an indemnity payment for a revenue loss.

In the crop insurance programs, behavioral responses by a policy holder characterized by moral hazard are considered to be especially problematic (Mas-Colell et al., 1995). Crop production involves a complex and lengthy process and a farmer should make a series of management decisions in consideration of a variety of risks involved in preplanting, planting, growing, harvest, postharvest, and off-season practices. In many circumstances, these decisions are altered now that the farmer holds an insurance policy, which is often hard to be distinguished by an insurance company.

A deductible is a standard tool used by an insurance company to limit behavioral changes caused by moral hazard. To be paid an insurance indemnity, a crop insurance policy holder is required to pay a deductible first. The inclusion of a deductible in the policy precludes an insurer's payment on small losses. If these small losses are arisen mostly because of managerial decisions influenced by moral hazard, the deductible can reduce moral hazard.

Recognizing perverse incentives in a crop insurance program, an area-wide insurance policy was suggested to address behavioral problems such as moral hazard and adverse selection (Halcrow, 1949). In this policy design, an indemnity payment is triggered by an area-wide, for example, US county, yield shortfall, instead of an individual farm's yield shortfall. The rationale for an area-wide crop insurance is that although an individual farm's yield of a grain is controlled to a large extent by farm decisions, a countywide yield of a grain is by and large outside the control of an individual farm.

Halcrow and others suggested that in an area-wide insurance policy, a farmer's purchase of an insurance policy is less motivated by the problem of adverse selection and the behaviors of the insured farmer are less influenced by moral hazard (Miranda, 1991; Skees et al., 1997; Miranda and Glauber, 1997; Mahul, 1999).

However, an area-wide insurance policy can lead to other types of perverse incentive problems. For example, due to geographic, geologic, and climatic variations across the land area upon which an area-based insurance policy is drawn, subarea A may experience a higher yield even in a drought year whereas subarea B may experience a severe yield shortfall. If area-wide yield does not fall sufficiently enough to trigger an indemnity payment, subarea B will not reap the benefits of the area-based insurance policy, although farmers in subarea B will have paid their premiums regularly. On the other hand, farmers in subarea A will not be interested in joining the area-wide insurance program and pay the premiums if the benefit of the insurance policy largely falls on subarea B.

In the insurance market, area-based crop insurance has not had noteworthy success. In the fiscal year 2011, countywide insurance policies made up only 2% of the total net insured acres in the crop insurance program (Sumner and Zulauf, 2012). A primary reason for the slow progress is reported to be that a countywide insurance policy faces competition from individual farm-based insurance policies whereas the latter are also offered high premium subsidies by the federal governments. Farmers choose an individually drawn insurance policy over a countywide insurance policy.

Be it yield-based or revenue-based, the basic structure of the US federal crop insurance program is as follows (Shields, 2013). A farmer chooses an insurance policy which covers a certain level of yield loss or revenue loss from an array of crop insurance policies offered by private insurance companies. For example, in a catastrophic coverage insurance policy, the insured farmer receives a payment for losses exceeding 50% of the "normal" yield and 55% of the estimated market price of the crop. The "normal yield" and the estimated market price are determined by the insurance company based on a certain computer model. A farmer should make regular premium payments, but taxpayers subsidize the total cost of the premium for a catastrophic coverage.

A farmer can "buy-up" a higher level of insurance coverage. For example, he/she can buy-up an insurance coverage for 75% of the yield losses and 100% of the estimated market price of that crop. In a buy-up insurance policy, insurance premium gets higher, the higher the level of coverage purchased. In a buy-up policy, taxpayers subsidize a lower percentage of the total cost of the premium, the higher the level of coverage (Shields, 2013). As can be seen in Table 7.2, most of the policies sold in the past two decades are buy-up insurance policies.

As such, taxpayers bear the burden of subsidizing much of the US federal crop insurance program. According to the recent report from the Congressional Research Service, US taxpayers subsidize around 60% of the total premium costs of the insured farmers across all the crop insurance policies. In addition, taxpayers subsidize the federal government's reimbursement of the administrative and operating costs incurred by the private crop insurance companies which amount to 22–24% of the total premiums. Further, taxpayers subsidize a significant share of the government's payments that go directly to producers in the event of a yield or revenue loss (Shields, 2013). According to the Risk Management Agency of the USDA, the total cost to taxpayers has increased significantly from US$3.1 billion in 2001 to US$14 billion in 2012. In the fiscal year 2014, a subsidy for crop insurance premiums accounted for about 72% of the total cost to taxpayers (USDA RMA, 2015).

Most certainly, crop insurance will influence the ways how an individual manager makes decisions in the face of climatic changes and other natural shocks. Observed yields, net revenues, and land uses at the present time in US agriculture are heavily influenced by the availability of the crop insurance and federal government subsidy program. However, the extensive crop insurance and subsidy programs available in the United States described up to now are not available in tropical low-income countries such as those in Sub-Sahara and South America (Anderson and Masters, 2009). Therefore, distortions in observed behaviors and outcomes such as crop yields, net revenues, and land uses by the availability of crop insurance and subsidy programs are most likely to be small in the low-latitude countries.

Availability of a crop insurance policy for a grain will lead to a downward bias in the observed yields of the insured grain in a downside weather event. That is, when severe drought strikes in a particular year, a farmer with an insurance policy for the grain will not make full efforts to protect themselves against a severe yield loss in that year. Instead, he/she is better off by letting the grain yield fall to the lowest yield and receiving an indemnity payment from the insurance company. The observed yields across the insured farmers will not, then, reflect the true yield responses to the downside weather event, that is, a severe drought. Therefore, severe drops in the yields of wheat, maize, cotton, and soybeans in the United States due to weather and climate realizations reported by some researchers can be ascribed, among other things, to the threshold behaviors that emerged from the US federal crop insurance and subsidy programs (Schlenker and Roberts, 2009; Fisher et al., 2012; Seo, 2013).

Will the crop insurance and subsidy program in US agriculture spur or hinder US farmers' adaptation behaviors to future changes in natural events including climatic changes? From a microbehavioral perspective, the answer seems to be straightforward even though detailed answers need further investigations. Existing crop insurance and subsidy programs will continue to subsidize crops, enterprises, and land uses that will be adversely affected by natural changes in the future. In the absence of the existing subsidy, a farmer is expected to switch efficiently to the best enterprise and practices under the changed natural condition. A continued subsidy received from the federal government will, however, give an incentive to him to stay put on the status quo.

7.6 THEORY OF A BUBBLE AND SPECULATIVE ASSET PRICES

Up to now in this chapter, the present author explained the theories of prices of various financial securities and portfolios, that is, public equities, portfolios, futures, options, and insurance premiums. A common thread to these theories is that market prices of the securities are efficiently determined. That is, market prices reflect fundamental values of the financial securities. This is known as the efficient market hypothesis (EMH) (Fama, 1970).

In the efficient market, the price of a security will incorporate all the information in the market and any change in the price is caused only by new information which has been not known or nonexistent previously. New information is by definition a shock to the market, that is, unexpected by market participants before revelation. A shock is by definition random. Therefore, the price trajectory of a financial security in the efficient market should exhibit a pattern characterized by random walks (Fama, 1970, 1991; Fama and French, 1992).

Eugene Fama introduced three forms of the EMH: weak form, semistrong form, and strong form of the EMH. In the weak form of the EMH, asset prices would fluctuate without any trend, therefore exhibit a random walk, as explained previously. With y_t being the asset price at a point in time and ε_t being the random term, the price of the asset is described as follows:

$$y_t = y_{t-1} + \varepsilon_t,$$
$$\varepsilon_t \sim N(0, \sigma^2).$$

$$(7.12)$$

In the semistrong form of the EMH, the price of a financial security in an efficient market fully reflects all publicly available information. Adjustments in prices occur at the speed of light in responses to public events such as stock splits, announcements of financial reports by firms, and new security issues. There is no further value in the publicly available information as they are already embedded in the current price of the security.

In the strong form of the EMH, all public and private information are fully reflected in security prices in the sense that no single individual can have a higher trading profit than others because he/she holds monopolistic access to some information. In the strong form of the EMH, no one can beat the market.

The EMH has been the most salient theory of asset prices in economics, but also challenged by many researchers since the beginning of this literature by Fama for theoretical as well as practical reasons. One of the most prominent critiques came from Robert Shiller who argued that observed actual price movements of major market indexes are highly volatile and very hard to be justified by the EMH (Shiller, 1979, 1981).

Fig. 7.5 recreates his figure presented in the first edition of the book entitled "Irrational Exuberance" published in 2000 which coincided with the burst of the dot-com bubble in the same year. Shiller argued that the S&P 500 real price index constructed by him from the market data since 1870

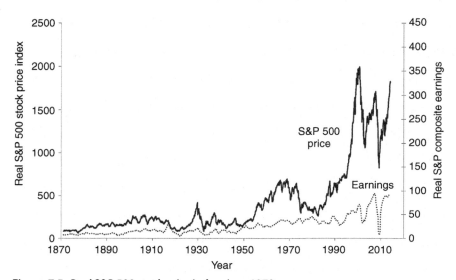

Figure 7.5 *Real S&P 500 stock price index since 1870.*

exhibits occasional "irrational exuberance" in the market which is hard to be justified by the rational and efficient market.

The figure shows two recent shocks in the 2000s: the burst of the dot-com bubble in 2000 and the burst of the real estate bubble in 2008. In both events, the S&P 500 stock index fell sharply in a short period of time while the index increased sharply just before the peak of the bubble.

The bubble theory of asset prices by Shiller states that the prices of assets are driven by speculation by market participants which build the ever larger bubble until it bursts. A bubble is defined by envy and a gambler's excitement (Shiller, 2000, 2014):

> *A situation in which news of price increases spurs investor enthusiasm which spreads by psychological contagion from person to person, in the process amplifying stories that might justify the price increases and bringing in a larger and larger class of investors, who, despite doubts about the real value of an investment, are drawn to it partly through envy of others' successes and partly through a gambler's excitement.*

In the theory of a bubble, market prices deviate from the fundamentals that determine the prices of assets (Shiller, 1981, 2000, 2005; Summers, 1986). In Fig. 7.5, historical real earnings data are plotted with the vertical axis on the right-hand size and overlaid on the S&P 500 stock index. In the times of bubbles, the figure shows that the real S&P 500 index sharply deviates from the real earnings during those times. Earnings is what is earned by the S&P 500 companies and is usually the 10-year average of earnings, which is used as a measure of the fundamentals in the economy. During the times of the bubbles and market crashes, the price-earnings (P/E) ratio sharply spikes, then crashes.

Another way to state that an asset price deviates from the fundamental value of the underlying asset is through the dividend theory of a stock price (Shiller, 1981). The ownership of a stock entitles an owner to the stream of dividends that would be earned by holding the equity. Therefore, the price of the equity should be determined as the expected value of the stream of dividends discounted over time (Fisher, 1906):

$$P_t = E_t \sum_{k=0}^{\infty} \frac{D_{t+k}}{(1+r)^{k+1}},$$
$$D = \text{Dividend},$$
$$r = \text{discount rate}.$$

(7.13)

The calculation of the real S&P 500 index price based on the afore-mentioned theory of dividends using Eq. (7.13) and the plot of it against the actual market index shown in Fig. 7.5 reveals excess volatilities of the actual market index against the theoretical market index (Shiller, 2014). This tells that the actual market price movements are hard to be justified by the theory of dividends and should be explained by other causes (Shiller, 1981).

The various research efforts with adjustable discount rates, consumption-based discount rates, and other attempts to replicate market behaviors of the actual stock index by the supporters of the EMH for more than three decades since the publication by Robert Shiller have not been successful in replicating the market price movement (Samuelson, 1998; Campbell and Cochrane, 1999).

The bubble theory and the empirical findings such as Fig. 7.5 pose serious challenges to the supporters of the EMH but also add much to an economic analysis of individuals' behaviors in the markets. The theory holds pertinence to the microbehavioral modelers.

What is the extent of speculative bubbles in the prices of agricultural and natural resource products? It should be noted that excess volatilities do not always occur in all circumstances. In the analysis of the real estate boom in the United States, Case and Shiller examines the speculative nature of the property prices in the major US cities before the real estate bubble which burst in 2008 (Case and Shiller, 1989, 2003; Shiller, 2005). They find that property values exhibit the bubble-like behavior in major cities of the United States such as New York, Los Angeles, Chicago, Boston, and San Francisco. However, the bubble-like behavior does not show up in a primarily rural state such as Wisconsin. Note that these studies focused on the residential housing markets in the major cities. What this implies is that the values of agricultural and natural resource assets are most likely primarily determined by market forces of demands and supplies.

In Fig. 7.6, the present author recreates the historical land value of the US farmlands since 1980 based on Nickerson and his coauthors from the USDA (Nickerson et al., 2012; USDA, 2014). The land values adjusted for price changes are overlaid against the net farm incomes through the years since 1980. As can be seen, the value of farmland does not exhibit excess volatilities, nor does it show signs of speculative asset prices as in Fig. 7.5.

Excess volatilities can be understood against the fundamentals in the economy. In Fig. 7.5 which demonstrates excess volatilities of the stock market index, the price movements are drawn against the earnings. Against the earnings data, the stock price seems highly volatile. By contrast, historical

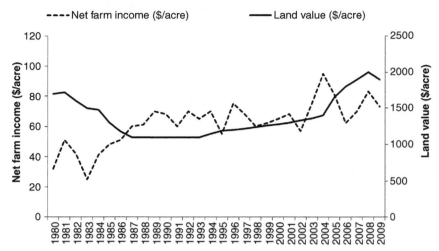

Figure 7.6 *Land values and farm sector net income, 1980–2009 (adjusted to the 2005 price level).*

land values in Fig. 7.6 do not seem to be more volatile than the historical farm net incomes. Indeed, the ratio between the land value and the farm net income is quite stable over the time period.

7.7 PROSPECT THEORY AND PSYCHOLOGY

The bubble theory or the theory of speculative asset prices is deeply rooted on psychological aspects of human behaviors. A bubble builds up through investors' enthusiasm, psychological contagion, envy of success, and gambler's excitement. Behavioral finance which is a broader field that includes the bubble theory is the study of economic activities and indices from the perspectives of psychological influences on decision making (Shiller, 2003, 2014; Thaler, 2015).

This literature draws insights from the psychological studies on decision making under uncertainties first elucidated by Kahneman and Tversky (1979, 1984). Kahneman and Tversky showed how an individual who is affected by psychological states may make a decision which is neither rational nor based upon expected value. Their arguments reveal a gap in the widely appreciated theory of decision making based on rational expectation of possible events and the probabilities that such events could occur (von Neumann and Morgenstern, 1947; Friedman and Savage, 1948; Nash 1950, 1951; Mas-Colell et al., 1995).

They point out that an individual has one's own value function which is different from the utility function. This function is quasi-concave but exhibits a kink at a reference point. That is, if the same amount of change occurs in the underlying quantity (eg, monetary return) at the reference point, the decrease in the value function is much steeper due to monetary loss than the increase in the value function owing to monetary gain. An individual perceives the loss more seriously than the same amount of gain at the reference point (Kahneman and Tversky, 1979).

Fig. 7.7 draws an individual's value function. In the reference point, the value function has a kink. The value function below the reference point has a steeper slope than the value function above the reference point. The value function doesn't have to be a linear function as shown in the figure. It may be a concave function above the reference point and a convex function below the reference point (Kahneman and Tversky, 1984)

One should note that, from the rational expectation theory, it is possible to construct a utility function with a kink such as the one in Fig. 7.7. However, the unique feature of the "prospect theory" which was the name given by Kahneman and Tversky (1979) is that the kink is shifting. The reference point may appear in any decision point. Indeed, the kink may exist in most situations which involve probabilistic outcomes such as a gamble.

The prominent feature of the prospect theory can be explained through a gamble which offers two different prospects, that is, outcomes. Let's consider the choice situation with the following two prospects:

Prospect 1: Win $1000 with 85% chance and win nothing with 15% chance.

Prospect 2: Win $ 800 with certainty.

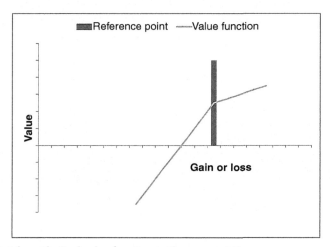

Figure 7.7 *A hypothetical value function in the prospect theory.*

A large number of individuals are shown, through experiments, to choose Prospect 2 over Prospect 1. This is despite the fact that the expected monetary gain is greater in Prospect 1 than in Prospect 2. The prospect theory argues that people do not evaluate the prospects by the expectation of monetary gains and losses but rather by the expectation of the subjective values attached to these outcomes. The subjective value of a gamble is a weighted average of the subjective value of each outcome in which the weight is probability.

Risky prospects are characterized by their possible outcomes and by the probabilities of these outcomes. Kahneman and Tversky distinguish decision weights from objective probabilities. They argue that people underweight as well as overweight possible outcomes depending upon the situations they are in. People may underweight moderate and high probabilities relative to sure things, which contribute to risk aversion in gains by reducing the attractiveness of positive gambles. The same effect also contributes to risk seeking in losses by attenuating the aversiveness of negative gambles. People may overweight low probabilities relative to moderate and high probabilities, which enhances the value of long shots and amplifies the aversiveness of a small chance of a severe loss (Kahneman and Tversky, 1984).

The prospect theory comes into the picture of a microbehavioral econometric modeling in the situations where a micro agent is in an attempt to make a transition from one enterprise to another enterprise (Seo, 2015a, b). Therefore, the theory has particular relevance to the study of adaptations to global warming and climatic changes. That is, adaptation calls for a transformation, that is, leaving one enterprise (system) and entering into a new enterprise (system) and the decision of transformation is the domain to which the prospect theory is particularly relevant. The process of adaptation must involve probabilistic outcomes as well as not-usual costs of investments and returns.

For example, let's suppose a farmer wants to make a transition from a crops-only enterprise to a livestock-only enterprise in order to cope with a potential predicted climatic change (Seo, 2010a, b). Because an array of inputs and outputs is by and large different in the two enterprises, a farmer must incur a significant sunk cost of transition. Once the decision to make a transition in order to adapt to a climatic change is made, then the sunk cost is a sure thing while future incomes generated from a new enterprise are probabilistic (Seo, 2015b).

Then, the prospect theory argues that the transition will not take place even if the discounted value of future profits exceeds the discounted value of all the costs including the sunk cost of investment because of psychological barriers (Kahneman and Tversky, 1984). From a national scale, the transition from a crops-only enterprise to a livestock-only enterprise will turn out to be slower than the rate of transition that the rational expectation theory would suggest.

This again means that the types and rates of adaptation should be empirically learned based on observed behaviors of individuals instead of assuming the types and rates of numerous adaptation measures (Seo, 2006, Seo 2011a, Seo, 2015b). The microbehavioral studies of adaptations as those presented in the preceding chapters would provide valuable insights as well as policy-relevant outcomes on the speeds of adaptations as well as the changes in profits from the enterprises which are chosen as an adaptation strategy (UNFCCC, 2008, 2011a, 2011b, 2015).

7.8 EXTREME EVENTS AND FAT-TAILED DISTRIBUTIONS

A primary message of the bubble theory of asset prices is that the prices will fall eventually when the bubble shall burst at some point. When the bubble pops unexpectedly, the fall in the price will be steep and very unusual, thereby shocking market participants as well as the overall economy. Some of the worst past market crash events are called an extreme event, an event that occurs with a very low probability. These extreme events in the markets will not go away as long as the market is driven by speculation and psychological contagion.

Extreme crash events in the stock markets have occurred occasionally. Examples are the stock market crash in the 1929 (the Great Crash), the market crash in 1988 (black Monday), the dot-com bubble burst in 2000, and the real estate bubble burst in 2008 (Galbraith, 1954; Shiller, 2000, 2005). These events are captured in Fig. 7.5 as precipitous falls in the S&P 500 stock index adjusted for inflation.

A consequence of speculative asset prices is to make the tail distribution of stock prices and stock returns fatter. To explain a "fatter' tail distribution, let X be a random variable of the return of the stock index. If the distribution of this random variable is a normal distribution, then it has a bell-shaped probability density function in which probability falls sharply as the outcome deviates from the mean of the distribution (Casella and

Berger, 2001). Let the mean of this random variable μ and the standard deviation σ. The probability of an event x to fall in the tails is defined as follows:

$$P\big[|x - \mu| \geq \sigma\big] < 0.33,$$
$$P\big[|x - \mu| \geq 2\sigma\big] < 0.05,$$
$$P\big[|x - \mu| \geq 3\sigma\big] < 0.003,$$
$$P\big[|x - \mu| \geq 4\sigma\big] < 0.0001.$$

(7.14)

In the normal distribution, the probability of a rare event falls sharply. In terms of rarity of an event, we can define x-sigma event. That is, one-sigma event is an event that falls outside one-sigma distance from the mean. Two-sigma, three-sigma, four-sigma events are defined accordingly (Nordhaus, 2011, 2013).

Note from Eq. (7.14) that the four-sigma event is extremely rare, so that the probability of occurring is almost nil, less than one in ten thousands, if the underlying distribution is a Gaussian. Even the probability of a three-sigma event is very rare. What it means is that the four-sigma event, when it occurs, will be quite a surprise and shocking to market participants.

The Gaussian distribution is considered a medium-tailed event distribution (Schuster, 1984). According to one definition, a thin-tailed distribution has a finite upper limit (such as the uniform distribution or the triangular distribution sometimes used in the mixed Logit model); a medium-tailed distribution has exponentially declining tails (such as the normal distribution); and a fat-tailed distribution has power law tails (such as the Pareto distribution to be explained presently).

A Pareto distribution has the following probability density function of a random variable X (Nordhaus, 2011):

$$f(X) = k \cdot X^{-(1+\alpha)}$$

(7.15)

where α is the "shape parameter" which captures the importance of tail events and k is a constant that ensures that the sum of probabilities across the values of X is 1. If α is very small, the distribution has fat tails. If α is very large, the distribution looks like a Gaussian distribution.

In a fat-tailed Pareto distribution, the probability of a rare event does not approximate zero asymptotically. In Fig. 7.8, the present author draws a fat-tailed distribution using the Pareto distribution in Eq. (7.15) and overlays it against a thin-tailed distribution again drawn from the Pareto distribution by varying the size of the shape parameter. Also, a (hypothetical) threshold is marked on the figure. In a thin-tailed distribution, the probability falls rapidly as the value of the random variable moves right along the horizontal axis. On the other hand, the probability does not decline quickly in the fat-tailed distribution.

In Fig. 7.8, a threshold value of the random variable is marked which may be thought of as a dividing line between a rare event and a usual event. A rare event is an event that lies on the right side of the threshold mark. It may be a five-sigma or even a six-sigma event which under a Gaussian distribution would occur extremely rarely. For example, a rare event may be a once-in-ten-thousand-year drought event.

How fat is fat for it to be considered a fat-tailed distribution? There is no formal rule on answering this question. However, in the ultimate case of a fat-tailed distribution, the variance of a fat-tailed distribution is undefined, in other words, infinite. One statistical example is a Cauchy distribution in which higher moments are not defined (Casella and Berger, 2001).

A slightly easier question to handle with regard to the fat-tailed distribution is whether the observed stock prices—or any other prices, for example, grain prices—are normally distributed. In other words, can we say that the

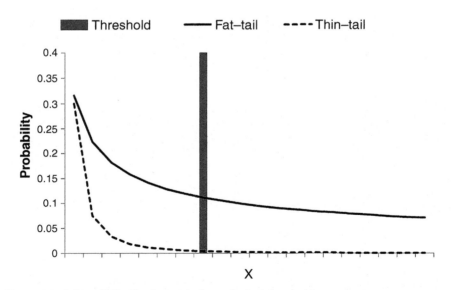

Figure 7.8 *A fat-tail distribution and a hypothetical threshold.*

observed prices of the stock index such as the S&P 500 index do not have a fat-tailed distribution (Mandelbrot, 1963; Mandelbrot and Hudson, 2004)?

In Fig. 7.9, the present author draws monthly returns calculated from the same S&P 500 index data used in Fig. 7.2. The observed monthly returns since the 1870s show that there are conspicuously large falls and spikes in the historical data. Do these unusual spikes and precipices make the distribution of the S&P 500 index a fat tailed?

To answer this question, on top of the observed monthly returns from the S&P 500 index, the present author simulates a normal distribution, that is, a nonfat-tailed distribution, using the same mean and standard deviation found in the observed monthly returns data. From the observed S&P 500 index, the mean is found to be +0.4% and the standard deviation is 4.1%. The simulated Gaussian returns are plotted in red and overlaid against the observed monthly returns.

What we are asking in this simulation experiment is whether the observed monthly returns can be said to have arisen from a Gaussian distribution with the same mean and variance. In Fig. 7.9, the simulated returns from 1871 to 2013 show that although almost all the realized (observed) returns are expected under the assumption of a normal distribution, some

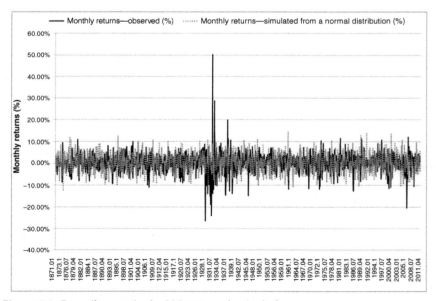

Figure 7.9 *Fat-tail events in the S&P 500 stock price index.*

events are not replicated. These nonreplicable events are prominent stock market crashes and spikes during the great depression in 1930, the market crash in 1988, the dot-com bubble burst in 2000, and the real estate bubble in 2008. The stock index plunges during these events are far out of the range simulated by the normal distribution.

What are the consequences of a fat-tailed distribution in terms of economic analyses? It has a grave consequence, indeed (Mandelbrot, 1963; Mandelbrot and Hudson, 2004). A fat-tailed event prevents a researcher from relying on the analysis based on a normal distribution or any well-defined distribution (Weitzman, 2009). In a policy analysis, a cost-benefit analysis based on the assumption of a Gaussian distribution gives a misleading conclusion. In an extremely fat-tailed distribution, a more proper policy option is what is often called a "precautionary principle" which means that a policy must be designed in a way that a threshold must not be crossed at any cost.

This "dismal" conclusion is not hard to understand. In a fat-tailed distribution, the probability remains significant even for an extreme value. This means that the expected value of the extreme outcome is unbounded. One analytical result from the fat-tailed distribution is called the dismal theorem developed in the context of global warming policy, according to Martin Weitzman, which is expressed as follows (Weitzman, 2009):

For any given n and k,

$$\lim_{\lambda \to \infty} E[M \mid \lambda] = +\infty. \tag{7.16}$$

Weitzman calls M a "stochastic discounting factor", the amount of present consumption an agent would be willing to give up in the present period to obtain one sure unit of future consumption. The λ is called the VSL (value of statistical life)-like parameter, approximately the value of statistical civilization as we know it or the VSL on Earth as we know it. The parameters n, k are roughly understood to be the number of available data and the number of prior data, respectively.

However, there is no formal rule on how fat a distribution should be for a cost-benefit analysis to break down (Nordhaus, 2011). Even in the case of the S&P 500 index which exhibits evidence against the normal distribution, an economic analysis can still be conducted with a nonfat-tailed distribution with additional specifications.

The dismal theorem in Eq. (7.16) is derived from several key assumptions. One of them is that all future predictions, regardless of whether they are done by an expert or a casual observer, are all equally valid. Second, scientific efforts cannot narrow down the probability of a catastrophic event, even with much resources and time devoted (Le Treut et al., 2007). Third, the future extreme event will end the life on earth. Fourth, behavioral responses by individuals, communities, governments, and international societies are meaningless in the context of a fat-tailed event.

A perhaps more policy pertinent question to ask is what event has a truly and extremely fat-tail distribution? We can safely say that the distribution of land values shown previously in Fig. 7.6 is not fat tailed. That is to say that all the realizations of the land value are reasonably expected from a Gaussian distribution. Do crop prices exhibit a fat-tailed distribution? Do oil prices exhibit a fat-tailed distribution? Do gold prices have a fat-tailed distribution? These are empirical questions that can be answered, but cannot be answered satisfactorily without taking into account a full complex economic and financial system comprehensively (Nordhaus, 2007; Wright, 2011). In any satisfactory analysis of the extreme events, the present author believes that microbehavioral responses and how to model these will play a central and pivotal role.

In the natural resources sectors, a researcher can ask whether a certain event is a rare event and how rare it is (NRC, 2013; Titley et al., 2016). A drought can be said to be one-sigma event, two-sigma event, three-sigma event, four-sigma event, and so on. A heavy rainfall event can be said to be a four-sigma event or a five-sigma event. Similarly, heat stress caused by an unusually high sustained temperature can be said to be an x-sigma event (Rahmstorf and Coumou, 2011). Or, a hurricane storm surge is said to be one-in-one-hundred-year event or one-in-one-thousand-year event (Lin et al., 2012).

Has the rainfall event in the United States or elsewhere perhaps in a tropical country such as Nigeria in Africa, India in South Asia, or Ecuador in South America a fat-tailed distribution? These countries are known for a highly volatile rainfall pattern. Historical rainfall data are available from the climatology studies and the national climate and/or weather organizations (Hulme et al., 2001; New et al., 2002; NOAA National Centers for Environmental Information, 2015). The amount of rainfall that falls on a location varies day by day and exhibits seasonal fluctuations over a year. Further, rainfall events over many decades are strongly influenced by multi-decadal swings in the global ocean currents (Ropelewski and Halpert, 1987; Janowiak, 1988; Shanahan et al., 2009; JISOA, 2015). El Nino Southern Oscillation (ENSO), Atlantic Multidecadal Oscillation (AMO), and Pacific Decadal Oscillation (PDO) are associated with the changes in rainfall swings over many decades in these countries.

That rainfall volatility, through heavy rainfall events and severe drought events, is associated with the underlying process, for example, multidecadal changes in ocean currents mean that rainfall extremes are cyclical events and should be interpreted with a long-term horizon of more than a century. Further, the nature of rainfall volatility, whether extreme or normal, should be researched only with a large geographical scale of, for example, a country considering the shifting nature of rainfall events across the landscape.

Microbehavioral models shed ample insights on the discussions of extreme events or fat-tailed events. That some events are tail events do not mean that a natural resource manager is without means to cope with such events. Sub-Saharan farmers show that they adapt to increased rainfall and temperature volatility through a mixed crops–livestock farming and/or managing animals instead of crops (Seo, 2012c). Australian natural resource managers have increased livestock management, especially sheep, in both hot and arid climate zones (Seo, 2015c). Indian farmers increased the ownership of goats in order to cope with the Indian monsoon climate which is characterized by an extremely heavy rainfall in the monsoon season followed by an extremely low rainfall in the nonmonsoon season (Seo, 2016). Adaptation measures such as an early warning system and a hurricane path projection helped coastal vulnerable areas to reduce the number of fatalities from severe hurricanes (Seo, 2015d; Bakkensen and Mendelsohn, 2015; Seo and Bakkensen, 2016).

Exercises

1. Using the historical record of land values in the United States shown in Fig. 7.6 or other historical land value data available, test the hypothesis that land value is primarily driven by speculations by market participants, therefore subject to the cycle of an ever larger bubble which eventually bursts.

2. Develop a set of climate-related risk indicators faced by natural resource and environmental managers, focusing on a specific natural resource sector in a specific country or region. For example, you may choose the 2012–14 California drought and agriculture. Test whether climate-related events are extreme events or fat-tailed events using the indicators you developed. Explain through microbehavioral econometric models how behavioral, market, and financial instruments help natural resource managers to deal with such risks and rare events.

REFERENCES

Aksoy, S., Attardo, G., et al., 2014. Genome sequence of the Tsetse fly (Glossina morsitans): vector of African Trypanosomiasis. Science 344 (6182), 380–386.

Anderson, K., Masters, W.A. (Eds.), 2009. Distortions to Agricultural Incentives in Africa. World Bank, Washington DC.

Arrow, K.J., 1971. Essays in the Theory of Risk Bearing. Markham Publishing Co, Chicago.

Arrow, K.J., Fisher, A.C., 1974. Environmental preservation, uncertainty, and irreversibility. Q. J. Econ. 88, 312–319.

Bakkensen, L.A., Mendelsohn, R., 2015. Risk and Adaptation: Evidence from Global Hurricane Damages and Fatalities. Yale University, New Haven, CT.

Barry, P.J., Elllinger, P.N., Baker, C.B., Hopkin, J.A., 2000. Financial Management in Agriculture, sixth ed. Interstate Publishers, Illinois.

Black, F., Scholes, M., 1973. The pricing of options and corporate liabilities. J. Pol. Econ. 81 (3), 637–654.

Bloomberg Business, 2015. Markets. Available from: http://www.bloomberg.com.

Campbell, J.Y., Cochrane, J., 1999. By force of habit: a consumption-based explanation of aggregate stock market behavior. J. Pol. Econ. 107, 205–251.

Case, K.E., Shiller, R.J., 1989. The efficiency of the market for single family homes. Am. Econ. Rev. 79 (1), 125–137.

Case, K.E., Shiller, R.J., 2003. Is there a bubble in the housing market? Brookings Pap. Econ. Act. 2003, 299–342.

Casella, G., Berger, R.L., 2001. Statistical Inference, second ed. Duxbury Press, CA.

Deschenes, O., Greenstone, M., 2007. The economic impacts of climate change: evidence from agricultural output and random fluctuations in weather. Am. Econ. Rev. 97, 354–385.

Deschenes, O., Greenstone, M., 2012. The economic impacts of climate change: evidence from agricultural output and random fluctuations in weather: Reply. Am. Econ. Rev. 102, 3761–3773.

Easterling, D.R., Evans, J.L., Groisman, P.Y., Karl, T.R., Kunkel, K.E., Ambenje, P., 2000. Observed variability and trends in extreme climate events: a brief review. Bull. Am. Meteorol. Soc. 81, 417–425.

Fabozzi, F.J., Modigliani, F.G., Jones, F.J., 2009. Foundations of Financial Markets and Institutions, fourth ed. Prentice Hall, New York.

Fafchamps, M., Udry, C., Czukas, K., 1998. Drought and saving in West Africa: are livestock a buffer stock? J. Dev. Econ. 55, 273–305.

Fama, E.F., 1970. Efficient capital markets: a review of empirical work. J. Fin. 25 (2), 383–417.

Fama, E.F., 1991. Efficient capital markets II. J. Fin. 46 (5), 1575–1617.

Fama, E.F., French, K.R., 1992. The cross-section of expected stock returns. J. Fin. 47, 427–465.

Fisher, I., 1906. The Nature of Capital and Income. Macmillan, New York.

Fisher, I., 1930. The Theory of Interest. Macmillan, New York.

Fisher, A.C., Hanemann, W.M., Roberts, M.J., Schlenker, W., 2012. The economic impacts of climate change: evidence from agricultural output and random fluctuations in weather: comment. Am. Econ. Rev. 102, 3749–3760.

Ford, J., Katondo, K.M., 1977. Maps of tsetse fly (Glossina) distribution in Africa, 1973, according to subgeneric groups on a scale of 1:5000000. Bull. Anim. Health Prod. Afr. 15, 187–193.

Fox, N.J., Marion, G., Davidson, R.S., White, P.C.L., Hutchings, M.R., 2012. Livestock Helminths in a changing climate: approaches and restrictions to meaningful predictions. Animals 2, 93–107.

Friedman, M., Savage, L.J., 1948. Utility analysis of choices involving risk. J. Pol. Econ. 56 (4), 279–304.

Fudenberg, D., Tirole, J., 1991. Games in strategic form and Nash equilibrium. In: Fudenberg, D., Tirole, J. (Eds.), Game Theory. MIT Press, Cambridge, MA.

Galbraith, J.K., 1954. The Great Crash 1929. Houghton Mifflin, Boston.

Geanakoplos, J., 2010. The leverage cycle. Acemoglu, D., Rogoff, K., Woodford, M. (Eds.), NBER Macro-economics Annual 2009, vol. 24, University of Chicago Press, Chicago.

Gibbons, R., 1992. Game Theory for Applied Economists. Princeton University Press, Princeton, NJ.

Gitay, H., Brwon, S., Easterling W., Jallow, B., 2001. Ecosystems and their goods and services. In: McCarthy et al., (Ed.), Climate Change 2001: Impacts, Adaptations, and Vulnerabilities. Cambridge University Press, Cambridge, pp. 237–342.

Goodwin, B.K., Smith, V.K., 2014. Theme overview: the 2014 farm bill—an economic welfare disaster or triumph? Choices 29 (3), 1–4.

Goswami, B.N., Venugopal, V., Sengupta, D., Madhusoodanan, M.S., Xavier, P.K., 2006. Increasing trend of extreme rain events over India in a warming environment. Science 314, 1442–1445.

Hahn, G.L., Gaughan, J.B., Mader, T.L., Eigenberg, R.A., 2009. Chapter 5: Thermal indices and their applications for livestock environments. In: DeShazer, J.A. (Ed.), Livestock Energetics and Thermal Environmental Management. ASABE, St. Joseph, Mich, pp. 113–130, Copyright 2009 American Society of Agricultural and Biological Engineers. ASABE # 801M0309. ISBN 1-892769-74-3.

Halcrow, H.G., 1949. Actuarial structures for crop insurance. J. Farm Econ. 31, 418–443.

Hansen, J., Sato, M., Reudy, R., Lo, K., Lea, D.W., Medina-Elizade, M., 2006. Global temperature change. Proc. Natl. Acad. Sci. USA 103, 14288–14293.

Hansen, J., Sato, M., Reudy, R., 2012. Perception of climate change. Proc. Natl. Acad. Sci. USA 109, E2415–E2423.

Hogg, R.V., Craig, A., McKean, J.W., 2012. Introduction to Mathematical Statistics, seventh ed. Pearson, New York.

Hulme, M., Doherty, R.M., Ngara, T., New, M.G., Lister, D., 2001. African climate change: 1900–2100. Clim. Res. 17, 145–168.

IPCC, 2012. Managing the Risks of Extreme Events and Disasters to Advance Climate Change Adaptation. A Special Report of Working Groups I and II of the Intergovernmental Panel on Climate Change. Cambridge University Press, Cambridge.

Intergovernmental Panel on Climate Change, 2014. Climate Change 2014: The Physical Science Basis, the Fifth Assessment Report of the IPCC. Cambridge University Press, Cambridge.

Janowiak, J.E., 1988. An investigation of interannual rainfall variability in Africa. J. Clim. 1, 240–255.

Joint Institute for the Study of Ocean and the Atmosphere (JISOA), 2015. Sahel Precipitation Index. JISOA, University of Washington, Seattle.

Kahneman, D., Tversky, A., 1979. Prospect theory: an analysis of decision under risk. Econometrica 47, 263–291.

Kahneman, D., Tversky, A., 1984. Choices, values and frames. Am. Psychol. 39 (4), 341–350.

Kazianga, H., Udry, C., 2006. Consumption smoothing? Livestock, insurance, and drought in rural Burkina Faso. J. Dev. Econ. 79, 413–446.

Keeling, C.D., Piper, S.C., Bacastow, R.B., Wahlen, M., Whorf, T.P., Heimann, M., Meijer, H.A., 2005. Atmospheric CO_2 and $^{13}CO_2$ exchange with the terrestrial biosphere and oceans from 1978 to 2000: observations and carbon cycle implications. In: Ehleringer, J.R., Cerling, T.E., Dearing, M.D. (Eds.), A History of Atmospheric CO_2 and its Effects on Plants, Animals, and Ecosystems. Springer-Verlag, New York.

Keynes, J.M., 1936. The General Theory of Employment, Interest, and Money. Palgrave Macmillan, London.

Le Treut, H., Somerville, R., Cubasch, U., Ding, Y., Mauritzen, C., Mokssit, A., Peterson, T., Prather, M., 2007. Historical overview of climate change. In: Solomon, S., Qin, D., Manning, M., Chen, Z., Marquis, M., Averyt, K.B., Tignor, M., Miller, H.L. (Eds.), Climate Change 2007: The Physical Science Basis. Contribution of Working Group I to the Fourth Assessment Report of the Intergovernmental Panel on Climate Change. Cambridge University Press, Cambridge.

Lin, N., Emanuel, K., Oppenheimer, M., Vanmarcke, E., 2012. Physically based assessment of hurricane surge threat under climate change. Nat. Clim. Change 2, 462–467.

Mahul, O., 1999. Optimum area yield crop insurance. Am J. Agric. Econ. 81 (1), 75–82.

Mandelbrot, B., 1963. The variation of certain speculative prices. J. Bus. 36 (4), 394–419.

Mandelbrot, B., Hudson, R.L., 2004. The (Mis)behaviour of Markets: A Fractal View of Risk, Ruin, and Reward. Profile Books, London.

Markowitz, H., 1952. Portfolio selection. J. Fin. 7, 77–91.

Markowitz, H., 1959. Portfolio Selection: Efficient Diversification of Investments. John Wiley & Sons, New York.

Mas-Colell, A., Whinston, M.D., Green, J.R., 1995. Microeconomic Theory. Oxford University Press, Oxford.

Meehl, G.A., Hu, A., 2006. Megadroughts in the Indian monsoon region and southwest North America and a mechanism for associated multidecadal Pacific sea surface temperature anomalies. J. Clim. 19, 1605–1623.

Mendelsohn, R., 2000. Efficient adaptation to climate change. Clim. Change 45, 583–600.

Mendelsohn, R., Nordhaus, W., Shaw, D., 1994. The impact of global warming on agriculture: a Ricardian analysis. Am. Econ. Rev. 84, 753–771.

Miranda, M.J., 1991. Area–yield crop insurance reconsidered. Am. J. Agric. Econ. 73, 233–242.

Miranda, M.J., Glauber, J.W., 1997. Systemic risk, reinsurance, and the failure of crop insurance markets. Am. J. Agric. Econ. 79, 206–215.

Modigliani, F., Pogue, G.A., 1974. An introduction to risk and return: concepts and evidence. Fin. Anal. J., 69–86, (May–June).

Nash, J., 1950. Equilibrium points in n-person games. Proc. Natl. Acad. Sci. USA 36 (1), 48–49.

Nash, J., 1951. Non-cooperative games. Ann. Math. 54 (2), 286–295.

National Research Council (NRC), 2013. Abrupt Impacts of Climate Change: Anticipating Surprises. The National Academies Press, Washington DC.

New, M., Lister, D., Hulme, M., Makin, I., 2002. A high-resolution data set of surface climate over global land areas. Clim. Res. 21, 1–25.

Nickerson, C., Morehart, M., Kuethe, T., Beckman, J., Ifft, J., Williams, R., 2012. Trends in U.S. Farmland Values and Ownership. EIB-92. U.S. Dept. of Agriculture, Econ. Res. Serv., Washington DC.

NOAA National Centers for Environmental Information, 2015. State of the Climate: Global Analysis for Annual 2014, published online January 2015. Available from: http://www.ncdc.noaa.gov/sotc/global/201413.

Nordhaus, W., 2007. Who's afraid of big bad oil shock? Brookings Pap. Econ. Act. 2, 219–240, 2007.

Nordhaus, W., 2011. The economics of tail events with an application to climate change. Rev. Environ. Econ. Pol. 5, 240–257.

Nordhaus, W., 2013. The Climate Casino: Risk, Uncertainty, and Economics for a Warming World. Yale University Press, New Haven, CT.

Pratt, J.W., 1964. Risk aversion in the small and in the large. Econometrica 32 (1–2), 122–136.

Rahmstorf, S., Coumou, D., 2011. Increase of extreme events in a warming world. Proc. Natl. Sci. Acad. USA. 108, 17905–17909.

Reilly, J., Baethgen, W., Chege, F., Van de Geijn, S., Enda, L., Iglesias, A., Kenny, G., Patterson, D., Rogasik, J., Rotter, R., Rosenzweig, C., Sombroek, W., Westbrook, J., 1996. Agriculture in a changing climate: impacts and adaptations. In: Watson, R., Zinyowera, M.,

Moss, R., Dokken, D. (Eds.), Climate Change 1995: Impacts, Adaptations, and Mitigation of Climate Change. Intergovernmental Panel on Climate Change (IPCC). Cambridge University Press, Cambridge.

Ricardo, D., 1817. On the Principles of Political Economy and Taxation. John Murray, London, England.

Ropelewski, C.F., Halpert, M.S., 1987. Global and regional precipitation patterns associated with the El Nino/Southern Oscillation. Mon. Weather Rev. 115, 1606–1626.

Rosenzweig, C., Iglesias, A., Yang, X.B., Epstein, P.R., Chivian, E., 2001. Climate change and extreme weather events: implications for food production, plant diseases, and pests. Global Change Hum. Health. 2 (2), 90–104.

Rosenzweig, M.R., Wolpin, K.I., 1993. Credit market constraints, consumption smoothing, and the accumulation of durable production assets in low-income countries: investments in bullocks in India. J. Pol Econ. 101 (2), 223–244.

Ross, S., 1976. The arbitrage theory of capital asset pricing. J. Econ. Theory 13 (3), 341–360.

Samuelson, P.A., 1998. Summing up on business cycles: opening address. In: Fuhrer, J.C., Schuh, S. (Eds.), Beyond Shocks: What Causes Business Cycles. Federal Reserve Bank of Boston, Boston, pp. 33–36.

Schlenker, W., Roberts, M., 2009. Nonlinear temperature effects indicate severe damages to crop yields under climate change. Proc. Natl. Acad. Sci. USA 106 (37), 15594–15598.

Schuster, E.F., 1984. Classification of probability laws by tail behavior. J. Am. Stat. Assoc. 79 (388), 936–939.

Seo, S.N., 2006. Modeling farmer responses to climate change: climate change impacts and adaptations in livestock management in Africa. PhD Dissertation, Yale University, New Haven.

Seo, S.N., 2010a. Is an integrated farm more resilient against climate change?: a micro-econometric analysis of portfolio diversification in African agriculture? Food Pol. 35, 32–40.

Seo, S.N., 2010b. A microeconometric analysis of adapting portfolios to climate change: adoption of agricultural systems in Latin America. Appl. Econ. Perspect. Pol. 32, 489–514.

Seo, S.N., 2010c. Managing forests, livestock, and crops under global warming: a micro-econometric analysis of land use changes in Africa. Austr. J. Agric. Resour. Econ. 54 (2), 239–258.

Seo, S.N., 2011a. An analysis of public adaptation to climate change using agricultural water schemes in South America. Ecol. Econ. 70, 825–834.

Seo, S.N., 2011b. A geographically scaled analysis of adaptation to climate change with spatial models using agricultural systems in Africa. J. Agric. Sci. 149, 437–449.

Seo, S.N., 2012a. Adapting natural resource enterprises under global warming in South America: a mixed logit analysis. Economia 12, 111–135.

Seo, S.N., 2012b. Adaptation behaviors across ecosystems under global warming: a spatial microeconometric model of the rural economy in South America. Pap. Reg. Sci. 91, 849–871.

Seo, S.N., 2012c. Decision making under climate risks: an analysis of sub-Saharan farmers' adaptation behaviors. Weather, Clim. Soc. 4, 285–299.

Seo, S.N., 2013. An essay on the impact of climate change on US agriculture: weather fluctuations, climatic shifts, and adaptation strategies. Clim. Change 121, 115–124.

Seo, S.N., 2014a. Evaluation of agro-ecological zone methods for the study of climate change with micro farming decisions in sub-Saharan Africa. Eur. J. Agron. 52, 157–165.

Seo, S.N., 2014b. Coupling climate risks, eco-systems, anthropogenic decisions using South American and Sub-Saharan farming activities. Meteorol. Appl. 21, 848–858.

Seo, S.N., 2015a. Micro-behavioral Economics of Global Warming: Modeling Adaptation Strategies in Agricultural and Natural Resource Enterprises. Springer, Cham.

Seo, S.N., 2015b. Modeling farmer adaptations to climate change in South America: a micro-behavioral econometric perspective. Environ. Ecol. Stat. 23, 1–21.

Seo, S.N., 2015c. Adapting to extreme climates: raising animals in hot and arid ecosystems in Australia. Int. J. Biometeorol. 59, 541–550.

Seo, S.N., 2015d. Fatalities of neglect: adapt to more intense hurricanes? Int. J. Climatol. 35, 3505–3514.

Seo, S.N., 2016. Untold tales of goats in deadly Indian monsoons: adapt or rain-retreat under global warming? J. Extreme Events 3. doi: 10.1142/S2345737616500019.

Seo, S.N., Bakkensen, L., 2016. Did adaptation strategies work? High fatalities from tropical cyclones in the North Indian Ocean and global warming. Nat. Hazards.

Seo, S.N., Mendelsohn, R., 2008a. Measuring impacts and adaptations to climate change: a structural Ricardian model of African livestock management. Agric. Econ. 38, 151–165.

Seo, S.N., Mendelsohn, R., 2008b. A Ricardian analysis of the impact of climate change impacts on South American farms. Chil. J. Agric. Res. 68, 69–79.

Seo, S.N., Mendelsohn, R., 2008c. Animal husbandry in Africa: climate change impacts and adaptations. Afr. J. Agric Resour. Econ. 2, 65–82.

Shanahan, T.M., Overpeck, J.T., Anchukaitis, K.J., Beck, J.W., Cole, J.E., Dettman, D.L., Peck, J.A., Scholz, C.A., King, J.W., 2009. Atlantic forcing of persistent drought in West Africa. Science 324, 377–380.

Sharpe, W.F., 1964. Capital asset prices: a theory of market equilibrium under conditions of risk. J. Fin. 19 (3), 425–442.

Shields, DA., 2013. Federal crop insurance: background. Congressional Research Service. R40532. US Congress: Washington DC.

Shiller, R.J., 1979. The volatility of long-term interest rates and expectations models of the term structure. J. Pol. Econ. 87 (6), 1190–1219.

Shiller, R.J., 1981. Do stock prices move too much to be justified by subsequent changes in dividends? Am. Econ. Rev. 71 (3), 421–436.

Shiller, R.J., 2000. Irrational Exuberance. Princeton University Press, Princeton, NJ.

Shiller, R.J., 2003. From efficient markets theory to behavioral finance. J. Econ. Perspect. 17, 83–104.

Shiller, R.J., 2004. The New Financial Order: Risk in the 21st Century. Princeton University Press, Princeton, NJ.

Shiller, R.J., 2005. Irrational Exuberance, second ed. Princeton University Press, Princeton, NJ.

Shiller, R.J., 2008. Financial Markets. Open Yale Courses. Yale University, New Haven.

Shiller, R.J., 2009. The Subprime Solution: How Today's Global Financial Crisis Happened, and What to do About it. Princeton University Press, Princeton, NJ.

Shiller, R.J., 2014. Speculative asset prices. Am. Econ. Rev. 104 (6), 1486–1517.

Skees, J.R., Black, J.R., Barnett, B.J., 1997. Designing and rating an area yield crop insurance contract. Am. J. Agric. Econ. 79, 430–438.

South Africa Futures Exchange, 2015. Available from: http://www.safex.co.za.

Summers, L.H., 1986. Does the stock market rationally reflect fundamental values. Econometrica 41, 591–601.

Sumner, D.A., Zulauf, C., 2012. Economic & Environmental Effects of Agricultural Insurance Programs. The Council on Food, Agricultural & Resource Economics (C-FARE), Washington DC.

Tebaldi, C., Hayhoe, K., Arblaster, J.M., Meehl, G.E., 2007. Going to the extremes: an intercomparison of model-simulated historical and future changes in extreme events. Clim Chang 82, 233–234.

Thaler, R.H., 2015. Misbehaving: The Making of Behavioral Economics. W. W. Norton Company, New York.

Titley, D.W., Hegerl, G., Jacobs, K.L., Mote, P.W., Paciorek, C.J., Shepherd, J.M., Shepherd, T.G., Sobel, A.H., Walsh, J., Zwiers, F.W., Thomas, K., Everett, L., Purcell, Gaskins,

R., Markovich, E., 2016. Attribution of Extreme Weather Events in the Context of Climate Change. National Academies of Sciences, Engineering, and Medicine. National Academies Press, Washington, DC.

Tobin, J., 1958. Liquidity preference as behavior toward risk. Rev. Econ. Stud. 25 (2), 65–86.

Udry, C., 1995. Risk and saving in Northern Nigeria. Am. Econ. Rev. 85, 1287–1300.

United Nations Framework Convention on Climate Change, 2011a. The Durban Platform for Enhanced Action. UNFCCC, Geneva.

United Nations Framework Convention on Climate Change, 2011b. Report of the Transitional Committee for the Design of Green Climate Fund. UNFCCC, Geneva.

United Nations Framework Convention on Climate Change (UNFCCC), 2015. The Paris Agreement. Conference Of the Parties (COP) 21, UNFCCC, Geneva.

United States Department of Agriculture, 2014. Land Values 2014 Summary. USDA, National Agricultural Statistics Service, Washington DC, August 2014.

United States Environmental Protection Agency, 2014. Heating and Cooling Degree Days. US EPA, Washington DC.

U.S. Risk Management Agency (RMA), 2015. Costs and Outlays of Crop Insurance Program. USDA, Washington DC, Available from: http://www.rma.usda.gov/aboutrma/budget/costoutlays.html.

von Neumann, J., Morgenstern, O., 1947. Theory of Games and Economic Behavior, second ed. Princeton University Press, Princeton, NJ.

Weitzman, M.L., 2009. On modeling and interpreting the economics of catastrophic climate change. Rev. Econ. Stat. 91, 1–19.

Wooldridge, J.M., 2010. Econometric Analysis of Cross Section and Panel Data. MIT Press, MA.

Working, H., 1953. Futures trading and hedging. Am. Econ. Rev. 43 (3), 314–343.

Working, H., 1962. New concepts concerning futures markets and prices. Am. Econ. Rev. 52 (3), 413–459.

Wright, B., 2011. The economics of grain price volatility. Appl. Econ. Perspect. Pol. 33, 32–58.

Wright, B., 2014. Multiple peril crop insurance. Choices 29 (3), 1–5.

Zilberman, D., 1998. Agricultural and Environmental Policies: Economics of Production, Technology, Risk, Agriculture, and the Environment. The State University of New York Press, Oswego, NY.

Ziska, L.H., 2003. Evaluation of yield loss in field-grown sorghum from a C3 and C4 weed as a function of increasing atmospheric carbon dioxide. Weed Sci. 51, 914–918.

CHAPTER 8

Gleaning Insights From Microbehavioral Models on Environmental and Natural Resource Policies

Throughout this book, the present author described microbehavioral econometric methods with both statistical theories and applications to economic decisions in agricultural and natural resource enterprises. As stated in the first chapter of this book, the primary objective of the book is to introduce microbehavioral statistical methods to the studies of environmental and natural resources which have increasingly become a pertinent research field for social discourses and policy decisions.

The final chapter of this book is devoted to discussions of policy implications and insights that can be gleaned from the applied microbehavioral econometric modeling efforts for designing environmental and natural resource policies. For this purpose, the present author will provide a comprehensive but not necessarily extensive survey of past and existing policies in the areas of agriculture, environment, energy, natural resources, climate change, and financial markets.

Let's begin with a brief summary of what this book has accomplished up to this point. The present author started with the need and pertinence of microbehavioral models in addressing environmental and natural resource problems that are of paramount importance to today's societies. As a representative example of these problems, the present author introduced to the readers the problem of global warming and climatic shifts, one of the most difficult and complex problems that confront the today's generations (Nordhaus, 1994; Keeling et al., 2005; Hansen et al., 2006; United Nations Framework Convention on Climate Change, 2009; United Nations Framework Convention on Climate Change, 2015; Intergovernmental Panel on Climate Change, 2014a; Le Treut et al., 2007; National Research Council, 2013).

Following up with the introductory chapter, the book explained a full array of microbehavioral econometric models in the succeeding two chapters (McFadden, 1974; Heckman, 1979; Dubin and McFadden 1984; Train 2003;

Cameron and Trivedi 2005). Chapter 2 gave an account of microbehavioral models from the perspectives of economic decisions whereas Chapter 3 explained each of the components in the microbehavioral models from the perspectives of statistical assumptions and considerations. The two chapters combined lay down a theoretical foundation for microbehavioral modeling.

The four chapters that followed provided examples of applied microbehavioral econometric models. The four chapters are intended to highlight different aspects of applied models. Chapter 4 began the application of microbehavioral models to agricultural and natural resource enterprises in South America. The chapter deals with an individual's decisions faced with climatic changes and global warming with regard to agricultural and natural resource enterprises. The chapter presents a microbehavioral model in which adoptions of the three enterprises are made explicit: a crops-only, a livestock-only, and a mixed crops and livestock.

Chapter 5 explained the importance of making adoption decisions explicit in economic modeling by comparing the microbehavioral model developed in Chapter 4 with the Ricardian model in which the full range of adaptation strategies is accounted for but is implicitly embedded.

In Chapter 6, the present author further develops a microbehavioral model in which adoptions of the six enterprises of agricultural and natural resources are made explicit: a crops-only, a livestock-only, a forests-only, a crops–forests, a crops–livestock, and a crops–livestock–forests. Individuals' decisions of adopting one of these enterprises are coupled with eco-system (or ecological) changes that are caused by climatic changes historically and predicted in the future.

In Chapter 7, the present author provided modeling efforts to capture risk, extremes, speculation, and uncertainties in the microbehavioral models. The chapter drew insights heavily from the literature on financial decisions as well as agricultural and natural resource decisions. Topics covered included climate risk, modern portfolio theory, attitudes toward risk, futures and options, insurance and subsidy, speculative asset prices, prospect and psychology, and extremes and fat-tail events (Weitzman 2009, Nordhaus 2011).

Microbehavioral econometric models described throughout this book are a superb tool for unraveling how microagents, that is, an individual, make decisions given external circumstances and change such decisions if circumstances are altered. The findings from the microbehavioral models have played a major role in numerous fields of policy decisions. Henceforth, the present author wishes to highlight some of these contributions to policy discourses.

First, a microbehavioral model can inform the public and policy makers of what decisions are made by the individuals given circumstances and how these decisions will be changed were these circumstances altered. In many public policy discourses, such information is vitally important.

For example, many concerned people seek information on how a farmer will cope with or adapt to a change in climate in the future. Microbehavioral models can provide knowledge on what portfolios (or enterprises) are held by individual mangers of resources at concerned locations and what factors explain the individuals' choices of these portfolios and changes of these choices (Seo, 2006, 2015b).

Adaptation has become one of the key pillars of the policy discussions on global warming and climatic changes in the international negotiations (United Nations Framework Convention on Climate Change, 2011a; United Nations Framework Convention on Climate Change, 2011b; IPCC 2012). Economists have long emphasized the role of adaptations in climate change discussions on agriculture (Rosenberg 1992; Mendelsohn 2000; Hanemann, 2000). Nonetheless, there have been few studies on adaptation strategies in agricultural and natural resources sectors using microbehavioral statistical models (Kurukulasuriya et al., 2011). Adaptation strategies are treated in an ad hoc manner in the climate economics models (Adams et al., 1999; Reilly et al., 2003; Parry et al., 2004; Butt et al., 2005). A few adaptation studies that are available examine historical changes in aggregate yields, leaving out individual's decisions (Olmstead and Rhode, 2011; Zhang et al., 2013).

As another example, earlier environmental studies used microbehavioral econometric models in the context of valuation of water pollution (Train, 1999). A discrete choice model is developed to model the choice of a fishing site by an individual as a function of explanatory variables which include relative distances to available sites, availability of camping sites, abundance of fish population, historical and cultural importance, and scenic beauty of fishing sites. A policy maker is often interested in whether and how much water pollution affects the visits by individuals to the sites because of diminished fish stock.

The second contribution of the microbehavioral models is that researchers are able to estimate correctly and tell to the public and policy makers about the profit function of the enterprise of concern and how it will be changed. Besides choices of enterprises or portfolios, policy makers are interested in expected changes in enterprise profit when an external factor is altered. James Heckman first showed that the estimation of an enterprise profit relying on the observed profits only is impossible due to the selection bias inherent in the observed profits (Heckman, 1979, 2000). A consistent and correct estimation of an enterprise profit becomes possible only when selection decisions are taken explicitly into account, which is one of the core elements of the microbehavioral models (Lee 1983, Dubin and McFadden 1984, Schmertmann 1994).

In the Heckman's example, a consistent estimation of the women's wage function cannot be done relying on the working women's wages alone. This is because nonworking women's wages cannot be treated as meaningless. In fact, a nonworking woman must have made a decision not to participate in the labor market because the highest wage offered to her in the market is lower than the "wage" earned by staying at home, that is, the value of work as a housewife such as child care, cooking, maintenance among other things. On the other hand, a working woman must have made a decision to participate in the labor market because the former is greater than the latter. Therefore, it is seen that there is a reference wage level for each woman, beyond which she is willing to participate in the labor market. Treating potential wages of nonworking women as meaningless is similar, although not same, to truncating the sample at a cut-off point in that both operations shift the mean of the error term from zero (Tobin, 1958).

The factors that increase the likelihood of Ms. Smith to participate in the labor market and decrease the likelihood of Ms. Taylor will increase the wage offered to Ms. Smith and decrease the wage offered to Ms. Taylor. The wage function of female workers then cannot be estimated correctly with the observed wages of working women alone. The error term in the wage function is correlated with the error term in the choice equation. As such, the mean of the error term of the working women's wage function is not zero. That is, the estimated wage function is biased.

In the examinations of agricultural resources, many researchers argued that major crops such as wheat, maize, rice, cotton, and soybeans are highly vulnerable to climatic changes (Rosenzweig and Parry, 1994; Parry et al., 2004; Auffhammer et al., 2006; Schlenker and Roberts, 2009; Welch et al., 2010; Lobell et al., 2011; Fisher et al., 2012; Deschenes and Greenstone, 2012). They predicted more than 80% fall in the yields of major grains in a severe climate change scenario. However, these individual crop-based analyses have not paid any attention to those who do not grow one of these grains or the areas where one of these crops are currently not grown. However, one should note that these areas are not used for these grains not because these grains cannot be grown there, but because alternative investments are more profitable than these grains. That is, an individual manager on this noncultivating area must have made a choice of what enterprise should be performed there. These decisions cannot be ignored (Seo, 2013).

Leaving out the choice of one of these grains that a researcher is concerned about will most likely lead to an overestimation of the impact of climate change on the grain. This is because a grain is chosen for cultivation on the most suitable conditions, physical or economic. A change in these favorable conditions due to climatic shifts will lead to a large damage on the grain of concern. Nonetheless, in the areas where this grain is not currently cultivated may benefit from a climatic shift if it makes the conditions in these unfavorable areas more suitable for the grain.

The third contribution of microbehavioral econometric models is that they are well suited for an analysis of the impact of climate change because they include all options available and fully accounting for possible adjustments in the portfolios individuals hold at present (Mendelsohn et al., 1994; Seo, 2015b). When it comes to an overall evaluation of the impact of a change in climate, microbehavioral models are superior to the other physically based models or individual crop-based models because these models are comprehensive of available portfolios, that is, not concentrated on a specific crop or enterprise. In addition, these models are comprehensive of adaptive changes of individuals and individual enterprises in response to changes in underlying conditions.

Applications of microbehavioral models indicate that the aggregate impact of climate change on agriculture will be much smaller than what other models have predicted (Seo, 2010b, 2015c). It is not hard to understand that since farmers are assumed to behave in a smart way by changing current portfolios in appropriate times, some of the severe impacts can be offset by these smart adaptive changes. For example, a currently cropping–dominated region may be able to transform to a mixed crops–animals enterprise if the climatic change turns out in a way to be more suitable for the latter enterprise (Seo and Mendelsohn, 2008; Seo, 2010a, 2015a). The overall impact of climatic change with such rearrangements will turn out to be much less severe than the overall impact of climatic change without such rearrangement and with sticking to the current practices.

From a policy perspective, this contribution is critically important because the aggregate impact of climatic change on agricultural and natural resources is considered by many a measuring stick of the impact of climate change on the globe. According to the IPCC, the impact of climate change on agricultural and natural resources accounts for more than one-third of the total impact of climate change on the society (Cline, 1992; Pearce et al. 1996). Agricultural and natural resources are deemed critically important because these are managed in the outdoors exposed directly to climate conditions. The most recent IPCC report also emphasizes amply catastrophic consequences of the impact of global warming on agriculture (Intergovernmental Panel on Climate Change, 2014b; Seo, 2014c; Schlenker et al., 2005, 2006).

From a practical policy viewpoint, this means that a correct estimate of the impact of climate change on agricultural and natural resources is a critical input into the integrated assessment models (IAM) of climate change such as the DICE (Dynamically Integrated Climate and Economy) model, the MERGE model (A Model for Evaluating the Regional and Global Effects of GHG Reduction Policies), or other widely used models (Nordhaus, 1992, 1994; Weyant, 2014; Weyant and Hill 1999; Manne and Richels 2001; Manne and Richels, 2004). The level of carbon price or tax, which is the primary output from these IAMs, hinges on the aggregate impact of climate change, that is, the shape and magnitude of the damage function. Put differently, the findings from the microbehavioral models are crucially important in answering the question of how stringently the world should cut global warming gases (Nordhaus, 2008, 2013).

The fourth contribution of microbehavioral models is concerned with options and conditions that serve as backgrounds for decision making. Market conditions and financial instruments that are existent at the moment of microlevel decisions are a key component of policy analyses and interventions. Financial instruments such as futures, forwards, options, and insurance give an individual with more options and capacities to manage various unexpected or rare risks and disasters (Barry et al., 2000; Fabozzi et al., 2009). Some individuals will purchase these instruments whereas others will not, considering external conditions that are prevalent in the respective regions.

Similarly, market conditions such as export markets, access to input and output markets, roads, communication networks, availability of schools, extension services, female labor participation, and other employment opportunities are key factors in numerous decisions that are made frequently in environmental and natural resource sectors.

The framework of microbehavioral models introduced throughout this book can incorporate any of these factors handily into the models (Udry, 1995; Seo, 2011b, 2012c, 2014a; Kala, 2015). This handiness comes from the premise that microbehavioral models are driven by individuals who make decisions faced with a great complexity of factors, physical or psychological.

In microbehavioral models, any of these factors is shown to affect, or not to affect, choices of individuals as well as outcomes of such choices. For example, availability of extension services to farmers in sub-Saharan Africa plays an important role in their decisions. Similarly, accessibilities of farmers to various markets for export, product sale, and inputs are major factors in farming decisions of sub-Saharan Africa. Policy makers in sub-Saharan Africa would heed to these results as a basis for improving road conditions and extension services.

This contribution or advantage that comes from microbehavioral perspectives should not be missed, especially in the context of environmental and natural resource studies. My researchers in the fields rely on biologically based models which stem from biological, ecological, or earth science models (Rosenzweig and Parry, 1994; Darwin et al., 1995; Reilly et al., 2003; Tubiello et al., 2007). Although these models are meaningful in some aspects and can incorporate some of these factors described earlier in an ad hoc manner, it is not possible to provide a comprehensive model taking into account the great variety of these options and market conditions.

The fifth aspect of the microbehavioral models that is meaningful in policy discussions is on psychological dimensions of decision making. Behavioral responses of individuals are often hard to quantify and predict because of psychological factors that drive individuals and markets (Kahneman and Tversky 1979, 1984; Shiller, 2003, 2005, 2014a; Thaler, 2015). An individual's decisions are driven oftentimes by prospects, framing, speculation, and story telling. These psychological effects make the markets irrationally exuberant, leaving market prices deviate from those supported by fundamentals. Markets will undergo a bubble-and-burst cycle repeatedly if speculation dominates market transactions.

The framework of microbehavioral models provides an appropriate platform on which behavioral decisions driven by speculation and bubble can be empirically examined and modeled (Seo, 2015c). As shown in the previous chapter, agricultural land markets even in the most developed nations such as the United States do not show the evidence that land prices are determined by the bubble-and-burst cycle (USDA 2014). In managing environmental and natural resource enterprises, especially in low-latitude developing countries, decisions driven by speculative motives and prospects seem to be rare because in part of long-term effects of such decisions which must be carefully considered in investment and management decisions (Seo, 2012c; Kala, 2015).

In contrast, in the biological models, human minds and psychological aspects are completely out of the model's purview (Tubiello and Ewert, 2002; Ainsworth and Long, 2005). In the biologically based models which integrate biological models with various social and economic models, the impacts of psychological and speculative drivers on the model outcomes become unmanageable because of a complex web of loose linkages embodied in the model through which these effects are transmitted.

The sixth aspect of the microbehavioral econometric framework is its capacity to integrate individuals' decisions with changes in ecosystems and ecological systems (Seo, 2014a). It is of great interest to policy makers to understand the clear relationships between the two components if a policy variable, for example, global warming, were to alter one of these components. As this book introduced in Chapter 6, changes in adoptions of natural resource enterprises can be coupled with changes in land covers or vegetations in the geographic region of concern (Seo, 2010c, 2012a,b, 2014b).

Scientific attempts to classify ecosystems and ecological zones turn out to be meaningful endeavors for microbehavioral modelers. Ecosystems may be understood in a broader terms of land covers (Matthews, 1983). Ecosystems can be defined for a more specific application such as crop productivity as have been done in the classifications of the agro–ecological zone (AEZ) and length of growing periods (LGP) (Dudal, 1980; Fischer et al., 2005; FAO, 2005).

In the policy dialogs, however, there has been one-sided emphasis on revealing changes in ecosystems and ecological systems (Gitay et al., 2001; Fischlin et al., 2007). Another half in this mutual relationship, that is, changes in behaviors, has received little attention, but is an important area of research in the future for those who are concerned about the interactions between human systems and natural systems (Seo 2014b).

Having discussed policy-relevant aspects and potential contributions of the microbehavioral modeling framework, the present author will provide a brief review of existing policies in the fields of agriculture, natural resources, climate, energy, and environmental protection from the microbehavioral perspectives in order to offer a few constructive suggestions for the future. The present author picked the policies described later because each of these policies contains fascinating microbehavioral storylines, either in the policy design itself or in the analysis of the policy consequences, which are often told by the researchers. Again, this is an endeavor to highlight microbehavioral dimensions in policy making and policy analyses which could be subjected to microbehavioral econometric analyses in the future.

Let's begin with a crop subsidy program. The crop insurance and subsidy program in the United States was explained in Chapter 7. Like any insurance programs, it leads to behavioral distortions such as moral hazard and adverse selection (Akerlof, 1970; Fabozzi et al., 2009; Sumner and Zulauf, 2012). The success of these programs, hence, hinges on embedding a set of mechanisms that minimize and even prevent such perverse behaviors into the insurance and subsidy program (Halcrow, 1949; Stigler, 1961; Spence, 1973). From the perspectives of microbehavioral incentives, a number of interesting observations emerge with regard to a crop subsidy program.

A farmer with a crop subsidy on, for example, maize, will not make the full effort to protect herself against a range of natural disasters such as drought and heavy rainfall, knowing that she is compensated by a government subsidy when the maize yield in a specific year falls below a critical level (Shields, 2013). In such a case, existence of a maize subsidy would lower the yields of the insured grain to be supplied to US consumers, not increase the yields, increasing the market price of maize. At the same time, a crop subsidy would put heavy burden of compensation to the consumers, equivalent to $15 billion annually (USDA, 2015). However, supporters of the crop subsidy program would argue that the program protects small subsistent farmers from going out of business due to a severe disaster that strikes in a single year, thereby increasing the supply of the crop to the country in the long-term and lowering the market price. This argument is weakened if US consumers can rely on imports from other major crop producing countries.

A crop subsidy program may cause a serious land use conundrum in a future with high uncertainty. In the existence of a crop subsidy, a farmer's land use decisions are determined by and large by existing land use patterns and subsidy supports from the government. In a future with high uncertainty, for example, with regard to climatic changes, optimal transitions from one land use to another will not occur, given the subsidy system in place. An efficient resource allocation that results will lead to welfare loss for the national economy.

Looking at the past as well as to the future, a heavy crop subsidy program has been and will be a trigger of conversions of land from forested zones and grasslands/pasturelands to croplands which are subsidized. Besides the inefficiencies that arise from such forced conversions, there will manifest environmental consequences in the form of increased pollution from carbon dioxide emissions and nitrous oxides emissions.

The second policy area to be reviewed is concerned with energy policy. The CAFE (Corporate Average Fuel Economy) standards, one of the key pillars of the US energy policy, are designed to improve automobile mileage driven per unit of energy used (Portney et al., 2003; McConnell, 2013). As a result, automobile mileages of the cars produced in the United States for the past decade have improved significantly, showing evidence that the policy of CAFE standards is forcing a technological innovation by automobile manufacturers.

With the CAFE standards, policy makers target primarily two policy objectives. One is the reduction of fossil fuels such as oil, natural gas, and diesel used, which is to maximize the utility of fossil fuels given the limited supply of fossil fuels in the world. The other is the reduction in a variety of automobile pollutions that result from these fuels assuming reduced uses of fossil fuels under the CAFE standards (United States Environmental Protection Agency, 2010).

From a microbehavioral perspective, however, an increase in automobile mileage per gallon of fuel means that he/she can drive a larger distance with the same amount of oil or natural gas used. This means that the CAFE standards may have inadvertently increased the number of miles driven by an individual. The intended reduction in the consumption of oil and natural gas through the CAFE standards is offset in part by the individual's response to the CAFE policy. By driving more hours, an individual increases the use of fossil fuels. A cheaper operation cost of an automobile because of reduced gasoline cost per mile driven can increase individuals' purchases of automobiles, further increasing the consumption of fossil fuels by the society. These behavioral responses are known as "rebound effects" (Portney et al., 2003; Tietenberg and Lewis, 2014).

Considering the rebound responses by individuals, a number of alternative policy instruments may be suggested which better incorporates microbehavioral decisions of individuals. For example, an appropriate level of energy and pollution tax could be imposed on the use of fossil fuels. The tax should be imposed on each ton of gasoline or natural gas burned in the use of these fuels, which would have the impacts of reducing the consumption of the fuels because of higher prices of fuels due to the embedded tax component. At the same time, automobile makers will strive to improve new car mileages in order to increase the sale of automobiles in the existence of the energy and pollution tax. Hence, this alternative policy instrument will likely better accomplish the policy goal of the CAFE standards, without directly forcing technological innovations of automobile manufacturers.

For the purpose of further analysis of this alternative policy instrument, let's consider a different type of tax scheme: a tax imposed on each mile driven by an individual, so-called a mileage tax. As each mile driven costs an individual, she will reduce the number of driving miles, *ceteris paribus*. She would prefer a higher mileage automobile as it reduces the cost of a mile driven as it reduces the fuel cost of the mile driven. That is, a higher mileage car burns less fuel than a lower mileage car for the same distance driven.

This mileage tax can be designed in a progressive manner as well. That is, a higher rate is charged for a larger number of miles driven. This would lead to an even more drastic reduction in the number of miles driven by an individual. However, the mileage tax does not achieve the policy goal of pollution control if new automobiles burn more fuels for the same distance. People would drive less, but pollute more. Similarly, the mileage tax would not achieve the policy goal of energy security if new automobiles call for burning more fuels for the same distance.

The point is that the three policy instruments—CAFE standards, energy and pollution tax, mileage tax—affect microbehavioral decisions in a different way. A policy instrument designed in a way that aligns behavioral responses well with policy targets should be preferred if policy makers intend to maximize society's welfare.

The third topic to review comes from a category of environmental policy. In a mega city of the world with more than 10 million people living in the city, driving one's own car to workplaces creates air pollution, congested roads, and wasted time on traffic delays. These problems become magnified during the rush hours of the day. Many major cities in the world have successfully achieved both better air quality and reduced road congestions and delays by devising environmental policies in a gradual manner that are responsive to people's behavioral patterns.

Many companies allowed their employees to have a flexible work hour. Deviating from the traditional 9 am–5 pm work hour, she is allowed to choose, for example, to arrive at the office at 7 am and leave at 3 pm. Or, she can choose to arrive at 11 am and leave at 7 pm. A flexible work hour was successful in spreading commuters across the day, reducing road congestions and traffic delays.

In some cities, a local government gave an exclusive lane for a public bus system during the weekdays in order to remove traffic or congestion delays for a public bus, which has increased the number of residents choosing a public bus ride instead of private passenger cars to workplaces. In addition, a local government created a linking of various public transportation modes such as bus, subway, light rails, boats, etc. The linked public transportation system allows an individual to switch from one mode of transportation to another mode "without paying additional fee." It created an incentive for an individual to take more often a public transportation system.

Further, a reduced rate for a public transportation system in the early hours, for example, from 5 am to 8 am, implemented by a local government creates an incentive for everyday commuters to go early to workplaces, reducing the number of commuters during the rush hours.

Establishment of a fully computerized public transportation system made a huge difference in making people to choose a public transportation system. In a fully computerized system, an individual can easily browse an electronic bus-stop board which displays which buses are available at each bus stop and where each of these buses is located currently and how many minutes will take for each of these buses to arrive at a specific bus stop. Therefore, the fully computerized public transportation system enables an individual to choose and switch efficiently across different modes of public transportation in the most efficient manner.

The variety of measures described earlier and similar measures enabled many mega cities to achieve far higher air quality, reduced congestion, reduced delays due to traffic, and improved amenity in general. The measures described earlier have been actually implemented in Seoul, South Korea in which 25 million people reside. These successful changes seemed unimaginable to the present author even 15 years ago.

The lesson here is that whether an environmental policy succeeds or not depends on how carefully behavioral responses are taken into account. The microbehavioral econometric methods described throughout this book provide both theoretical and empirical foundations for policy makers and analysts.

From a large number of policy instruments implemented over the past four decades around the world, the field of transportation and environment is an interesting subject in that one of the first applied works in discrete choice models was to explain individual choices of transportation modes (Boyd and Mellman, 1980; Cardell and Dunbar, 1980; Ben-Akiva et al., 1993).

The fourth policy area is global warming. As mentioned earlier in this chapter, adaptation has gradually become one of the key pillars of the climate change policy dialogues across the globe. From conceptual discussions in the early years of the United Nations' Framework Convention on Climate Change (UNFCCC), some progresses have been made in recent years to the formation of the Green Climate Fund (GCF) (United Nations Framework Convention on Climate Change, 1992; United Nations Framework Convention on Climate Change, 1998; United Nations Framework Convention on Climate Change, 2009; United Nations Framework Convention on Climate Change, 2011b; United Nations Framework Convention on Climate Change, 2013). The GCF promises to collect about $100 billion per year which should be allocated to mitigation and adaptation projects around the world. The GCF secretariat is chosen to be located in Songdo city of South Korea and the World Bank is chosen as the trustee of the GCF.

However, there has been no guideline at all on how this fund will be allocated to which projects in which countries. This has become a biggest hurdle in the climate change negotiations in the recent rounds of climate talks. Poor countries in Africa, South Asia, and Latin America are all waiting for these funds to be allocated to their individual countries as a precondition for participation in any global legal framework to be formed in the future. The gap between developed nations and developing nations has widened over the years on account of the nature of allocations of this fund.

Microbehavioral econometric models developed in this book provide an adequate empirical and analytical framework on how this fund should be distributed. The microbehavioral models show how an individual manger will adapt to the changes in climate in an efficient manner. However, it does not mean that an individual owner is well versed in this type of knowledge (Seo, 2015b). In general, individual managers do not have this knowledge. Microbehavioral models offer an empirical framework through which such knowledge is acquired and distributed.

Even with the sufficient knowledge provided by local and federal governments based on scientific research, a transition from one enterprise to another enterprise can incur substantial cost of transition which is one-time sunk cost to a manager (Seo, 2015c). Financial as well as psychological barriers will hinder efficient adaptations of individuals to changed climate systems.

Local governments as well as financial institutions can play a significant role in this regard by providing a long-term funding to selected adaptation projects which is to be returned overtime by the individual managers of such projects. In addition, local governments may provide adequate information on the cost of transitions and resulting benefits from such transitions.

Further, an adaptation project would be in some cases coordinated at the community level (Seo, 2011a). For example, an irrigation system may be coordinated among the community members in order to reduce the costs of individual irrigations. In such a community project, local governments may develop and provide appropriate loans and technical supports.

The fifth area to discuss is the study of financial markets. For the microbehavioral econometric modelers, this field should be treated as one of the key areas of microbehavioral economics upon which microbehavioral econometric methods are founded. Indeed, behavioral economics (and finance) originated from the study of financial markets (Markowitz, 1952; Shiller, 1981, 2003; Shiller, 2014a; Thaler, 2015).

The key conclusion of behavioral finance is that market prices will deviate from fundamentals in the markets if speculation and psychological elements would drive investor's decisions (Fama, 1970; Shiller, 1981, 2014a). When these elements are dominant, a bubble is created, which becomes ever bigger until it eventually bursts when the mood suddenly swings in the markets. Some of the prominent empirical evidence of behavioral finance includes the 1930 great crash, the dot-com bubble burst in 2000, and the real estate bubble burst in 2008.

The painful effects of speculative markets are amplified by a great deal in the absence of financial instruments that provide investors with means to hedge against a catastrophic event. These financial instruments include bonds, futures, forwards, options, and insurance (Fabozzi et al., 2009). The recent real estate bubble burst in 2008 and the following global financial crisis occurred in part because there was no proper financial instrument which can hedge the real estate owners during a great crash in housing prices (Shiller 2009, 2014b). When property prices fell drastically, house owners became unable to sell the property in order to pay the mortgage because house prices fell far below the mortgage debt. Many property owners defaulted on the loan and subsequently the properties were foreclosed by the lenders.

If a house owner had purchased a put option, an option to sell the property at a certain price at a future date, then he/she could have sold the property at the agreed price when the house price fell below the agreed price level. In this way, a property owner will be protected from a severe drop in her property prices. If the property price would remain above the agreed level, the owner will simply not exercise the option to sell the property at the agreed price. A potential owner would purchase the property along with a put option with additional cost, which is done at the owner's discretion considering the risk he/she faces.

A put option on property was not available in the real estate markets during the real estate bubble burst in 2008 (Case and Shiller, 2003; Shiller 2009; Shiller, 2014b). However, it is a financial instrument that can protect property buyers in the future. Similarly, a call option on property would have a similar effect.

The literature on property markets and more broadly financial markets extends seamlessly to land markets and other natural resources markets, the areas in which environmental and natural resource scientists are engaged who are also primary readers of this book.

Up to this point, the present author gave a broad overview of the policy areas where microbehavioral models make meaningful contributions with some suggestions: agriculture, energy, environment, global warming, and financial markets. This is neither an exhaustive nor comprehensive list of policy fields of interests, but nonetheless is enough to showcase microbehavioral aspects in policy designs and results.

In a grand conclusion, I would emphasize that the field of microbehavioral econometric methods is both a subfield of economics and a subfield of statistics in which microbehavioral decisions and outcomes are examined through probabilistic and statistical methods. Both aspects, that is, microbehavioral decisions and statistical methods, are explained in great detail in this book. For the researchers of environmental and natural resources, both of these aspects should be an essential part of their academic trainings and scholarly pursuits.

Exercises

1. The book began with the description of the problem of global warming in Chapter 1, which is one of the most prominent environmental and global issues today. Discuss why global warming is a problem of a global public good and why adaptation is a meaningful concept in the approach to coping with global warming. Explain how the recent agreement in the Paris meeting convened by the United Nations Framework Convention on Climate Change addresses the needs for adaptation.

REFERENCES

Adams, R., McCarl, B.A., Segerson, K., Rosenzweig, C., Bryant, K., Dixon, B.L., Conner, R., Evenson, R.E., Ojima, D., 1999. The economic effects of climate change on US agriculture. In: Mendelsohn, R., Neumann, J. (Eds.), The Impact of Climate Change on the United States Economy. Cambridge University Press, Cambridge.

Akerlof, G.A., 1970. The market for lemons: quality uncertainty and the market mechanism. Q. J. Econ. 84 (3), 488–500.

Ainsworth, E.A., Long, S.P., 2005. What have we learned from 15 years of free-air CO_2 enrichment (FACE)? A meta-analytic review of the responses of photosynthesis, canopy properties and plant production to rising CO_2. New Phytol. 165, 351–371.

Auffhammer, M., Ramaathan, V., Vincent, J.R., 2006. Integrated model shows that atmospheric brown clouds and greenhouse gases have reduced rice harvests in India. Proc. Natl. Acad. Sci. USA 103, 19668–19672.

Barry, P.J., Ellinger, P.N., Baker, C.B., Hopkin, J.A., 2000. Financial Management in Agriculture, sixth ed. Interstate Publishers, Illinois.

Ben-Akiva, M., Bolduc, D., Bradley, M., 1993. Estimation of travel model choice models with randomly distributed values of time. Transport. Res. Rec. 1413, 88–97.

Boyd, J., Mellman, J., 1980. The effect of fuel economy standards on the U.S. automotive market: a hedonic demand analysis. Transport. Res. A 14, 367–378.

Butt, T.A., McCarl, B.A., Angerer, J., Dyke, P.T., Stuth, J.W., 2005. The economic and food security implications of climate change in Mali. Clim. Change 68, 355–378.

Cameron, A.C., Trivedi, P.K., 2005. Microeconometrics: Methods and Applications. Cambridge University Press, Cambridge.

Cardell, S., Dunbar, F., 1980. Measuring the societal impacts of automobile downsizing. Transport. Res. A 14, 423–434.

Case, K.E., Shiller, R.J., 2003. Is there a bubble in the housing market? Brookings Pap. Econ. Act. 2003, 299–342.

Cline, W., 1992. The economics of global warming. Institute of International Economics, Washington, DC.

Darwin, R.F., Tsigas, M., Lewandrowski, J., Raneses, A., 1995. World Agriculture and Climate Change: Economic Adaptations. U.S. Department of Agriculture (USDA). Economic Research Service, Washington DC.

Deschenes, O., Greenstone, M., 2012. The economic impacts of climate change: evidence from agricultural output and random fluctuations in weather: Reply. Am. Econ. Rev. 102, 3761–3773.

Dubin, J.A., McFadden, D.L., 1984. An econometric analysis of residential electric appliance holdings and consumption. Econometrica 52 (2), 345–362.

Dudal, R., 1980. Soil-Related Constraints to Agricultural Development in the Tropics. International Rice Research Institute, Los Banos.

Fabozzi, F.J., Modigliani, F.G., Jones, F.J., 2009. Foundations of Financial Markets and Institutions, fourth ed. Prentice Hall, New York.

Fama, E.F., 1970. Efficient capital markets: a review of empirical work. J. Fin. 25 (2), 383–417.

Fischer, G., Shah, M., Tubiello, F.N., van Velhuizen, H., 2005. Socio-economic and climate change impacts on agriculture: an integrated assessment, 1990-2080. Phil. Trans. R. Soc. B 360, 2067–2083.

Fischlin, A., Midgley, G.F., Price, J.T., Leemans, R., Gopal, B., Turley, C., Rounsevell, M.D.A., Dube, O.P., Tarazona, J., Velichko, A.A., 2007. Ecosystems, their properties, goods, and services. Climate change 2007: impacts, adaptation and vulnerability. In: Parry, M.L., Canziani, O.F., Palutikof, J.P., van der Linden, P.J., Hanson, C.E. (Eds.), Contribution of Working Group II to the Fourth Assessment Report of the Intergovernmental Panel on Climate Change. Cambridge University Press, Cambridge.

Fisher, A.C., Hanemann, W.M., Roberts, M.J., Schlenker, W., 2012. The economic impacts of climate change: evidence from agricultural output and random fluctuations in weather: comment. Am. Econ. Rev. 102, 3749–3760.

FAO, 2005. Global agro-ecological assessment for agriculture in the twenty-first century (CD-ROM). FAO Land and Water Digital Media SeriesFAO, Rome.

Gitay, H., Brwon, S., Easterling, W, Jallow, B., 2001. Ecosystems and their goods and services. In: McCarthy et al.,(Ed.), Climate Change 2001: Impacts, Adaptations, and Vulnerabilities. Cambridge University Press, Cambridge, pp. 237–342.

Halcrow, H.G., 1949. Actuarial structures for crop insurance. J. Farm Econ. 31, 418–443.

Hanemann, W.M., 2000. Adaptation and its management. Clim. Change 45, 511–581.

Hansen, J., Sato, M., Reudy, R., Lo, K., Lea, D.W., Medina-Elizade, M., 2006. Global temperature change. Proc. Natl. Acad. Sci. USA 103, 14288–14293.

Heckman, J., 1979. Sample selection bias as a specification error. Econometrica 47, 153–162.

Heckman, J., 2000. Microdata, Heterogeneity and the Evaluation of Public Policy. Nobel Prize Lecture for Economic Sciences, Stockholm University.

IPCC, 2012. Managing the Risks of Extreme Events and Disasters to Advance Climate Change Adaptation. A Special Report of Working Groups I and II of the Intergovernmental Panel on Climate Change. Cambridge University Press, Cambridge.

Intergovernmental Panel on Climate Change, 2014a. Climate Change 2014: The Physical Science Basis, The Fifth Assessment Report of the IPCC. Cambridge University Press, Cambridge.

Intergovernmental Panel on Climate Change, 2014b. Climate Change 2014: Impacts, Adaptation and Vulnerability, The Fifth Assessment Report of the IPCC. Cambridge University Press, Cambridge.

Kahneman, D., Tversky, A., 1979. Prospect theory: an analysis of decision under risk. Econometrica 47, 263–291.

Kahneman, D., Tversky, A., 1984. Choices, values and frames. Am. Psychol. 39 (4), 341–350.

Kala, N., 2015. Ambiguity Aversion and Learning in a Changing World: The Potential Effects of Climate Change from Indian Agriculture. PhD dissertation, Yale University.

Keeling, C.D., Piper, S.C., Bacastow, R.B., Wahlen, M., Whorf, T.P., Heimann, M., Meijer, H.A., 2005. Atmospheric CO_2 and $^{13}CO_2$ exchange with the terrestrial biosphere and oceans from 1978 to 2000: observations and carbon cycle implications. In: Ehleringer, J.R., Cerling, T.E., Dearing, M.D. (Eds.), A History of Atmospheric CO_2 and its Effects on Plants, Animals, and Ecosystems. Springer Verlag, New York.

Kurukulasuriya, P., Kala, N., Mendelsohn, R., 2011. Adaptation and climate change impacts: a structural Ricardian model of irrigation and farm income in Africa. Clim. Change Econ. 2, 149–174.

Le Treut, H., Somerville, R., Cubasch, U., Ding, Y., Mauritzen, C., Mokssit, A., Peterson, T., Prather, M., (2007). Historical overview of climate change. In: Solomon, S., Qin, D., Manning, M., Chen, Z., Marquis, M., Averyt, K.B., Tignor, M., Miller, H.L. (Eds.), Climate Change 2007 The Physical Science Basis. Contribution of Working Group I to the Fourth Assessment Report of the Intergovernmental Panel on Climate Change. Cambridge University Press, Cambridge.

Lee, L.F., 1983. Generalized econometric models with selectivity. Econometrica 51, 507–512.

Lobell, D., Schlenker, W., Costa-Roberts, J., 2011. Climate trends and global crop production since 1980. Science 333, 616–620.

Manne AS, Richels RG (2001) U.S. rejection of the Kyoto Protocol: the impact on compliance costs and CO_2 emissions. AEI-Brookings Joint Center Working Paper No. 01-12.

Manne AS, Richels RG (2004) MERGE: an integrated assessment model for global climate change. Stanford University. Available from: http://www.stanford.edu/group/MERGE/GERAD1.pdf.

Markowitz, H., 1952. Portfolio selection. J Fin. 7, 77–91.

Matthews, E., 1983. Global vegetation and land use: new high-resolution data bases for climate studies. J. Clim. Appl. Meteorol. 22 (3), 474–487.

McConnell V (2013) The new CAFE standards: are they enough on their own? Resources for the Future Discussion Paper. RFF DP 13–14. RFF, Washington DC.

McFadden, D.L., 1974. Conditional logit analysis of qualitative choice behavior. In: Zarembka, P. (Ed.), Frontiers in Econometrics. Academic Press, New York, pp. 105–142.

Mendelsohn, R., 2000. Efficient adaptation to climate change. Clim. Change 45, 583–600.

Mendelsohn, R., Nordhaus, W., Shaw, D., 1994. The impact of global warming on agriculture: a Ricardian analysis. Am. Econ. Rev. 84, 753–771.

National Research Council, 2013. Abrupt Impacts of Climate Change: Anticipating Surprises. The National Academies Press, Washington DC.

Nordhaus, W.D., 1992. An optimal transition path for controlling Greenhouse Gases. Science 258, 1315–1319.

Nordhaus, W.D., 1994. Managing the Global Commons: The Economics of Climate Change. MIT Press, Cambridge, MA.

Nordhaus, W.D., 2008. A Question of Balance: Weighing the Options on Global Warming Policies. Yale University Press, New Haven, CT.

Nordhaus, W.D., 2011. The economics of tail events with an application to climate change. Rev. Environ. Econ. Pol. 5, 240–257.

Nordhaus, W.D., 2013. The Climate Casino: Risk, Uncertainty, and Economics for a Warming World. Yale University Press, New Haven, CT.

Olmstead, A.L., Rhode, P.W., 2011. Adapting North American wheat production to climatic changes, 1839–2009. Proc. Natl. Acad. Sci. USA 108, 480–485.

Parry, M.L., Rosenzweig, C.P., Iglesias, A., Livermore, M., Fischer, G., 2004. Effects of climate change on global food production under SRES emissions and socioeconomic scenarios. Global Environ. Change 14, 53–67.

Pearce, D., Cline, W.R., Achanta, A., Fankhauser, S., Pachauri, R., Tol, R., Vellinga, P., 1996. The social costs of climate change: greenhouse damage and benefits of control. In: Bruce, J., Lee, H., Haites, E. (Eds.), Climate Change 1995: Economic and Social Dimensions of Climate Change. Cambridge University Press, Cambridge.

Portney, P.R., Parry, I.W.H., Gruenspecht, H.K., Harrington, W., 2003. The Economics of Fuel Economy Standards. RFF DP 03-44. Resources For the Future, Washington DC.

Reilly, J., Tubiello, T., McCarl, B., Abler, D., Darwin, R., Fuglie, K., Hollinger, S., Izaurralde, C., Jagtap, S., Jones, J., Mearns, L., Ojima, D., Paul, E., Paustian, K., Riha, S., Rosenberg, N., Rosenzweig, C., 2003. U.S. agriculture and climate change: new results. Clim. Change 59, 43–69.

Rosenberg, N.J., 1992. Adaptation of agriculture to climate change. Clim. Change 21, 385–405.

Rosenzweig, C., Parry, M., 1994. Potential impact of climate change on world food supply. Nature 367, 133–138.

Schenkler, W., Hanemann, M., Fisher, A., 2005. Will US agriculture really benefit from global warming? Accounting for irrigation in the hedonic approach. Am. Econ. Rev. 95, 395–406.

Schenkler, W., Hanemann, M., Fisher, A., 2006. The impact of global warming on U.S. agriculture: an econometric analysis of optimal growing conditions. Rev. Econ. Stat. 88 (1), 113–125.

Schlenker, W., Roberts, M., 2009. Nonlinear temperature effects indicate severe damages to crop yields under climate change. Proc. Natl. Acad. Sci. USA 106 (37), 15594–15598.

Schmertmann, C.P., 1994. Selectivity bias correction methods in polychotomous sample selection models. J. Econ. 60, 101–132.

Seo S.N., 2006. Modeling farmer responses to climate change: climate change impacts and adaptations in livestock management in Africa. PhD Dissertation, Yale University, New Haven.

Seo, S.N., 2010a. Is an integrated farm more resilient against climate change?: a microeconometric analysis of portfolio diversification in African agriculture? Food Pol. 35, 32–40.

Seo, S.N., 2010b. A microeconometric analysis of adapting portfolios to climate change: adoption of agricultural systems in Latin America. Appl. Econ. Perspect. Pol. 32, 489–514.

Seo, S.N., 2010c. Managing forests, livestock, and crops under global warming: a microeconometric analysis of land use changes in Africa. Austral. J. Agric. Resour. Econ. 54 (2), 239–258.

Seo, S.N., 2011a. An analysis of public adaptation to climate change using agricultural water schemes in South America. Ecol. Econ. 70, 825–834.

Seo, S.N., 2011b. A geographically scaled analysis of adaptation to climate change with spatial models using agricultural systems in Africa. J. Agric. Sci. 149, 437–449.

Seo, S.N., 2012a. Adapting natural resource enterprises under global warming in South America: a mixed logit analysis. Economia 12, 111–135.

Seo, S.N., 2012b. Adaptation behaviors across ecosystems under global warming: a spatial microeconometric model of the rural economy in South America. Pap. Reg. Sci. 91, 849–871.

Seo, S.N., 2012c. Decision making under climate risks: an analysis of sub-Saharan farmers' adaptation behaviors. Weather, Clim. Soc. 4, 285–299.

Seo, S.N., 2013. An essay on the impact of climate change on US agriculture: weather fluctuations, climatic shifts, and adaptation strategies. Clim. Change 121, 115–124.

Seo, S.N., 2014a. Evaluation of agro-ecological zone methods for the study of climate change with micro farming decisions in sub-Saharan Africa. Eur. J. Agron. 52, 157–165.

Seo, S.N., 2014b. Coupling climate risks, eco-systems, anthropogenic decisions using South American and Sub-Saharan farming activities. Meteorol. Appl. 21, 848–858.

Seo, S.N., 2014c. Adapting sensibly when global warming turns the field brown or blue: a comment on the 2014 IPCC Report. Econ. Affairs 34, 399–401.

Seo, S.N., 2015a. Adapting to extreme climate changes: raising animals in hot and arid eco-systems in Australia. Int. J. Biometeorol. 59, 541–550.

Seo, S.N., 2015b. Micro-behavioral Economics of Global Warming: Modeling Adaptation Strategies in Agricultural and Natural Resource Enterprises. Springer, Cham.

Seo, S.N., 2015c. Modeling farmer adaptations to climate change in South America: a micro-behavioral economic perspective. Environ. Ecol. Stat. 23 (1), 1–21.

Seo, S.N., Mendelsohn, R., 2008. Measuring impacts and adaptations to climate change: a structural Ricardian model of African livestock management. Agric. Econ. 38, 151–165.

Shields, D.A., 2013. Federal Crop Insurance: Background. Congressional Research Service. R40532. US Congress, Washington DC.

Shiller, R.J., 1981. Do stock prices move too much to be justified by subsequent changes in dividends? Am. Econ. Rev. 71 (3), 421–436.

Shiller, R.J., 2003. From efficient markets theory to behavioral finance. J. Econ. Perspect. 17, 83–104.

Shiller, R.J., 2005. Irrational Exuberance, second ed. Princeton University Press, Princeton, NJ.

Shiller, R.J., 2009. Subprime Solution: How Today's Global Financial Crisis Happened and What to do About it. Princeton University Press, Princeton, NJ.

Shiller, R.J., 2014a. Speculative asset prices. Am. Econ. Rev. 104 (6), 1486–1517.

Shiller, R.J., 2014b. Why is housing finance still stuck in such a primitive stage? Am. Econ. Rev. 104 (5), 73–76.

Spence, M., 1973. Job market signaling. Q. J. Econ. 87 (3), 355–374.

Stigler, G.J., 1961. The economics of information. J. Pol. Econ. 69 (3), 213–225.

Sumner, D.A., Zulauf, C., 2012. Economic & Environmental Effects of Agricultural Insurance Programs. The Council on Food, Agricultural & Resource Economics (C-FARE), Washington DC.

Thaler, R.H., 2015. Misbehaving: The Making of Behavioral Economics. W.W. Norton Company.

Tietenberg, T., Lewis, L., 2014. Environmental & Natural Resource Economics. Prentice Hall, New York.

Tobin, J., 1958. Estimation of Relationships for Limited Dependent Variables. Econometrica 26 (1), 24–36.

Train, K., 1999. Mixed logit models for recreation demand. In: Herriges, J., Kling, C. (Eds.), Valuing Recreation and the Environment. Edward Elgar, Northampton, MA.

Train, K., 2003. Discrete Choice Methods With Simulation. Cambridge University Press, Cambridge.

Tubiello, F.N., Amthor, J.A., Boote, K.J., Donatelli, M., Easterling, W., Fischer, G., Gifford, R.M., Howden, M., Reilly, J., Rosenzweig, C., 2007. Crop response to elevated CO_2 and world food supply. Eur. J. Agron. 26, 215–223.

Tubiello, F.N., Ewert, F., 2002. Simulating the effects of elevated CO_2 on crops: approaches and applications for climate change. Eur. J. Agron. 18, 57–74.

Udry, C., 1995. Risk and saving in Northern Nigeria. Am. Econ. Rev. 85, 1287–1300.

United Nations Framework Convention on Climate Change (1992) The United Nations Framework Convention on Climate Change. New York.

United Nations Framework Convention on Climate Change, 1998. Kyoto Protocol to the United Nations Framework Convention on Climate Change. UNFCCC, Geneva.

United Nations Framework Convention on Climate Change, 2009. Copenhagen Accord. UNFCCC, Geneva.

United Nations Framework Convention on Climate Change, 2011a. The Durban Platform for Enhanced Action. UNFCCC, Geneva.

United Nations Framework Convention on Climate Change, 2011b. Report of the Transitional Committee for the Design of Green Climate Fund. UNFCCC, Geneva.

United Nations Framework Convention on Climate Change, 2013. Report of the Green Climate Fund to the Conference of the Parties and Guidance to the Green Climate Fund. UNFCCC, Warsaw.

United Nations Framework Convention on Climate Change (2015) The Paris Agreement. Conference Of the Parties (COP) 21, UNFCCC, Geneva.

United States Department of Agriculture 2014. Land Values 2014 Summary (August 2014). USDA, National Agricultural Statistics Service, Washington DC.

United States Environmental Protection Agency, 2010. The 40th Anniversary of the Clean Air Act. USEPA, Washington DC. Available from: http://www.epa.gov/airprogm/oar/caa/40th.html.

U.S. Department of Agriculture, Risk Management Agency. 2015. Costs and Outlays of Crop Insurance Program. Available from: http://www.rma.usda.gov/aboutrma/budget/costsoutlays.html.

Weitzman, M.L., 2009. On modeling and interpreting the economics of catastrophic climate change. Rev. Econ. Stat. 91, 1–19.

Welch, J.R., Vincent, J.R., Auffhammer, M., Moya, P.F., Dobermann, A., Dawe, D., 2010. Rice yields in tropical/subtropical Asia exhibit large but opposing sensitivities to minimum and maximum temperatures. Proc. Natl. Acad. Sci. USA 107, 14562–14567.

Weyant, J., 2014. Integrated assessment of climate change: state of the literature. J. Benefit-Cost Anal. 5, 377–409.

Weyant, J., Hill, J. (Eds.), 1999. The costs of the Kyoto Protocol: a multi-model evaluation, The Energy J. (special edition). International Association for Energy Economics, Dallas.

Zhang, W., Hagerman, A.D., McCarl, B.A., 2013. How climate factors influence the spatial distribution of Texas cattle breeds. Clim. Change 118, 183–195.

INDEX